Theory of Practical Cellular Automaton

Xuewei Li · Jinpei Wu · Xueyan Li

Theory of Practical Cellular Automaton

北京交通大学出版社
http://press.bjtu.edu.cn

Springer

Xuewei Li
Beijing Union University
Beijing
China

Xueyan Li
Beijing Jiaotong university
Beijing
China

Jinpei Wu
Wuyi University
Jiangmen, Guangdong
China

ISBN 978-981-10-7496-7 ISBN 978-981-10-7497-4 (eBook)
https://doi.org/10.1007/978-981-10-7497-4

Jointly published with Beijing Jiaotong University Press

The print edition is not for sale in China Mainland. Customers from China Mainland please order the print book from: Beijing Jiaotong University Press.

Library of Congress Control Number: 2017964426

Printed on acid-free paper

This Springer imprint is published by the registered company Springer Nature Singapore Pte Ltd.
part of Springer Nature
The registered company address is: 152 Beach Road, #21-01/04 Gateway East, Singapore 189721, Singapore

Preface

Today, mankind's understanding of external world has reached a staggering level. In macrocosmic view, astronomers can observe and study the universe that is hundreds of millions of light years away. On the contrary, in microscopic view, quantum physicists could dive into the magic world of stratum and quark. Without exception, all these brilliant scientific achievements were the results of human's processing of the information collected from the physical world surrounding us, with wisdom and proper thinking. However, the scientific explorations of the nature and our own society not only depend on how much we have known but also depend on how much we have not known, to a greater degree. In contrast to the deep understanding of the world surrounding us, the mankind's understanding of ourselves, especially the understanding of the essence of life and wisdom, is still at a rather naive and primitive stage.

In the 1950s, father of the computer von Neumann invented the cellular automata and successfully solved the problem of machine self-replication. This made him a pioneer in the scientific field of artificial life, which is not the study of natural lives that are made of the carbohydrate, but concentrates on simulating or "creating" lives by means of computing. Do people believe that one day in future, science and technology will create a machine with life characteristics? The question has attracted scientists from various fields and has become one of the most attractive scientific research topics for them. It is also one of the most significant challenges for the modern science and technology.

A cellular automaton is a system composed of a large number of cells. The local interactions among the cells decide the characteristics of the whole system's behavior. Because any characteristics of the system behavior are not equal to the linear superposition of the characteristics of individual cellular behavior, we cannot analyze the system using traditional mathematical equations or statistical regression. In step with the development of highly advanced computing technology, it was found that a cellular automaton can use a simple, locally ruled, and discrete method, with the help of computing technology, to transform nonlinear relationships among various factors into executable programs, thus to simulate a complex, global, and continuous system. Therefore, a cellular automaton has become an effective way to study a dynamic complex system to date. At the same time, a series of methods that are based on simple rules, including the elementary cellular automata, will become a practical tool to study the science of complex systems, and will be applied in more and more scientific disciplines extensively.

The content of this book is divided into three parts:

Part I (Chaps. 1–4) systematically elaborates the conceptual origin of the cellular automata, their working principles, modeling methods, and complexity analysis. With these, we try to provide fundamental theoretical knowledge for our readers who intend to understand the cellular automata in depth.

Part II (Chaps. 5–7) discusses mutual combination and interaction as well as mutual penetration between the cellular automata and genetic algorithm, neural network, and intelligent agent, thus draw upon each other's strength.

Part III (Chaps. 8–9) discusses the fields of common applications for the cellular automata. In this part, we will mainly introduce the typical applications of the cellular automaton in the fields such as economy, urban traffic management, and disease transmission. Finally, in the concluding remarks, we lay out the outlook for future prospect of the cellular automata.

This book can be used as a reference for college and university teachers, students as well as researchers in the fields of information science and engineering, artificial intelligence and computer science, systems engineering and complexity management, and related fields.

Completion of this comprehensive book was the result of the joint efforts of the teachers and graduate students of the authors' research teams in recent years, especially, Prof. LI Xuewei proposed the framework, major elements and details, then reviewed, and finalized the book, graduate student ZHAO Yun, who took part in the writing of Chaps. 4 and 9, based on his research for doctor degree; Dr. GUO Juanqiong, Dr. LI Jie, and Dr. ZHU Minghao who took part in the writing of Chap. 8; doctor degree graduate students DOU Shuihai, FENG Yunqing, WEI Gongding, and QIU Heting were responsible for proofreading of the book; Prof. Li Xuemei provided many valuable refinements to the book after carefully reading the whole manuscripts. It is their hard work and great contribution that enabled the book to be published promptly. We are much obliged to all of them.

In particular, we would like to express our gratitude to Mr. ZHANG Minsheng who translated this book into English.

In the writing process of this book, we took references of and cited a large number of related domestic and foreign publications and research proceedings. It would be impossible for us to complete this book without previous research results in the field. We are very grateful to all the experts and scholars whose work we have referenced or cited in the book. In addition, we want to thank the related leadership at Beijing Jiaotong University Press and the editor for this book Chen Yueqin, their generous help made this book published smoothly.

The researches conducted that were related with the writing of this book had been supported by the Chinese National 863 project—"professional component and system development of complex equipment operation and maintenance services", and had been carried on the exploratory trials on high-speed EMU health monitoring, and had laid a good foundation for further applications in engineering.

Finally, it is important to point out that, writing a book on a new inter-discipline subject like this, one has to be in constant contact of new knowledge, and in constant exploration of new topics. Due to the limitation of our knowledge, impropriety in the book may be unavoidable. We sincerely hope that experts and readers could kindly point out such impropriety, for the improvement of the book.

Beijing, China Xuewei Li

Contents

Chapter 1
The Conceptual Origin of Cellular Automata

1.1 A Way of Thinking in Complexity: Complex Thinking

1.1.1 Simplicity and the Principle of Simplicity

Since ancient Greece, simplicity has always been a beacon for scientists to the truth. Aristotle said in his book of "metaphysics" that: "an academic theory with less principles is more accurate than those alike with more complimentary principles". Later, some scientific pioneers inherited and developed the thought of Aristotle. For example, British philosopher William Occam proposed the famous "Occam razor", that was: "entities should not be multiplied unnecessarily." His logic was that we should shave off unmercifully those that are redundant and useless." In modern times, Newton (Newton) unified the complex principles of universe and earth movements with simple Three Laws of Motion and the Law of Universal Gravitation. He put forward in "the mathematical principle of natural philosophy" that: "Nature does nothing in vain, and more is in vain when less will serve; for Nature is pleased with simplicity, and affects not the pomp of superfluous causes". In the era of relativity, Albert Einstein liked simplicity more in thinking. He said: "one comes closer to the preeminent goal of science, that of encompassing a maximum of empirical contents through logical deduction with a minimum of hypotheses or axioms". He also points out that: "the simplicity of natural law is an objective fact", and: "The right conceptual system must be balanced in terms of the subjective and objective aspects of the simplicity". Considering simplicity as a fact of objective world, Albert Einstein took pursuit of simplicity as the highest goal of his life. He was willing to spend all the energy of the second half of his life to study the unified field theory, in which he tried to use geometric method to unify the interaction between gravitation forces and electromagnetic forces. In summary of aforementioned scientific pioneers' descriptions, thinking in simplicity developed into the Principle of Simplicity. The connotation is that in forming and evaluating a scientific theory, one should try the best to use fewer basic concepts, axioms, and

X. Li et al., *Theory of Practical Cellular Automaton*,
https://doi.org/10.1007/978-981-10-7497-4_1

assumptions; with the simplest mathematical languages, symbols and equations; but come up with the content covering the experiences, facts and phenomena as extensive as possible. The Principle of Simplicity stipulates that in the system of scientific deduction, general principles should obey the need of simplicity. This is because: first, the fewer basic concepts and basic laws used, the easier to determine the logic completeness of the entire theory system, and the easier to eliminate the conflict within the system itself. Secondly, the simpler the way in expressing the law of nature, the easier to verify through experimental observations, this brings the experiment the advantages of easy duplicating and repeated verifications. Thirdly, use as fewer basic concepts and basic laws as possible, this means that each concept obtained may contain as many experiences as possible, so that the theoretical system thus formed will have wide range of applications. It can be said that the Principle of Simplicity has been an important tradition for modern time scientific research. It also has been a driving force for the development of science.

For a long time, guided by the Principle of Simplicity, people have tried to probe into the simplicity of material composition, the simplicity of the laws of the movements, as well as the simplicity of the scientific methods. It can be said that the Principle of Simplicity has become a kind of paradigm for human scientific thinking. The so called paradigm is the spiritual pillar and the common belief accumulated together by a generation of scientists. It is also a general view or a framework as well as the guidelines for common compliance for these scientists in their scientific activities. It determines the ways scientists to observe, to ask questions, as well as to think and to solve the problems. In past hundreds of years, scientists have always been taking the Principle of Simplicity as the dominant ideology, and have made amazing achievements in scientific practices under the guidance of the principle. For example: the Quantum Physics views the world as various combinations of quarks and leptons, sums up the complex relationships among objects as four basic interactions; in Mechanics, a very complex machine is decomposed into various simple mechanical repetitions; in Optics, a riot of rich magnificent colors is decomposed into three kinds of primary colors of red, green and blue; in Chemistry, nearly 550 million compounds discovered in the world are considered as compositions of 112 kinds of elements, and various elements, and elements in turn, are only various combinations of electrons, neutrons and protons, etc. In summary, the Principle of Simplicity has made distinctive contributions to human understanding of the objective world. It has become a symbol of the truth. So far, the Principle of Simplicity is still regarded as an important part of the rationality of science. It is a principle of methods in establishing, evaluating and choosing scientific theories. However, it is no longer the sole principle in this aspect.

The Principle of Simplicity considers that the world as a whole is unified and harmonic, dominated by a few principles of very simple logic. One can grasp the laws of development for things once these principles have been found. No matter how complex the world is, its complexities should be, and also can be digested with the analysis guided by the Principle of Simplicity. These complexities are subject to the law of simplicity, can be quantified and also can be described with the languages or symbols. However, following the advancement of science and the improvement of human knowledge, it has become more and more apparent that the Principle of Simplicity's thinking of the world in a single mode has its limitations, as manifested in the following forms:

1. **Processing the whole as the sum of its parts**

The Principle of Simplicity is closely related with the Reductionism, the basic idea of which is that, in studying a complex object, the first thing we need to do is to divide this object into numerous components, according to certain principles. We will keep doing this kind of division until the sub components we obtained from division can be studied strictly and thoroughly. Physicists, for example, break a crystal down into atoms, and in turn break them down into smaller particles—the nuclei and electrons. It is generally believed that if all these smaller components have been fully understood, then a full understanding of the entire system has been reached.

The Reductionism processes complex things in simple ways. This kind of processing methods is influenced by the world view of the Mechanism, which views the universe as a machine or a big clock. Human beings are machines, or screws on a machine. According to the Mechanism, in order to understand this machine or this clock, we need first to break the system into parts or make the system detachable. This is obviously a simplification of the complex things. It considers that the only way to get the overall understanding of the whole is to start from the study of the characteristics of the parts, viewing the whole as the sum of the parts. In order to get characteristics of the whole, one only needs to detach the parts from each other and does study on these individual parts. In doing this, the nonlinear coherence among the parts of the system have been ignored.

The Reductionism has the potential of assuming that, whether belong to the same category or not, things can always be decomposed into more basic components or elements. In the process of decomposition, the original information will be preserved. Therefore the theory holds that through analysis on materials of lower level and the material movements with low level of complexity, people can understand the materials of higher levels, as well as the material movements with high level of complexity. In fact, in using this top-down and step by step method for decomposition and refinement, we cannot tackle the questions originated from high levels and from the entirety, and also cannot understand the emerging issues with the characteristics of the system as a whole.

2. **Handling the nonlinear problems in linear ways**

The method for the Principle of Simplicity in processing many nonlinear problems is to linearize the problems, and to approximate the nonlinear models with linear models. For example, in solving the problem of docking a boat, the classical mechanics uses linear differential equation and uses the simplified form of damping medium, thus the result obtained predicts that the movement of the boat docking follows an exponential curve, with the boat infinitely getting closer to the shore. Strictly speaking, the time for the boat really touches the shore is infinite according to this kind of theory. Obviously, this is an idealized model. The actual situation is much more complicated in which the boat would move further away from the results of the calculation based on this kind of theory, so long as there is a small wave.

Linear differential equation is a mathematical form commonly used by the Principle of Simplicity. It is commonly known that the solution of a differential equation can be obtained through integration. A differential equation is a function, thus a curve in the plane or the space of geometry. We can describe a system's movement in details based on the shape and various characteristics of mathematical curve we obtained about the system, thus to understand the nature, the characteristics and the patterns of the system's movements.

However, mathematicians found that the vast majority of the differential equations were not solvable. That is to say, their integral expressions could not be found thus they are not integratable. Scientists wish that we have as many integratable differential equations as possible, and in the contrary, have as fewer non-integratable differential equations as possible. Then in the end how many differential equations are there that are not integratable? Mathematicians compared the differential equations that are integratable with those that are not, and found that the amount of integratable differential equations is almost not measurable. What does this mean? If we put all the integratable differential equations as well as the non-integratable differential equations into a pocket, then every time we pick an equation out of the pocket, it must be non-integratable, with almost no chance of picking up an integratable.

Because that vast majority of differential equations are non-integratable, we should consider the nature of the world as non-periodic and nonlinear. In the past, the concerns of the Principle of Simplicity theory were on linear and periodic activities, therefore it was a theory about integratable systems. However, the systems in our real world are almost all non-integratable.

3. Viewing non-equilibrium as abnormal state

The classic science dominated by the Principle of Simplicity views the equilibrium state the only normal state, and views the non-equilibrium as abnormal state caused by disturbance, and tries to extend the conclusion of linearity obtained from the equilibrium state to the non-equilibrium state.

Belgian scientist and Nobel Prize winner Ilya Prigogine invented the Dissipative Structure Theory (DST), which as a pioneer theory, broke the limitation of the Physics of the Equilibrium State. The DST revealed the intrinsic mechanism of material movement from chaotic to orderly, from instable, disharmonic to stable and harmonic. Ilya Prigogine considered that in nature, there was no absolute order. As long as there was a breeze, it would stir up ripples on the calm water surface of a pond. Even for boundless torpid sea, with swift currents lurks underneath, its bottom was not calm.

Prigogine pointed out that "order arises from chaos." Everything in the universe is not balanced in the process of development. The balance is generated from imbalance, the two states one comes after the other. The nonlinear mechanism occurs only when the system is far from equilibrium, and coherence effect will be generated. Departing from linear function of the numerical superposition, the nonlinear mechanism is generated through the cooperation of the key elements of the system, to form a new integrated effect, thus resulting in the formation of new qualities and new structures with order.

4. **Treating chaos as random noise**

The principle of simplicity considers that the stable state of a system can only be at equilibrium or periodic, none periodic movement is transitional, will gradually disappear with the system approaching the steady state. Limited by this view, this theory treats the non-periodic chaos as random noise, although such phenomena commonly exist in nature and in human society. American meteorologist E. N. Lorenz was the first person who broke the limitation of this traditional view. In weather forecast, he discarded the concept that simplified the chaos as random noise in treatment. He acknowledged that although a system that could be described by a definitive equation, without any random factors added and the initial conditions were definitive, the system itself might generate a phenomenon that was chaotic and looked like random. The none-periodic movement might be a stable state of the system. Speaking in more accurate terms, chaos is a kind of pseudo random for a definitive system. Chaos is not simple disorder but without apparent periodicity, an orderly structure with rich inner layers. Ignoring the intrinsic disorder and complexity of a chaotic movement as superficial phenomenon and simplify it as orderly periodic movement (Hu 2010), or as a random disturbance, this belongs to the methodology of the Principle of Simplicity. The discovery of chaos forecasted a new revolution in scientific thinking. It revealed that the simple pursuit of order, linearity, as well as simplicity for the Principle of Simplicity does not fit the objective reality. The world we are facing is full of disorders, complexities and countless amazement.

5. **Treating segment shape as near-orderly pattern**

For objects with regular shapes, people have been using Euclid geometrical method to build up various ideal models (they were almost all linear), thus to put all these problems into the solvable domain. Such approximation method has been very effective in many situations, thus lead to fruitful results in scientific researches. However, if we look around, various kinds of objects in nature are almost not regularly shaped. For example, mountains, sea shores, rivers, snow-flakes, clouds in the sky, trees and woods, as well as the human bodies are all non-regularly shaped. According to the processing method of the Principle of Simplicity, we should choose a proper scale and ignore all the irregularities as well as nonlinearities that are less than the scale we have chosen and to discard them as exceptional objects, thus we transform the complex shaped patterns into relative regular patterns that are at least smooth curved in segments. In doing this, although the problems are greatly simplified, the intrinsic irregularities and complexities of the objects have been artificially illuminated as well. French mathematician Bennoit Mandelbrot worked against such principle. He collected the complex objects with patterns closer to nature shapes as his research objects, and did theoretical and philosophical study on them, and put forward the concept of segmental pattern. By directly taking non-linear complex objects as starting point, he tried to study the inner nature of the objects without simplification and absolution of them, and established the science of Fractal geometry. It can be said that Fractal geometry is a kind of geometry that is more close to the nature.

Fractal has two basic characteristics: irregularity (roughness) and self similarity (similarity between parts and the whole). For example, the stock price fluctuates, there seems to be no rules. By staring at the price every minute, you really cannot see any clue. However, by tracing the stock price change within a week, or even within a month or within a year, you will find some commonality, as well as certain similarity between the parts and whole. Unlike Euclidean geometry, Fractal geometry has no basic elements such as points, lines and surfaces. It departed from the long time habit of people's thinking about the objects in their lengths, sizes or scales. A fractal is described by algorithms and programs, and is transformed into a geometry form by computing. Because of the self similarity of fractal, many of these algorithms are recursive and iterative.

Fractal theory points out the dialectical relationship between parts and the whole in the objective world, which breaks the diaphragm separating the parts from the whole, and finds the media and the bridge from the parts to the whole, that is the similarity between the parts and the whole.

The fractal theory led human's understanding of the relationship between the parts and the whole from linear development to nonlinear, and provides a new method for the understanding of the unlimited from limited knowledge.

In short, taking the whole as the sum of its parts, the nonlinearity as a deviation from linearity, the non-equilibrium as the disturbance to the equilibrium state, the chaos as random noise, the fractal as a regular pattern in complex form, all these are treating the complexity as the simplicity, the results of which can only be failures. In twentieth Century, through in-depth study of vast amount of complex objects, the scientific community gradually realized that although the Principle of Simplicity had been effective and fruitful, it could not handle many issues in various fields such as biology, economics and social affairs. The limitations of the Principle of Simplicity gradually became apparent with the scientific development and social progress. In particular, in 1980s, the international academic community made a trend in the research of the complexity. Breaking the limitation of Principle of Simplicity and its thinking method had become a common desire among the scientists.

1.1.2 Complexity and Complex Thinking

1. **The rise of complexity research**

In entering the twenty-first Century, a question arose on what kinds of world outlook and methodology mankind will use to observe, to study and to change the world?

A famous British scientist Stephen Hawking considered that the twenty-first Century is the century of complexity science. A well known US scientist, Nobel laureate G. Cowan praised the complexity science as "the science of twenty-first Century." This is because that all the contemporary major natural and social problems have very strong relevance, and are increasingly integrated and complex.

People not only need to understand individual factors or individual objects, but also need to study and solve the problems of complex systems based on the understanding of the entirety of the system. It can be said that in the analysis of social structure, in handling of large industrial production, as well as in planning of the national economy and the study of biological, ecological and climate issues, there is almost no single complex object that is not included within the study of complexity research. Therefore, the rise of the exploration of complexity marked a new dialogue between people and society as well as between mankind and nature (Cao 2005).

Obviously in the universe, the most complex system that is the most difficult to explore by traditional scientific methods is human being. As the French scholars of the complexity study have pointed out: human beings cannot simply be consider as "men of making tools", or technically put on a face of "wise man" theoretically. On the face of a human being, we should be able to see the myth, the festival, the dance, the song, the obsession, the love, the death, the indulgence, the war, etc. A real person exists between a Homo sapiens and a fanatics. For this reason, only a theory of the system complexity will be able to integrate the inharmonic human phenomena in a harmonious way, and only this theory could rationally imagine the non-rational things.

In fact, complexity is emerging in many areas, the following examples will describe this.

In biological fields, we want to analyze the mechanism of interaction between biological molecules. For this, we cannot use the traditional methods of analyzing the physical systems. On the contrary, we should treat it as a complex system and analyze it using the theories of complex systems. This is because that modern researches have already revealed that the biological creatures have the characteristics of complex systems, no matter in the macrocosmic or the microscopic views. In fact, this issue was raised when people started to study nucleic acid DNA. Because DNA is the most basic level of our biological research, the research on all creatures can be deduced to this level. Are DNA sequences the complex systems? Recent studies have found that a complete DNA sequence has the characteristics of self similarity, which can be described by fractal dimensions. This shows that the micro-performances of the biological organisms have the nature of complex systems. Scientists also analyzed the beating of the heart and the ECG, and analyzed the activity of the brain and the data of EEG. The results showed that the data has the characteristics of chaotic dynamics, the nature of complex systems, and the activities reflected are chaotic activities. In addition, analysis on the respiratory cycle, sleep cycle and reproductive cycle of life creatures also have been conducted and it was found that all these macro-behaviors have chaotic characteristics. This means that the biological systems have the characteristics of complex systems on the macro view. As professor John Gribbin of the University of Cambridge in UK said: "chaos leads to complexity, complexity leads to lives". In short, only by the view of complex systems, the self-organizing phenomenon of biological molecules can be explained, why the process of the occurrence of biological creatures and lives in nature suddenly changed from chaotic to orderly, from unstructured into a structured can be explained. Therefore, the analysis methods of complex system can help us to understand various complex problems of biological systems.

In the field of information, mankind's study of the laws of thinking was focused on the development of the computers and mathematical logic. The inventers of computers attempted to simulate human's thinking process by using mathematical languages. But there is still a big difference between the computers and the human brains. A human brain is good at imaginary thinking. Its advantage is to be able to consider the problem from the entirety, using imagination, association, metaphor, intuition, inspiration for processing of the issues. To date, the computers are much inferior in comparison with human brains in imaginary thinking. Computers lack creative thinking because they are still in the stage of studying from and simulating human beings. Although there is no much difference on the level of information processing, why computers are so inferior in the capacity of imaginary thinking? One important reason is that human brains that are operated on biological platforms are vastly complex systems, while the computers that are operating on machinery platforms, still lack the various behaviors of complex systems. Computers can be fully utilized only when they are assigned proper tasks by human beings. Computers can only solve the problems that human beings understand thus come up with proper algorithms. So called creativity and inspirational thinking are all related with complex systems. The nonlinear emergent characteristics of complex system could only be possessed by human brains, so that they can think with nonlinear methods based on the consideration of entirety. All these cannot be achieved by a computer yet by now, for a computer is still operated on linear processes. The researchers of artificial intelligence believe that the difference between a human brain and an existing computer is mainly in the aspect of complexity, so the research on the characteristics of complex system of the computers becomes a very important and a key direction. Only by this way, the essence of the intelligence, that is, the essence of the complex system can be studied.

In the field of ecology, people are increasingly inclined to grasp different levels of natural system from its entirety. For example, in our research on earth, isolated researches on its crust, hydrosphere or atmosphere are no longer considered desirable. This is because that some of the natural systems cannot be separated from each other, or we can say that we can't get the behavior of entire system from studying partial behaviors. To reveal the mystery of the nature of the objects, the mystery of association and the relationship, the mystery of the complexity, it requires us to change our study from traditional single discipline studies to the study of the entirety of the natural system on different levels.

In economic field, the mainstream thinking of the traditional economics was based on the linear models. Linearity and equilibrium were the paradigms of the traditional economics. These specific assumptions reduced the complexity of the economic reality, but brought disguise to the economy. In fact, the economic system is more complex than the system of physics. The economic process is a complex process that cannot be described and accurately predicted by linear equations. By investigating the economic equilibrium and evolutionary dynamics, economists have put forward a non equilibrium, evolutionary, and nonlinear complex economics. The complex and rich and colorful phenomena of economics in life can be described by the methods based on nonlinear science and information science and can be explained in the terms of self-organization, fluctuation, and amplification. This shows that complexity is becoming a new paradigm in economics.

In the field of management, a management system is a system whose activities involved human beings that have consciousness and initiative. It has the attributes of the nature and in the mean time, possesses the complexity of having social attributes and human culture attributes. The new organizations are replacing traditional simple, mechanical organizations, and the most notable feature of the new organizations is their complexity. In fact, some concepts and ideas that are contained in the complexity science, such as integrity, nonlinearity, emergence, self-organization, self similarity, provide a valuable metaphor and methods for management science. This reveals that complexity is becoming a core element in organization and management.

In social fields, the objects of social science such as individual, group, organization, society, identity, status, functionality, all contain numerous layers and interactions, the study of which cannot avoid the concept of complexity. Although through setting up of the organizations, the society could weaken the complexity brought by the individual randomness and disorder, this on the other hand increased the layers of social organizations thus brought about a more and more complex social structure based on enormous organizational complexity. One step further, we can see that the eternal thread brought by disorder brings the society the characteristics of complexity—forever reorganizing.

In the field of engineering and technology, many large engineering projects are not pure engineering. Taking Three Gorges project as example, in the planning and construction stages, the project not only took full account of the needs of power generation, flood control, irrigation, shipping, fisheries, etc., but also needed to address the complex factors and relationships such as relocation of the people affected by the projects, pollution and environmental protection, in order to maximize the social and economical benefits and ecological benefits. For another example, the objects for the planners of construction engineering are not only houses. The famous architectural expert from Tsinghua University, a member of both Academy of Science and Academy of Engineering, professor Wu Liangyong once put forward the idea of "the science of human settlements". In his view, a construction project must consider overall living environment which includes architecture, urban and regional issues, thus the project is an open and complex giant system. In the course of its development, the project needs to face the complicated natural and social problems, needs the help from the methods of complexity science to explore and to solve the problems.

In short, a new paradigm of complexity is brewing in various fields. Although this paradigm is still in its infancy and in development stages, yet it has not become a mainstream paradigm in some areas, but its development trend has been highlighted. So, what is the significance of our study of complexity?

From the process of scientific study, people would always study the relatively simple systems first, and then studied the systems with relative complexity. Since 1990s, not only in the fields of natural sciences, but also in the fields of humanities, social sciences, philosophy, "complexity" has quietly coming into our sights, and now there is no area for which it does not have its own complexity and study the complexity is a task for the area. Some of the objects that were considered not perplexing by the observations of simple sciences now suddenly became understandable by revealing the objects' complex natures. Therefore, complexity science has become the frontier and trend of modern scientific research.

In non-complex systems, the processes of evolution can be neglected. The guiding ideology of the entire scientific system is deterministic, which believes that the world's development and changes are controlled by some definitive laws, and therefore, same causes will produce same results, time is reversible. Uncertainty is either a kind of myopia or illusion. When it comes to complex systems, however, evolution has become the center and key to our understanding of problems. It is therefore necessary to reexamine the original natural laws.

In the fields such as cosmology, physics, chemistry, biology, ecology, or any other fields in the social sciences and the humanities, we have observed instability, fluctuation, bifurcation and limited predictability on all levels of observation. It can be seen everywhere that the past and the future play different roles, and here the natural laws defined by determinism are severely challenged. New natural laws believe that the natural world is constantly evolving, and from either a temporal or spatial perspective, it is full of uncertainties. Evolution, emergence and complexity are the basic tones for all natural processes on all levels. Various individuals emerge from the whole, such as, towns emerge out of villages, while they are embedded in the villages where they come from. Such phenomena are against to the deterministic ideology, which holds that evolution is independent of its environment. Life always needs air and water. We have always had the interaction between "lives" and "non-lives." In the past, we were used to designing a fixed tool system for implementation of a defined practical goal. This could only complete specified tasks in a pre-determined environment, and the shift among tasks was controlled by determining conditions. In the scientific era when deterministic ideology was dominating, such an approach was without rebuke. In an environment where the complexity of evolution cannot be neglected, however, such design principle is impracticable. The so called complex systems are those which are comprised of complex elements, structures, relations and behavior. Such systems are not deterministic, but evolutionary. What, however, are the structures and laws of variation of these complex systems? How to design a system which can work self-adaptively in a constantly evolving and uncertain complex environment? These are new challenges mankind are facing.

Regarding complexity, the following opinions and methods are especially worth noticing: from determinism to evolution, from reductionism to emergence, from organization by others to self-organization, from the time reversible to irreversible, from centralism to dispersion, from an optimum solution to a satisfactory one, from substance centrism to relational centrism, etc. As we study these variations further, we will possibly bring about new reformation and elevation of human thinking methods.

2. **The Transformation of the Ways Human Think**

About half a century ago, the movements in nature scientists concerned about were either movements towards a fixed point, or periodical, quasi-periodical, or even random movements. The fixed-point, periodical or quasi-periodical movements all reflect a Newtonian world view, i.e., deterministic. It stipulates that as long as we find the motion equations of them, and determine their initial conditions by measurement, we can predict their behaviors precisely. Random movements, however, are non-deterministic. Still, so long as we can figure out their statistic equations, not only can we understand their behavior, but also we can predict the probability of the event occurrence, though we may not be able to predict the occurrence of the event with certainty. In recent decades, scientists discovered, however, apart from the several modes of movement mentioned above, chaotic movements and chaotic systems not only are present in nature and in social phenomena, but also are prevalent instead of being exceptional. They exist commonly in nature, in water stream and air stream, in the movements of planets, in global climatic changes, in the thinking of human brain, in social changes, in economical activities, even in the children's play on the swing. Although this kind of equations is definitive, not including any random elements, the behavior of the system is non-periodical, unpredictable. In addition, many movements that were originally categorized as random movements are actually chaotic. The discovery of chaos demonstrates that the motions in the material world around us are the dialectical coexistences of orderliness and disorderliness, of definiteness and randomness, of simplicity and complexity. It can be seen that, classical science which pursued order, linearity, precision, and simplicity, is not in accordance with the objective reality. The exploration of complexity represents our new efforts to change the scientific understanding and methods which dominated our research before, so as to establish a new mode of thinking for mankind.

1) **The Unity of the Opposites between Order and Disorder**

Physics points out: Order generally refers to the regular relations and movements, either among the elements inside an object or among the objects; irregularity, however, refers to the chaotic and irregular combinations and dynamic changes among the composite elements of things or the relations among them. In everyday life, people often use the two words "order" and "disorder" to describe the different states of things. For example, a melody is orderly, while noise is disorderly; a chunk of ice is orderly, while vapor is disorderly; life's regular movement is orderly, and death is disorderly; the harmony and steady development of national economy is orderly, and its imbalance is disorderly. The "orderliness" and "disorderliness" defined in physics are the same as our direct daily experiences.

For a long time, people had considered that things only existed in the world in two modes: orderly or disorderly. They even believed that the world was originally orderly and regular, and the task of science was to discover the orderly essence through the disorderly phenomena, so as to describe a completely regular and self-organized world. Even if it was a step back from the ideal situation, efforts were made to draw a blueprint in which the disorders were ignored. The discovery of chaos, however, deeply revealed the unity of opposites of the orderly and disorderly. Orderliness and disorderliness are relative, for any orderliness can become disorderly if being put in either a bigger or smaller domain. By the same token, any disorderliness, being put in bigger or smaller domain, can exhibit orderly behavior, as long as the observation means and methods are precise enough. For example, observing the water from the perspective of chemical structure, H_2O is orderly. Yet observing from the angle of entirety, a drop of water in the ocean or a drop of water in the rain is disorderly. The warm current underneath the ocean moves in an orderly manner, while the drops of water in the current move disorderly. And yet the drops of water moving disorderly have an orderly structure. In short, disorderliness contains orderliness, while orderliness contains disorderliness. The famous scientist Parigogine said: "Orderliness and disorderliness always occur together, which is the rule upon which the universe was set up." The French scholar Edgar Morin said about the relationship between orderliness and disorderliness in his book *Complex Thinking: The Science of Self-Consciousness*: "a universe based on strict determinism is an universe in which only orderliness exists, in which there are no changes, no innovations and no creations. On the other hand, in a purely disorderly universe any organizations cannot be formed, therefore is not suitable for maintaining newborn things thus is not suitable for evolution and development. A completely deterministic world and a completely random one are both one-sided and defective. The former cannot evolve, while the latter cannot generate new things." Therefore, orderliness and disorderliness both have their limitations. "We need to rethink in a complex way, so as to reconsider the problem of orderliness and disorderliness. Rethinking such problem will help us rethink other problems in a complex way."

Everything in the universe is constantly evolving from disorderliness to orderliness. Disorderliness nurtures orderliness, while orderliness is born from disorderliness. Regarding human creativities, they developed through the permutations of disorderliness and orderliness. People's knowledge structure is under constant adjusting and changing. It may form a fixed knowledge structure within a period of time with fixed notions. This may be counted as orderly, and yet such a structure cannot stop people thinking. Under fixed notions, there can be various explorations and thinking, or even skepticism of existing views. Once in touch with new situations and new knowledge, armed with new ideas, new energy will be generated. Orderliness and disorderliness are under constantly mutual transformation. The orderliness of a theory or a concept will definitely develop into a disorderly state with the emergence of new technology and new theory, and will form theories and technologies of higher level. Science is ever changing and has been developing in a spiral way.

2) **The Unity of the Opposites between Certainty and Randomness**

Newtonian mechanics describes the laws of motion as simple and deterministic, and definitive equations will lead to definitive results. According to such a theory, we can predict the future of the world based on our current knowledge. The statistical mechanics and probability theory developed since 19th century began to put randomness as research object. It aims to come up with the laws of statistics from numerous random events. It believes that an individual event still obeys the deterministic laws of Newtonian mechanics. But in studying numerous events as a whole, the statistics Law of large numbers will dominate. Randomness is an external interference for deterministic equations; it is a kind of noise or fluctuation. Individual motions obey set Newtonian laws, while collective motions comprised of multiple individual motions obey the law of statistics. Definitive equations get definitive answers; on the other hand, random equations obtain statistical solutions. This shows that the relationships between determinacy and randomness, and between certainty and randomness, are still external and parallel.

The discovery of chaos shows that, definitive equations may produce non-definitive results. Such situation is due to the innate behavior of definitive non-linear equations, and not due to external disturbances or noises. Because of the high sensitivity and dependency of chaotic motions on their initial states, when there is a tiny variation of the initial values, for example, a tiny variation of 10^{-7}, although the future values still can be predicted within a short period of time, looks unlike the random processes, in the long run, however, their states will be completely unpredictable, causing definitive equations to produce uncertain results. Such situations are caused by the non-linearity factors, as well as the non-definitive results from interactions among numerous definitive factors. People call such seemingly non-definitiveness as pseudo-randomness, and sometimes defines chaos as the innate randomness of definitive systems. Therefore, the discovery of chaos unifies certainty and randomness, determinism and non-determinism on a higher level.

3) **The Unity of Opposites between Analysis and Synthesis**

For a long time, traditional science has believed that as long as characteristics of all parts of an object were known, a combination of them would retrieve a unified view of the object as a whole. Therefore, traditional science adopted a purely analytic method. For example, in the field of physics, such a method enabled mankind's understanding of substances evolved from molecules to atom, from atom to elementary particles, from bigger elementary particles to smaller ones such as quarks. In biology, human understanding evolved from organs to cells, from cells to bio-macromolecules, then to penetrate DNA to find the genetic codes. This analytic (or reductionist) method uses the quantitative analytic method frequently used in logic thinking, so as to guarantee the rigor and precision of scientific theories. But analysis without synthesis limits us to only seeing individual trees instead of seeing the entire forest. In fact, any analysis has to start from an overall view, and cannot deviate from the guidance of the overall understanding of the studied object. Otherwise, the analysis will have great blindness. In short, any kind of analysis is not the ultimate goal of a scientific research, but only a way to get to know things. Therefore, our research and understanding of the objects cannot stop at the mere stage of analysis, but has to proceed to synthesis stage so as to disclose the essence of the object and the laws of its movements.

The science of complexity regards objects as organisms with parts interconnected, mutually restricted and harmonic. It also views an object's various connections with its surrounding as a complex but integrated system, and this is the holistic ideology, which emphasizes the comprehensive research of an object or a system from its entirety. Holistic ideology thinks that the essence of everything in the universe can only be examined and understood from its entirety and from a macro view. Once an object is divided into parts, and a part is studied in isolation and its connections with other parts ignored, the "live" state of an object will be turned into a "dead" state and the characteristics reflecting the object as a whole but not on individual parts will be lost. By the same token, when an object is isolated from its environment and its connections with surrounding objects are cut off, the complex and complete system formed by the coexistence of the object with its surrounding objects is destroyed, and the object loses its original characteristics.

And yet the synthetic method uses imaginary thinking as its way for think, emphasizing to understand things through empirical experiences, insights, intuition and inspiration, from macroscopic view. This kind of understanding in some sense is ambiguous and imprecise, but overall its conclusion is definitive. Therefore, synthesis needs analysis as its basis. Without analysis, a concrete thought can only be empty and abstract.

Obviously, only by combining the analysis method and synthesis method, or combining the reduction theory and the holistic theory, we can overcome the shortcoming of each method, or the short coming of each theory, to take complimentary advantage. This is the inevitable trend of future development. In fact, this is the way people practice to dialectically combine precise thinking and fuzzy thinking, to proceed in the way of "analyzing—synthesizing—analyzing again—synthesizing again".

The rise of complexity science has an important influence on the way of traditional scientific thinking. The simple thinking of the traditional science can get satisfactory results in a certain range when dealing with numerous practical problems. However, it is at the cost of discarding a variety of nonlinear factors, or at the cost of only putting the weak nonlinear problems into considerations. The limitation of the simple thinking lies in the way it reduces complexity of life and society to linear, orderly, single, reversible and deterministic things; breaking the natural connected things into unrelated things, taking a compartmentalized view of the world. Simple thinking has made great contributions in the history of human science, but based on our measurement of solvability for things, the scale of solvability for a simple thing is almost zero. So, simplicity is like an island, and complexity is like a sea.

Complex thinking is based on modern nonlinear science. For nonlinear nature of objective things, it is a new thinking that does not give out simplified explanation that neglects various nonlinear factors. It expresses a kind of thinking of associated synthesis and analysis on non-reductive and beyond-reductive, paying more attention to the association, the diversity, the difference among things; to the critical state and fluctuation, the imbalance and the non reversibility, of the things; to chaos and the emergence; to bifurcation and evolution, and so on.

Complex thinking is more real, more comprehensive and more sophisticated than the simple thinking. But the complexity is not exclusive of simplicity. It simplifies things from another dimension, from another perspective, with a different way. This kind of expression of simplification will get the result closer to the reality when the object is transformed back into its original state. Complexity is a very important concept. It is the inevitable trend of people to further understand the objective world. But complexity is not a master key. We should not make things more complex for the sake of the complexity, using complexity to kick up a cloud of dust, inflicting a pseudo complexity. This is not the scientific attitude in seriously exploring the complexity. Anthropologist Clifford Geertz, in his book of "cultural interpretation", said plainly and calmly that: "at the place where it can be applied and can be expanded, apply your effort and expand your effort; just stop at the place where your effort cannot be applied and expanded." This should be our attitude in facing a new field or a new concept.

1.2 A Computing Mode Originated from Complexity—Computation by Rules

1.2.1 The Complexity of Computation

No one's life, study, and work can function without computation. Whenever we encounter a practical problem, our usual response is "let me calculate it." Mathematics was born from the calculations of practical problems. Mathematicians have always been pursuing the general solutions of problems through computation. From the simple calculation of the area of a triangle to the solutions of complex equations which describe all kinds of natural and social phenomena, quantitative methods have infiltrated all walks of life. In complex science, computation and its algorithm have especially important significance.

Computation is a physical operational process, the completion of which needs basic computational time and space (Ben 2002). So called computational complexity refers to the cost of computer resources in solving a problem, and such cost is a measure of the efficiency of the algorithms used in the computation. In general, temporal complexity means how many steps a computer takes to solve a problem, while spatial complexity means how much memory or storage a computer needs for such an operation. The existence of both temporal and spatial complexity tells us that time and space are the most basic limiting physical factors of computation. Both computational time and space are limited, and they are closely related to the reasonable scales of time and space of human activities. Beyond this reasonable scale of time and space, computation will become unrealistic and impossible. For example, if computational time takes so long as several years or tens of years, the computation is unrealistic, not to mention that there is no guarantee that new problems will not occur during this period.

The complexity of computation is determined by the complexity of algorithms. In determining whether a problem is a complex problem that is difficult to solve, we must examine whether we have algorithms for the problem, that is, whether its operational time and the space it occupies exceed the reasonable scale. Therefore, the computation complexity is to transform the complexity of a system into the issue of how much time or space will be needed in solving a problem. Thus, we can see that all the problems tackled by the research of computational complexity are about algorithms. The same problem of computation often has many different algorithms for its solution. Regarding a large amount of data, numerous time and space needed for computation can be saved if we can find the optimum algorithm.

An algorithm is a computational method for solving certain kind of problems. Traditional science did not believe that any new things could be discovered through computation. Therefore, computational methods were just regarded as auxiliary methods. Complexity research, however, has changed people's outdated ideas, for many phenomena and laws of complexity have been discovered through computing. Many branches of complexity theory, such as cellular automata, the Game of Life, artificial life, complex adaptive systems and so on are all based on computation or algorithms, and are all typical cases of the applications of computational methods. Therefore, computational methods (or computational modes) are important methods for complexity research.

1.2.2 Two Computational Modes for Complexity Research

1. **Analytic Methods for Solving Mathematical Equations**

We all know that mathematics is the science of studying real world quantitative relations and spatial forms. In this regard, there are two kinds of the most basic problems in mathematics: those need solutions and those need proofs. The search for solutions consists of algorithmic design and computation; while the search for proofs consists of logical reasoning and deductive proving. Both are indispensable for the development of accurate human thinking. People experience "calculation" more easily, since it is the basic activity for scientific research and engineering design. It appears everywhere in people's lives and work. For instance:

When you stared at night sky, did you realize that the tracks of numerous celestial bodies could be described and calculated through mathematical equations?

When you listened to news broadcast, did you realize that the electromagnetic waves floating in the air owe their initial discovery to the solution of a group of differential equations?
When you went for a physical examination in a hospital, did you realize that the inventions of many widely used medical diagnosis equipments depended on certain mathematical principles?
When you wandered in the business world or in stock market, did you believe that mathematics could help you avoid risks, gain profits, and succeed by using the right strategies?
….

In summary, the progress of human civilization has sufficiently proven that only mathematics is able to describe scientific phenomena and laws precisely and succinctly with its unparalleled and irreplaceable language (concepts, formulas, theorems, algorithms, models, etc.). Just like the famous saying of the great scientist G. Galilei: "The book of nature is written in the language of mathematics."

Scientific progress was so rapid. By mid 20th century, almost all relatively simple scientific questions had their answers. The theory of general relativity and quantum mechanics explained the operating mechanism of the universe on both grand and minute scales. The understanding of the structures of nucleic acid molecules' DNA and their roles in the genetic replication mechanism made it simple to explain life phenomena on a molecular level (a level more microscopic than the cellular level). When the simple questions had been answered, naturally, scientists started trying to challenge more complex problems. As an important research method for people to explore unknown natural laws, mathematics also faced the challenge of complexity. As we know, natural evolution follows a mysterious way, which is completely different from any mathematical analytic method invented by men. For example, it is vitally important for the human body to maintain a constant temperature of 36.8 °C, and even a deviation of 0.5 °C is enough to make a person sick. Within the wide range from 0 to 100 °C, what makes the human body arrive at such an accurate optimum body temperature? This absolutely cannot be solved by analytic algorithms such as gradient descent. Yet, we believe that current analytic methods are far from being adequate to describe the body temperature, or to describe the complex relations between human body structure and the environment.

In order to make up for the inadequacy of the analytic methods, scientists needed to expand the concept of computation, and the key was to establish a new computational mode to extend but not to replace the analytic methods which are based on mathematical equations.

2. **Computer Simulation Method Using the Simple Rule of Repeated Iterations**

Complexity research shows that under certain conditions, repeated iteration of the simplest elements, relations and laws can simulate life, and even may simulate all existing complexity and diversity in the universe exhaustively (Huang 2005). That is to say, the repeated application of simple rules can possibly result in very complex behavior. We can summarize it with a formula: complexity = simplicity + iteration. This reminds us of the Chinese game of Go and the *Book of Changes*. The rules in the game of Go are very simple, but with very complex variations; also, the ideas in the *Book of Changes* are very plain, but with infinite unpredictable permutations and combinations of Yin and Yang. By the same token, in human society, a simple confrontation between individuals can result in various complex social cooperation and social structures by repeated (iterative) game playing.

Just as K. Steven said, "Whenever you observe very complex physical and biological systems, you will discover that their basic elements of composition and basic rules are very simple. The occurrence of complexity is due to the automatic and constant interactions among these simple elements."

Iteration plays an important role in the research of complex systems. It is a kind of computation which repeatedly operates on a system's behavioral states. We can use the language of functions to express the changes of a system's states. Suppose the change from state (a_0, t_0) to state (a_1, t_1) is the result of the operation of an operator, i.e. $a_1 = T(a_0)$, then, a_0 is called pre-image (counter image), a_1 is called conversion image (mapping image), T is called operator. Obviously, with the operator's repeated operations, the mapping image obtained from the previous operation must be regarded as a pre-image for the operator's current operation. Such repeated application of the operator on the states of a counter image is called iteration. During the successive conversion process, the consequently obtained states a_0, a_1, a_2, … can be seen as the results of applying the operator's functions repeatedly to the system. If the operator functions in n steps, then we will get

$$a_n = T^n(a_0)$$

From the point of view of system science, what is an iteration? It means to repeatedly use the same rule to apply a certain object or system. The result from iteration research indicates that: even if such an object or system is controlled and determined by some very simple rules, there will still be quite complex, even chaotic and unpredictable results. In the biological world, iteration corresponds to reproduction. In complex systems, iteration expands its roles to include in the growth of economic systems, the increase of antibodies in immune systems, the strengthening of certain neuronal synapses in the human brain, as well as the sustaining of certain form of interconnection in the nerve system, and so on. Therefore, some scholars regard system iteration as one of the three major characteristics of complex system behavioral interaction, the other two being diversity and adaptability (Wu and Li 2010).

J. H. Holland, founder of the theory of complex adaptive systems, seizes this point and proposed that: The key for emergence of generation process is through a procedure whereby great complexity, emergent properties, unpredictable novelty and irreducible entirety are produced by a great deal of interaction and iteration of entities which are governed by a few simple rules. Accordingly, Holland gave a precise description of the emergence of constrained generation process in a complex system.

First, the functions of adaptive individuals in a system need to be expressed by simple behavioral rules, i.e., transfer functions: $f: I \times S \rightarrow S$. Here, f is a function using input and states as independent variables, and its current state is produced from its previous state, i.e.

$$\mathrm{S(t+1) = f(I(t), s(t))}$$

Here, S represents the limited possible states of an element, i.e. $S = \{S_1, S_2, \ldots\}$; I represents the many input possibilities, i.e. $I = \{I_1, I_2, \ldots, I_j, \ldots, I\mathrm{k}\}$. Every input, on the other hand, has many possible state values, i.e. $I_j = \{I_{j1}, I_{j2}, \ldots I_{jh}, \ldots\}$. I_{jh} is the number h possible state value of input j.

Second, interactions among the elements need to be expressed as interface function:

$$I_{ij}(t) = g_{ij}(S_h(t))$$

That is to say, element h, at moment t, by its state $Sh(t)$, through interface function g, determines input j, thereby gets connected with element i. The transfer of element states and element interactions can be local and simple, but through the iteration with time $t = 0, 1, 2\ldots$, complex system modes, structures, and functionality are produced.

The above analysis method is based on the establishment of simple rules and then using computer iteration to realize the analysis of the development process of a system, instead of analytical analysis through setting up precise mathematical equations of the system.

3. **The Connotation of Computation by Rules (Iteration)**

What is Computation by Rules?

It is not a model strictly defined by mathematical equations or functions, but a model formed by a series of rules. Through the repeated computation by a computer of the simplest rules, the model can be developed into a hugely complex one and be able to explain most of the phenomena in nature.

The basic ideas of iteration are as follows: many complex structures, phenomena, and processes in nature and the human society are after all caused by the simple interactions among numerous basic elements. We may simulate them by just using some simple models (or pure program codes).

We have all seen a group of geese flying in the sky—gathering at one time and scattering at another, displaying fantastic and harmonic motions. They sometimes form a straight line, and at another time, they may form like a Chinese character "人". It is obvious that the geese fly in an orderly manner, but where comes this order? One explanation is that it is due to the lead and coordination of the leading bird. The leader assures the beautiful array of the group by sending out direct orders. Some believe, however, natural evolution enables every goose in the group to memorize the entire arrangement of the queue. In fact, nonlinear scientific research shows that every flying goose obeys three simple rules: ① separation, i.e., try not to bump into other fellow geese; ② coordination, i.e., try to remain in the same direction as fellow companions; ③ attraction, i.e., try to move towards the center of fellow companions. Constrained by these simple rules, the interactions among the geese enable the natural harmony of the group. In a system, although every individual may be quite simple, and yet when they get together through nonlinear interactions, some wonderful characteristics in the aspects of behavior, functionality and structure, that belong to a group but not any individual will emerge, and this is the concept of "emergence."

In nature, such examples are everywhere. Schools of fish can migrate quickly and orderly on a large scale. Ants can discover the optimum route to food by following some simple rules. A bunch of fireflies can twinkle at the same pace. These systems usually consist of a large number of individuals, but each individual has a simple structure, with neither a central controller nor monitor, and only possesses the ability to detect local information. The retrieval and exchange of the information are just carried out among part of the individuals, and the process is probably dynamic. However, it is exactly such simple local information based actions or controls that may produce expected macro actions. This is just like a great battle victory without unified plan and command, without a wise commander or without professional advisers. How can it be possible? It is the power of self-organization in nature. Hence we can give a definition of complex systems: They are systems with behaviors of emergence and self-organization. The key question for complexity research is that, "how do the behaviors of emergence and self-organization happen?"

4. **Scientific Thoughts Contained in Computation by Rules**

1) *Repeatedly applications of simple rules can produce behaviors or diagrams of tremendous complexity.*

As a well known example, the iteration of one-dimensional non-linear functions causes chaos. Regarding one-dimensional iteration:

$$x_{\mathrm{n}+1} = \mathrm{f}(x_{\mathrm{n}}) \tag{1.1}$$

There is only one variable x here, and $f(x)$ is a known function with a given initial value x. Using $x = f(x_0)$, we get x_1, and by putting x_1 into the previous formula as initial value, we get x_2, then, by analogy, x_3, x_4, …, x_n. The common expression is:

$$x_n = f(x_{n-1}) = f^{(n)}(x_0)$$
$$f^{(n)}(x_0) = f\{f\{\cdots f\{f(x_0)\}\cdots\}\}$$

In this formula, x_n is the result of computation starting from x_0 and using function f for n times, i.e., using one number to replace another, and then a new number to replace the previous one …Even for simple parabolic functions such as $x_{n+1} = f(x_n) = a - x_n^2$, as the exponent increases with every iteration, the form of functions will become more and more complex. Iteration amplifies the complexity of non-linear functions. Once parameter a exceeds a certain number, $f(x)$ will display astoundingly complex patterns of change and fluctuation according to the changes of n, so much so that its innate laws are difficult to understand or grasp. Obviously, the complex solutions of functions result from repeated iteration. Therefore, complexity does not come from seeking the solution for an equation once, but from repeated simple computation thousands of times. In fact, many complex things and phenomena are backed up by simple laws or simple rules. Their complexity is the result of long time and repeated occurrence and evolution of very simple things. Although complex structures in nature are everywhere, it does not necessarily imply there is corresponding complexity for creating physical beings. Rather than saying that the universe was complex from its beginning, it is better to say that there exists a kind of simple formula in the universe and within individual lives, and it was the endless iterations of such formulas as feedback loops that brought about splendid and colorful appearances of the modern world. Based on the principle of computation by iteration, cellular automata seized the main conflict between simplicity and complexity in the objective world and revealed that: colorful and rich objects and phenomena in nature do not necessarily mean that the basic laws creating them are complex. Rather, numerous repetitions of simple laws (or regulations) can cause the emergence of different characteristics on different levels. That is to say, the simplicity of basic laws does not mean the they can only produce ordinary results. On the contrary, simple basic laws, utilized for a long time by systems consisting of a great number of elements will generate tremendous complexity, reflecting the many characteristics of objects, such as linear and non-linear, certainty and randomness, orderliness and chaos, self-organization or organization by others, etc. (Mitchell 2011).

2) *By using a bottom-up modeling method, we may get a model closely imitating a complex system.*

For simple systems, people think their components are static, passive and non-evolutionary, and therefore, no new quality will emerge and no new orderly structure will be formed in such system. But complex systems have emergent, dynamic, self-adaptive and unpredictable characteristics. How should people do analysis and research in facing such systems? We should consider the elements of such systems as "live" individuals, because only adaptive individuals are the original driving forces of a macro system for development and evolution. For example, cells in biological organisms, investors in stock markets, drivers in municipal transportation systems, animals and plants in the ecosystem…all of them can make self-adaptive judgments or decisions based on their living environment and the information they receive, and by their own rules. Inspired by these, we use the method of computer simulation to imitate individual behaviors in complex systems, letting a group of such individuals interact and evolve in the virtual world created by computers, thereby enabling the complex behavior of the entire system to emerge bottom-up.

3) *Computation by rules has expanded the concept and methods of computation, thereby becomes an important tool for studying complex systems.*
In order to explore the complexity in nature and in our society, scientists have established various complicated system models from different perspectives and with different methods. In differential equations established by mathematical analytic methods, time and states are continuous, which are based on the philosophical understanding that time and space are continuous. A great deal of important scientific laws have been deduced and expressed by differential equations. But modern computer science is founded on the basis of discreteness: differential equations must be transformed into difference equations in the process of computation by self-discretization; or, to be expanded into power series equations and intercept part of the expansion; or, to apply certain type of transformation to express continuous variables in the form of discrete structures. Such processes of transformations not only are complex, but also make the differential equations lose their most important characteristics—precision and continuity. On the contrary, models built up by extracting rules from real systems already possess discreteness in time and states, and do not need pre-discretization. Thus they are quite suitable for computer modeling and simulation. Commenting on computer models, Holland says: "Computer models possess both characteristics of abstractness and concreteness. The definitions of these models are abstract, same as mathematical models, using numbers, the connections among these numbers and the time variation of the numbers to define them. At the same time, these numbers are 'written into' computer registers accurately, instead of being represented symbolically. Therefore we can obtain these specific records that are very close to the records obtained through carefully performed procedures in the laboratory. As a result, computer models possess at the same time both theoretical and experimental characteristics." Because computer models possess such characteristics, Holland believes that they are "a major tool for the scientific research of emergence." Many models in complexity research, such as Holland's emergence model, J. H. Conway's "Game of Life" model, C. Langton's "artificial life" model, etc., are all models based on computation by rules, which all need to be simulated in computers, and are all new models set up by going beyond analytic methods. In a computational environment dominated by modern computers, discrete computational methods based on the iteration of rules are more advantageous in finding solutions, especially in the simulation of complex dynamic systems.

1.3 A Discrete Dynamics Model Originated from Complexity—Cellular Automata

Complex systems usually consist of many relatively simple components or elements of the same kind. The behavior of parts or elements is usually easy to comprehend, but the behavior of the whole or a system is often hard to be explained simply. Moreover, the systematic behavior of the system as a whole cannot be predicted from the understanding of the behavior of its parts. This means that for the complex behavior of the whole, not only there is no clear overall algorithm, but also it is more difficult to establish a mathematical equation of the whole. Why is that? How is complexity formed? We had not had a good explanation for this in the past. In the 1950s, the father of computers, John von Neumann, proposed a model without fixed mathematical formula, i.e. cellular automata. It gave out the simplest and most standard cases to clearly explain how complexity and complex behavior were generated and developed from the simplicity of elements. Since this kind of research is the research of models, we can avoid questions such as: although an immune system is complex, its components—lymphocytic cells are not simple either; although a biological system is complex, its components—species groups are also not simple; although a stock market is complex, speculators are not simple too. Therefore, we can assume that the composing elements of a system are completely simple. To use rule models to represent this simplicity and to use computers to simulate it, we can observe how complexity is formed from it. By now we have got an abstract computational system, which is temporally and spatially discrete; the states of its elements and the rules governing these states are very simple in computation. The overall modes and structures composed by these simple elements, however, can simulate all the complexities in reality. Therefore, we can utilize this tool (cellular automata)to analyze the formation of complexity and its behavior by discrete dynamics (Paton et al. 2004).

Cellular automata are idealized complex systems, and their structures are completely different from those of modern computers. Taking Diagram 1.1 as an example, it seems like a series of light bulbs arranged on a board, and every bulb is connected to the bulbs around it and those on the diagonal. We only draw the connections of one bulb here as an example. The states of the bulbs can be either on or off. Assuming that the whole arrangement is circular, i.e., the bulb on the leftmost is actually right next to the bulb on the rightmost, and the bottommost and the topmost bulbs are also next to each other, and so on.

In Diagram 1.2, the light bulbs board on the left demonstrates the initial set up of the bulbs, and for simplicity, we did not draw the lines connecting the bulbs. Some bulbs are already turned on from the beginning. Then, the bulbs continuously "renew their states" according to rules—choosing either on or off. All the bulbs change state simultaneously. This light bulb array can be seen as a twinkling model of fireflies. Each firefly adjusts its twinkling state—light or off, according to the conditions of the fireflies around it. This array can also be regarded as the triggering

Diagram 1.1 Light bulb array

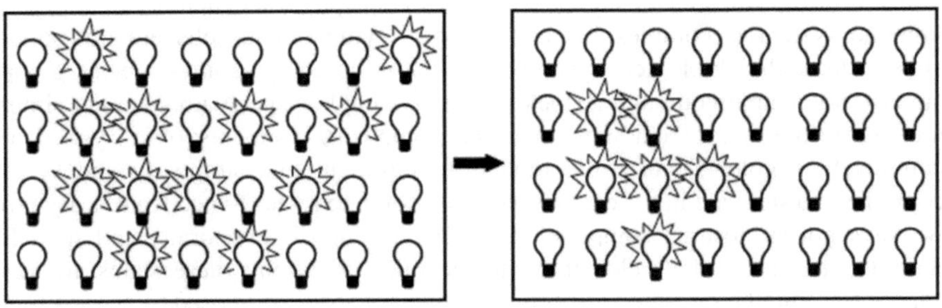

Diagram 1.2 Light bulb states variations

model of neural elements, in which every neuron is triggered or suppressed by the states of its adjacent neurons.

As we have said before, in order to let every bulb have 8 neighbors, the four sides of the array of the bulbs are circularly connected. It can be imagined as that the top and bottom sides are connected, and the left and right sides are connected, so as to form the shape of a donut. In this way, each bulb has eight neighbors.

Then, how does each bulb "decide" whether it is on or off at every step? They all follow certain rules, such as, the next state (on or off) is to be decided by the states of the adjacent 8 bulbs and its own current state.

For example, the rule can be: "If more than half (including itself) of the bulbs in its neighborhood are on, then it turns on (if it is already on, then no change); otherwise, it turns off (if it is already off, then no change)." That is to say, if five or more of nine neighboring bulbs are on, then the next state of the bulb in the middle is on.

Now let us see how the light bulb array will change at next step. According to the aforementioned rule: "Adopting the majority state of the neighbors," then, the initially prescribed states of the bulbs (shown in the left diagram in Diagram 1.2) change to the states as shown in the right diagram in Diagram 1.2 after one time change of the states.

We may also use more complex rules, such as, "Turn on if no fewer than two and no more than seven light bulbs in the neighborhood are on, otherwise turn off." Now the variation of the light bulb array will be different. Or, the rule can be changed to "turn on if one and only one bulb is off, or four are on, otherwise turn off." There are numerous possible rules.

Exactly how many possible rules are there? As we are going to mention later, in order to define a rule, the next state of the bulb as decided by the states of the bulbs in the neighborhood must be clarified. There are eight surrounding bulbs plus the middle bulb itself in the neighborhood, and each bulb has two states, either on or off. Therefore, the number of possible combinations of states is $2^9 = 512$. For every combination of states, the next state of the middle bulb can be either "on" or "off." Therefore, the possible number of corresponding rules for all 512 combinations is $2^{512} \approx 1.3 \times 10^{154}$. The number is many times greater than the number of atoms in the universe. Therefore, in order to study various cellular computational rules, we must categorize these rules. We will discuss the problem of categorization later in this book.

The light bulb array described above is actually a cellular automaton. Cellular automata are grids consisting of cells. Every cell chooses its states of on or off according to states of cells in its neighborhood (generally speaking, the number of states of the cells can be freely prescribed, but here we only discuss two states, i.e., on/off). All cells follow the same rule, which is also called the renewal rule of cells. The rule decides the next states of a cell according to the current states of cells in its neighborhood.

Why do we say that such a simple system is the ideal model for complex systems? Like the complex systems in nature, cellular automata also consist of numerous simple individuals (cells). There is no central control, and every individual only interacts with a few other individuals to generate complex collective behavior and complex information processing by using simple operating rules. Moreover, their behavior is hard or even impossible to predict with their renewal rules.

References

Ben, S. (2002). Getting the behavior of social insects to compute. *Science, 295*(5564), 2357.

Cao, N. (2005). *Listening to lectures at Tsinghua: Episode II*. Beijing: Tsinghua University Press.

Hu, S. (2010). *Scientific spirit*. Shanghai: Shanghai Science and Technology Press.

Huang, X. (2005). *Study of methodology for complexity science*. Beijing: Tsinghua University Press.

Mitchell, M. (2011). *Complexity: A guided tour*. Translated by Lu Tang. Changsha: Hunan Science and Technology Press.

Paton, R., Bolouri, H., Holcombe, W. M. L., et al. (2004). *Computation in cells and tissues: Perspectives and tools of thought*. Berlin: Springer.

Wu, J., & Li, X. (2010). *An introduction to the development of system science*. Beijing: Tsinghua University Press.

Chapter 2
The Working Principle of Cellular Automata

2.1 The Invention of Cellular Automata

What exactly is life? How do we define the essential difference between a life system and a non-living one? This has been a long-lasting question for scientific research. In the 1950s, a famous mathematician and computer scientist Von Neumann proposed that self-reproduction is the unique characteristic of living things, and also the necessary condition for anything to be considered life. At that time, the mechanism of biological self-reproduction was not fully understood yet, therefore, such a theory demonstrated Von Neumann's genius foresight.

Von Neumann was one of the scientists who perceived deeply the connection between computation and living organisms at the earliest time. He was dedicated to finding the solution for machines of self-reproduce. In order to design such a machine, with the suggestion from his colleague Stanislaw Ulam, Von Neumann gave up the research on specific elements and operational problems of such a machine. Instead, he focused on how to construct a machine within a mathematical framework, so that it could make copies of its own information and by doing that, reproduce a new machine. Von Neumann started to consider solving the problem within a temporally and spatially discrete framework consisting of many cells. Within this framework, each cell had its own internal state and was composed of a limited number of discrete values. By using only simple rules, the internal states of the cells at a new moment could be calculated. In addition, the state of each cell would only vary according to the states of the cells in its neighborhood. It reflected the interactions among cells within a close distance. Each cell would follow the same rules and update its state simultaneously with those nearby. Numerous cells produced the dynamic evolution of a system by simple interactions among themselves. This temporally and spatially discrete dynamic system proposed by Von Neumann was called Cellular Automata (CA). Before his death, Von Neumann proved that "there exists at least one kind of cellular automata which can self-reproduce and evolve." He successfully solved the problem of machines'

X. Li et al., *Theory of Practical Cellular Automaton*,
https://doi.org/10.1007/978-981-10-7497-4_2

self-reproduction. In 1966, Von Neumann's colleague Arthur Burks edited and published the book *Theory of Self-Reproducing Automata*, which included all the research achievements concerning cellular automata.

The original model of a cellular automaton proposed by Von Neumann was extremely complex, which consisted of thousands of two-dimensional cells, and each cell consisted of 29 different states. It could not be realized by the simulation capacity of any computer at the time. And yet the fact that such a model really existed solved the difficult mathematical problem. Moreover, later research proved that this model was amazingly similar to the self-reproducing mechanism of living organisms. Von Neumann therefore is considered one of the real pioneers in the science of artificial life.

Once people had an affirmative answer to the question "whether machines can self-reproduce," scientific research headed towards a completely new direction of using cellular automata to construct machines which have life characteristics. Some scholars followed Von Neumann's research direction and achieved landmark results.

In the 1970s, British mathematician John Horton Conway at Cambridge University devised "Game of Life." It was not an ordinary game, but its rules were far simpler than those of chess. In this game, there was no winner or loser. Its inventor Conway wanted to use it to demonstrate how the most complex phenomena—possibly even living things, evolved from the simplest rules (Rendell 2002).

The Cellular automaton Von Neumann invented was very complex, with each cell being composed of 29 possible states. Conway, on the other hand, wanted to see what processes of change would happen in a quite simple virtual world. He designed a two-dimensional orthogonal grid of square cells similar to that of a Go board. Each cell in it only has two possible states: "alive" or "dead," which are represented by the colors of "black" and "white." Every cell interacts with its 8 neighbors, which are the cells that are horizontally, vertically, or diagonally adjacent, and only respond according to a set of very simple rules. There are 3 main rules:

1. If a cell has exactly 2 live neighbors, it will maintain its current state (that is to say, the cell will still be alive if the original state is alive, it will be dead if the original state is dead).
2. If a cell has exactly 3 live neighbors, the new state of the cell will be alive, even if its original state is dead.
3. If the number of live neighbors of a cell is neither 2 nor 3, then the cell new state of the cell will be dead, even if its original is alive.

Above rules may seem simple, but the evolution of which is very close to the evolution of the rules of surviving and reproducing rules of living orgasms: when the density of life is very low, that is, when a cell's live neighbors are fewer than 2, survival will be threatened due to loneliness, the lack of help and chances for breeding and reproduction, therefore, the state of the cell changes from live to dead.

When the density of life is high, that is, when a cell has more than 3 live neighbors, survival will also be threatened due to scarce resources, worsened environment and intensified competition. Therefore, the state of the cell also changes from live to dead. Only when the number of live neighbors is proper, namely, either 2 or 3, can organisms maintain a healthy surviving environment and keep on living and reproducing, therefore even a dead cell becomes alive by reproduction. Because this model can simulate complex phenomena in life such as survival, competition and extinction, it gets the name of "Game of Life."

Game of Life can be easily converted to computer programs, and demonstrates the growth mode of cells within the grid on a computer screen. The most famous one is called "glider," which can continuously generate new "gliders" just like reproducing new lives.

From the simple Game of Life, we can see a new domain of designing cellular automata. It has begun to be transformed into technology and has found its applications in many fields. At the same time, it also has become a new perspective for people to understand life and has paved the way for a new branch of science —"artificial life."

Since the 1980s, led by mathematician and computer scientist Christopher Langton, a group of scientists have conducted research on creating artificial life in the virtual environment of computers with the prototype of the 29-state cellular automaton invented by Von Neumann. The prototype was later simplified by computer expert E. F. Codd to the one with only 8 states. An artificial life is a man-made life and not a natural life organically composed by carbohydrates. Langton thought that the science of artificial life is a science about artificial systems which can demonstrate the behavioral characteristics of natural life systems. Creating artificial life models in the virtual environment of computers has to have the following basic characteristics:

(1) An artificial life is composed of simple programs or a group of single individuals which have predetermined behavior;
(2) There is no program of central control, all the programs are loosely connected;
(3) Each program describes in detail the mode of the local reaction of a simple individual towards other individuals;
(4) The system does not contain rules prescribing the global behaviors;
(5) Any global behavior that is higher than the individual layer emerges on its own, and is unpredictable.

Therefore, the evolutionary model of life proposed by Langton should start from simple things like bacteria, and not from complex equations like those in mathematics. With repeated iteration of simple elements and simple behavioral rules, various complex structures of virtual life can be formed.

Langton raised an essential question regarding the creation of virtual life: what enables life—whether natural or artificial, to continuously reproduction?

He thought that the flow of information was at least a very important aspect for the successful reproduction of life. Therefore, he studied the topic about under what kind of conditions, the dynamic behavior of cellular automata information would lead to spontaneous emergence of vital signs, and lead to the construction of a self-reproductive cellular automaton on a computer. For a one-dimensional cellular automaton, Langton found a parameter of λ for the amount of information a CA contains. In order for a life system to operate well, the information amount parameter λ must be set to a right value. If the value is too low, all the previous generation's information will be transferred to the next generation completely unaltered, then the system will be relatively static without change, just like crystals. If the value is too high, the information transferred from the previous to the next generation will be disorderly, resulting in a chaotic state and losing the original explicable life mode. A relatively proper λ parameter value not only can provide appropriate variation, but also can maintain relative stability, thus creating lifelike phenomena.

Langton believed that evolution meant a process in which life was getting more capable of controlling its parameters, getting itself more capable of maintaining balance on the edges. Langton created a famous concept of "life on edge of chaos" to describe this very important state. When a system is in an Edge of Chaos state, the system will display complex behavior: within this layer, the behavior of the system determines that the constituent elements of the system never are fully locked in one place, while the system will never disintegrate into chaotic state. Such a system has both enough stability to store information and enough fluidity to transfer information. Such a system has basic characteristics of self-organization and self-reproduction. Langton believed that complex phenomena such as life existed and emerged at "Edge of Chaos". Neither orderliness nor disorderliness was complex. Complexity existed at the edge of disorderliness. Currently, "Edge of Chaos" has become an important achievement and landmark catchphrase for the research of complexity science. Some scientists believe that complex dynamics at "Edge of Chaos" is the ideal explanation for natural and social evolutionary behaviors.

In short, the development of the theory of cellular automata gave birth to the science of artificial life. Today, various technologies based on the research of artificial life have infiltrated all aspects of the world, from the design of online games with various roles of complicated characters, to the research of complex robots, to using simulation systems in disease control centers to demonstrate the worldwide prevalence of the flu so as to regulate and control it ahead of time, all reflect the idea and technology of artificial life. It can be predicted that Langton's work will inspire people to try harder to understand the essence of life, and the research will never stop.

In the 1990s, a famous mathematician and physicist Stephen Wolfram fully concentrated his research on a kind of single-dimensional cellular automata (which were called elementary cellular automata). He studied not just one, but hundreds of such cellular automata. The more of them he studied, the more modes he saw, and the more firmly he believed that the phenomena he observed had extensive adaptability. Wolfram finally decided on what he wanted to do: using computers to explore and simulate how surprisingly complex behavior emerged from simple algorithms. He believed that it was impossible to use complex mathematical equations to perfectly represent the complex structures studied by physics and cosmology. On the contrary, computers could help him find a completely different solution. After ten years of in-depth yet lonely study, in 2002, Wolfram published a 1280-page scholarly work on cellular automata: *A New Kind of Science* (Wolfram 2002). He extensively challenged the science at his time with his own research and ideas. He believed that it was probably not appropriate to study natural phenomena by observing the calculations of data and thereby obtaining equations. Nature was likely to accomplish the emergence of complex behavior through a set of simple rules. Therefore, people needed to look for these simple rules, and to study how complex behavior emerged out of them. Eventually Wolfram proposed that nature was like a computer, which could derive all kinds of complex behavior by using many simple but powerful programs. Therefore, the entire universe was nothing but a huge cellular automaton. Wolfram started to use this way of thinking to study nature and tried to initiate a new scientific revolution. Wolfram's "new kind of science" gave rise to heated debates in scientific circles, and his theory and ideas were not widely accepted. Nevertheless, his research achievements effectively pushed forward the development of the theories and applications of cellular automata. Although "new science" was not able to simply replace existing science (science based on formulas and equation expressions), it could make traditional science richer and more prosperous. It could probably provide scientists with a new tool instead of "a new kind of science."

2.2 The Definition of Cellular Automata

Cellular automata result from the concerted work of physicists, mathematicians, computer scientists and biologists. Therefore, we can interpret the meaning of them from different perspectives. Physicists regard them as discrete dynamic systems with infinite dimensions. Mathematicians regard them as the opposite of partial differential equations which describe continuous phenomena, a mathematical model with discrete time and space. Computer scientists regard them as a branch of the emerging science of artificial intelligence and artificial life, which can process information in a synchronize way, particularly suitable for parallel computation, and can possibly become the rudimentary form of the next generation parallel computers (Mitchell 2006). Biologists, on the other hand, regard them as an abstraction of life phenomena. We will give the mathematical and physical definitions of cellular automata in the following context.

2.2.1 Mathematical Definition

To make it easier for narration and understanding, we only discuss the definition of one-dimensional cellular automata here, and the definitions of multiple-dimensional cellular automata can be derived from it.

On a bilateral infinite straight line, there are an infinite number of cells which are distributed at different points on the integer lattice, every cell has k states, represented by 0, 1, …, $k - 1$.

Let S = {0, 1, …, $k - 1$} represents the state set of every cell. The bilateral infinite sequence

$$x = \ldots x_{-2}x_{-1}x_0x_1x_2\ldots \quad x_i \in S$$

is called the configuration of the cellular automata, and the set contains all configurations is called configuration space, denoted as s^z, here **Z** is a set of integers.

We suppose time is discrete, and for a configuration, every cell changes simultaneously. Suppose x_i^{t+1} is the state of cell i at time $t + 1$, and it is completely determined by the state of cell i at time t and the states of a number of $2r$ adjacent cells with a neighboring distance not more than r to cell i. To express it with a formula:

$$x_i^{t+1} = f(x_{i-r}^t, \ldots, x_{i-1}^t, x_i^t, x_{i+1}^t, \ldots x_{i+r}^t)$$

Here, f has nothing to do with i and t. Actually, f is a mapping from S_t^{2r+1} to S_{t+1}.

$$f : S_t^{2r+1} \rightarrow S_{t+1}$$

The dynamic evolution of the cellular automaton is determined by the partial evolutionary rule f of individual cells. That is:

$$F : S_t^z \rightarrow S_{t+1}^z$$

We give the above discussion the following definition, which is:

Definition : Mapping F: $S_t^z \rightarrow S_{t+1}^z$ is called a cellular automaton, and suppose there exist $r > 0$ and f: $S_t^{2r+1} \rightarrow S_{t+1}$ to enable any configuration $x = \ldots x_{-1}x_0x_{+1}\ldots$ to satisfy

$$F(x)_i = f(x_{i-r}, \ldots, x_{i-1}, x_i, x_{i+1}, \ldots x_{i+r})$$

In the formula, f is called the partial rule of the cellular automaton; r is called the neighborhood radius; while F is called the overall rule of the cellular automaton. By now, we have obtained a model of cellular automata.

If a cellular automaton can be regarded as the evolution of a certain phenomenon, the existence of its local rule can be explained as: the occurrence of a thing is only dependent on the conditions in its limited surroundings, and has nothing to do with time or location. It shows the locality, steadiness, and spatial homogeneity of cellular automata.

Suppose the radius of a cellular automaton's neighbors $r = 1$, the number of states $k = 2$, i.e., the set of states has only two elements $\{0, 1\}$, a cellular automaton so defined is called an elementary cellular automaton. Its partial mapping is expressed as:

$$x_i^{t+1} = f(x_{i-1}^t, x_i^t, x_{i+1}^t) \quad \forall\, i \in z$$

The above formula stands for the evolutionary formula of a one-dimensional cellular automaton with two values and three neighbors, i.e., the state of every cell at the next moment is determined by its own state at the current moment and the states of $2r = 2$ adjacent cells.

From this we can see that one-dimensional elementary cellular automata have two distinctive characteristics:

(1) The interactions among cells are local interactions within the immediate neighborhood;
(2) The cells only have two values—0 and 1, and can only have one value at any moment.

2.2.2 *Physical Definition*

Cellular automata are defined as dynamic systems in a cellular space consisting of discrete cells with a limited number of states, and evolve in a discrete temporal dimension according to certain local rules.

Specifically, the parts composing cellular automata are called "cells." Every cell has a certain state, and this state can only come from a certain set of limited states, such as "live" or "dead," or one of the seven colors, etc. All cells are orderly aligned on a spatial grid. The grid is discrete, and each grid can only hold one cell. The states of the cells will vary according to time, and the variation of each cell's states is only affected by the states of its several close neighbors. All the cells update their states according to the same rules in a synchronized way. Through simple interactions, numerous cells constitute the dynamic evolution of cellular automata.

We know that, a system, whether as gigantic as the Milky Way galaxy or as minute as subnuclear particles, as long as it is changing over the time, we call it a power system (or dynamic system). These systems exist extensively in nature and in human society, for example:

- The solar system (the positions of the planets vary according to time);
- The human heart (periodical pulsation);
- The human brain (continuous triggering of the neurons);
- The stock market (the rise and fall of stock prices);

...

The purpose of research on power systems is to understand the present, and to predict the future. For ordinary power systems, their models are established by strictly defined physical equations or functions. But in the research of complex systems, because the variables are complex and diverse, and are nonlinear and non-continuous, sometimes are even impossible to measure and can only be qualitatively described, the changes of states are often discrete. Cellular automata are discrete power systems. The construction of their models does not have fixed mathematical formulas, but is composed of a series of evolutionary rules (Berlekamp et al. 1982). The key to the emergence and the generation of a cellular automaton is a process in which numerous cells, under the control of a number of simple rules, with their interactions and repeated iterations, produce enormous complexity, emergent properties, unpredictable novelty and irreducible integrity. Such examples include the generating processes of gliders in a cellular automaton, a swarm of ants, a stock market, etc. Why is this? This is because many systems in nature have similar micro mechanisms, and cellular automata can produce related complex behavior on a macro level by simulating these simple micro mechanisms.

In Short, physics studies systems from the perspective of movement and evolution, while cellular automata are temporally and spatially discrete local dynamic systems, which can easily describe the interaction among cells without creating and solving complex differential equations. They only need to establish simple local rules. Therefore, they are quite suitable for simulation of time-space evolutionary processes of complex systems. Cellular automata provide an important method for studying complexity science. They provide an effective means for theoretical exploration and computer simulation of complex phenomena.

2.3 The Composition of Cellular Automata

Cellular automata are composed of cells (squares), cellular space (grid), neighbors (adjacent cells r), evolutionary rules of the cells (state variation function) and cell states ($S_1, S_2, \ldots, S_k$, a limited number), as shown in Diagram 2.1.

As shown in above diagram, cellular automata are information processing systems composed of a great deal of simple elements, simple links, simple rules, limited states and local interactions. They can nevertheless simulate most complex phenomena in the world, therefore have huge potentials both in theory and in practice.

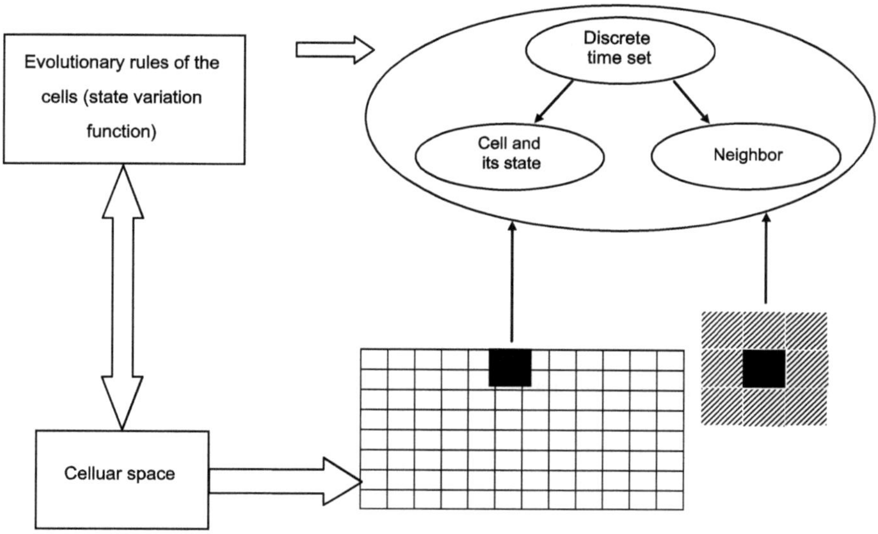

Diagram 2.1 Diagram of the composition of cellular automata

2.3.1 Cells

Cells are also known as units or elementary units, which are the most basic components of cellular automata. Cells are distributed on discrete one-dimensional, two-dimensional or multi-dimensional grids in Euclidean space.

The states of the cells can either be in binary forms such as {live, dead}, {black, white}, {on, off}, etc., or in the form of a discrete set consisting of integers $\{S_1, S_2, \ldots, S_i, \ldots, S_k\}$. Strictly speaking, the cells of cellular automata can have only one state variable each, but in actual application, it is often expanded. For example, in the cellular automaton model constructed by Ziyou Gao and others for the study of traffic, the cells representing vehicles were given additional state variables such as vehicle position and speed (Jia et al. 2007).

2.3.2 Cellular Space

Cellular space is a set of grid points in space representing the distribution of cells.

1. **The Geometrical Division of Cellular Space**

Theoretically, cellular space can be a regular division of Euclidean space of any dimension. Current research mainly focuses on one-dimensional and two-dimensional cellular automata. For one-dimensional cellular automata, cellular space has only one kind of division. As for two-dimensional cellular automata,

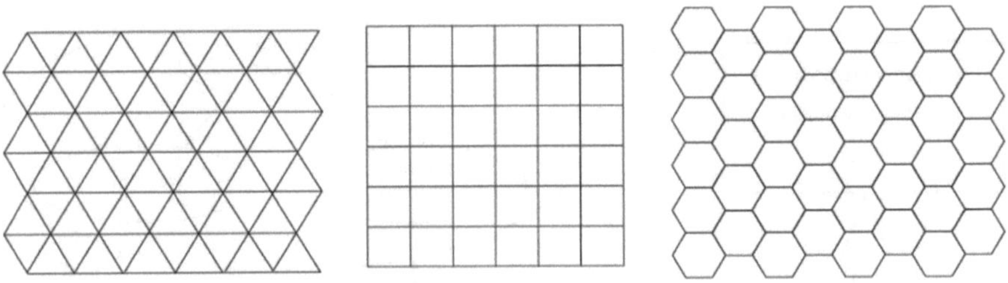

(a) Triangular Lattice (b) Square Lattice (c) Hexagonal Lattice

Diagram 2.2 Three lattice divisions of two-dimensional cellular automata

cellular space can take the shape of triangular, square, or hexagonal lattices, as shown in Diagram 2.2.

The above three geometrical divisions of cellular space have different advantages and disadvantages in regard of modeling.

(1) The advantage of the triangular lattice is that it has relatively fewer numbers of adjacent cells and is easy for dealing with complex boundaries. This is quite useful on certain occasions. Its disadvantage is that it is inconvenient for computer expression and display, and must be converted into a square lattice.
(2) The advantage of the square lattice is that it is intuitive and simple. In addition, it is especially suitable for expression and display in the current computer environment. Its disadvantage is that it cannot well simulate the phenomenon of isotropy, for example, the HPP model in lattice gas automata.
(3) The advantage of the hexagonal lattice is that it can simulate the isotropic phenomenon relatively well, therefore, models can be more natural and real, such as the FHP model in lattice gas automata. Its disadvantage is the same as that of the triangular lattice, i.e., it is relatively difficult and complicated to be expressed and displayed on a computer.

2. **Boundary Conditions**

Theoretically speaking, cellular space is supposed to be able to extend infinitely in all dimensions. This is for the convenience of theoretical research and reasoning. However, in practical applications, we are unable to implement such an ideal condition on computers. Because it is impossible to deal with infinite networks, cellular space has to be limited and has boundaries. To sum up, there are mainly three types of boundaries: periodical, reflective, and constant. In applications, sometimes in order to simulate actual phenomena more objectively and naturally, we may also use random boundary, i.e., to generate real-time random values at the boundaries.

(1) Periodic boundary: a cellular space in which boundaries opposite each other are connected. For one-dimensional space, cellular space appears as a circle with the two ends joining together. For two-dimensional space, cellular space is

Diagram 2.3 Reflective boundary

formed with top and bottom connected, as well as left and right connected, forming a torus like the shape of a tire or donut. A periodic space comes closest to an infinite space, therefore, in theoretical discussions, it is often used as a test, for related theoretical analysis and simulation.

(2) Reflective boundary: here the state of a neighbor cell outside the boundary is a specular reflection of the cell on the other side with the boundary as the axis. For example, Diagram 2.3 shows the boundary situation in one-dimensional space and when the neighbor cell's radius $r = 1$.

(3) Constant Boundary: all cells outside the boundary take a fixed value such as 0, 1, etc.

What needs to be pointed out is that in practical applications, especially in modeling cellular automata of two or more dimensions, these three kinds of boundaries can be used together. For example, in two-dimensional space, top and bottom boundaries can be reflective, while left and right boundaries can be periodic.

3. **Configuration**

Configuration is the spatial distribution and combination of all the states of all cells in the cellular space at a certain moment. Usually, it can be mathematically represented by a multi-dimensional integer matrix $\mathbf{Z}_d$. Here d stands for the dimensions of the cellular space, and $\mathbf{Z}$ is a set of integers. That is to say, all the cells are in a space of d dimensions, and their positions can be determined by a matrix of integers with d elements.

2.3.3 Neighborhood

Cells and the cellular space only show the static elements of cellular automata. In order to introduce "dynamics" into the system, it is necessary to add evolutionary rules. In cellular automata, evolutionary rules are defined within a local range, i.e., the state of a cell at the next moment is determined by its own current state and the states of its neighbors. Therefore, before determining the rules, it is necessary to define the sizes of the neighbors and make clear which cells belong to the neighbors of the cell in question. Neighborhood refers to the spatial domain a certain cell needs to search before updating its state. In one-dimensional cellular automata, neighborhood is usually determined by radius r. All the cells within radius r of a certain cell are considered that cell's neighbors. The definitions of neighborhood in two-dimensional cellular automata are more complicated, but usually include the following types.

1. **The von Neumann Neighborhood**

The four cells which are horizontally and vertically adjacent to a cell are that cell's neighbors. Here, the neighborhood radius $r = 1$, which is equal to the four neighborhoods and four directions in image processing, as shown in Diagram 2.4a.

2. **The Moore Neighborhood**

The Moore neighborhood expands the von Neumann type by including, in addition to the four cells which are horizontally and vertically adjacent to the central cell, another four cells from upper left, upper right, bottom left, and bottom right, and which are diagonally connected to the central cell, so that a cell has altogether eight adjacent cells as its neighbors. The neighborhood radius is still 1, and it equals the eight neighborhoods and eight directions in image processing, as shown in Diagram 2.4b.

3. **Extended Moore Neighborhood**

By extending the radius of the Moore neighborhood r to 2 or greater, we get the extended Moore neighborhood, as shown in Diagram 2.4c. In this diagram, the black cell represents the central cell, and the grey ones are its neighbors. The state of the central cell at the next moment needs to be calculated by both the current state of itself and the current states of its neighbors together.

4. **Margolus Neighborhood**

This neighborhood type is completely different from the above introduced neighborhood types. It does not consider single cells, but treats 2×2 neighboring cells as a cell unit. When the states of the cells need to be updated, the cells within the

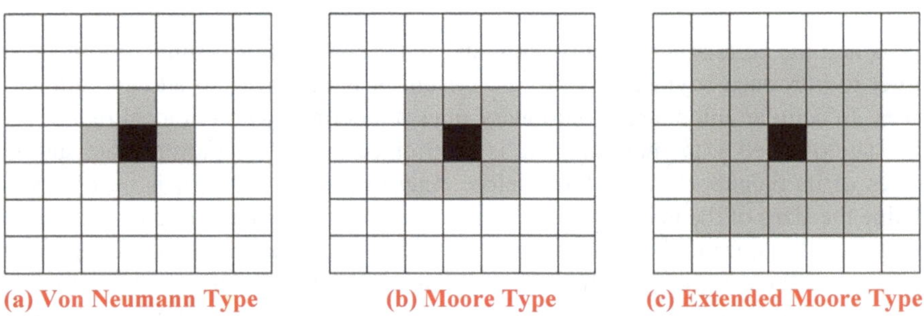

Diagram 2.4 Commonly used neighborhood types of cellular automata

cell unit only update their states according to the state of the cell unit; they have no direct connection with the states of neighborhood cell units. That is to say, the cells are only responsive to the states of the neighbors in positions of their upper left, upper right, bottom left and bottom right. The method of dividing space into units can reduce the complexity of rules, while at the same time prevent the long distance influence. The modes of network divisions vary with the evolution of time: the modes of odd time step unit division and even time step unit division interchange to enable the transmission of information across the boundaries of units, as shown in Diagram 2.5. In this diagram, the solid lines and dotted lines represent the alternative changes of two divisional modes. The cells within a cell unit are marked as ul (upper left), ur (upper right), ll (bottom left), lr (bottom right). At the next time step, due to the change of divisional mode, the cell marked as lr will change to ul.

2.3.4 Rules of Evolution

A dynamic function which determines the state of a cell at the next moment according to its current state and the states of its neighbors is called the rule of evolution. Simply put, it is a state transfer function, which can be expressed as

$$f : S_i^{t+1} = f(S_i^t, S_N^t)$$

Here, f stands for the state transfer function (or the rule of evolution), S_i^t stands for the state of cell i at moment t; S_N^t stands for the states of cell i's neighbors at moment t.

Cellular automata are dynamic systems. Although as time goes, systems' physical structures themselves do not change each time, their states do change. If we use a mathematical formula to represent cellular automata, it can be expressed as an equation with four unknowns:

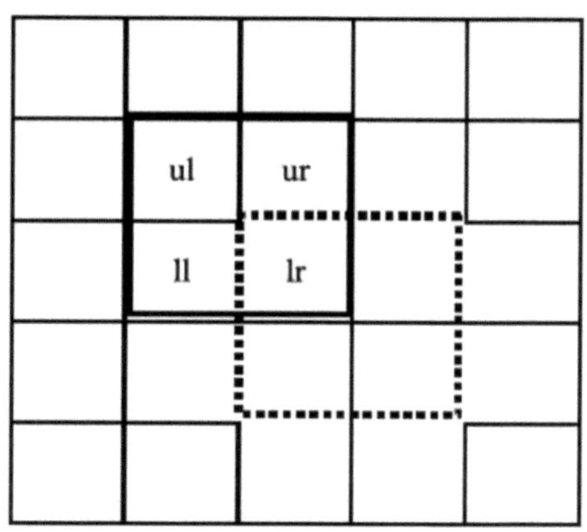

Diagram 2.5 Margolus neighborhood

$$A = (L_d, S, N, f)$$

Here, A stands for a cellular automaton system; L_d stands for the cellular space, and d is the spatial dimensions; S is a limited and discrete set of cell states; N stands for the combination of all the cells in the neighborhood (including the central cell); f is the state transfer function, i.e., the rule of evolution.

Rules of evolution are a set of conditions we prescribe beforehand for limiting the states of cellular automata. In practice, the success of a cellular automaton model depends on proper design of its rules, on whether they can objectively reflect the internal essential characteristics of an actual system. Therefore, the design of the rules of evolution is the core of the overall analysis of cellular automata.

2.4 Working Process of Cellular Automata

Suppose we take a strip of lattice in the cellular space: each square is a cell, and each cell has a state Si, which is among k number of limited possible states. The lattice is discrete square by square (spatially discrete), and its time also jumps forward step by step (temporally discrete) from …, $t-1$, to t, then $t+1$, …. The temporal dimension extends downward as shown in Diagram 2.6.

Suppose the state of cell i at moment $t-1$ is S_i^{t-1}, there are r neighbors on its left, marked as S_{i-1}^{t-1}, S_{i-2}^{t-1}, …, S_{i-r}^{t-1}. There are also r neighbors on its right, marked as S_{i+1}^{t-1}, S_{i+2}^{t-1}, …, S_{i+r}^{t-1}.

How, then, is the next state of cell S_i^{t-1}, which is S_i^t, determined?

$$S_i^t = f(S_{i-r}^{t-1}, \ldots S_{i-1}^{t-1}, S_i^{t-1}, S_{i+1}^{t-1}, \ldots, S_{i+r}^{t-1})$$

Now let us consider the simplest and most common situation: suppose the number of a cell's states is $k = 2$, i.e., the cell has only two possible states $\{S_1, S_2\}$. Since the specific symbols used in S are not important, for example, they can be {static, mobile}, {live, dead}, {black, white}, etc., we commonly transcribe them as

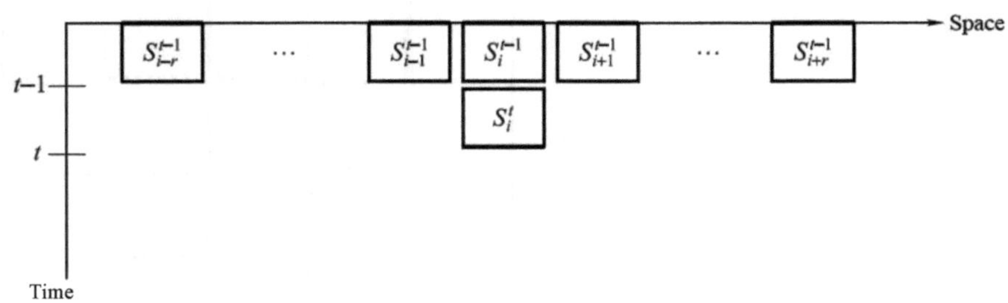

Diagram 2.6 Working process of one-dimensional cellular automata

{0, 1}; neighborhood radius $r = 1$, i.e., any cell has only two neighbors (on the left and on the right). The working process of a cellular automaton is: the updating of the state of a cell (from moment $t - 1 \rightarrow$ moment t) is jointly determined by the states of itself and its neighbors at the previous moment. Therefore:

$$S_i^t = f(S_{i-1}^{t-1}, S_i^{t-1}, S_{i+1}^{t-1})$$

Or

$$S_i^{t+1} = f(S_{i-1}^t, S_i^t, S_{i+1}^t)$$

That is to say, the next state of each cell is determined by the state of itself at the current moment and the states of $2r = 2$ cells which are its neighbors.

Therefore, a cellular automaton can be completely determined by S, r and f. There are three state variables in the state transfer function, and each state variable has 2 states. Therefore, there are altogether $2^3 = 8$ ways of combinations. As long as values of f are given on all the 8 ways of combinations of independent variables, f is completely determined. Diagram 2.7 uses two colors black and white to demonstrate the eight possible combinations of the input states of one-dimensional cellular automata.

It can also be represented by numbers, as shown in Diagram 2.8.

Every input condition gives out two output states 0 or 1. There exist overall $2^8 = 256$ output state combinations. That is, for one-dimensional cellular automata, there are 256 rules as shown in Diagram 2.9.

Every combination is marked as a_i, in which, $i = 0, 1, \ldots, 7$. They are aligned in an order of $a_7a_6a_5a_4a_3a_2a_1a_0$ to represent a binary number. Its corresponding decimal number is

$$R = \sum_{i=0}^{7} a_i 2^i$$

Diagram 2.7 Eight possible input state combinations of one-dimensional cellular automata (represented by colors black and white)

111 110 101 100 011 010 001 000

Diagram 2.8 Eight possible input state combinations of one-dimensional cellular automata (represented by numbers)

Diagram 2.9 Possible output states of one-dimensional cellular automata

t	→	111	110	101	100	011	010	001	000
		↓	↓	↓	↓	↓	↓	↓	↓
		1	1	1	1	1	1	1	1
$t+1$	→	or	or	or	or	or	or	or	or
		0	0	0	0	0	0	0	0
		α_7	α_6	α_5	α_4	α_3	α_2	α_1	α_0

Diagram 2.10 R_{126}

t	→	111	110	101	100	011	010	001	000
		↓	↓	↓	↓	↓	↓	↓	↓
$t+1$	→	0	1	1	1	1	1	1	0

R's size represents the numerical size of the rule. Now we give a possible rule: 01111110.

We now calculate:

$$R_{126} = a_7 a_6 \ldots a_1 a_0$$
$$= \sum_{i=0}^{7} 0 \times 2^0 + 1 \times 2^1 + 1 \times 2^2 + 1 \times 2^3 + 1 \times 2^4 + 1 \times 2^5 + 1 \times 2^6 + 0 \times 2^7 = 126.$$

This is Rule No. 126 R_{126}. The value of S_i^{t+1} is determined by the eight combinations of the rule, as shown in Diagram 2.10.

As long as the initial state of a cellular automaton is given, the evolution of its states can be derived by R_{126}. We may use algebraic methods to analytically calculate the results, however, several steps of evolution further, it might become rather difficult to use analytic algebra to get the desired result. Therefore, on most occasions, the search for solutions of the evolution of cellular automata uses the method of numeric iteration and let it be performed by computers. Now suppose we have an one-dimensional cellular automaton, there are only two cells with states of 1, i.e., $S_1 = 1$, $S_2 = 1$, while the states of all the other cells on both sides S_3, S_4, … and S_{-1}, S_{-2}, … are 0. Here we use black to represent 1 and white to represent 0. Applying R_{126} to this initial state, we can write out the first few diagrams of the evolution of cell states during the first several steps in time, as shown in Diagram 2.11. The simulation of R_{126} and the relatively long time steps of evolution starting from state "11," however, have to be accomplished on computers. Nowadays, such a task can be easily accomplished b using cellular automata software.

In summary, cellular automata models are built on a simple state set and a set of local interaction rules. They are systems which can self-develop, self-improve and continuously expand. In actual applications, in addition to one-dimensional cellular automata, cellular automata of two dimensions, three dimensions or higher

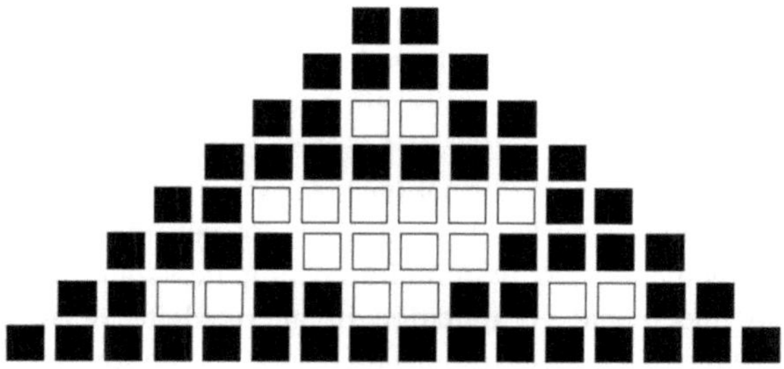

Diagram 2.11 Simulation of and the evolution of the first few time steps of initial state "11"

dimensions can be constructed according to the dimensions of cellular space, and they are all built based on this simple method.

2.5 Information Processing in Cellular Automata

From the perspective of computing, any variation of information is computation. Obviously then, the state change of each cell in a cellular automaton is a form of computation. We can completely regard cellular automata as systems of information processing or system of computation.

In the sense of traditional computing, the information processing or computing is performed through programs. This can seen from two levels: the level of machine code and the level of program language. On the machine code level, programs are composed of specific step by step low level instructions for the machine to accomplish, for example, "move data with address *n* from ROM to register *j* in the CPU." "Operate on or perform logical process to data stored in registers *j* and *i* in the CPU, and save the results to address *m* in ROM."

On the program language level, programs are configured by advanced language commands such as BASIC or Java, so as to make them more comprehensible. For example, "multiply a certain variable by 2, and give the result to another variable." A high-level language command usually needs several lower level commands to implement, and the actual way of implementation may vary by computer types. Therefore, high-level language programming can be translated into machine codes in different ways. High-level program language is a more abstract description of information processing. But this kind of high-level language description enables us to easily understand information processing (or computing) on the machine code or hardware level.

To compare information processing in cellular automata with that in traditional computers, we can say that the information in cellular automata is the combination of the state of the cell grids at each step. Input information is the combination of the initial states of the cells, and output information is the combination of the final states. Information generated during every intermediate step is to be transferred and processed in the neighborhood according to the rules of cellular automata.

The significance of information processing comes from people's understanding of the task at hand, as well as their interpretation of the mapping from input to output. For example, "'The cells will eventually become white' means that the white cells are the majority in the initial state combination."

To describe information processing at this level is like to describe it on the "machine code level," and it cannot help people understand how computation is implemented. As with tradition computers, here we also need a high-level language to understand computation in intermediate steps, so as to describe the specific details of the working mechanism at the bottom level in an abstract way in cellular automata.

One of the reasons that computation in traditional computers is easy to describe is because programming language and machine code can interchange without ambiguities. The design of computers makes such interchanges quite easy. Computer science provides tools for self-translation and decompiling, enabling us to understand how specific programs process information.

Cellular automata, however, do not possess such translation or decompiling tools, nor have any practical and universal high-level language for designing "programs." That is to say, when we prescribe a specific computational task, it is impossible for cellular automata to tell a computer directly how to operate in the way of traditional programming. This is the current difficulty of understanding the information processing in cellular automata. In recent years, however, scientists proposed a computational method using "particles," trying to describe the information processing of cellular automata with the interactions among particles. It is similar to a high-level language in traditional computing sense. Information is transmitted through the movement of particles, and their collisions are the processing of information. Thus, the intermediate steps of information processing gain significance through people's interpretation of the actions of particles. In fact, such descriptions provide a high-level language for cellular automata.

Particle description let us see things we cannot see by simply observing the evolutionary rules of cellular automata or their temporal-spatial evolution pattern variation. They let us understand how cellular automata perform computations from the perspective of information processing. Particles are descriptions we impose on cellular automata, and not anything actually happening within them. Luckily, American physicist J. P. Crutchfield at UC Berkeley has derived rules to explain the behavior of cellular automata with particle information processing using genetic algorithm. His research told us that: every cell in a cellular automaton can only accomplish its own simple individual computational task. However, these cells accomplish overall computations through the interaction among themselves. Why is that? Further research by Crutchfield pointed out that one of the most important reasons that such simple parallel and interacting cells can accomplish overall computation was that they could communicate across domains through "particles," so as to achieve the overall coordination and cooperation of two or more cells in different domains. Only by connecting originally scattered individual cells into an integrated body, complex tasks of information processing (or computing) can be accomplished.

Crutchfield once wrote *Twenty Questions of the Theory of Cellular Automata*, the last question of which is "Can there be high-level descriptions of the information processing by cellular automata?" What he wanted was to possibly use particles and their interactions as a language to explain the distributional computation with one-dimensional cellular automata as a background. In fact, most complex systems have micronized structures, which are composed of numerous relatively simple individual elements. The individuals cooperate in a highly parallel mode. Therefore, although using "particles" to understand information processing does not conform to normal practice, it is useful for computation on numerous simple individuals that are scattered and without central control. The idea of using computation of particles to understand high-level information processing of cellular automata only appeared in recent years, which has not become a systematic computing theory, and needs further study.

2.6 Basic Characteristics of Cellular Automata

1. **Basic Characteristics**

Cellular automata's characteristics are their temporal, spatial and state discreteness. Every cell has only a limited number of states, and the rules for the updating of states are local and synchronous, specifically:

(1) **Spatial discreteness**: The cells are distributed on discrete grid points which are divided according to certain rules. The variations of the states of the cells are represented by definitive rules. The cells are distributed in similar manners, their sizes and forms are also similar, and their distribution is regular and orderly.
(2) **Temporal discreteness**: The evolution of the system proceeds at equal time intervals, and the state configuration at moment t only affects the state configuration at the next moment $t + 1$.
(3) **Limited state discreteness**: The state parameters of cellular automata can only take a limited number (k) of discrete values, S_1, S_2, …, S_k. Compared to dynamic systems with continuous states, it does not need to be coarse-grain-treated and can turn into a symbol array directly.
(4) **Parallelism**: The state change of every cell at moment $t + i$ ($i = 1, 2, \ldots$) is independent and does not need to be aligned according to any universal standard. The actions of the cells are in parallel and do not affect each other. If we treat the state variations of cellular automata as data processing, then such processing is synchronous and particularly suitable for parallel computation.
(5) **Temporal and spatial locality**: The state of every cell at a certain moment is determined by the states of cells within its neighborhood of radius r at the

previous moment. It mainly reflects the interactions among cells within a close distance, i.e., local interactions.

(6) **High-Dimensionality**: If a cell has k states, and the update of its states is determined by its current state plus the states of n neighborhood cells, then there will be number of k^{k^n} possible evolutionary rules. It usually is a large number, making it a necessary condition for simulating complex phenomena. Therefore, high-dimensionality is a typical characteristic of the study of cellular automata.

2. **Major Advantages of Cellular Automata (CA)**

1) **CA is suitable for information processing and system modeling of non-structured issues**

What are structured issues? They are problems which can be described and solved by structured ways (or using formulas). The route to solutions of structured issues is known or can be easily obtained, for example, to solve a quadratic equation with one unknown is a structured issue, the same as using operational research to solve the problem of resource optimization.

Non-structured issues are hard to be described by clear mathematical formulas. The processes and methods for their solutions do not have any regular rules to follow. For example, psychological consultation is a non-structured issue with incomplete definition.

In real life, problems for information processing such as low measurability, blurred boundaries, unclear goals, incomplete definitions and hard for modeling are everywhere. In these situations, mathematical analytic methods are usually ineffective, but solutions can be obtained with the CA method. This is because CA has good adaptability, and its rules are easily described by computers, making them particularly suitable for the computer simulation of discrete phenomena.

2) **There is no error accumulation in the CA simulation**

The errors in traditional simulation will accumulate with the increase of time, but CA has no error accumulation through innumerable iterations. Therefore, we can discover the regularity of a complex system through long duration simulation.

3) **CA do not need prior discretization**

CA establish discrete models by directly drawing rules from actual systems, whereas traditional numerical calculations depend on the discretization of continuous equations. Usually, such equations have to be converted into difference equations or expanded into power equations and intercepting part of the expanded form. Such a process of conversion is not only complicated, but often impossible to accomplish. CA, on the other hand, uses computers to perform computations naturally and reasonably. They even become the prototype for the next generation parallel computers.

4) **CA are parallel operational systems**

In CA, the state updating of every cell is synchronous according to rules, in other words, the information processing of every cell in CA does not need to be aligned according to any standard or protocol. On the contrary, it is information processing in parallel and distributional, which is also the future direction of computer development.

5) **The locality of cellular interaction**

The state updating of every cell in CA depends on its own state and the states of its surrounding neighbors. This is short-range communication (short-range interaction). If we treat every cell as a CPU, and put many of them on a semiconductor chip, then only the communications among the adjacent CPUs are needed. In this way, cost can be saved and the complexity of a system can be reduced.

In short, CA provides a new paradigm for the methodology of scientific research: using simple, local rule-governed, and discrete methods to describe complex, global and continuous systems. Therefore, CA have exerted enormous influence on the science of information systems and many related fields, and obtained wide-spread applications, reaching to various fields in natural and social sciences.

In real applications, however, the key for using cellular automata well is to determine the rules. We can consider that the evolutionary rules are the soul of cellular automata. The success of a cellular automaton model depends on the reasonableness of the design of its rules, and whether it objectively reflects the inherent essential characteristics of the real system (Gan 2005). If we meet a situation where the rules are difficult to be ascertained, we can test several different rules to observe whether the evolutionary result on the macro scale of the system matches the real process.

Let us see a popular example: in order to improve the quality of teaching, teachers can prescribe rules for classroom teaching. One senior teacher prescribes the following three "no-teaching rules," ① If the students can understand the concepts by reading the textbook, no teaching; ② Even if students cannot understand the concepts by reading the textbook, but can figure them out by thinking, then, no teaching; ③ If, by reading or thinking, the students still cannot figure out the ideas, but can understand them by discussing with fellow classmates, then, no teaching. These three rules actually prescribe the relationship between teaching and learning, and will eventually cause the significant increase of students' self-learning abilities. Long-term teaching practice has actually passed down many written or unwritten rules. We can reexamine these rules from a new perspective and try to adjust or rewrite the established rules, or propose new ones beyond conventions.

2.7 Three Classical Types of Cellular Automata

2.7.1 Elementary Cellular Automata by Wolfram

Wolfram used to be called the genius in physics and obtained his Ph.D. at California Institute of Technology in theoretical physics in 1979 when he was only 20 years old. Two years later, he received the famous "Macarthur Genius Fellowship," making him the youngest receiver of this prestigious award. Later, he led a group to develop the famous software "Mathematic," which was widely applied to various areas in mathematics and engineering. From the 1980s, Wolfram committed himself to use computer to explore and simulate the emergence of amazingly complex behavior out of simple algorithmic rules. He focused on comprehensive and systematic study of an one-dimensional cellular automata and discovered that it was impossible to use complex mathematical equations to perfectly represent complex structures he used to study in physics and cosmology. On the contrary, various amazingly complex modes can be generated by the system with simple rules. He therefore believed that cellular automata could help him to go on a completely new way of solutions (Wolfram 1983a, b, 1984, 1985).

1. **Typical Wolfram Rules:**

Suppose the number of states of a certain cell is k, i.e., $S = (S_1, S_2, \ldots, S_k)$, and the neighbor radius is r, which means there are $2r + 1$ cells in the neighborhood. Thus, the possible inputs are

$$N_{input} = k^{2r+1}$$

Every input condition corresponds to k output conditions, making the total number of rules

$$N_{rule} = k^{k^{2r+1}}$$

For elementary cellular automata, suppose there are $k = 2$ states and the neighbor radius $r = 1$, then there are $2^{2^3} = 256$ kinds of output combinations. That is to say, there are 256 rules in total for elementary cellular automata.

When studying these cellular automata, Wolfram numbered them. How did he do that? As we mentioned before, he aligned the output state a_i of every input condition in an order of $a_7a_6a_5a_4a_3a_2a_1a_0$ and regarded it as an eight-digit binary number. Therefore, the number of an evolution rule can be calculated as follows:

$$R = \sum_{i=0}^{7} 2^i a_i$$

The decimal number to which this eight-digit binary number corresponds is the number of the rule.

Obviously, elementary cellular automata have 256 differently numbered rules, i.e., R is within a range of [0, 255]. A possible evolution rule: $R = 01101110$, i.e. $a_7 = 0$, $a_6 = 1$, $a_5 = 1$, $a_4 = 0$, $a_3 = 1$, $a_2 = 1$, $a_1 = 1$, $a_0 = 0$, the number of this rule is

$$R = \sum_{i=0}^{7} 0 \times 2^0 + 1 \times 2^1 + 1 \times 2^2 + 1 \times 2^3 + 0 \times 2^4 + 1 \times 2^5 + 1 \times 2^6 + 0 \times 2^7 = 110$$

This rule is thus named Wolfram Rule No. 110, marked as R_{110}, as shown in Diagram 2.12. If we use colors black and white to represent numbers {1, 0}, then No. 110 cellular automaton rule can be described as: if at moment t, a cell is the same color as its two adjacent neighbors, or, if the cell and the neighbor on its right are both white, then this cell will be white at moment t + 1; otherwise it will be black.

We now introduce three evolution rules of elementary cellular automata. In simulation research, we discovered that, the result of evolution has to do with both the time of evolution and the sizes of the cells participating in the evolutionary process.

1) Rule 90:

Its rule of evolution is described by means of mapping as follows:

$$\begin{array}{cccccccccc} t & \rightarrow & 111 & 110 & 101 & 100 & 011 & 010 & 001 & 000 \\ t+1 & \rightarrow & 0 & 1 & 0 & 1 & 1 & 0 & 1 & 0 \end{array}$$

Corresponding black and white expression:

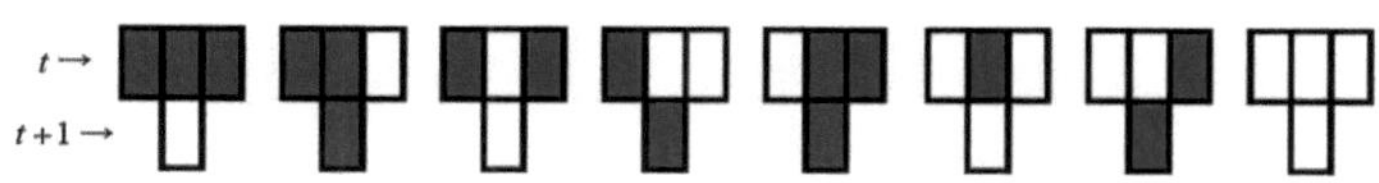

$$\begin{array}{cccccccccc} t & \rightarrow & 111 & 110 & 101 & 100 & 011 & 101 & 001 & 000 \\ & & \downarrow & \downarrow & \downarrow & \downarrow & \downarrow & \downarrow & \downarrow & \downarrow \\ t+1 & \rightarrow & 0 & 1 & 1 & 0 & 1 & 1 & 1 & 0 \end{array}$$

(a) Numerical Representation

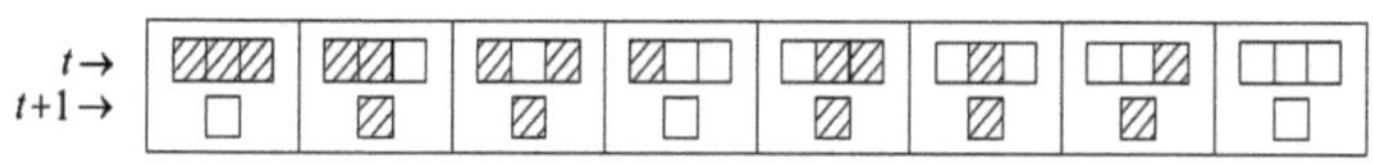

(b) Black and White Representation

Diagram 2.12 Wolfram's No. 110 rule

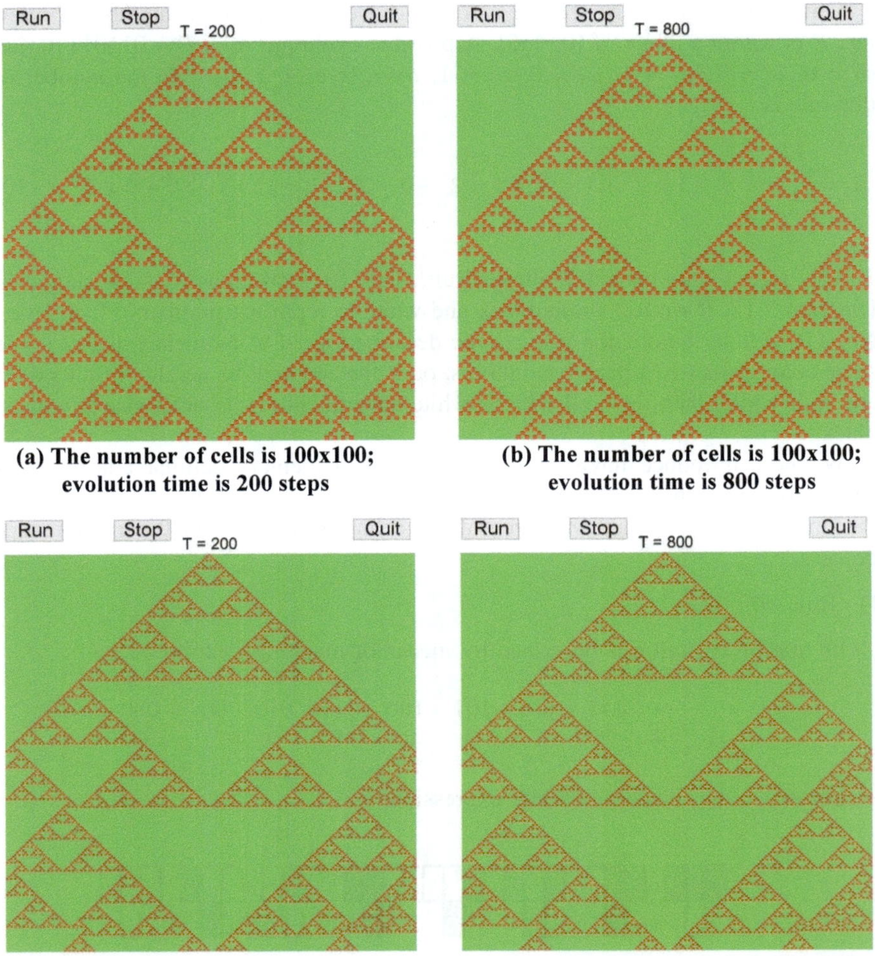

(a) The number of cells is 100x100; evolution time is 200 steps

(b) The number of cells is 100x100; evolution time is 800 steps

(c)The number of cells is 200x200; evolution time is 200 steps

(d) The number of cells is 200x200; evolution time is 800 steps

Diagram 2.13 Evolutionary result of Rule 90

R_{90} can be described by words as: If at moment t, only one of a cell's neighbors is white, then the color of this cell at moment $t + 1$ is black; otherwise it is white. Diagram 2.13 shows the result of its evolution.

Under Rule 90, suppose that the initial value of the central cell in line one is 1, the values of the others are 0, then the cells' expanding growth evolution displays a complex pattern. When both the number of cells and their time of evolution increase, the pattern will become more complex, and yet the complex pattern is very regular. In fact, the pattern is formed by many triangles interlocked together. Every triangle is a miniature of the entire pattern. Such a structure is commonly called "fractal" or "self-simulation," and the structure of such evolution is predictable.

2) Rule 30:

Its rule of evolution can be described using the mapping method as follows:

$$\begin{array}{cccccccccc} t & \rightarrow & 111 & 110 & 101 & 100 & 011 & 010 & 001 & 000 \\ t+1 & \rightarrow & 0 & 0 & 0 & 1 & 1 & 1 & 1 & 0 \end{array}$$

Corresponding black and white expression:

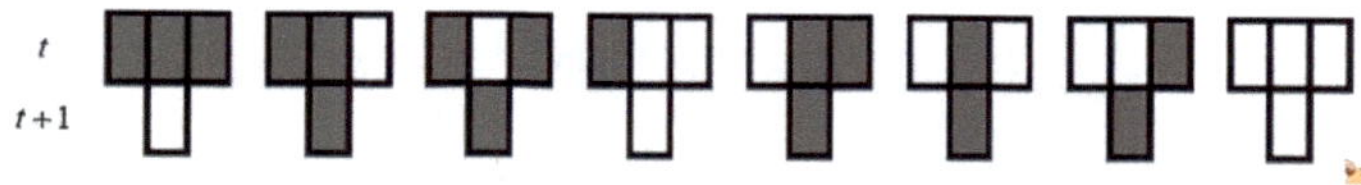

R_{30} can be described by words as: first, examine the states of a cell itself and the neighbor on its right at moment t, if they are both white, the cell at moment $t+1$ will take on the color of its left neighbor at moment t; otherwise, take on the opposite color of the left neighbor at moment t. Its evolutionary result is shown in Diagram 2.14:

Under Rule 30, we take the initial value of the central cell in the first line as 1, others as 0, the cells exhibit an evolutionary expanding pattern of growing from top to bottom, and their growth pattern is disorderly. After a while, the states of all cells tend to become stable. It is not difficult to expect that as the number of cells increases, such an expanding evolutionary mode will sustain. Even though we cannot predict the color of a certain cell at a particular moment, as a whole, the probability of any cell being black or white is relatively equal.

3) Rule 110:

Its evolutionary rule is as follows:

$$\begin{array}{cccccccccc} t & \rightarrow & 111 & 110 & 101 & 100 & 011 & 010 & 001 & 000 \\ t+1 & \rightarrow & 0 & 1 & 1 & 0 & 1 & 1 & 1 & 0 \end{array}$$

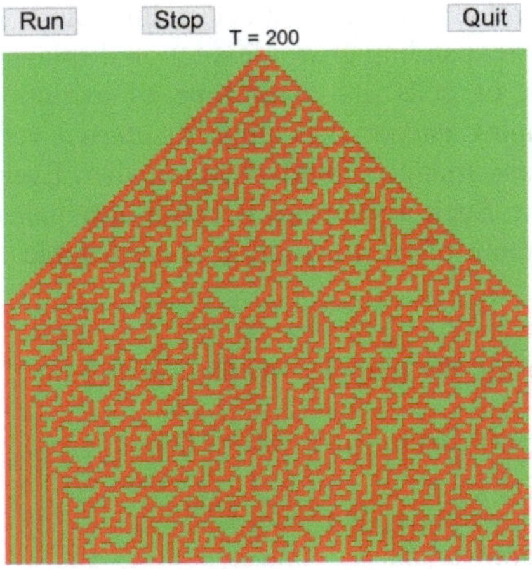

(a) The number of cells is 100x100; evolution time is 200 steps

(b) The number of cells is 100x100; evolution time is 800 steps

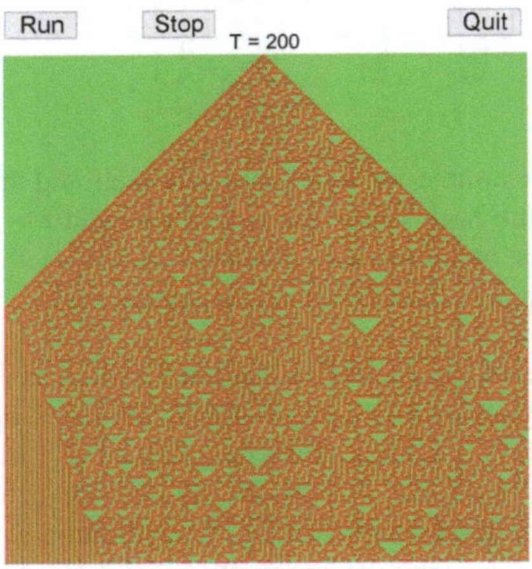

(c) The number of cells is 200x200; evolution time is 200 steps

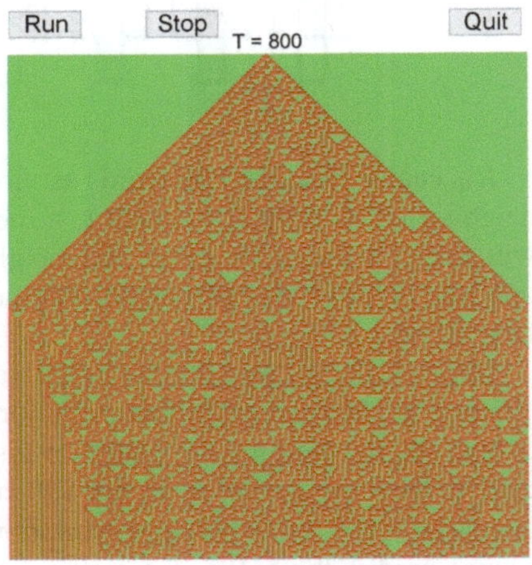

(d) The number of cells is 200x200; evolution time is 800 steps

Diagram 2.14 Rule 30 evolution result (1). Rule 30 evolution result (2)

(a) The number of cells is 100x100; evolution time is 200 steps

(b) The number of cells is 100x100; evolution time is 800 steps

(c) The number of cells is 200x200; evolution time is 200 steps

(d) The number of cells is 200x200; evolution time is 800 steps

Diagram 2.15 Evolutionary result of Rule 110

Corresponding black and white expression:

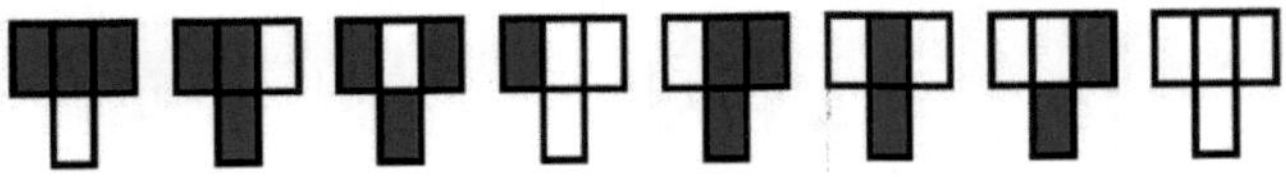

Under Rule 110, the initial values of the cells are that the cell at the rightmost on the first line as 1, all the others as 0, the cells expanding evolve from top to bottom. After a while, the states of all cells become stable. In observing Diagrams 2.15c and d, it is easy to see that as the number of cells increase, the diagrams of cellular design are a combination of regularity and randomness. Near the left side, a diagonal stripe will appear after every several time steps, but on the right side, the patterns are chaotic and basically random. Therefore, it is hard to predict what the configuration of the patterns will become after a certain number of steps of evolution under Rule 110.

We now have a conclusion after comparing the evolutionary situations of cellular automata operated on three different rules.

(1) The rules for R_{30} and R_{90} are quite simple: the initial state starts from a black cell, the evolutionary patterns of R_{30}, however, are much more complicated than the patterns of R_{90}. Where does this complexity come from? We never used any method to add complexity-inducing conditions to the system. Wolfram discovered similar phenomena many times during his research, i.e., even though the internal rules of a system are quite simple, the initial state is also very simple, and yet the system can still display very complex behavior. Therefore, Wolfram thought that it was a miracle that such complexity could emerge out of simple rules. Later he said that "The cellular automaton based on R_{30} is the most amazing thing I have ever encountered in science…, I have spent several years to understand its importance. At last, I realized that this diagram (of pattern) contains the clue to a long-time riddle in all scientific subjects—where does the complexity in nature come from?"

(2) The evolutionary behavior of the cellular automata under R_{110} is more complicated. Their evolutionary patterns are neither completely regular, nor totally random, but a combination of the two. Wolfram believes No. 110 cellular automaton is universally adaptable, the same as a universal Turing machine. No. 110 cellular automaton can produce complex mode of patterns from simple rules and simple initial conditions.

Wolfram's research of cellular automata always concentrated on a central theme: every process in the universe complies with simple calculation, and such operational rules possibly belong to No. 110 cellular automaton. He believes that despite all sorts of strange things happen in nature, most of the complex phenomena are determined by certain simple internal rules. In letting a computer repeatedly iterate the simple rules, extremely complex models can be developed, and most of complex phenomena in nature can be explained. We attach MATLAB emulation program of Rule 110 below:

```
w=100;
m=2;
for i=1:w
    for j=1:w
        if i==1&j==w
            cell(i,j)=1;
        else
            cell(i,j)=0;
        end
    end
end
cellx=zeros(w+m,w+m);
for i=1:w
for j=1:w
cellx(i+m/2,j+m/2)=cell(i,j);
end
end
for i=1:w
    for j=1:w
        if(cellx(i,j)==1&&cellx(i,j+1)==1&&cellx(i,j+2)==0)
        ||(cellx(i,j)==1&&cellx(i,j+1)==0&&cellx(i,j+2)==1)
        ||(cellx(i,j)==0&&cellx(i,j+1)==1&&cellx(i,j+2)==1)
        ||(cellx(i,j)==0&&cellx(i,j+1)==1&&cellx(i,j+2)==0)
        ||(cellx(i,j)==0&&cellx(i,j+1)==0&&cellx(i,j+2)==1)
        cell(i,j)=1;
        end
    end
end
for i=1:w
    for j=1:w
        cellx(i+m/2,j+m/2)=cell(i,j);
    end
end
```

2. **The classification of cellular automata by Wolfram**

We know that classification is necessary for in-depth study of any subject in science, and is important for promoting and developing science. Due to the lack of fixed mathematical formula for modeling and too many ways in configuration, as well as complex behaviors, the classification of cellular automata is rather difficult. There is not a universally accepted classification method except that based on the dimensions of the cells. Wolfram proposes that "In a certain sense, to classify cellular automata is like to classify matter into solids, gases and liquids, or to classify organisms into animals and plants." At first, the classification only stayed on a superficial level. But later as more and more attributes were discovered, they were found to be closely related to classification. Therefore, Wolfram thought that it was possible to make the original definitions for cellular automata more precise, according to the detailed properties. After numerous computer experiments, he studied all 256 kinds of elementary cellular automata. Wolfram started from their different initial states and let them run for a relatively long period of time in order to observe their variations, until becoming stable. Eventually, he categorized them into four types:

(1) The Stable Type: disregard of its initial state, after a period of running, the cellular automaton will almost always stop at an eventual pattern, such as totally black or white, as Rule 8 prescribes. Evolution causes a homogeneous condition which will not change. It is the same as the evolution towards an attractor at a fixed point in system dynamics.
(2) The Periodic Type: disregard of its initial state, after a period of running, the cellular automaton will either stop at a fixed pattern, or circulate among several patterns. The specific final pattern depends on the initial state, as described by rule 56. It is the same as the evolution towards the limit cycle in system dynamics.
(3) The Chaotic Type: starting from any initial state, after a period of running, the cellular automaton will produce a non-periodic pattern or self similar fractal pattern. It is obviously random just like an abnormal TV channel that will continuously produce snowflake interference. The cellular automaton evolves into a chaotic state as rule 30 describes. This is the same as evolving towards the strange attractor in system dynamics.
(4) The Complex Type: starting from any initial state, after running for a period, the cellular automaton will evolve into a mixed structure of order and randomness: the local structures are quite simple, but they can move and interact with other structures in complex ways, as described by rule 110. This is the same as evolving towards the "edge of chaos" in system dynamics. The behavior of the system is neither completely random, nor completely orderly. This is the basic characteristic of the complex type.

Since the invention of cellular automata, the classification of them has always been an important and essential subject for their research. Wolfram first used the theory of system dynamics to describe their evolution and discovered the regular dynamic rules of their classification. His discovery that the dynamic behavior of almost all cellular automata can be classified into only four types is quite significant. It reflects that such classification may have certain universal meaning. Many physical or biological systems may all be studied according to this classification method. Even though actual details may vary, behaviors in each classification are the same qualitatively.

3. **Wolfram's "New Science"**

Wolfram used ten years to finish his great work *A new kind of Science.* When it was published in 2002, it immediately created a sensation in society and scientific circles. Soon it became the best seller on Amazon's website and stayed so for a long time.

In the preface of *A new kind of Science,* Wolfram made some bold pronouncements and predictions. He claimed that his work would cause a new scientific revolution. He said: Three centuries ago, people believed that the natural world could be described by mathematical equations. With the guidance of that idea, radical transformation happened in science. Now, I write this book in order to start a similar revolution, which is to introduce a new kind of science. This new kind of science is based on such an idea: many complex general rules can all be expressed specifically by simple computer programs. What Wolfram mentioned as the scientific transformation which happened three centuries ago is what we often refer to as "scientific revolution." It started with Copernicus' book *On the Revolutions of the Celestial Spheres*, and reached the climax when Newton published *Mathematical Principles of Natural Philosophy*. Wolfram believed that "traditional science" such as mathematical equations failed to establish theories to explain the complexity of the universe. Therefore he wanted to start a new "scientific revolution," and its purpose was to use simple computer programs to replace mathematical equations. The core of the simple computer programs Wolfram loved was cellular automata.

A new kind of Science received both praises and criticism. There appeared two extreme views: some readers thought the book was brilliant and revolutionary; others thought it was blindly arrogant without substance and originality. For example, critics pointed out that physicists K. Zuse and E. Fredkin proposed that the universe was a cellular automaton as early as the 1960s.

Wolfram connected cellular automata with the surrounding real world based on a great deal of data simulation and theoretical analysis, for example: the randomness in billiards, card games, Brownian motion, three body problem and others can all be explained by cellular automata; fluid turbulence, growth behavior of crystals, the rise and fall of Wall Street stock prices can all be simulated by cellular automata; the forms and designs of almost all things in nature such as trees, leaves, shells or snowflakes can all be generated by cellular automata precisely, and cellular automata can also explain why they are formed in that way. Wolfram even believed anything which could be done by analytic calculation could also be done by regular computation. Therefore he boldly predicted that: "Within fifty years, more technology will be invented based on my science instead of traditional science. People will learn the theory of cellular automata before they learn algebra."

Wolfram's view caused heated debates and questioning in international scientific circles. He continued to insist on his "new science" idea, thinking his new science "can penetrate every currently existing scientific field with few exceptions." Therefore, debates and questioning will continue.

How should we regard the relationship between "traditional science" and "new science"? As we mentioned before, Wolfram's fourth type cellular automata has an important characteristic, which is the unpredictability of the designs they generate. Since Rule 110 cellular automaton which belongs to the fourth type has universality, according to his "principle of computational equivalence," any complex system equaling Rule 110 cellular automata will be married off. Therefore, systems as gigantic as the universe of it or as tiny as a bucket of rusty nails, all their behavior is unpredictable. If people want to know what is the result of step 30,000 of a rule 110 cellular automaton, they must wait until it runs to step 30,000. If they want to know where tomorrow's moon will be, then just wait patiently until tomorrow. Wolfram admitted frankly that in certain situations, if someone wanted to know where tomorrow's moon would be, he/she only needed to use a simple formula based on Newton's law to get a satisfactory answer. People depended exactly on mathematical equations to advance the cognition of the essence of the universe step by step. This is because real science should be able to predict things instead of only describe them. Equations still provide the easiest way for us to understand more general concepts such as force, speed, vibration or friction. Equations can also help scientists understand new problems according to phenomena already understood. Wolfram wanted to use the language of cellular automata which represented "new science" to replace the language of "traditional science"—mathematical formulas, yet he did not have enough experience and theoretical evidence to prove how much adaptability his idea had.

In fact, there are two methods for describing complex systems: one is deduction by establishing precise mathematical equations; another is induction through repeated iterations of simple rules by computers. Cellular automata are a result of repeatedly computing simple program codes, i.e. a result of induction. Deduction and induction are two basic methods for people to know the world. They support and complement each other and there is no question of which should replace which.

People's understanding usually starts by studying individual objects, and from numerous facts summarizes general rules. For example, we see copper's volume increases after being heated, the same with aluminum and iron, …, then we form the idea that the volume of all metals will increase after being heated. This is the method of induction.

Induction is widely used in the research of natural science, especially physics. Scientists always make inferences about endless subjects from a limited number of experiments and observations, that is, from individual to general. The results are often correct. Wolfram used cellular automata to simulate leaves, snowflakes, shells, fluid turbulence, billiard balls …, and also obtained correct results. From that he concluded that: the forms and designs of nearly all things, from large scale to small scale, can be simulated by cellular automata; nearly all systems which are complex enough equal rule 110 cellular automata, and therefore equal a universally adaptable Turing machine. The method used by Wolfram in his research of the theory of cellular automata is induction.

We would like to ask, however, are the results obtained by induction dependable? In the example we gave before, regarding the volume of metals will increase when being heated, we did not heat all kinds of metals one by one, we only heated a tiny fraction of all metals, how then, can the characteristic of all metals be induced from the characteristic of such a tiny fraction of metals? What to do? The correct conclusion needs to be drawn under the guidance of the method of deduction.

Deduction reasons from generality to individuality and is based on inevitability. This is because its reasoning is premised on generality and conclusion is about individuality. Generality includes individuality. Any general characteristic a kind of things possess, every individual of the kind inevitably possesses. Therefore, we can reason like this: in nature, when metals are heated, the cohesion of their molecules are weakened, causing an increase of the distance between them, so the volume of the metals will increase. This is the conclusion by deductive reasoning. For another example, all matters in nature are divisible, elementary particles are a kind of matter in nature, therefore, they are divisible. In geometry, only propositions proven by deductive reasoning starting from axioms or postulations are regarded as truth. Axioms or postulations (for example, "a finite straight line can be extended infinitely," "two equal amounts each plus the same amount, their sums are still equal, etc.) are all basic facts based on people's long-term practical experience and believed do not need any proof. From a few self-evident axioms, through logic connections to derive thousands of theorems, that is the logical thinking mode of deductive reasoning. The world of mathematics only accepts deductive reasoning, thinking that knowledge obtained by observations is not truth, no matter how many individual examples there are. On conclusions drawn by deduction are certain and universal.

In order to obtain knowledge, get to know truth, which method should be used? Induction or deduction? This subject used to cause heated debates in the history of Western philosophy. Two opinions debated long and repeatedly. The result is that they complement each other and gradually come closer: induction and deduction are a unity of opposites. Induction emphasizes perceptual knowledge. Based on scientific experiments and empirical facts, it is a practical and reliable way to obtain knowledge; deduction emphasizes rational cognition and reveals the internal connections of things. It makes us see the essence behind phenomena and deepens our understanding. Induction and deduction are two methods to arrive at truth. They are different but closely connected; they depend on each other and complement each other so that our understanding comes closer and closer to truth.

Traditional mathematical equations (such as differential equations) derive from deduction. Their advantages are: theoretically comprehensive, rigorous, precise. Cellular automata are a kind of temporally and spatially discrete mathematical model. They use computers for computation, and are quite natural and reasonable. Nonetheless, there is no comprehensive theoretical support for formations to satisfy particular purposes, and their construction is often a process of intuition. The mode of calculation of differential equations is analytic and the mode of computation of cellular automata is iteration of rules. They are opposite but not conflicting, and possibly are complementary and mutually improving. They both have advantages and disadvantages, but both have reasons to exist. Faced with complex problems in nature and society, people established two scientific descriptive systems and computational modes. They have different basis, different contents, different methods and forms, but are equally important and useful as powerful tools for the research of complex systems. However, in current computer environment, cellular automata, as a discrete computational mode at a relatively young stage, have huge theoretical and practical potentials. They need more attention and support.

2.7.2 Conway's "Game of Life"

As mentioned before, although von Neumann successfully designed a cellular automaton capable of self-reproduction, he used thousands of cells with 29 states each and wrote a design manual of over 150 pages. Conway's goal was to reconstruct it. Wouldn't it be better if machines' self-reproduction can be realized by a simplest kind of cellular automaton. He used a two-dimensional cellular automaton. It is like an infinite broad chessboard, with every grid as a cell. Every cell has only two states, i.e. $k = 2$: "live" and "dead," "1" and "0." Every cells has 8 neighbors which are horizontally, vertically and diagonally adjacent, that is the Moore Neighborhood. The evolutionary rules determining a cell's state is extremely simple:

1. Any live cell with fewer than two live neighbors dies, as if caused by under-population;
2. Any live cell with two or three live neighbors lives on to the next generation.
3. Any live cell with more than three live neighbors dies, as if by over-population;
4. Any dead cell with exactly three live neighbors becomes a live cell, as if by reproduction.

The evolutionary rules in the Game of Life can be expressed by the following mathematical formula:

$$\begin{aligned} &\textit{if} \quad S^t = 1 \quad \textit{then} \quad S^{t+1} = \begin{cases} 1, & S = 2, 3 \\ 0, & S \neq 2, 3 \end{cases} \\ &\textit{if} \quad S^t = 0 \quad \textit{then} \quad S^{t+1} = \begin{cases} 1, & S = 3 \\ 0, & S \neq 3 \end{cases} \end{aligned}$$

The states of Conway's two-dimensional cells and these behavioral rules which simulate ecological principles are quite simple. But who expects such simple behavior, by interaction and iteration, can simulate various life forms and phenomena, possible and realistic, natural and artificial, and perform the functions of a general computer? We are going to use the evolutionary diagrams of the Game of Life to briefly explain this.

Suppose that we start from a huge grid on which live or dead cells are randomly distributed. We turn on the computer program to let the cells behave according to the above evolutionary rules. After running for a period of time, you will discover many "life forms." We will only enumerate three of them in the following.

(1) The evolutionary diagram of "The Game of Life" (see Diagram 2.16)

From Diagram 2.16, it is not hard to discover that under the functioning of the evolutionary rules of the Game of Life, the survival rate of the cells is gradually lowered, but they will not all die. Eventually, after a series of steps of evolution, the number of live cells becomes stable.

(2) Flash Diagram (see Diagram 2.17)

The "flash" as shown in Diagram 2.17 is a simple diagram that varies periodically. In every evolution, the cells on the left and right of the central cell die, while the one on its top and the one at its bottom live. The cycle repeats endlessly.

(3) Glider Diagram (see Diagram 2.18)

Diagram 2.18 is the famous "glider" evolutionary diagram. This is a form composed of cells and can move across the cellular space like a tiny worm. In the evolutionary process, the initial configuration moves along the diagonal lines in the cellular space through deformation. After a period of time, it changes back to the initial configuration. The entire process resembles a glider gliding through space, therefore it gets the name. It can be seen in the diagram that there is a glider moving towards southeast. Of course, the cells do not move. They are fixed. What moves is a non-dissipating shape formed by live cells.

Conway blazed a trail for the research of two-dimensional cellular automata, and realized von Neumann's ideal of inventing machines which can self-reproduce by a very simple method (Von Neumann 1966). Complex life functions such as growth, metabolism, reproduction or diversity are all simulated by the iteration of the simplest cells and simplest behavioral rules. Furthermore, through such simple game of life, we can see a brand new field for the design of cellular automata. It also paves the way for new experiments on "artificial life" and the comprehensive theoretical research on emergent behavior (Tu and Yin 2004).

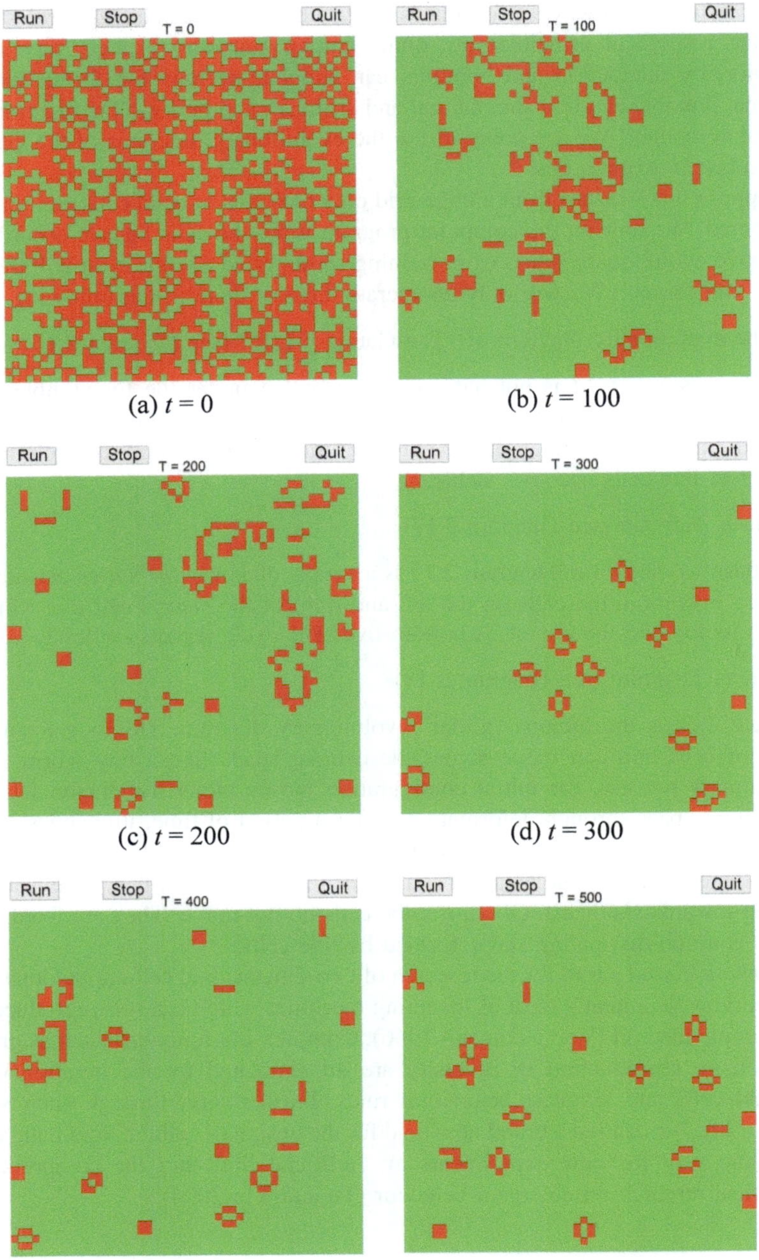

(a) $t = 0$ (b) $t = 100$

(c) $t = 200$ (d) $t = 300$

(e) $t = 400$ (f) $t = 500$

Diagram 2.16 Evolutionary diagram of the game of life

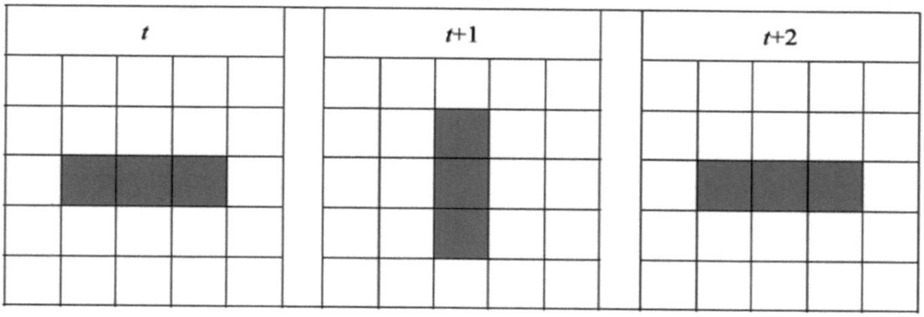

Diagram 2.17 Flash diagram

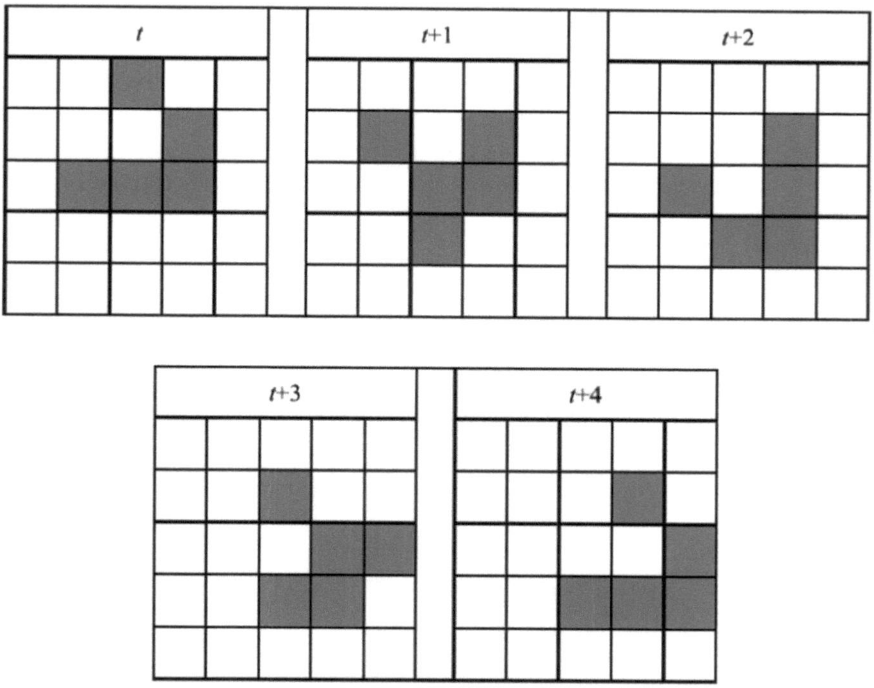

Diagram 2.18 Glider diagram

Now we attach MATLAB simulation program of "The Game of Life" below:

```
w=50;
m=2;
cell=randsrc(w,w,[0 1]);
cellx=zeros(w+m,w+m);
for i=1:w
    for j=1:w
        cellx(i+m/2,j+m/2)=cell(i,j);
    end
end
for i=1:w
for j=1:w
    if cell(i,j)==1
        if cellx(i,j+1)+cellx(i+2,j+1)+cellx(i+1,j)+cellx(i+1,
          j+2)+cellx(i,j)+cellx(i,j+2)+cellx(i+2,j)+cellx(i+2,j+2)
==2||cellx(i,j+1)+cellx(i+2,j+1)+cellx(i+1,j)+cellx(i+
1,j+2)+cellx(i,j)+cellx(i,j+2)+cellx(i+2,j)+cellx(i+2,j+
2)==3
        cell(i,j)=1;
        else
           cell(i,j)=0;
        end
elseif cell(i,j)==0
      if cellx(i,j+1)+cellx(i+2,j+1)+cellx(i+1,j)+cellx(i+1,
       j+2)+cellx(i,j)+cellx(i,j+2)+cellx(i+2,j)+cellx(i+2,j+2)
       ==3
            cell(i,j)=1;
    else
            cell(i,j)=0;
        end
     end
     end
 end
 for i=1:w
for j=1:w
    cellx(i+m/2,j+m/2)=cell(i,j);
     end
 end
```

2.7.3 Langton's "Virtual Ants"

A single ant's behavior is quite simple. Biologists point out that it has only a dozen or so behavioral rules, such as emitting a certain scent when discovering food (ectohormone). Other ants act according to this scent, etc. But the systematic behavior of a colony of ants is very complex and orderly: taking the shortest route to get to where the food is; building a nest of several meters high on the level ground in Africa; using building material in the most reasonable way; maximizing the propagation of its own species, so much so that their total amount occupy one-third of the total population of wild animals, and so on. How is this emergent phenomenon possible? Chris Langton used cellular automata to simulate the behavior of ants. Such simulated ants are also called virtual ants or Vants. Vants is a new word invented by Langton.

The environment for virtual ants is:

(1) There is a finite and unbounded square lattice, just like the cellular square lattice in "The Game of Life" we mentioned earlier;
(2) Every square can be either white or black;
(3) Every virtual ant is faced with four adjacent squares to the east, west, south and north, into which the ant may move.

Behavioral Rules are:

(1) The ant moves forward;
(2) When the ant moves into a white square, its direction will turn 90° left, and flip the color of the square to black;
(3) When the ant moves into a black square, its direction will turn 90° right, and flip the color of the square to white;

The establishment of these rules was possibly led by stimulus source left by the ants, and also may be inspired by the way in which an ant can change the behavior of others.

Diagram 2.19 shows how simple the behavioral rules for a single ant is, and such movement is also temporally reversible (step 8 in Diagram 2.19 can be reversed to step 1). So the autonomous individual actor has simple behavioral rules and a simple structure of time and space. But once a single ant interacts with the effect of its past behavior, the overall simplicity is completely broken.

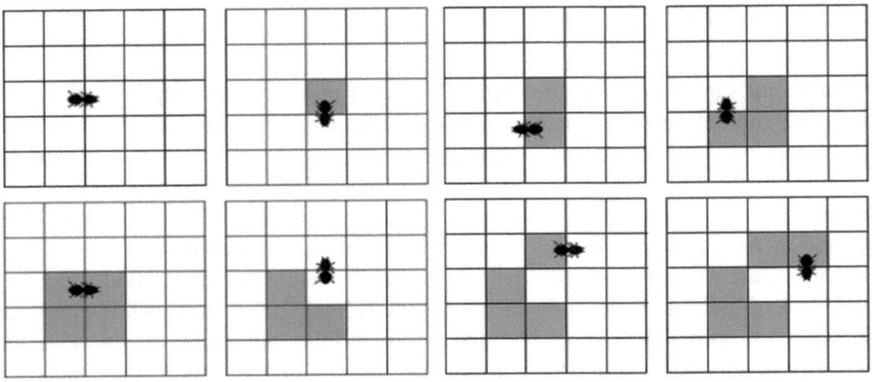

Diagram 2.19 A single virtual ant moves 8 steps from the initial square of the cellular lattice

Suppose a single ant departs from a completely white lattice square and walks 500 time steps, and actually returns to the original point. At this time, due to the interaction between the ant's action and the effect of its past action (turning the squares to black or white), soon things go into a chaotic state, so the ant's action is unpredictable. Suppose we change the initial condition just a little bit, taking out a black square somewhere, for example, the entire behavior will change dramatically thereafter. Therefore, the unpredictability mentioned before is related to the extreme sensitivity towards the initial condition. But if we continue to simulate on Diagram 2.19 another 10,000 time steps, the ant suddenly displays extremely regular and orderly behavior. It has escaped the stage of "initial chaos," and starts what James Propp described as building a highway. Propp first discovered that such a highway and the spatial lattice form an angle of 45°, and can have four directions. Diagram 2.20 shows that, at the beginning of evolution, the ant displays very complex behavior, and its movement is unpredictable. After 10,000 time steps, however, the ant displays very regular behavior. It moves far away from the initial position and builds a "highway," which is at a 45° angle to the spatial lattice. If the lattice space is infinite, then the ant will walk to infinity along the highway; but since our cellular space is a "finite and unbounded" Einstein universe, its four edges will roll up, and the highway will eventually intersect with the lattice space where the ant used to move. This will force the ant back into a chaotic state. But after it stays there for a certain period of time, it will automatically start building another highway. Once the highway is finished, other ants can use it to move quickly.

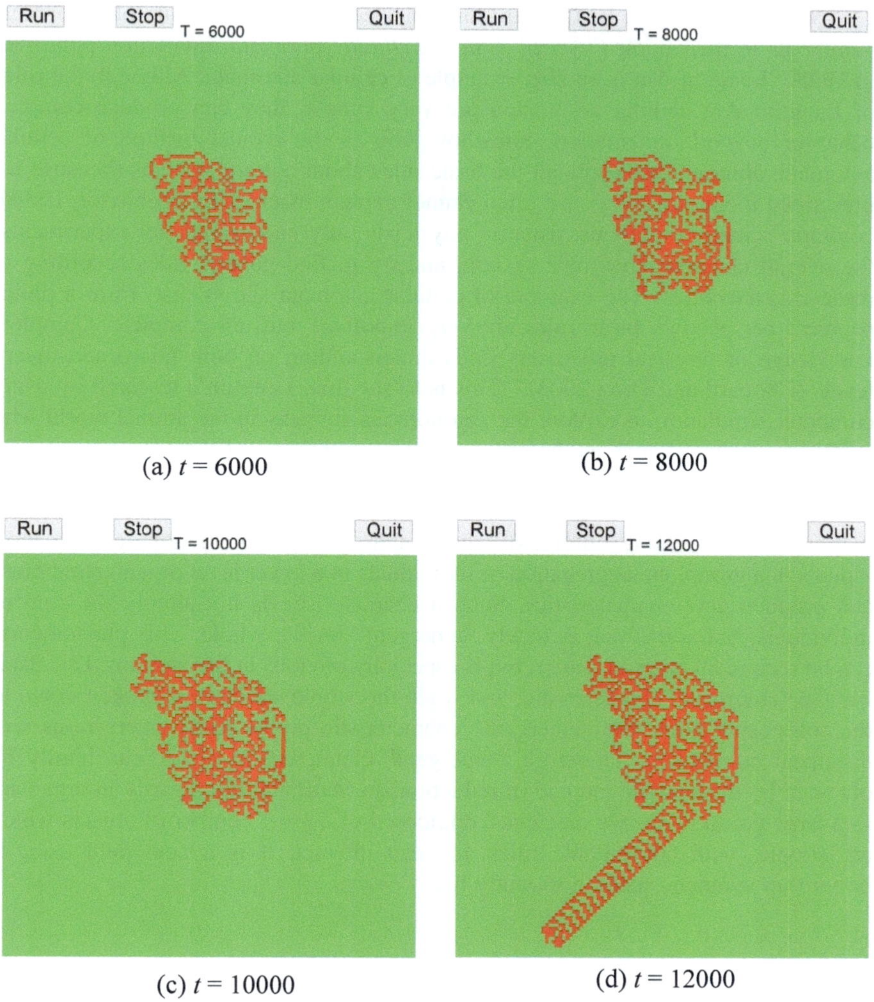

(a) $t = 6000$ (b) $t = 8000$

(c) $t = 10000$ (d) $t = 12000$

Diagram 2.20 The evolutionary process of “Langton” Ant

About Langton Ant, B. Chopard and M. Deoz made some quite philosophical comments in their book *Physical System Cellular Automata Simulation* published in 1998: “Langton Ant is another example of cellular automata. Although the rules of Langton Ant cellular automaton are very simple, they can produce complex behavior beyond imagination. Somehow, this is the typical method of cellular automata: although we know all the basic rules about control systems (because we prescribed them ourselves), we often cannot explain macroscopic behavior. Unlike common scientific methods, usually, physicists only understand (by experiments) the overall characteristics of a system, and try to find general rules according to these characteristics. The example of cellular automata shows that, from a philosophical perspective, basic rules are very important, but not complete. Complete knowledge of physical processes needs understanding on both micro and macro levels (Chopard and Droz 2003).” This is to say that, Langton’s research by using computer simulation to explore the autonomous subjects in the animal world who go their own ways, such as the self-organization problem of the ants, cannot only rely on traditional science’s reductionism to get a clear explanation. It needs to be complemented by idea of emergent.

Langton ant cellular automaton shows that through interactions among individuals in a group, the aggregation of individuals in a lower level organization often can produce new characteristics. Such a characteristic is not simply the sum of individuals, but something is newly “emergent” on the whole. This phenomenon can be seen in all areas in nature, but is especially obvious in life systems. Life itself has the “emergent” characteristic, and when the whole structure is broken down to the composing parts, the “emergent” characteristic produced by interactions will disappear completely. Therefore, “emergent” characteristic of life can hardly be obtained by the analytic method of reductionism. Artificial life regards an organism as a large group of simple machines, composed of a great number of objects which are simple, with controllable rules and can interact. It is a new field using a bottom-up synthetic method to study life.

Now we attach the MATLAB simulation program of Langton Ant as below:

```
width=120;
length=120;
cell=zeros(width,length);
%storage of ant directions, "1" represents north; "2" represents east; "3" represents south; "4" represents west
direction=zeros(width,length);
%==========ant's departure point=========
a=width/2;
b=length/2;
direction(a,b)=2; %walking towards east at the beginning
%=========evolution starts=============
 while (t<=T)
 if cell(a,b)==0
        cell(a,b)=1;
        if direction(a,b)==1;
            a=a;
            b=b-1;
            direction(a,b)=4;
        elseif direction(a,b)==2;
            a=a-1;
            b=b;
            direction(a,b)=1;
        elseif direction(a,b)==3;
            a=a;
            b=b+1;
        direction(a,b)=2;
    elseif direction(a,b)==4;
        a=a+1;
        b=b;
        direction(a,b)=3;
    end
elseif cell(a,b)==1
    cell(a,b)=0;
    if cell(a,b)==1;
        a=a;
        b=b+1;
        direction(a,b)=2;
    elseif direction(a,b)==2;
        a=a+1;
          b=b;
          direction(a,b)=3;
       elseif direction(a,b)==3;
          a=a;
          b=b-1;
          direction(a,b)=4;
       elseif direction(a,b)==4;
          a=a-1;
          b=b;
          direction(a,b)=1;
       end
end
```

2.8 The Philosophical Implications of Cellular Automata

1. **Inevitability and Contingency**

One of the difficult problems philosophers face is to precisely define inevitability and contingency (or definitiveness and randomness). Just as G. W. Leibniz, one of the inventors of calculus, says, there are two mysteries in the world which puzzle rationality: one is how to coordinate inevitability and randomness, the other is how to integrate continuity and indivisibility.

For a long time, there are two opposite scientific views regarding the relationship between inevitability and contingency. The discovery of the phenomenon of chaos shows that: even for some completely definitive systems, with no random factors added, with determined initial conditions, can still produce random behavior internally. The scientific fact that randomness exists in definitiveness as revealed by the phenomenon of chaos, forcefully proves that an objective entity can have both definitiveness and randomness. This provides a scientific answer to questions being debated for a long time such as "Is the world definitive or random,inevitable or haphazard, orderly or chaotic?" "Can the world be divided half and half?" According to dialectical materialism, the objective world exist both inevitability and contingency, and there is no unbridgeable gap between them. On the contrary, they are a dialectical unity. The behavior of cellular automata again provides perfect proof of this idea.

On the one hand, we see that for certain elementary cellular automata, their initial configurations are randomly formed, but as long as the rules are determined, their evolutionary laws are definitive. This demonstrates that definitiveness can come from randomness. On the other hand, we can also discover that uncertainty can emerge from the interaction among plenty of definitiveness. It seems like a random phenomenon on the surface, yet its essence follows definitive rules. The third type cellular automata, for example, are systems which operate according to definitive rules. And yet during the process of evolution, completely uncertain and random behavior emerge. Strictly speaking, these are chaotic systems that unify definitiveness and randomness.

2. **Simplicity and Complexity**

Is the world ultimately "complex," or "simple" from its nature? Searching for the answer to this question has always been the ultimate goal of science.

From the perspective of physics, the projection of physical processes from a high-dimensional space to a low-dimensional space will create complexity; on the contrary, to add new parameters or variables to physical processes can reduce complexity. The improper use of the methods of understanding will also make simple things complex.

Hence, a question naturally arises: is the "complexity" demonstrated by things their inherent characteristic, or caused by people's deficiency in understanding or improper approaches?

Chaos theory and fractal theory show that complex phenomena are possibly controlled by very simple rules. Things can produce complex behavior or phenomenon under simple rules, and this inspires us to simulate complex objects or processes through simple rules.

From evolutionary logic, it is generally believed that the world is gradually formed from simple to complex. Then can we say that the essence of the world is simple, and complexity is only the result of later evolution? Just as American physicist and Nobel Prize winner Gell Mann says: "The behavior of extremely complex nonlinear systems usually will also demonstrate actual simplicity, but such simplicity is typically formed and does not appear at the beginning."

The theory of cellular automata led us to the discovery, to our great surprise, that the simplest elements, relationships and rules, under certain conditions, by repeated iteration, can generate extremely complex behavior or characteristics. The states of cells and their rules are so simple, and yet they can simulate any complex process. From biological evolution to the rise and fall of the stock market, to the formation of snowflakes, to the rusting of iron nails…It makes us further understand that many complex structures and processes in nature are ultimately caused by simple interactions among a great number of basic components." This further strengthens our belief that "things seemingly complex on the surface may be very simple in essence," thereby inspire us to persevere in discovering simplicity from within complexity, so as to better understand the real nature of the objective world (Cook 2004).

3. **Existence and Evolution**

The major goal of traditional science is to study existence. However, scientific development requires us to study not only the existence of things, but their evolution.

From a philosophical perspective, the existence of the universe is definite, yet the evolution of the universe is random (Poundstone 1984). Nonlinear science repeatedly shows that existence is evolutionary existence, and evolution is existential evolution. The essence of matter is existence, but matter is neither born nor dying, which reflects its evolutionary characteristic.

Traditional science studies the existence of things by mainly focusing on their states. Modern science believes that in order to understand an object deeply, it is necessary to understand its entire evolutionary history and the entire dynamics of the environment in which it exists. That is to say, we need to examine the evolutionary behavior of systems and not just their states at a certain moment. Instead, we need to form a way of thinking which takes process as the perspective of study. In many cases, the ultimate state of an object is unknown, and whether such an ultimate state exists is also unclear. Philosopher G. W. F. Hegel once said that to understand the history of a science is to understand the science itself. Langton also said: "You should observe how a system operates instead of observing what it consists of."

Cellular automata has a time dimension, thus they reflect a process. Their particular characteristics do not manifest themselves at a certain static moment. These characteristics only appear in a dynamic evolutionary process. When we analyze these characteristics, such as making a dynamical classification, for certain cellular automata, the process of observation has to be long enough to truly discover the laws of their operations.

4. **Centrality and Dispersion**

What is centralized control?

Generally speaking, a highly organized system must be a system with centralized control: life is controlled by its DNA blueprint; animals are centrally controlled by their various levels of nervous systems; human behavior is uniformly controlled by the brain; a country has a head of government to lead all government branches. Such means of control is centralized control.

In both nature and human society, however, centralized control is not the only means of control. For example, bees build beehives, ants build ant hills, and yet these activities are not centrally controlled by the order or information sent out by their queens. The activity of the entire group is dispersedly controlled by every participant bee or ant according to its own relatively simple behavioral rules. Therefore, it is called distributed or dispersed control. If a "controller" exists, then everyone is, thus there is no central controller. By the same token, in a free and non monopolistic market composed of numerous independent manufactures and consumers, the price of a certain product is not centrally controlled and is also impossible for it to be controlled centrally. It is dispersedly controlled by every manufacturer or consumer, although people involved may not realize that they are consciously controlling the prices of the goods, for the phenomenon arises naturally instead of forming under a central command. Once the government fixes a price by official order, or some monopoly group raises or lowers prices by exerting its monopolistic power, it is no longer market economy.

Cellular automata are composed of a large number of cells, and their behavior is an emergence of the evolutionary behavior of the individual cells. These cells are of equal status, and evolve concurrently according to rules without the need of centralized control. In such a situation with no centralized control, they can effectively realize self-organizational and disperse control, leading to the emergence of diverse complex and novel behavior on the whole. This inspires us: centralized control is not the only means to manipulate a system for realizing certain goal. Especially in complex systems, disperse control is the unstoppable trend, because it has advantages such as robustness, tenacity, and self-autonomy.

Admittedly, centralized control has its advantages, too. During the process of designing a decision-making mechanism, on the one hand, people need to make it display the dispersibility of control within a system, stimulate the initiative and creativity of the various subsystems to react timely to the fast changing external environment, so as to make the system on the whole fully dynamic and competitive. On the other hand, people take advantage of centralized control under uncertain conditions, so as to achieve the optimum overall effect of dispersive control.

5. **Continuity and Discreteness**

Things in the world are changing constantly, but we can still know A is A, B is B. This is because things change little by little. They usually do not adopt a completely different shape all of a sudden. It gives us the impression that the variation of things is continuous. We can think that the change of time is continuous and movement is continuous. If a point runs from one end of a line segment to the other end, it should pass all the points on the segment. The problem of continuity is closely related to the problem of infinity. But how to establish the concept of "continuity" used to be a difficult problem for philosophers.

The continuity of change for things is our perception. But this perception may not be accurate. A film actually consists of many different frames and its change is not continuous. But because the difference between two consecutive frames is slight, we perceive the whole film as continuous. In fact, if matter is composed of molecules or atoms, the growth of things cannot possibly be continuous. For another example, the activities of someone in a day such as getting up, morning exercise, going to class, finishing class, eating, taking a nap, playing basketball …, may be the sum of his states during a day. They are discrete. Based on the above reasons, in modern mathematics, variables are classified into continuous value and discrete value, and also may be classified into one can be expressed by numerical value while the other cannot.

Differential equation, which has a history of more than three hundred years, is founded on the concept of "continuity." It has become the language of modern science and one of the most important tools for scientific research. Even though many complex phenomena in the real world are completely different, they have the same mathematical form and can usually be expressed by differential equation (Heims et al. 1980). Just as Friedrich Engels, coauthor of the Communist Manifesto, says: "The unity of nature is manifest in the surprising similarity of the use of differential equation by various phenomena." A great number of important scientific laws are reasoned and expressed by differential equation.

Differential equation is based on the philosophical understanding of the continuity of time. Its theory is complete, rigorous, and precise. When it comes to human calculation, composed of symbols, differential equation can flexibly perform arithmetic operations such as symbol reduction to get precise quantitative solutions. This is its advantage. However, modern computers are digital information processing systems, built on discreteness. This poses an awkward problem for differential equation when it tries to perform computation by using computers. This means that it has to discretize itself.

Cellular automata are temporally and spatially discrete models which are particularly suitable for computer simulation. They are even the prototype for next generation parallel computers. Therefore, in the computing environment of modern computers, discrete computing method represented by cellular automata has more advantage in getting solutions, in particular, in the simulation of complex dynamic systems.

The computation modes corresponding to differential equation and cellular automata: the continuous analytic calculation and discrete iteration of rules is a pair of opposite computing methods. But as physicist N. H. D. Bohr says: "Opposites are not necessarily incompatible. They may be complementary and perfecting each other." Both of them are powerful tools for scientific research, especially the research of complex systems.

From a philosophical perspective, the emergence of cellular automata advanced people's renewed understanding of continuity and discreteness.

References

Berlekamp, E., Conway, J. H., & Guy, R. (1982). *Winning ways for your mathematical plays* (Vol. 2). San Diego: Academic Press.

Chopard, B., & Droz, M. (2003). *Cellular automata based modeling of physical systems* (Y. Zhu & X. Zhao, Trans.). Beijing: Tsinghua University Press.

Cook, M. (2004). Universality in elementary cellular automata. *Complex systems, 15*(1), 1–40.

Gan, T. (2005). *Cellular automata and algorithms in modern science*. Beijing: China Renmin University.

Heims, S. J., Neumann, J., & Weiner, N. (1980). *From mathematics to the technologies of life and death*. Cambridge, MA: MIT Press.

Jia, B., Gao, Z., Li, K., et al. (2007). *Model building and simulations of a cellular automata based traffic control system*. Beijing: Science Press.

Mitchell, M. (2006). Complex systems: Network thinking. *Artificial Intelligence, 170*(18), 1194–1212.

Poundstone, W. (1984). *The recursive universe*. New York: William Morrow.

Rendell, P. (2002). Turing universality of the game of life. In *Collision-based computing* (pp. 513–539). London: Springer.

Tu, X., & Yin, Y. (2004). *Artificial lives and their applications*. Beijing: Beijing University of Posts and Telecommunications Press.

Von Neumann, J. (1966). *Theory of self-reproducing automata*. Urbana: University of Illinois Press.

Wolfram, S. (1983a). Cellular automata. *Los Alamos Science, 9*, 2–21.

Wolfram, S. (1983b). Statistical mechanics of cellular automata. *Reviews of Modern Physics, 55*, 601–644.

Wolfram, S. (1984). Cellular automata as models of complexity. *Nature, 311*, 419–424.

Wolfram, S. (1985). Twenty problems in the theory of cellular automata. *Physica Scripta, T9*, 170–183.

Wolfram, S. (2002). *A new kind of science*. Champaign, IL: Wolfram Media.

Chapter 3
Model Building Method of Cellular Automata

3.1 Computer Models

What are mathematical models?
Mathematical models apply mathematical ways of thinking to simplify and abstract problems needing to be solved, and use mathematical symbols, formulas, diagrams to describe the essential characteristics and inherent rules of things. When people solve a specific problem, they do not rely on observations and experiments, but turn the problem into a mathematical topic and use mathematical analytic method to find the answer. For example, the variations of the electric current and voltage of a circuit system do not need to be actually measured, but are obtained by establishing a mathematical model of differential equation according to the laws of electromagnetics, and then substituting known data for the unknowns in the model for a solution.

Generally speaking, simple systems are often ideal systems for easy mathematical processing, while complex systems are difficult to be processed by mathematics alone. However, with fast growing speed, fast dropping price, as well as fast growing functionalities of computers, it becomes possible to construct computer models for complex systems and perform simulations (Axelrod 1997). Pioneers in computer science such as Alan Turing, Von Neumann, Norber Wiener, etc. all hoped to use computers to simulate systems that could reproduce, develop, think, learn and evolve. Along with the rapid development of computers, a new science was born. In addition to theoretical science and experimental science, a new science branch of computational science was born.

Before the appearance of computers, two methods of creating knowledge—experimentation and theory, had always occupied dominant positions in scientific research. Galileo and Newton laid the foundations for experimental science and theoretical science separately, which were vitally important for the development of the science and technology for mankind. Theoretical science mainly researches the inherent laws of various natural phenomena, intending to describe these laws (such

X. Li et al., *Theory of Practical Cellular Automaton*,
https://doi.org/10.1007/978-981-10-7497-4_3

as Newton's laws of motion, etc.) by rigorous mathematical models, and to seek accurate solutions under certain conditions. Further, the results thus obtained are used to judge whether a mathematical model formed realistically reflects natural phenomena, or whether it leaves room for improvement.

Experimental science is mainly for studying and making of various equipments and instruments. It simulates various natural conditions to design controllable and repeatable experiments. In analyzing the experimental results, the science judges the results, on whether they conform to reality, or whether they meet the requirements.

The development of computational science has been completely catching the boat downwind of computers. Taking advantage of the super tool such as computers, the science simulates on computers various phenomena in the objective material world. Especially in the exploration of complexity, computers made possible the first time that many complex systems became the objects of scientific research. The research carried out in the Santa Fe Research Institute in the U.S. on artificial life is the most well known example of such kind.

Although in the past, at present, and in future, the experimental and theoretical scientific methods all had, have and will have quite important functions, they had, have and will have their limitations, too. In reality, many of the research subjects are either too large or too small in size, or too quick or too slow in moving speed. Further, some things are impossible to be described precisely in theory or to be made in experiments. For example, in the research of nuclear weapons, it was very difficult to measure the detailed reaction process of nuclear weapons through one nuclear experiment. This is because that the nuclear explosion process and reaction process were both carried out under high-temperature, high-pressure conditions. The temperature could reach as high as tens of millions of centi-degrees, and the pressure could reach as high as several million of earth atmospheric pressure. There were no available equipments capable of measuring the various internal condition changes within such a nuclear weapon. On the other hand, the mathematical model describing such physical process of nuclear reaction was composed of a set of very complex nonlinear partial differential equations, for which a precise solution is impossible. Thus it was only possible to get a numerical value simulation of the physical process on computers. Therefore, computational science broke the limitations of experimental and theoretical sciences (Shi 2000).

A main direction of the research on complex systems is the study of ideal models, i.e., to understand general concepts through relatively simple models. For example, genetic algorithm is the ideal model for studying adaptability, or the ideal model for E. Darwin's theory of evolution. H. V. Koch's curve is the ideal model for studying fractal structures such as coastal lines, snowflakes, etc. This model is temporally and spatially discrete, the cell states and the rules determining these states are quite simple in computation. However, the overall modes and configurations composed can simulate all the complexity of the real world.

For most complex systems, it is impossible to perform real experiments on them, and it is also difficult to conduct mathematical research on them. Therefore, computer models are the only feasible way to study them. It can be said that the method of using computer models is the main method for studying complex systems. In evaluating computer models, Holland said: "Computer models have both abstract and concrete characteristics. The definitions of these models are abstract, just like mathematical models, which are defined by numbers, the connections among numbers and the variations of numbers with time. At the same time, these numbers are precisely 'written into' the register of a computer instead of only being expressed symbolically … We can obtain these concrete records, and they come very close to the results of carefully performed operations in a laboratory. Thus, computer models possess both theoretical and experimental characteristics." Because of such characteristics of computer models, he thought that they were "a major tool for scientific research of emergence."

To examine whether a computer model is correct, the best method is to see whether the result obtained from modeling is repeatable. That is to say, the same results can be obtained from the models completely reconstructed by others. R. Axelrod once said: "repeatability is the cornerstone of science accumulation." Repeatability can be used to test the dependability of a simulation result, i.e. the same result can be obtained by repeating the process from the start. Otherwise, the results obtained from computer models must have distorted the object of simulation. Repeatability is also very useful for testing the stability of a model.

3.2 Models of Cellular Automata

Cellular automata models are a new kind of computer models for simulating complex structures and processes. They mainly adopt the analytic way of thinking of modern systems, i.e., to use the idea of turning a system into a system of cells as the basis of application. At the same time, cellular automata incorporate the objective laws of the evolution of systems into the core of algorithm, i.e., when the model of a system is divided into numerous tiny cells, the characteristics and behavior of each cell are always influenced by the characteristics and behavior of its adjacent cells, or, the evolution of the states of a cell is determined by the states of the few cells adjacent to it.

Cellular automata models provide a new way of thinking and a new method for studying complexity. Traditional methods always try to use precise mathematical analysis. This top-to-bottom method of system analysis often uses mathematical models to describe complexity, and to solve problems caused by complexity. For example, to repeatedly simplify a practical system, starting from the description of the system, the essence of system complexity would have been lost. The basic belief of cellular automata is: the complexity of a system does not exist in any single element, but in the combination of elements and their interactions. It is just as the complexity of human life does not come from the complexity of genes, for human genes are no more complex than the genes of many other inferior organisms. Individual characteristics of a human being do not mainly come from the characteristics of his or her genes. Genes exist as independent individuals, but their interactions and mutual influences will display extremely complex phenomena. We can draw a concise conclusion from this: the complex behavior of a system emerges from the interactions of numerous simple composite elements. In everyday life, people have already realized that when certain objects gather together, some new phenomena which cannot be obviously derived from their original characteristics will emerge. Cellular automata are exactly a kind of models that can form various complex systems due to numerous elements interacting in accordance with simple rules. As K. Mainzor points out in his book *Thinking in Complexity*: "Cellular automata are not only beautiful computer games. They are also models which describe the discretization and quantization of their dynamic evolution's complex system of nonlinear partial differential equations." "As the complexity of nonlinear systems increases, and solving differential equations or even calculating approximate numerical values so as to determine the system's behavior becomes more and more hopeless, cellular automata become very flexible and effective modeling tools."

Cellular automata are non-deterministic. That is to say, it is impossible to give a general answer of the ultimate state of the evolution pattern of cellular automata by limited program steps. But cellular automata have powerful computational functionality, and their parallel computational methods have shown a bright future for the modeling of complex systems. The characteristics of cellular automata models can be summarized as: abstractness, adaptability, and self-organization.

3.2.1 The Abstractness of Cellular Automata Models

Cellular automata are an important complement for the method of system analysis. They mainly define the state of a complex system by making it into an abstract model. The stock system is such an example. Cellular automata can make us reexamine certain traditional research methods in a new perspective. They are not like common mathematical physical methods which rigidly describe or simulate a system. It may be very difficult, or even impossible to use mathematical physical methods to analyze a relatively complex system. The method of cellular automata, however, adopts some new ideas to simplify the process of analysis, and at the same time can achieve better computer simulation effect. Such a method also can possibly become a stable and dependable method.

Many real complex systems can be abstracted as cellular automata systems. For example, the research of artificial life simulation is the abstraction of the basic dynamics of life characteristics, so as to study life science. R. Dawkins, a scholar of the theory of evolution at Oxford University proposed using cellular automata to simulate the evolution of life. He constructed a cellular automaton which could simulate the evolution of insects to observe their mutation, reproduction, and swallowing each other on a computer screen, and unexpectedly portrayed the processes of evolution and extinction of life on the computer which is amazingly similar to the real biological world. Of course, not all practical complex systems can be simulated by using cellular automata systems, such as the problem of the testing and synthesis of super scale integrated circuits, the problem of computation by large parallel computers and the prediction as well as simulation of complex dynamic systems, etc. If the mathematical models established by these problems cannot reflect the system's complexity, the results obtained are often different from reality. Cellular automata models, on the other hand, can not only reduce the difficulty of system analysis, but also increase the efficiency of solving problems (Mitchell 2011).

3.2.2 The Adaptability of Cellular Automata Models

Because of the limited resources in the world, not all different kinds of organisms, subjects of action and complex systems have chances to self-reproduce and self-regenerate, hence there inevitably exist the problems of choosing environments and "survival of the fittest". If a system can adapt to its environment, we regard the system as having adaptability.

In the beginning of the 1960s, Holland started the research of the theory of adaptability. He drew on the basic ideas of E. Darwin's theory of evolution and G. Mendel's laws of heredity, and extracted, simplified, as well as abstracted them. He thus proposed an algorithm which could perform computer simulation of biological genetics and natural selection—Genetic Algorithm. It could adapt to different environments, different problems, and obtain relatively effective and satisfactory solutions in most cases. In genetic algorithm, the problem under study is expressed as a string of symbols (or string of codes), consisting of a certain limited fixed set of symbols. As the genetic algorithm starts, first, it generates a number of symbol strings randomly, and then calculates the adaptability of every single string of symbols, so as to grade each string according to the quality of the calculation results (the degrees of adaptability). Strings of high quality (high adaptability) are used for reproducing offspring, while strings of low quality (low adaptability) automatically die out. The process goes on generation after generation until the string of symbols which can perfectly solve a problem eventually gains dominance. Genetic algorithm seems simple, but it has been applied to solve many difficult problems in science and engineering, even in the arts, music, and architecture. Later, many scholars made various improvements of the algorithm in actual applications.

Still, genetic algorithm has the following limitations:

(1) The adaptability measuring function for the algorithm is prescribed beforehand, while real adaptability should be local, naturally formed in the survival struggle of individuals against the environment, change along with the variation of the environments. The natural selection mechanism in genetic algorithm is at most only artificial selection instead of real natural selection.
(2) It only considers the competition among organisms, and does not consider the possibility of cooperation among them. In real situations, competition coexists with cooperation. This is so called synergistic evolution. Biological evidence

shows that synergistic evolution has greatly quickened the course of evolution of organisms. In genetic algorithm, the structures of all organisms are prescribed strings of symbols. Such a system cannot realize infinite evolutions, and all things which can possibly happen within the system are in the control of its designer.

(3) The copying and hybridization mechanisms of the algorithm are too simple. The so called copying is to make an accurate copy of the original, while hybridization gets parts from the individuals to be hybridized and combines them into the next generation.

At the end of the 1970s, Holland proposed a cognitive model based on genetic algorithm—the system of classifier. It follows three basic rules: ① knowledge can be expressed as structures similar to rules, and these rules are always in competition; ② experience makes useful rules more and more powerful, and useless rules weaker and weaker; ③ new rules come out of the combination of old ones.

Genetic algorithm and classifier algorithm are simulations of the evolutionary adaptability and learning adaptability of complex adaptive systems in nature. The fact that such simulation can effectively solve scientific and engineering problems as well as problems of various management systems proves that there is a common law in all natural and artificial systems: the law of the evolution of adaptability. To a certain degree, evolution is a process of adaptation, because natural selection functions in every generation. Cellular automata can completely be seen as the best examples of the simulation of the evolution of adaptability. For example, for a two-dimensional cellular automaton, "black" or "white," "0" or "1" are its states. As long as the rules for the change of cell states are determined, with the addition of free input under the initial condition and a certain number of cells interacting with each other and changing states under the limitation of simple rules, infinite complex systems and formation processes of emergence can be generated, such as the growth process of gliders in cellular automata, the formation process of an ant colony or a stock market, etc.

The most interesting thing about the study of evolutionary adaptability is how complexity can gradually evolve from a simple initial state. It is just as Lao Tsu once said in his *Classics of the Virtue of the Dao*: "The Dao is the underlying principle behind the creation of the myriad things. The order of the process giving rise to the myriad things began with the Dao producing a kind of generative force." The view of evolution, in the most general sense, means to grasp the essence of the object of study from its history, development and change, instead of separating history and reality. This has great significance for the guidance of complexity study.

3.2.3 The Self-organization of Cellular Automata Models

In nature and in human society, especially in the biological world, we see relatively stable system organizations, structures, modes and forms everywhere. For example, stars in the sky, mountains on earth, human families, communities, or markets, the snowflake crystals or layers of clouds, as well as various species in the physical and biological worlds, are very orderly. However, such orders are obtained from their autonomous internal interactions under certain conditions, without any external imposed interference and particular outside instructions. We call this phenomenon as self-organization. On the contrary, the organization, which is formed by the control and domination of external factors, is called "none-self-organization." This mode can possibly get us far away from nature, even be on the opposite side of nature, and causes serious environmental and ecological problems. The modes of operation of "none-self-organization" systems include "central-control", "unified management", "overall communications", 'macro strategic decision-making" and "sequential operation". How to explain the phenomenon of none-self-organization? Some newly emerged theories of science give explanations:

(1) According to the theory of dispersive structures, an open non-linear system that is far from the equilibrium state can raise the degree of orderliness of itself and lower the content of entropy by exchanging matter and energy with the outside world. This theory believes that "non-equilibrium is the source of orderliness."
(2) According to synergistic theory, systems composed of a great deal of tiny units, under certain external conditions, through interactions among the various units, can automatically coordinate the behavior of the various units, and this will lead to the appearance of macro spatial structures, temporal structures and functional structures. This theory believes that in a critical state, occasional ups and downs will be enlarged, and this will facilitate the emergence of orderliness.

In development of cellular automata theory, von Neumann thought of live organisms as a self-reproducing network of cells, he thus first proposed the idea of establishing a mathematical model for them. This idea was further expanded by John Conway and others into the method of computer modeling and simulation for the study of the macro behavior and rules of systems composed of numerous parallel individual elements similar to biological cells. Cellular automata vividly show how random initial configurations evolve into stable and orderly spatial structures through the local interactions among cells, micro decision-making, parallel coordination and repeated iterations. We know now that the dynamic behavior of cellular automata can be basically classified into four types:

(1) The evolution of cellular automata reaches an even and stable state which does not vary with time, i.e., every cell is in the same state as the others;
(2) The evolution of cellular automata produces a periodic structure, in which a limited fixed number of states recycle themselves infinitely;
(3) The evolution of cellular automata causes the appearance of chaotic behavior, and this is a non-periodic random mode;
(4) The evolution of cellular automata produces a complex local structure, which is a kind of mixed structure combining orderliness and randomness.

The above four developmental prospects are the “attractors” of cellular automata’s evolution under random initial conditions. The first three types are approximately analogous to stationary attractors, limit cycles and exotic attractors for continuous dynamical systems. Even though the four structures are different, they all belong to orderly structures. The form and characteristics of every structure need to be determined by the properties of its corresponding attractor. The development from a disorderly initial state to an orderly structure means that cellular automata’s evolution can completely be used to describe the process of self-organization.

As introduced before, although the rules of the cellular automaton of Langton’s ants are very simple, they can generate complex behavior beyond imagination. We can often observe similar phenomena in nature. If you have ever observed the behavior of animal groups: schools of fish in water, flocks of birds in the sky, beasts on land, their collective behavior demonstrates the optimization of the group as a whole and behavioral diversity. It is like one single gigantic monster in action. Why does this happen? This is nature, and especially the power of self-organization in the world of lives.

In 1987, computer scientist and researcher of evolutionary computation Craig Reynolds, inspired by Lanton’s idea, created a computer model to study the self-organizational behavior of animal groups. He named the individuals in a flock of birds “Boids.” This word is not in the dictionary. “Boids” means “group companions.” In group actions, the goal and behavioral rules of “Boids” are quite simple, as follows:

(1) Anti-collision: Boids keep a certain distance between each other during collective flight, so as to avoid collision due to crowdedness;
(2) Imitation: in order to form a queue in flight, Boids fly by imitating the average speed and direction of their adjacent companions;
(3) Flock to the center: move towards the center of Boids as close as possible, and the result is that their outer exposure is minimized.
(4) Visual field: move away from Boids who block the view so as to see other Boids as much as possible.

Under the collective restrictions of aforementioned four rules, a virtual bird flock is created, which is like a real bird flock. Individuals in the flock can keep the same pace with others when flying over various barriers and they form a flock in the shape of the Chinese character “人”.

The above simulation shows that, the formation of a flock of birds does not need a leader. It only needs every bird in the flock to follow certain simple interactive rules, then the cluster phenomenon emerges as a whole group mode from the local interactions of individuals. The overall mode of a complex system is not the simple accumulation of individuals, but the newly “emerged” characteristic on the entirety of the system. Such phenomena can be seen in many fields in nature and in society. The twinkling of a group of fireflies, the chirping of a group of crickets, the pulsing of the pacemaker cells in the heart, how do these achieve same-pace coordination without central control? How do individual cases of a disease develop into an epidemic? How does an individual idea become a social trend? That is to say, how does individual behavior become collective behavior? This is one of the most basic and prevalent questions in the entire scientific field. It is difficult to obtain the "emergent" properties of complex systems with the traditional reduction theory. Models based on cellular automata provide a completely different solution. In this method, time, space, and even variables describing the state of a system are all discrete. It is a synthetic bottom-up method. The characteristic of "emergence" in the process of self-organization it reveals can completely rival that provided by differential equations or iterative mapping.

3.2.4 The Configuration of a Cellular Automaton Model

Cellular automata are discrete dynamic systems composed of an array of cells and their evolution rules. Cellular automata divide the space of a model into many units (cells) in a certain lattice configuration. The states of every cell are expressed by discrete values. If every cell is given an initial state, and a group of evolution rules is defined, the process of a system's evolution with time can then be studied.

Simply put, a cellular automaton equals the lattice division of space plus evolution rules. Therefore, the construction a cellular automaton model mainly includes: to divide the system into a lattice configuration, to determine the initial state and to define the evolution rules.

(1) **Dividing a System into a Lattice Configuration**: In using a cellular automaton to simulate a complex system, time is divided into a series of discrete moments, and space is divided into a kind of regular lattice. Every lattice can take states of "0" or "1" in simple situations, and take multiple values in complex situations. Different lattice shapes, different state sets and different evolution rules will configure different cellular automata models. In one-dimensional cellular automata models, a line is divided into numerous equal Fsections to represent cells respectively; two-dimensional cellular automata models divide a plane into many cells in square or hexagon shapes; three-dimensional cellular automata models divide space into many 3-D cells.
(2) **Determining the Initial State**: An initial state refers to the initial value of each cell's evolution which has already been determined. It is the source influencing the evolutionary configuration of cellular automata. Suppose we gave a different initial state at the beginning, the entire result of the evolution would be quite different. This proves that the initial state is a factor influencing the state of the system.

(3) **Defining the Evolution Rules**: Simply put, the rule is a dynamic function which can determine a cell's state at the next moment according to its state and the states of its neighboring cells at the current moment. It can be expressed as

$$f : S_i^{t+1} = f\left(S_i^t, S_N^t\right)$$

In this formula, S_I^t represents the state of the central cell i at moment t, S_N^t represents the combination of the states of neighborhood cells at moment t. Thus we call f the local mapping or local rule of cellular automata. Unlike ordinary models in dynamic study, cellular automata models are not restricted by strictly defined physical equations or functions. Instead, they are models formed according to a series of rules. Therefore, the determination and perfection of the rules are the cores of a cellular automaton in analyzing the system as a whole. They directly relate to the result of the evolution of the system's state.

In order to obtain a meaningful result of the states of the system's evolution, it is necessary to restrict the rules of evolution. Specifically:

(1) The rules of cellular automata's evolution must satisfy the resting condition. If the initial states of all cells are "0," their subsequent states are also "0." Otherwise, it will be generating something from nothing. We all know that if you have not put the seed in the soil, there will be no plant coming out. Anything out will be illegal. This is called the Resting Condition of cellular automata.
(2) The rules of evolution must be in reflective symmetry. It can be defined as such as: neighborhood domains 00011 and 11000 are the same, i.e., for the central cell "0," whether the cell on its left is "00" and is "11" on its right, or the cell on its left is "11" and is "00" on its right, their next states are the same. Such a restriction guarantees the homogeneity and uniformity of the cellular automata. Mapping according to such a method reduces the rules by half.
(3) Evolution rules must follow the principle of totality. It prescribes the state of every cell, which is only related to the sum of the states of its adjacent neighbors. Then, adjacent neighbors 11010 and 10011 are the same, because for the central cell "0," the sum of the states of cells in its neighborhood always equals 3. It conforms to the characteristics of certain things in reality, e.g., in "The Game of Life," the method used was the rule of sums. The mapping in this way can reduce the quantity of rules from the degree of exponential to polynomial. Wolfram proved that cellular automata described by the rule of sums could display the functions of all possible dynamic behavior of all cellular automata.
(4) The alignment of cells on a straight line is always limited. Therefore, certain boundary conditions are needed. For example, at moment $t-1$, set the line segments outside the left and right boundaries of the cells as 0, and then find the

edge value at the moment of t according to the rule of operation previously determined. The boundary condition can also be set to have two ends of the line meet each other, or to form a periodical boundary condition, etc.

3.3 The Modeling Process of Cellular Automata

Cellular automata adopt a modeling way of bottom-up, self-organizational.

3.3.1 Determining the Characteristics of the System Being Studied

1. **Is the System a Self-organizing System?**

If a system is a self-organizing system, that is, there are only local interactive elements inside the system and no external relative elements, (invariable and fixed relative elements), then the system will display relative stability, which is beneficial for the synthetic analysis of the whole system. For example, the control of traffic signals in a city is a system consisting of a limited number of intersections. They form special inseparable mutually dependent and interactive connections. The whole system has the basic characteristics of self-organization. Therefore, we can apply the idea of cellular automata's self-organization to the modeling of a city's traffic control.

2. **Is the System Static or Dynamic?**

Determining a system static or dynamic is an important factor for system modeling. This is because the modeling of a static system and that of a dynamic system are completely different. The internal structure of a static system is stable, while that of a dynamic system is unstable, possibly its characteristics are convergent. For example, the traffic control system of a city is a dynamic system, with its traffic flow, vehicle speed and density varying constantly. Therefore, the coordination and cooperation among various intersections need to be adjusted at any time.

3. **Is the system one-dimensional, two-dimensional, three-dimensional or multi-dimensional?**

The state of a system is closely related to its dimensions. And the applications of the methods of cellular automata also vary by their dimensions, possibly including integral dimensions and fractal dimensions. For example, the system of a city's traffic control divides intersections into units, therefore, this system is a two-dimensional system with its units being interconnected.

In addition, dimensions are basic factors for determining evolution rules. Only when the dimensions of a system are determined, can we consider what basic rules to start with, as well as to consider whether a cell is under linear or non-linear influence, or a combined influence of both (Wang 2004).

3.3.2 *Lattice Division of a System*

The key of this process is to divide the entire system into innumerable tiny individuals, then classify and also abstract them into cells, with each cell having optional states. When we choose the initial states of the cells to analyze, we must pay attention to every cell interactions with the others. That is, determining the central cell and the number of its interactive neighbors, and guaranteeing this number is far smaller than the total number of cells of the entire cellular automaton system.

After such division of the system, the lattice of cells and the cellular space ($n \times n$) are determined. Of course, the actual size of the lattice has to be determined by specific conditions and the processing capacity of the computer.

3.3.3 *Determining Initial States of the Cells*

Initial states refer to the cells that are already determined and classified, their initial evolutionary values. It is like in some board games, an initial state and a series of rules are given. Then the players choose different rules according to the current state of the game, and base their decision on predicting the next state. Hence, the initial states we give are just like the different arrangements of pieces in board games, and these arrangements are the sources which will influence later arrangements. The initial states of cellular automata can be Boolean values or a series of continuous variable values. The key is to pay attention that the initial states must be representative and general.

3.3.4 *Determining the Evolution Rules of a System*

When determining the evolution rules of cells, the following must be considered:

(1) Cells' Neighbors. Generally, when using cellular automata for analysis, the types of cells' neighbors must be determined. That is, a cell will respond to the state change of which adjacent cells, what are the ranges of such responses? For example, the radius of a one-dimensional cellular automaton is the range of a few cells in the front and back respectively which influence the states of other

cells, while a two-dimensional cellular automata can establish a circular or square range of its radius.

(2) Cells' Responses and Attributes. Generally, a local cell's state at the next moment is influenced by the states of its neighbors and the state of its own. Hence, possibly a response of a local cell is a superposition of responses to multiple states and multiple attributes. Then it is necessary to synthesize every response as well as each attribute.

(3) The Temporal and Spatial Processing of Cellular Rules. When a cellular automaton processes a system and makes the evolution of its states, it is necessary to consider how to deal with segments of time and space. Since cells' responses are related to time and space, eventually, the states of a system's evolution are also related to time and space. The evolutionary process of cellular automata on the temporal dimension uses the method of the simulation clock to simulate the progress of the temporal dimension. Simulation clock t is the integral value on interval $[0, T]$. The initial value is 0, step length is 1, while the end value is T. With every forward movement of the simulation clock, the state of the cellular automaton will vary according to relevant rules.

Cellular automata's processing of time and space has the characteristics of being synchronous and local. For example, information at all the intersections in a city's traffic system is processed in parallel in one time interval, thus, the pace is synchronous; the local rules are applied to the entire system, so that to reach optimum in space for the system.

(4) The Structural Source of Cellular Rules. How the rules are determined is the core of the entire rule structure. Whether the rules are determined correctly directly affects the result of the evolution of a system's states. When analyzing a relatively complex system, we usually choose a representative, relatively small and not very complex system to analyze first, by methods such as the observation of experiments to determine a series of useful relationship networks (rules). Generally we believe such analysis is correct, and then apply these rules to the complex system. This makes the analysis of complex systems much easier.

In short, the problems of studying cellular automata can be put into two categories: the first is to study their characteristics and behavior once their rules are prescribed. These are the problems of developing the dynamic behavior of the entire system from local rules. The second category of the problems is looking for rules of cellular automata whose functions are given. This is the inverse problem of cellular automata. The study on the inverse problem is relatively complex and difficult, and so far there is no generally accepted method for structuring the rules. The determination of rules often depends on experience, but lacks effective theoretical guidance.

The determination of rules is a process of learning and improving. In recent years, many scholars think that the solutions to most inverse problems (i.e. determining rules) can make use of evolutionary computation.

Mitchell proposed a method of using genetic algorithm to determine rules for cells. Since the mode of definition of the chromosomal structure in genetic algorithm is basically consistent with the mode of defining the rules for cellular automata, in order to find solutions effectively, we only need to regard the binary rules of cellular automata as chromosomes and establish corresponding adaptive functions. The key here is to change a inverse problem into a problem of optimization, establish appropriate adaptive functions to find the cellular automaton with given functions.

3.4 Simulation of the Evolution of Investment Strategies in Stock Market

According to the modeling method of cellular automata, the steps for constructing a two-dimensional evolutionary model based on cellular automata for the investment strategies in stock market are as follows.

1. **Background for Modeling**

As a typical example of complex system, stock market has always been a hot focus of research. Its basic principle is that the local behavior of investors brings out the complex behavior of the entire market. In stock market, there are usually two types of investors—fundamental investors and technical investors. Certainly, such a division is not rigid, and the choice of investment strategies can be influenced by other investors around. An investor often decides his future strategy according to profits made by others around. This causes the phenomena of strategy evolution. Although this is a relatively simple mechanism of action, still, after a certain period of time, the market will generate complex and interesting overall behavior, and the specific result of its evolution becomes unpredictable.

Cellular automata have the features such as space discreteness, time discreteness, state discreteness, and synchronous evolution. They can realistically reflect the subtle structural mode of interactions among numerous individuals, and generate complex phenomena through simple cells and rules. Thus, they are capable of simulating a system as complex as the stock market (Amilon 2008; Zhu 2009).

2. **System Analysis**

To analyze a system is to determine its nature. This can be done through consideration of three aspects.

(1) Is the stock market a self-organizing system? If it is, the interactive elements only exist within the system itself. There are no external factors to influence it. Such a system will demonstrate stability and is suitable for synthetic analysis of

the system. Strictly speaking, the stock market is not a completely self-organizing system, because during the process of its evolution, the system is influenced by the guidance of stock prices, which plays an important role in causing complexity.

(2) Is the system static or dynamic? The internal structure of a static system is stable, while that of a dynamic system is unstable, but possibly its system nature is convergent. Obviously, the stock market is a typical dynamic system, because the states of every investor at different moments are full of changes. In addition, the output of the system—the prices of the stocks, also change with time.

(3) How many dimensions does the system have? The state of a system is closely related to its dimensions. And the methods of cellular automata application also vary with the system's dimensions. The distribution of investors in the stock market can be visually mapped onto a two-dimensional cellular automaton.

3. The Construction of a Cellular Automaton Model

1) The Lattice Division of the System

The group of investors in the stock market can be regarded as innumerable small cells, and every cell should have optional states. In addition, it is important to pay attention to the interactions of every cell with others. At the same time, the number of cells interacting with each cell in consideration must be far smaller than the total number of cells in the cellular automaton system.

After the division of the system, the cells (stock investors) and the cellular space $(n \times n)$ lattice are also determined. Of course, the size of the lattice needs to be determined by the specific conditions and the processing capacity of a computer. The larger the space of the lattice is, the slower is the computer's speed of simulation. But if the space is too small, the result of simulation will be hard to be seen. Here we set the lattice as 50×50.

2) Determining Initial States

After making a lattice division of the system, we need to determine the initial states of the cells. The states of the cells are values used for examining certain characteristics of the cells. We can establish a two-dimensional space of cell states according to the characteristics of investors, so as to determine its attributes and states.

There are two kinds of investors (fundamental and technical) in the market. We use a uniform set of states to describe the attributes of the investors in more detail, since there are plenty of discrete state variables involved.

$$S_{i,t}^{h} = (h_{i,t}, D_{i,t}^{h}, U_{i,t}^{h}, \pi_{i,t}^{h}, L_{i}^{c}) \tag{3.1}$$

In this, $h_{i,t} \in \{f, c\}$ represents types of investors: f represents fundamental investors, c represents technical investors. $D_{i,t}^{h}$ represents the risk asset demand (order) of investor i at moment t; $U_{i,t}^{h}$ represents the strategy evolution effect of investor i at moment t; $\pi_{i,t}^{h}$ represents the profit of investor i at moment t; L_i^c represents the length of the moving average used by investor i when he becomes a technical investor.

3) **The Dynamic Model of the System**

(1) Investors

Here we use the classical framework of the capital asset pricing model proposed by Carl Chiarella et al. For fundamental investors, the function of their risk asset demand is defined as:

$$D_{i,t}^{f} = \alpha\left(P_{i,t}^{*} - P_t\right) \tag{3.2}$$

In the formula, P_t is the stock price at moment t.

For technical investors, the function of their risk asset demand is defined as:

$$D_{i,t}^{c} = \tanh\left[a\left(P_t - ma_{i,t}^{L_i^c}\right)\right] \tag{3.3}$$

Formula (3.3) is Carl Chiarella's model (general).

For a group of investors within a discrete cellular space, $P_{i,t}^{*}$ can be understood as the fundamental investors' basic belief in the basic value of their stocks. α is the risk tolerance factor of investors for wrong pricing. Of course, individual beliefs of investors inevitably deviate from actual information, which is expressed as follows:

$$P_{i,t}^{*} = P_t^{*}\left(1 + \delta_\varepsilon \varepsilon_{i,t}\right) \tag{3.4}$$

In this formula, $\delta_\varepsilon \geq 0$ is a constant, $\varepsilon_{i,t} \sim N(0,\, 1)$. Unlike fundamental investors, technical investors use technical means such as moving average of historical prices to make decisions. Here, technical investors use the moving average method, at moment t, the moving average result of window length L_i^c is

$$ma_{i,t}^{L_i^c} = \frac{1}{L_i^c}\sum_{i=0}^{L_i^c - 1} P_{t-i} \tag{3.5}$$

In formulas (3.3) and (3.5), when a is very small, technical investors are quite cautious about signals of long-term or short-term investments. They tend to wait for a stable state of signal variation. That is, if within a short time, the frequency of investment signal variation is very high, they will try their best to minimize their transactional cost.

(2) Market Makers

In the framework of the capital assets pricing model proposed by Carl Chiarella and others, P_t is used to represent stock prices at moment t; $n_{h,t}$ is used to represent the proportion of h type investors at moment t ($h_{i,t} \in \{f, c\}$), and $\sum_{h-1}^{H} n_{h,t} = 1$; D_t^h represents the demand of h type investors at moment t; when prices are determined by market makers, stock prices at every moment are determined according to overall demand:

$$
\begin{aligned}
P_{t+1} &= P_t(1 + \sigma_\varepsilon \varepsilon_t) + \mu D_t \\
&= P_t(1 + \sigma_\varepsilon \varepsilon_t) + \mu \sum_{h=1}^{H} n_{h,t} D_t^h
\end{aligned}
\tag{3.6}
$$

In this formula, $\varepsilon_t \sim \mathrm{N}(0, 1)$, representing the random fluctuation of prices caused by unknown information or noise investors; $\sigma_z \geq 0$ is a constant; parameter $\mu > 0$ represents the market makers' speed of price adjustment according to demand; D_t is the total number of orders in the market at moment t.

Now we use a cellular automaton model to discretize above analytic model, abandoning the "population proportion" expression $n_{h,t}$ in Carl Chiarella's original model (Chiarella et al. 2006). Instead, we apply the "real" population of investors of various types in the cellular space and the total number of orders as the moving power of price updates, so that the subject of study is refined from "a kind of people" to "a person". The stock price update is expressed as follows:

$$
P_{t+1} = P_t(1 + \sigma_\varepsilon \varepsilon_t) + \mu \left\{ \sum_{i=1}^{N_t^f} D_{i,t}^f + \sum_{i=1}^{N_t^c} D_{i,t}^c \right\} \tag{3.7}
$$

Here, N_t^f and N_t^c represent respectively the number of fundamental investors and technical investors in the cellular space at moment t, and the temporal variation of the basic value of stocks is as follows:

$$
P_{t+1}^* = P_t^*(1 + \delta_\lambda \lambda_t) \tag{3.8}
$$

In it, $\lambda_t \sim N(0, 1)$; $\delta_\lambda \geq 0$ and is a constant.

(3) Profits

Using state variables $\pi_{i,t}^f$ and $\pi_{i,t}^c$ to represent the profits of fundamental investor i and technical investor i at moment t, we get

$$
\left.
\begin{aligned}
\pi_{i,t}^f &= D_{i,t-1}^f (P_t - P_{t-1}) \\
\pi_{i,t}^c &= D_{i,t-1}^c (P_t - P_{t-1})
\end{aligned}
\right\} \tag{3.9}
$$

4) The Structure of Evolution Rules

Unlike the dynamic model of the system as described above, evolution rules are mapping of the states of the central cell's neighbors to its own state at the next moment. The key point is the state change of the cell. When determining the evolution rules of cellular automata, the following must be considered:

(1) The response radius of a cell: this is also the type of a cell's neighborhood, i.e., a cell will respond to which adjacent cells' state stimuli, and what is the scope of stimuli. Here we use the Moore Neighborhood, as shown in Diagram 3.1, in which each cell interacts with its eight surrounding neighbors.

(2) Response and its attributes: in general situations, the state of a cell at the next moment is influenced by the states of its neighbors, its own state and the control variable, which can be expressed by the following formulas:

$$S^{h}_{i,t+1} = F(S^{h}_{i,t}, S^{t}_{iL}, R) \tag{3.10}$$

$$S^{t}_{iL} = (S^{t}_{iL(1)}, \ldots, S^{t}_{iL(n)}) \tag{3.11}$$

$S^{h}_{i,t+1}$ stands for the state of the cell at position i in the cellular space at moment t + 1; vector S^{t}_{iL} stands for the state of neighbor L of the cell at position i in the cellular space at moment t; R is the control variable; F stands for the cellular automaton's evolution rules; n is the number of neighboring cells.

(3) Rule description: in the study of analytic models by Carl Chiarella et al. and Henrik Amilon, the strategic adjustments by both kinds of investors are seen as a kind of overall behavior of the market. They also designed the "function of the effect of strategy evolution" to determine market proportions occupied by

$(a-1, b-1)$	$(a-1, b)$	$(a-1, b+1)$
$(a, b-1)$	(a, b)	$(a, b+1)$
$(a+1, b-1)$	$(a+1, b)$	$(a+1, b+1)$

Diagram 3.1 Moore neighborhood

the two kinds of investors. Here we introduce this function of the effect of strategy evolution into the cellular space based on the Moore Neighborhood, giving individual investors the ability to evaluate the amount of profits, which can guide their choice of strategy. For investor i, his "effect of strategy evolution" is expressed as follows:

$$\left.\begin{array}{l} U_{i,t}^{f} = \pi_{i,t}^{f} + \eta U_{i,t-1}^{f} \\ U_{i,t}^{c} = \pi_{i,t}^{c} + \eta U_{i,t-1}^{c} \end{array}\right\} \tag{3.12}$$

Here, $\eta \in [0,1]$, representing the memory factor of investors' memory of past effects. An investor's action at the next moment is determined by his judgment of the profits of all nine people including his eight neighbors and himself. Let the coordinates of central cell i be (a, b), then at moment t, among the central cell itself and its eight neighbors (nine people in total), the total effect of investors choosing the fundamental strategy is $\sum_{m=a-1}^{a+1}\sum_{n=b-1}^{b+1} U_{m,n}^{f,t}$; the total effect of investors choosing the technical strategy is $\sum_{m=a-1}^{a+1}\sum_{n=b-1}^{b+1} U_{m,n}^{c,t}$.

(4) Specific rules: at moment $t + 1$, central cell i has a probability of $p_{i,t}^{f}$ in changing to a fundamental investor; and has a probability of $p_{i,t}^{c}$ in changing to a technical investor:

$$p_{i,t}^{f} = \frac{e^{\beta \sum_{m=a-1}^{a+1}\sum_{n=b-1}^{b+1} U_{m,n}^{f,t}}}{e^{\beta \sum_{m=a-1}^{a+1}\sum_{n=b-1}^{b+1} U_{m,n}^{f,t}} + e^{\beta \sum_{m=a-1}^{a+1}\sum_{n=b-1}^{b+1} U_{m,n}^{c,t}}} \tag{3.13}$$

$$p_{i,t}^{c} = \frac{e^{\beta \sum_{m=a-1}^{a+1}\sum_{n=b-1}^{b+1} U_{m,n}^{c,t}}}{e^{\beta \sum_{m=a-1}^{a+1}\sum_{n=b-1}^{b+1} U_{m,n}^{f,t}} + e^{\beta \sum_{m=a-1}^{a+1}\sum_{n=b-1}^{b+1} U_{m,n}^{c,t}}} \tag{3.14}$$

Here, $\beta \geq 0$, which represents the intensity of investors' adjustment between the two investment strategies. Especially, if $\beta = 0$, it means there is no changeover between the two strategies. While $\beta = \infty$ means all investors always choose the optimum investment strategy immediately.

4. **Computer Simulation**

1) Determining Simulation Parameters

Without special notice, the values of simulation parameters are all set according to Table 3.1.

2) Initial State (as shown in Diagram 3.2)
3) Process of Evolution and Result (as shown in Diagram 3.3).

Table 3.1 The setting of simulation parameters

Parameter symbols	Significance of parameters	Values taken
N	Number of investors	900
μ	Speed of price adjustment	0.1
α	Risk tolerance factor of fundamental investors	0.01
a	Technical investor's degree of sensitivity of price changes	0.01
β	Intensity of strategy evolution	0.5
η	Memory factor of the strategy evolution effect	0.3
P_1	Initial prices of stocks	10
T	Time of evolution	200
L_i^c	Average moving window length of technical investors	[5, 30]
σ_ε	Price noise	0.01

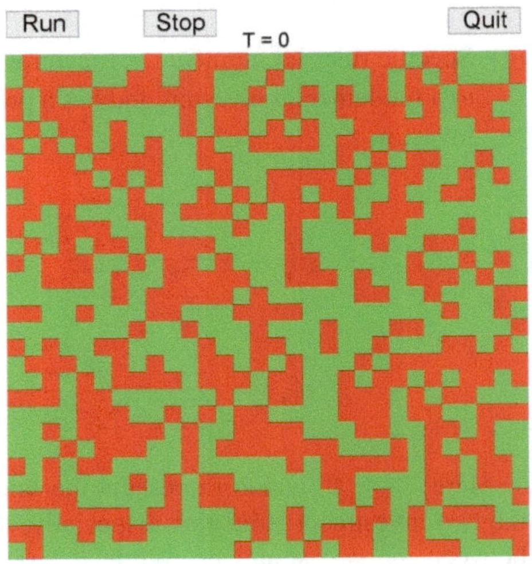

Diagram 3.2 Initial state of the cellular space (dark color: fundamental investors; light color: technical investors)

Here we specially design a control group, i.e., the types of investors do not vary with time (no evolution rules), in order to compare the variation of the average profits of investors in the market before and after the addition of evolution rules, as shown in Diagram 3.4.

It is not difficult to see that, evolution rules based on the "strategy evolution effect function" enable investors to alternately use the two strategies, based on their judgment of profits. The interplay between the two strategies affects prices, making the market average profit level significantly improved than the level when strategies stay unchanged, as shown in Table 3.2.

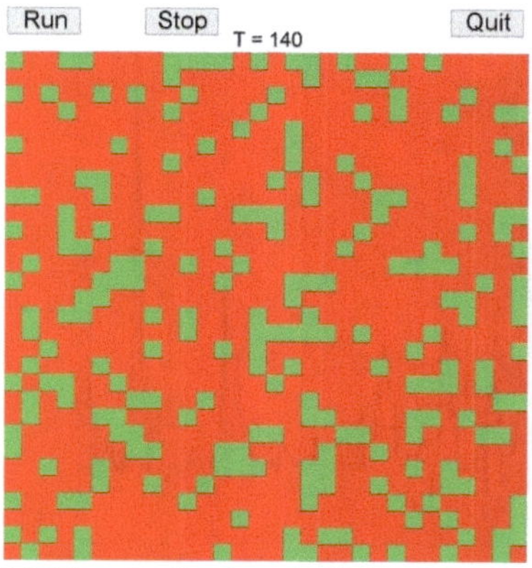

(a) When the Fundamental Is Predominant

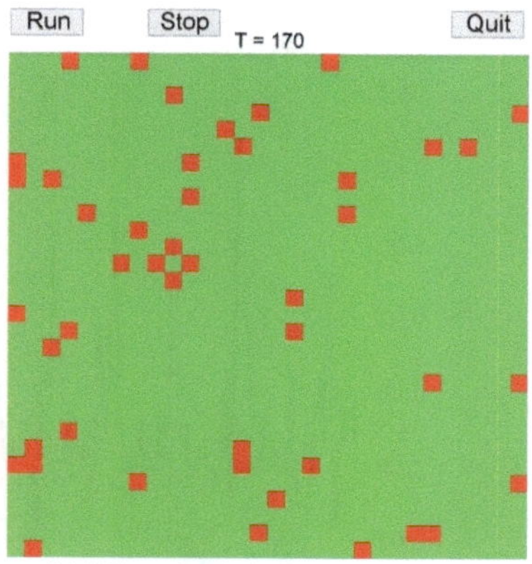

(b) When theTechnical Is Predominant

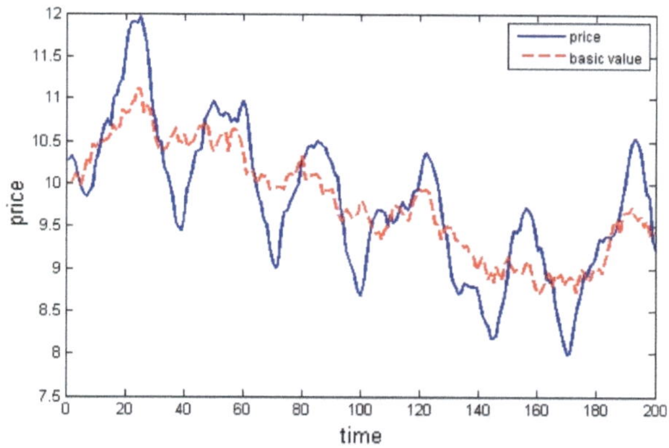

(c) stock price

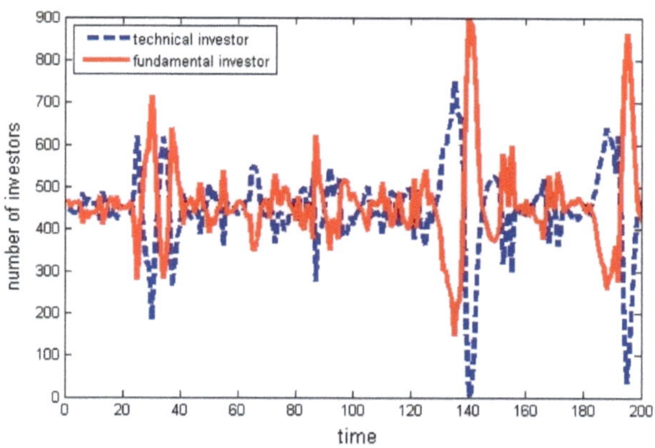

(d) the variation of the numbers of the two kind investors

Diagram 3.3 Result of evolution

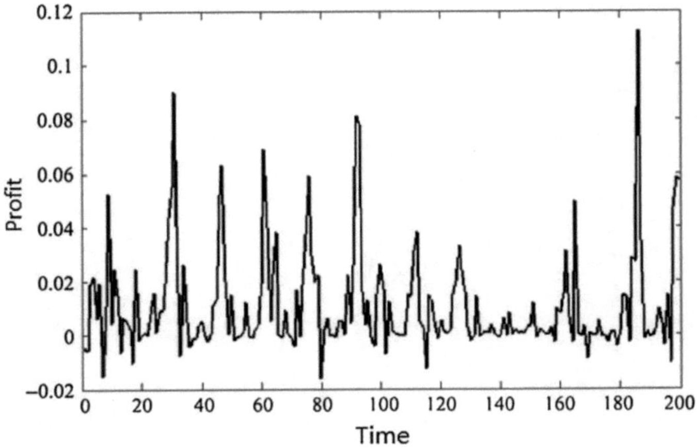

(a) Without Evolution Rules

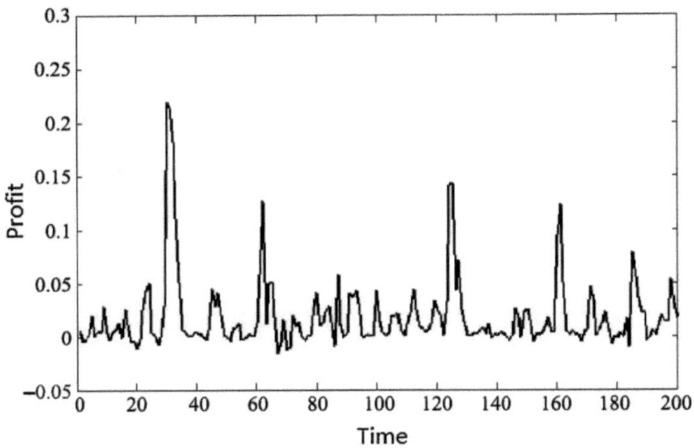

(b) With evolution Rules Based on the "Function of Strategy Evolution Effect"

Diagram 3.4 Profit situations

Table 3.2 Average profit of investors

Evolution mechanism	Minimum value	Maximum value	Average value	Standard deviation
No evolution rules	0.022	0.137	0.057	0.020
Function of strategy evolution effect	0.029	0.265	0.083	0.031

References

Amilon, H. (2008). Estimation of an adaptive stock market model with heterogeneous agents. *Journal of Empirical Finance, 15*(2), 342–362.

Axelrod, R. (1997). Advancing the art of simulation in the social sciences. *Complexity, 3*(2), 16–22.

Chiarella, C., He, X., & Hommes, C. (2006). A dynamic analysis of moving average rules. *Journal of Economic Dynamics and Control, 30*(9&10), 1729–1753.

Mitchell, M. (2011). *Complexity: A guided tour* (L. Tang Trans.). Changsha: Hunan Science and Technology Press.

Shi, Z. (2000). *The third kind of scientific method: Scientific computation in the age of computers*. Beijing: Tsing Hua University Press.

Wang, A. (2004). *The analysis and modeling of complex systems*. Shanghai: Shanghai Jiaotong University Press.

Zhu, M., Chiarella, C., He, X., et al. (2009). Does the market maker stabilize the market? *Physica A, 388*(15&16), 3164–3180.

References

Chapter 4
The Complexity of Cellular Automata

Introduction
Numerous complex systems exist in nature. The structure of every single component of these systems may be very simple, but because the existence of certain connections (or so called coupling) among various parts, the eventual display of the overall state is quite complex. Cellular automata are the ideal mathematical model for studying complex systems. Through modeling based on the complex system of cellular automata, we can simulate complex systems' evolutionary phenomena and mechanisms. But at a deeper level, although the evolution of cellular automata simulates the phenomena of the development and the variation of complex systems, for model building itself, it is not capable of analyzing the ultimate cause for complex systems in generating complexity. The mechanism of the generation of complexity is still unknown and indescribable. Only by further analyzing and describing the mechanism of the generation of cellular automata's complexity, can we explain and analyze the complexity of various systems in depth.

4.1 The Complexity in Nature and Formal Languages

4.1.1 Coarse-Grained Description and Symbol Set

Scientific research cannot start from definitions but from the analysis of facts. Observing intuitively, from atoms, molecules, crystalline and amorphous solids to "soft" matters such as macro-crystals and liquid crystals, to "live" matters that organisms are composed of, even to human brain, to human being's consciousness and mode of thinking, the objects of scientific research have indeed been escalating the ladder of complexity, at the same time gaining more special characteristics. It is these special characteristics that give an object its rich content. This reminds us again that the study of complexity should not be discussed in a superficial way.

X. Li et al., *Theory of Practical Cellular Automaton*,
https://doi.org/10.1007/978-981-10-7497-4_4

The following observations will be helpful for constructing an effective framework for the analysis of complexity (Jackson 1991).

In seeing six lowercased letters u, d, c, s, b, t, people studying elementary particles will immediately identify them as the names of the six kinds of quarks, and will associate the letters with mass, electric charge and other characteristics of the quarks. More scholars use p, n, e to represent proton, neutron and electron, knowing their characteristics such as electric charge, mass, spin, magnetic moment, etc. However, these scholars may not care which three quarks compose the proton and neutron respectively.

When chemists see symbols of elements such as H, C, N, O, P, S, they will think of their atomic numbers, ionic radius, chemical valence and affinity, etc. As we see the compound molecular formulas written with element symbols, such as H_2O, NO, CO_2, etc., we associate them with a certain amount of molecular weight, and they are either transparent liquid or colorless odorless gas. When encountering not even a big nucleotide molecule, however, if we have to write out the element symbol of thirty to forty atoms every time, it is neither convenient nor necessary.

People use a, t, c, g to represent four different kinds of nucleotide, and notice that when they form the double helix structure of DNA, a and t are connected by two hydrogen bonds, called weak coupling; while c and g are connected by three hydrogen bonds, called strong coupling. The genetic genes of various organisms on earth are all composed of these four nucleotides "encoded" in different sequences. The genetic information of a tiny Escherichia coli is a long series of 4,639,221 symbols, even though they are all within the four letters a, c, g, t. All the genes of a human being are aligned separately within 23 pairs of chromosomes, consisting of approximately three billion letters. All proteins are formed in cells according to information encoded in genes. Every single protein is a macromolecule consisting of twenty kinds of amino acids aligned according to a particular sequence. A single amino acid is a bit smaller than nucleotide, consisting of 10–27 atoms, which can be represented by one letter. Insulin is a very small kind of protein, and when we study its three-dimensional structure, we need to know the positions of thousands of atoms. When we compare the insulin of people, cows and pigs, we can examine similar sequences composed of 51 symbols, while when we discuss the metabolic process of glucose, however, insulin is often represented by one symbol.

Such narration can continue to extend several levels. On the other hand, ways of "starting from the beginning," i.e., trying to start from quarks to explain the things in biosphere, or to treat the universe as a "gigantic complex system," do not really deepen our understanding of nature or enrich people's scientific knowledge too much. The above observations reveal profound guidelines for research:

(1) When we study natural phenomena, we must focus on a particular level for coarse-grained description. Differences on finer levels are taken as certain characteristic parameters from the focused level, such as the heat conduction coefficient; (96)

(2) Coarse-grained description inevitably uses symbols and symbol sequences, and on many occasions form one-dimensional symbol sequences. In fact, for sequences composed of a limited number of symbols, "multi-dimensional" can be boil down to one-dimensional sequence with distant neighbor relationships;
(3) Sequence of symbols can be naturally integrated into "formal language" framework;
(4) Formal language can be classified according to the gradation of grammatical complexity, and the specific research of various symbol sequences can also enrich the complexity of grammar.

4.1.2 Formal Language and Grammatical Complexity

Let us first briefly introduce the concepts of language and grammatical complexity. First there has to be a particular letter set, such as letters R and L or numbers 0 and 1, as we mentioned before, can both be used to form a letter set of two symbols. 26 capitalized Latin letters, with 26 such letters in the lowercase, plus 13 punctuation marks, form a letter set of 65 symbols. The symbols in the letter set do not have any meaning themselves any more.

We usually consider a letter set composed of a limited number of symbols. Taking the symbols in such a set to form all possible strings of symbols, including an empty string with no symbol, this forms a large collection of infinite number of elements. Any subset in this large collection is called a language. This is the definition of the formal language.

Starting from such a general and abstract definition does not get us very far. It has to be pointed out that the languages we care about are formed by strings of symbols or "letters." In principle, languages composed of a limited number of letters can be described by the exhaustive method. Some infinite languages are also easy to describe. For example, set $\{Rn\ Ln,\ n\ \geq\ 1\}$is a language based on the letter set $\{R, L\}$. A more effective method is to prescribe one or several initial letters and a group of "generation rules," to repeatedly use the generation rules on the initial letters and newly formed letters to generate the entire language. This is language defined by "generation grammar."

Generation rules can be serial or parallel. In the 1950s, N. Chomsky gave a complete classification of serial generative grammar. All languages formed by serial generative grammar, including many program design language which people are familiar with, can be classified into four categories, and languages in every category can be accepted (or implemented, identified) by a type of automaton. The four categories are:

(1) Formal language (RGL), accepted by a finite automaton which does not need memory;
(2) Context-free language (CFL), accepted by a computer with stacked (also called last-in-first-out) memory. Frequently used algorithmic languages such as FORTRAN belong to this category;
(3) Context-sensitive language (CSF), accepted by a "linear bounded automaton" whose memory capacity is in proportion to input volume; (97)
(4) Recursive enumerable language (REL), accepted by a Turing machine with infinite memory.

The top down classification gives the Chomsky hierarchy from simplicity to complexity. Symbol sequences obtained through the coarse graining of physical observation, if their generative grammar can be clarified, we get a criterion for complexity with a rigorous mathematical background. The Chomsky hierarchy is not an unchangeable standard. To analyze specific questions specifically can often enrich its content, so as to refine the classification in certain hierarchy.

It is not difficult to see that the period and ultimate periodic orbits in the mapping of one-dimensional parabola correspond to the simplest formal language. Chinese scholars Huimin Xie and others have proven the more difficult inverse proposition, i.e., orbits corresponding to formal language only belong to these two categories. The limits of many orbits which correspond to formal language, such as the infinite limit of the period doubling bifurcation sequence, skip context-free language and reach the complexity of context-sensitive language. People thus guess: there is no context-free language in the symbol sequence generated by the mapping of one-dimensional parabola. We can also make use of the finer attributes of grammar or automaton (for example, the number of enable words or disable words, the number of nodes in finite automata, especially their growth rate) to compare the degree of complexity of different symbol sequences. The evolution of a symbol sequence can be described by a transfer matrix. The block structure of an infinite transfer matrix provides another way of examining complexity exceeding formal language. Therefore, knowledge of the classification of orbit complexity in the mapping of parabola has far exceeded the level of the early 1990s.

In the 1960s, Dutch developmental biologist L. Lindenmayer observed the developmental processes of certain multicellular algae, including anabaena catenula, which belongs to the genus Anabaena. The direction of its cell division has polarity. Small cells divide once they grow up, and pass on the polarity to newly born small cells. At the same time, their own polarity turns to the opposite direction and the next time, new small cells are split off at the other end. Therefore, starting from a small cell with a certain kind of polarity, after a number of divisions, an anabaena with special arrangement patterns of its size and polarity is formed. Lindenmayer used four letters to represent cells of different sizes with polarities from left to right and wrote down the variation rules among them. The result obtained by repeatedly using these rules completely agrees with the observation obtained under a microscope. Soon, people realized that this method could be generalized into a system of parallel generative grammar. The classification of it generated a different classification system for formal language unlike Chomsky's. It is called the L System. Possibly the L System has wider applications for biological topics.

A simpler level of Lindenmayer's classification can possibly surpass various complex "ladders" of Chomsky's classification. Some seemingly "simple" languages might be quite complex on a higher level, for example, $\{R_n\ L_n,\ n \geq 1\}$ is not a formal language but context-free language, while $\{R_n\ L_nM_n,\ n \geq 1\}$ reaches the level of context-sensitive language. This proves from another aspect what we discussed before, i.e., there is no absolute standard for measuring complexity. The classification of formal languages also is not limited to the two systems we introduce here.

4.1.3 Formal Languages and the Equivalence Theory of Automata

According to aforementioned relationship between formal languages and complexity, it can be seen that certain connection can be established between the level of grammatical complexity of formal languages and the complexity of cellular automata. Considering that cellular automata are a development of the theory of automata, it is necessary to clarify the equivalence relationship between automata and formal languages.

1. **Regular Language RL Is Equivalent to the Limited Condition Automata DFA (or NFA)**

Regular language has five models of equivalence: regular grammar RG, regular expression RE, definitive limited state automata DFA, uncertain limited state automata NFA, and ε–NFA, a type of limited state automata with action ε (Hopcroft and Lllman 1979). The interchanging relationships among these five equivalent models of can be shown by Diagram 4.1:

The direct interchange among the five equivalent models of regular languages can be summarized into six situations:

Diagram 4.1 Interchanging relationships among five models of equivalence of regular language

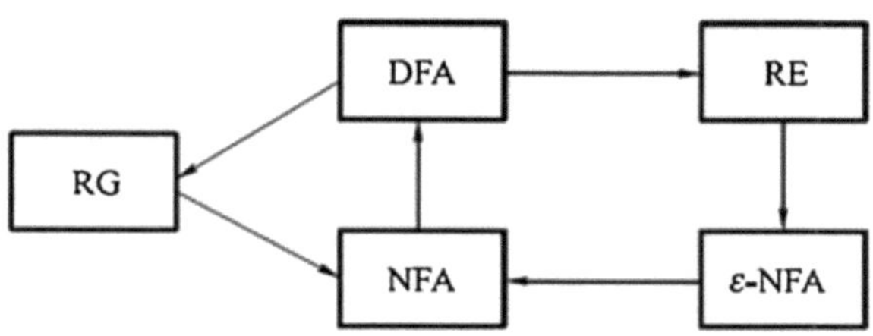

1) **Definitive Limited State Automata DFA Changes to Regular Grammar RG**

Suppose L is a limited state language FSL, and $L = L$ (DFA), let

$$DFA = \left(Q, \sum, \delta, q_0, F\right)$$

Regarding the state of automata as the non-terminal symbol of grammar to construct the right linear grammar:

$$\mathrm{RG} = \left(\sum, \mathrm{Q}, \mathrm{q}_0, \mathrm{p}\right)$$

In above equation, p is $\{\mathrm{q} \rightarrow \mathrm{xq}' | \delta(\mathrm{q,x}) = \mathrm{q}'\} \cup \{\mathrm{q} \rightarrow \mathrm{x} | \delta(\mathrm{q,x}) \in F\}$. Specially, $q_0 \rightarrow \varepsilon$ if the initial state is also the accepting state.

2) **Regular Grammar RG Changes to Uncertain Limited State Automata NFA**

If L is a regular language, and $L = L(G)$, let $G = (\Sigma, V, S, P)$ for constructing NFA. Taking the non-terminal symbol of the grammar as the state of NFA, and adding an accepting state q (if $S \rightarrow \varepsilon$ is in grammar G, i.e. $\varepsilon \in L$, then the initial state S is also the accepting state), make

$$DFA = (Q, \sum, \delta, \mathrm{Q}_0, F)$$

In above, $Q = V \cup \{q\}$, $F = \{q\}$, $\delta(A, x) = \{B | B \in V, A \rightarrow xB \text{ in } P\} \cup \{q | A \rightarrow x \text{ in } P\}$, $Q_0 = \{S\}$.

3) **Definitive Limited State Automata DFA Changes to Regular Expression RE**

To properly process the state change diagram of DFA: add two states X and Y: state X is the new initial state, and the cut-in degree is 0; state Y is the only new accepting state; then process the state diagram accordingly, until only states X and Y remain, and there is only one possible arc from state X to state Y; the regular expression marked on this arc is the regular expression corresponding to the language accepted by DFA; if the arc does not exist, the language accepted by DFA is $\varnothing$, and the corresponding regular expression is $\varnothing$.

4) **Regular Expression RE Changes to Limited State Automata with ε Action ε-NFA**

Regular language is effectively closed to three arithmetic operations: join operation, concatenation operation and closure operation. As for regular expression R, there is an equivalent limited state automaton with ε action ε-NFA.

5) **Limited State Automata with ε Action ε-NFA Changes to Uncertain Limited State Automata NFA**

Suppose language L is accepted by a limited state automaton ε-NFA with empty movement, let

$$\varepsilon\text{-}NFA = (Q, \sum, \delta, \mathrm{q}_0, F)$$

Construct a limited state automaton NFA without ε action

$$NFA = (Q, \sum, \delta_1, \mathrm{q}_0, F_1)$$

In the equation above:

$$\delta_1(q,a) = \delta^*(q,a); \mathrm{F}_1 \begin{cases} F \cup \{q_0\} \ldots s.t. F \cap \varepsilon\text{-}CLOSURE(q_0) \neq \Phi \\ F \ldots s.t. F \cap \varepsilon\text{-}CLOSURE(q_0) = \Phi \end{cases}$$

6) **Uncertain Limited State Automata NFA Changes to Definitive Limited State Automata DFA**

Suppose language is accepted by NFA, let

$$NFA = \left(Q, \sum, \delta, \mathrm{Q}_0, F\right)$$

Construct

$$NFA' = (Q', \Sigma, \delta', \mathrm{q}_0{}', F')$$

In above equation,

$$Q' = 2^Q; \delta'(\mathrm{p,x}) = \cup\{\delta(\mathrm{q,x})|\mathrm{q} \in \mathrm{p}\}; \mathrm{p} \in \mathrm{Q}', \mathrm{x} \in \sum; q_0' = Q_0 \in Q';$$
$$F' = \{p' | p' \in Q' \; and \, p' \cap F \neq \Phi\} \subset Q'$$

2. **Pushdown Automata Accept Context-Free Language**

Pushdown automata and context-free grammar can interchange, since they both belong to context-free language.

Suppose context-free grammar is in the GNF mode (if it is not, it needs to be converted to the GNF mode first), it is possible to construct a single-state PDA to accept language L. The GNF mode has three generative algorithms, which correspond to the three state transfer functions of PDA respectively. If the generative algorithm of the GNF mode is $S \rightarrow \varepsilon$, the single-state PDA has state transfer function $\langle \varepsilon, S, \varepsilon \rangle$. If the generative algorithm of the GNF mode is $A \rightarrow b$, the single-state PDA has state transfer function $\langle b, A, \varepsilon \rangle$. If the generative algorithm of the GNF mode is $A \rightarrow bW$, the single-state PDA has state transfer function $\langle b, A, W \rangle$, and $A \in V$, $W \in V^+$.

3. **Linear Bounded Turing Machine and Context-Sensitive Language**

Linear bounded Turing machine and context-sensitive grammar can interchange, since they both belong to context-sensitive language.

4. **Turing Machine and Phrase Structure Language**

Turing machine and phrase structure grammar can interchange, since they both belong to phrase structure language.

4.1.4 General-Purpose Computation of Cellular Automata and the Turing Machine

Generally speaking, calculation is a conversion from input to output. If we regard everything as information, calculation is the conversion of information. Specifically, from a known INPUT value, according to certain rules, through limited steps of evolution, an OUTPUT value can be obtained from it. Such a process of conversion is calculation. For example, to convert a symbol string "1 + 1" to "2" is addition, to convert "1 + 1 = 2" to "True" is logical calculation. Translation between languages is calculation, to change x to function $F(x)$ is also calculation. Even the process of a little ball being thrown to the ground and bouncing back is calculation, because here we regard the ground as a system, the ball thrown to the ground is an input, and the bouncing back ball is an output.

Calculability theory is a mathematical theory studying the common characteristics of calculation (Boccara et al. 1991). The process of calculation is a process of applying algorithms. The central question of calculability theory is designing mathematical models for calculation, so as to study what is calculable and what is not. Since calculation is related to algorithms, calculability theory is also called algorithmic theory. In 1936, Turing designed the model of the Turing machine, and proposed that the Turing machine was equivalent to various computer systems which stored instructions, or to put in another way, that the Turing machine was equivalent to intuitive algorithms. However, intuitive algorithms only have the characteristics such as finiteness, mechanical enforceability, certainty and the ability to terminate, and these are not sufficient for the formalized description of algorithms. Therefore, it is impossible to prove the equivalence between the Turing machine and algorithms in intuitive sense. Nevertheless, as a universally accepted computational model, the Turing machine enables us to focus algorithms on computations which can be described by it. Therefore, the question of computability can be seen as equal to the question of computability by the Turing machine. By encoding a problem with a symbol string in a finite alphabet, we can turn the problem into judging whether a language is a recursive language. If the language of a problem is recursive, we call this problem decidable, otherwise, it is non-decidable. We proved before that the evolution languages of cellular automata are all context-sensitive languages, meaning they are recursive languages. Therefore, theoretically speaking, cellular automata can all use the common Turing machine to perform computations.

The Turing machine has been proven to be able to describe any algorithm. We will now explain the computability of cellular automata by constructing a Turing machine of a Rule No. 110 cellular automaton. Suppose a one-dimensional cellular automaton evolves on a limited number of cells. There are N numbers of cells, and the boundary condition is a constant value "J" (the same can be discussed of other boundary conditions). Suppose a basic triad Turing machine are: $A = \{0, 1, \beta_L, \beta_R\}$, $Q = \{q_0, q_1, q_2, q_3, \ldots q_9, q_F\}$, $V = \{l, r, h\}$, and the basic Turing machine is: $M = \{Q, A, V, \delta, q_0, q_F\}$. In it, A represents a letter set, among the four letters, β_L is the left boundary condition of value "1", β_R is the right boundary condition of value "1", Q is a set of states. Among the eleven internal states, q_0 is the initial state, q_F is the final state, V is a set of actions. l represents the read-write head moving left one square, r represents the read-write head moving right one square, h represents the read-write head not moving, δ represents the move function of the Turing machine. Suppose the number of squares on the band of the Turing machine is $N + 2$, and the computation sequence of the squares is from left to right. When the N numbers of squares are all processed, the read-write head will return to the initial position on the left. The process can be expressed as

$$\begin{array}{ccc} \downarrow q_0 & & \downarrow q_F \\ \beta_L S \beta_R & \Rightarrow & \beta_L S' \beta_R \end{array}$$

Here, S, S' represent the original configuration and new configuration respectively, "$\Rightarrow$" represents the entire computational process. The steps needed for processing N squares are not more than $4N + 3$. For the next computation, we only need to change q_F to q_0. The instructional format of the Turing machine is expressed as

$$q_i, a', v, q'$$

In it, $a' \in A$, $v \in V$, $q' \in Q$.

For the Turing machine simulating the evolution of R_{110} cellular automata with the left and right boundaries of the constant value "1", we can use the following instructions:

q_0, β_L, r, q_1; $q_1, 1, r, q_2$; $q_1, 0, r, q_3$; q_1, β_R, h, q_F; $q_2, 1, r, q_2$; $q_2, 0, r, q_3$; q_2, β_R, h, q_F; $q_3, 1, l, q_4$; $q_3, 0, l, q_5$; q_3, β_R, l, q_9; $q_4, 1, r, q_6$; $q_4, 0, r, q_6$; $q_5, 1, r, q_7$ $q_5, 0, r, q_7$; $q_7, 1, l, q_4$; $q_7, 0, r, q_7$; q_7, β_R, l, q_9; $q_6, 0, r, q_3$; $q_6, 1, l, q_8$; q_6, β_R, l, q_9 $q_8, 1, r, q_2$; $q_8, 0, r, q_2$; q_9, β_R, r, q_F

Every single computational result of any initial configuration by program T above equals one evolutionary step of the initial configuration under R_{110}. Such computation can be described by Diagram 4.2:

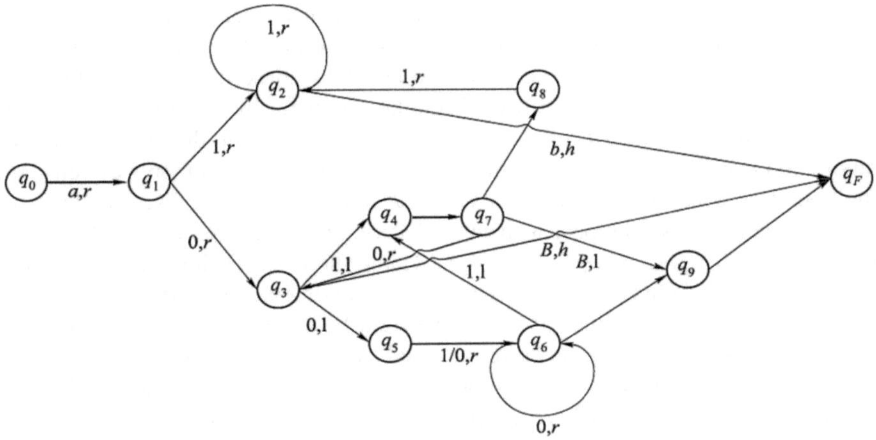

Diagram 4.2 State transfer diagram of the Turing machine which simulates cellular automaton No. 110

For the common Turing machine UT, the input not only can be some initial configuration S with computation, but also can be a certain specific program T. Therefore we can see that the common Turing machine can actually simulate the evolution of all cellular automata. At the same time, due to equivalence between a cellular automaton and phrase structure grammar, it can be proven from a computational perspective that the grammatical level of the languages a cellular automaton can accept will not exceed recursive enumerable languages in the Chomsky system (Culik et al. 1990).

Cellular automata are a special computational model, which display discreteness and dynamics. They can simulate phenomena such as self-organization, self-reproduction, signal transmission, information storage, and so on. Their computational ability is equivalent to the universal Turing machine. Therefore, they are widely used in the research of the systems of organisms.

Following the advice of the famous mathematician Stanislaw Ulam, von Neumann designed and used the cellular automaton with twenty-nine states and five neighbors. He first proposed the concept of universal computation by cellular automata, the outline of which is shown in Diagram 4.3. The model has three components: first is the tape, which includes the description of the machine to be constructed. In a situation of self-reproduction, the tape includes the description of the constructor itself. Second is the universal constructor itself, which is a very complex machine that can read and interpret the content on the tape. Third is the construction arm which follows the instruction of the constructor. It is used for constructing the next generation machine described by the tape. The construction arm moves across space and at the same time sets the values of the next generation machine's components.

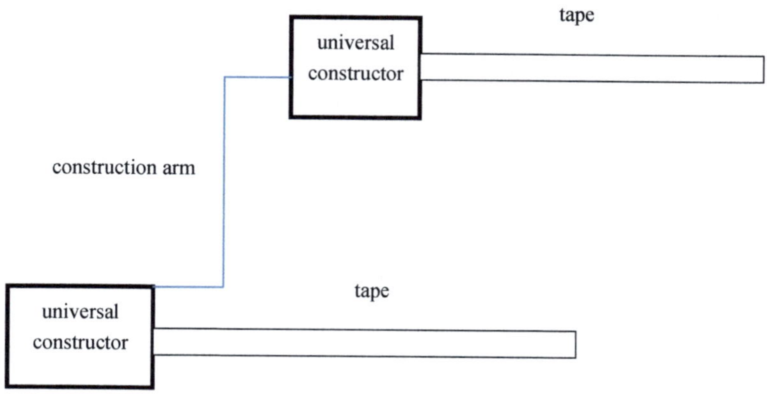

Diagram 4.3 Von Neumann's cellular automata model

4.2 The Complexity of Cellular Automata's Evolutionary Configuration

4.2.1 The Complexity of Cellular Automata's Languages

Cellular automata are a kind of models, which can make numerous simple cells generate various complex systematic states under certain simple innate rules (Culik and Yu 1988). Usually, a cellular automaton is an n-dimensional combination (n is a natural number) of a set of squares. A limited state automaton exists in every square, and every automaton uses the state of its adjacent limited state cell square as an input. It then outputs a state which is of the same limited state set as itself. This can be expressed as follows:

$$\{s_1, s_2, \ldots, s_n\}^{\sum} \Rightarrow \{s_1, s_2, \ldots, s_n\}$$

In this formula, Σ stands for the subset composed of limited states s_1, s_2, …, s_n; n is the number of limited states. That is to say, the states of a cellular automaton are the result of interactions with the states of those automata interacting with it.

A cellular automaton model is built on the basis of a simple state automaton and a set of local rules of interactions.

It is an automaton that can self-develop, self-improve, and evolve continuously, and it can describe system states and predict system future according to certain rules. After modeling the "Game of Life" cellular automaton, a cell's value a at any moment t, is determined by the following formula:

$$a_{i,j}^{t} = f(a_{i,j}^{t-1}, a_{i-1,j}^{t-1}, a_{i-1,j-1}^{t-1}, a_{i+1,j}^{t-1}, a_{i,j+1}^{t-1}, a_{i-1,j+1}^{t-1}, a_{i,j+1}^{t-1}, a_{i+1,j}^{t-1}, a_{i+1,j+1}^{t-1})$$

The cellular automata defined by such local evolutionary rules are two-dimensional. Cellular automata models of one, two, three or multi dimensions can all be defined in the same manner. From this we can see that cellular automata are constructed by a simple method, and yet they can simulate large-scale complex systems. At the same time, from the perspective of arithmetic relationships, cellular automata models actually evolved from limited state machines, but they can process at a higher level the evolutionary states of complex systems of one, two or higher dimensions (Hopcroft and Lllman 1979).

1. **Cellular Automata's Limit Languages**

In 1984, for studying cellular automata, Wolfram first introduced formal languages and the theory of cellular automata (Wolfram 1984a). From then on the research on the complexity of cellular automata's languages started. Here we will first introduce the concept of dynamic language, and then the basic concept of limit language and related background.

Definition 4.1 If language L satisfies the following two conditions, it is called a dynamic language:

(1) If $x \in L$, then any the substrings of x is also in L;
(2) If $x \in L$, then there exists $a, b \in S$, which enables $axb \in L$.

Definition 4.2 Suppose L is a dynamic language, if string d satisfies the following two conditions, then it is called an excluded word of L's:

(1) $d \notin L$;
(2) any real substring of d is in L.

An excluded word is used to describe a word which will never appear in a language, but any of its real substring is bound to appear in the language.

Let $\Omega_0 = S^Z, \Omega_{t+1} = F(\Omega_t)$, here $t \geq 0$. It is easy to see that for any $t \geq 0$, the following relationship exists:

$$\Omega_{t+1} \subset \Omega_t$$

Let $\Omega = \bigcap_{t=0}^{\infty} \Omega_t$ and $L_t = \ell(\Omega_t), L = \ell(\Omega)$, here $l(\Omega)$ is a set composed of all the limited long substrings of every configuration in Ω. Similarly, $l(\Omega_t)$ is a set composed of all the limited long substrings of every configuration in Ω_t. It has been proven that Ω must not be empty, and it is the largest invariant set. Therefore, L is a non-empty dynamic language. And the following proposition exists:

Proposition 4.1 *If sets L_t, L satisfy the above definition, then*

$$L = \bigcap_{t=0}^{\infty} L_t$$

Definition 4.3 Call Ω the limit configuration of cellular automata, L as the limit languages of cellular automata, L_t as the limited step languages of cellular automata.

From the definition we can see, the symbol strings in the limit languages are exactly the symbol strings that always remain after any times of evolution of a cellular automaton. Therefore, limit languages approximately reflect the forms that cellular automata can display when time is long enough. Wolfram proved that the limited step languages L_t of cellular automata were all formal languages. Using automata theory, he defines the formal complexity of cellular automata as the number of states of the smallest limited automaton which accepts the limited step languages L_t.

He deducted the limit language of a cellular automaton from the variations of such formal complexity. First, in a simple situation, if the measurement of such complexity increased in the form of a polynomial (such as a linear polynomial and a quadratic polynomial) as t changes, he would guess that its limit language was a formal language. If the increase of the measurement of such complexity exceeded the increase of a polynomial (maybe it increased exponentially) as t increased, he would guess that its limit language was informal (Wolfram 1984b).

Wolfram studied many cellular automata, including 256 elementary cellular automata. He discovered that the formal complexity of the limited step languages of many cellular automata increased exponentially, such as cellular automata No. 104, No. 164, No. 94, No. 18, No. 22, etc. Therefore, he proposed that informal limit languages existed in elementary cellular automata. In 1900, Hurd presented two non-elementary cellular automata and proved that their limit languages were context-free language and context-sensitive language respectively. Later, someone even constructed a number of cellular automata and proved that their limit languages were either recursive enumerable or non-recursive enumerable. But, for a long time, whether informal languages definitely exist in the limit languages of elementary cellular automata has not been strictly proven (Wolfram 1986).

For a symbol string x, in order to decide whether $x \in L$ can be proven, innumerable times of the verification of $x \in L_i$, $\forall\, i > 0$ have to be done. Therefore, the question of limit language's Membership is not an ordinary question.

From the work of Kari and others we know that, for common cellular automata, the question of Membership is definitely undecidable. Moreover, any uncommon proposition about cellular automata is undecidable. Here, the meaning of an undecidable question is that it does not have an algorithm. The answer to this question for all cellular automata can be either "yes" or "no". And yet it does not rule out the possibility of a thorough analysis of one cellular automaton or one type of cellular automata on the same problems.

However, for any random symbol string $x \in S^*/L$, a natural number n exists, which enables $x \in S^* L_n$, that is, for a finite number of times it can be decided that x is in the complementary set of cellular automata's limit languages, so that S^*/L is a recursive enumerable language which can be accepted be the Turing machine. Therefore, even though the limit languages of cellular automata may not be recursive enumerable languages, their complementary languages are within recursive enumerable languages. Using theories such as skew period (i.e. s-period), it can be proven that the limit languages of cellular automata No. 94 and No. 22 are both informal, and the limit language of cellular automaton No. 122 is not a context-free language.

2. **Cellular Automata's Evolution Language**

In the 1920s, M. Morse first successfully studied mathematical problems by using the symbolic dynamical system. Since then, this method has been used in ergodic theory, differential dynamic systems and some other natural science fields. Eventually, this idea named by physicists as "Coarse Graining" has become an important method for studying dynamic systems. A famous example of it is the "Smale Horseshoe", and another typical example is the coarse graining of Single Hump Mapping. This method has been proven quite successful.

It is highly important to properly coarse grain a system (Marr and Hutt 2005). Such propriety mainly depends on the system and the goal of our research. If the information lost during the process of coarse graining is irrelevant to our research goal, such coarse graining is proper. It can help us get rid of much useless interfering information, so that we can more easily grasp the essence of the problem. On the contrary, if too much information is lost during the process of coarse graining, this symbolic system can sometimes become too simple, and the conclusion thus obtained may be quite ordinary.

Cellular automata can be seen as discretization (coarse graining) models of complex systems. In the following we will coarse grain their evolution orbits one more time, i.e., just like with the coarse graining of single hump mapping, to use a unilateral infinite symbol sequence to represent an orbit (Delorme and Mazoyer 1998).

Let S^Z represent a set of configurations, $x = \ldots x_{-1}\, x_0\, x_1\, x_2 \ldots$ is a configuration of S^Z, marked as

$$S_0 = \{x_0 = 0 | x \in S^Z\}, S_1 = \{x_0 = 1 | x \in S^Z\}$$

Then, S_0, S_1 are two non-intersecting sets of S^Z that are both open and closed (below the product topology), and $S^Z = S_0 \cup S_1$.

Coarse grain orbit $(x, F(x), F^2(x), \ldots)$ into $a_0 a_1 a_2 \ldots$ In it

$$a_i = \begin{cases} 0, & if \quad F^i(x) \in S_0 \\ 1 & if \quad F^i(x) \in S_1 \end{cases}$$

This is called coarse graining with width 1.

Usually, we consider coarse graining with width n, let

$$S^n = \{\alpha_0 \alpha_1 \alpha_2 \ldots \alpha_{n-1} | \alpha_i \in S, 0 \le i \le n-1\}$$

In it, $\alpha_0 \alpha_1 \alpha_2 \ldots \alpha_{n-1}$ is seen as a new symbol, i.e. S^n is a set of symbols, therefore, the set composed of the entirety of all these symbols is marked as S^n. There are 2^n different symbols in S^n, then divide the configuration set S^Z into 2^n different sets which are both open and closed.

$$S_{\alpha_0\alpha_1\alpha_2\cdots\alpha_{n-1}} = \{x_0x_1\ldots x_{n-1} = \alpha_0\alpha_1\alpha_2\ldots\alpha_{n-1}|x \in S^Z\}$$

Here $\alpha_0\alpha_1\alpha_2\ldots\alpha_{n-1}\in S^n$

Similarly, orbit (x, $F(x)$, $F^2(x)$,...) is coarse grained to $\alpha_0\alpha_1\alpha_2\ldots$, here $\alpha_i = \alpha_0\alpha_1\alpha_2\ldots\alpha_{n-1}$, if $F'(x) \in S_{a_0a_1a_2\ldots a_{n-1}}$

Defining coarse grain function $T_n : x \to a_0a_1a_2\ldots$, the definition domain of T_n is S^Z, and T_n (x) is a unilateral infinite sequence in symbol set S^n.

Definition Given a cellular automaton F: $S^Z \to S^Z$. Let

$$A_n = \{T_n(x)|x \in S^n\}$$

$E_n = \{u \in (S^n)^* | u$ is a limited long symbol string of y, here $y \in A_n\}$

Here we call every unilateral infinite sequence in A_n an evolution sequence with a width of n (shortened as n-evolution sequence), and E_n is an evolution language with a width of n (shortened as n-evolution language). The $(S^n)^*$ in the above definition are all the limited long symbol strings (including the empty string ε) of S^n.

From another point of view, the evolution sequence obtained above after coarse graining is actually equal to the observation window sequence proposed by R. H. Gilman and others. The width of the observation window is what we mentioned above. Many experts including Gilman and others have done much work regarding the complexity of cellular automata's evolution language, among which, Gilman proved the following propositions, which is equivalent to defining the upper limit of the evolution language (Eloranta and Nummelin 1992).

Proposition 4.2 *The Evolution Languages of Cellular Automata Are All Context-Sensitive Languages*

In fact, it is not easy to prove that the evolution language of a cellular automaton (even if it is an elementary cellular automaton) is informal. Gilman proposed a non-elementary cellular automaton, and pointed out that its evolution language was neither formal nor context-free.

Among elementary cellular automata, there exist many whose evolution languages are formal. But there also exist many whose evolution languages are informal. However, such informality has not been strictly proven. In later context, we will continue to discuss the complexity of the evolution languages of cellular automata No. 110 and No. 126, which are of important utilizing values.

4.2.2 *Proof of the Complexity Levels of Several Types of Cellular Automata*

In this section, we will use the describing methods of several kinds of formal languages that are closely associated with cellular automata, as discussed in previous context, to select representative and frequently used cellular automata rules, and discuss their degrees of language complexity. This includes the proof and analysis of the degree of language complexity,and descriptive analysis of the degree of computational complexity, to describe the complexity of cellular automata from several different aspects. In Wolfram's classification of cellular automata, No. 7, 9, 22, 25, 26, 37, 41, 54, 56, 62, 73, 74, 110 are all classified into the fourth type, while relatively complex cellular automata rules which can simulate most complex systems also mostly appear in the fourth type. Therefore, we choose the relatively representative Rule No. 164 and at the same time choose a less complex Rule No. 126 which belongs to the third type.

1. **Analysis of the Language Complexity of Cellular Automaton No. 126**

In this section, we mainly study the complexity of elementary cellular automaton No. 126. Its local rule is defined as follows:

$$111, 000 \to 0;\ 001, 100, 010, 110, 011, 011 \to 1$$

The study of elementary cellular automata can be done from two aspects. First, from the angle of universally applicable languages, we will study the ultimate language and evolution language of cellular automaton No. 126. Second, start from an applied cellular automaton model, we will study the complexity of evolutionary configuration of one-dimensional cellular automata with N variables, so as to prove the complexity of cellular automata from the perspective of formal languages and lay the theoretical foundation for the application of cellular automata (Xie 2001).

Theorem 4.1 *The Evolution Language of Elementary Cellular Automaton No. 126 Is a Formal Language*

Theorem 4.2 *When $n \geq 2$, the n-Evolution Language of Elementary Cellular Automaton No. 126 Is Not a Formal Language*

In order to prove Theorem 4.1, we only need to prove that for any $x \in A^*$, there exists $a \in A^*$, making $a \in CP_1(x)$.

For any $aa \in (00 + 11)$, $a \in A$, the additional operations are defined as:

$$00 + 00 = 00, \quad 00 + 11 = 11, \quad 11 + 11 = 00, \quad 11 + 00 = 11$$

For any aa, bb, $cc \in (00 + 11)$, it is easy to prove $aa + bb \in (00 + 11)$, and from local rule M we can get, if $f(bbcc) = aa$, then

$$f(bbcc) = bb + cc = aa \tag{4.1}$$

That is, the third can be decided by any two, and the evolution of any symbol string in $(00 + 11)^*$ satisfies formula (4.1). Next, we prove Theorem 4.1.

Proof For any $x \in A^*$, suppose $|x| = n$, let $x = x_n^0 \ldots x_2^0 x_1^0$, in it, $x_i^0 \in A$.

If i is an odd number, add symbol x_i^0 to the right of x_i^0;

If i is an even number, add symbol x_i^0 to the left of x_i^0.

From formula (4.1) can get: $x_2^1 x_2^1$ can be decided by $x_1^0 x_1^0$ and $x_2^0 x_2^0$, $x_3^{-1} x_3^{-1}$ can be decided by $x_2^0 x_2^0$ and $x_3^0 x_3^0$; $x_3^1 x_3^1$ can be decided by $x_2^1 x_2^1$ and $x_3^0 x_3^0$. Similarly,$x_4^{-1} x_4^{-1}$,$x_4^1 x_4^1$, $x_4^2 x_4^2$, $x_5^{-1} x_5^{-1}$, $x_5^{-2} x_5^{-2}$ can be decided one by one. Therefore, to move upward one by one, we can get a central right limit primary image $\mathrm{CRP}_1\left(x_n^0 \ldots x_2^0 x_1^0\right)$ of $x_1^0 x_2^0 \ldots x_n^0$ We mark it as d.

If n is an even number, let $n = 2k$, then $d = x_{2k}^{-(k-1)} x_{2k}^{-(k-1)} \ldots x_{2k}^0 x_{2k}^0 \ldots x_{2k}^{k-1} x_{2k}^{k-1} x_{2k}^k x_{2k}^k$;

If n is an odd number, let $n = 2k^{-1}$, then $d = x_{2k-1}^{-(k-1)} x_{2k-1}^{-(k-1)} \ldots x_{2k-1}^0 x_{2k-1}^0 \ldots x_{2k-1}^{k-1}$;

Therefore, $\mathrm{CP}_1\left(x_n^0 \ldots x_2^0 x_1^0\right) \neq \varnothing$. So E_1 is a formal language. End of proof.

Proposition 4.3 *For Every Positive Integer n, in the Chomsky Hierarchy, E_n Is Not More Complex than E_{n+1}.*

Theoretically, if we can solve the Membership problem of E_2, i.e., for any symbol string in A, if we can decide whether it belongs to E_2, we can then decide the exact grammatical level of E_n. In fact, it is difficult to completely solve this problem, since it involves many steps of cellular automata evolution under uncommon situations. And yet we do not have to completely solve the Membership problem in order to decide the level of a language in Chomsky's hierarchy. Consider a special subset of E_2, $(00 + 11)^*$, i.e., a set of limited symbol strings composed of only 00 and 11 in A2. We are going to prove that in $(00 + 11)^*$ R_{E2} has an unlimited number of equivalence classes, i.e. the index of R_{E2} is unlimited. Therefore, according to the Myhill–Nerode Theorem we know that E_2 is an informal language (Hanson and Crutchfield 1992).

By studying the grammatical complexity of the evolution language of elementary cellular automaton No. 126, we discover that while studying the evolution languages of cellular automata, their grammatical levels are often difficult to be decided. This demonstrates that the characteristic of cellular automata is a computational model rather than a theoretical deductive model. It is difficult to analyze cellular automata only from an abstract deductive perspective, therefore, in the study of cellular automata, we should be guided by their practical applications and the purpose of theoretical analysis is to serve practical computational applications.

2. **The Complexity of the Limit Language of Cellular Automaton No. 164**

In the 1980s, Wolfram first applied formal languages and the theory of automata to the study of cellular automata, and made many assertions and guesses about their limit languages. But most of those lacked strict mathematical proofs. To completely ascertain the limit language of a cellular automaton, however, is not an easy matter. This is true even for some elementary cellular automata with simple rules and two states only (Jiang 2001).

Elementary cellular automata are one-dimensional cellular automata with a neighborhood radius of 1 and with 2 states (usually represented by numbers 0 and 1). The evolutionary rule f of cellular automaton No. 164 is defined as:

$$000 \to 0, 001 \to 0, 100 \to 0, 110 \to 0$$
$$011 \to 0, 101 \to 1, 010 \to 1, 111 \to 1$$

We now briefly introduce some frequently used concepts and symbols in formal languages. Let $A = \{0,1\}$, $A^* = (0 + 1)^*$ stand for all the limited long symbol strings composed of symbols in A. ε represents an empty string, which is also within A^*. Expand the definition domain of f to A^*, i.e. $A^* \to A^*$. Any symbol string $x = x_1x_2x_3 \ldots x_n$ acted upon by f is

$$\begin{cases} \varepsilon \\ f(x_1x_2x_3)f(x_2x_3x_4)\cdots f(x_{n-2}x_{n-1}x_n) \end{cases}$$

Use symbol f^k to represent k times of the compounding of f, $f^1(x)$ represents all the primary images of x, $|x|$ represents the length of x. Obviously $|\varepsilon| = 0$. In addition, formal expression is used.

The limit language L of cellular automaton No. 164 is defined as: $L = \{y \in A^* | \forall n, \exists x \in A^*$, making $f^n(x) = y\}$.

From the definition of L we know that whether a string y is in L depends on whether it has an infinite number of primary images, i.e. whether an infinite number of symbol strings $\{x - n\}_1^\infty$ exist to satisfy

$$\cdots x_{-n-1} \xrightarrow{f} x_{-n} \xrightarrow{f} x_{-n+1} \xrightarrow{f} \cdots \xrightarrow{f} x_{-1} \xrightarrow{f} y$$

It is easy to see that L is a D type language, i.e. if $y \in L$, then any substring of y is in L. This proposition and its converse negative proposition will often be used in this book.

Let $a = a_1a_2\ldots a_n$, then $a_n \ldots a_2a_1$ is called the mirror image of a, marked as a^R. From the evolutionary rule of L, we can see $f(x) = y \Leftrightarrow f(x)^R = y^R$. This characteristic is called the mirror characteristic of cellular automata. It shows that cellular automaton No. 164 has the mirror characteristic. For all cellular automata with the mirror characteristic, there is the following conclusion: $a \in L \Leftrightarrow a^R \in L$.

Let $n \geq 1$, $j \geq 2$, we call $10(11)^n\,10$ as elementary particle type I, 10^j1 elementary particle type II, and both are collectively called elementary particles. (111) $101^i0^j1^k01$($i + j + k$ is an even number) is called particle cluster type I, while $101^i0^j1^k01$($i + j + k$ is an odd number) is called particle cluster type II or defective particles (shortened as the defective). Obviously, particle cluster type I and the defective both have elementary particles type II as their substrings. Use #(x) to represent the number of elementary particles in string x, for example, string 010110101001 only contains two elementary particles: 101101 and 1001, so we have #(010110101001) = 2.

If string x satisfies $f(a_1xa_2) = x$ ($\forall a_1, a_2 \in A$), x is called an unchanging string. Obviously, if x is an unchanging string, then we have $x \in L$.

Using the definition of L, we can directly verify the following conclusions.

Lemma 4.1 *For any positive integer k, it can be established that*

$$f^{-1}(10(11)^k01) = 10(11)^{k+1}01$$

Lemma 4.2 *Suppose string X has 00 as its prefix and suffix, and X does not include 11 and 101, then X is an unchanging string, and all unchanging strings are in L.*

Proof Now for X, by the only local rules in effect, we have: $000 \to 0$, $001 \to 0$, $100 \to 0$, $010 \to 1$, so it is easy to verify that X is an unchanging string. An unchanging string has at least one primary image which is also an unchanging string, therefore, unchanging strings are bound to be in L.

Note: After detailed discussions, it can be proven that all unchanging strings satisfy the conditions of Lemma 4.2. Therefore, the formal expression of unchanging strings can be written as $00^+(100^+)^*$, and 00 is the shortest unchanging string.

If unchanging string X satisfies the following conditions, we call x the maximum local unchanging string of string y: (1) X is the substring of y; (2) X is an unchanging string; (3) any random unchanging string of y does not have X as its substring. For example, string 101001000100 has many unchanging strings, such as 00,000, 000100,001000100 and so on, yet obviously, only 001000100 is the maximum local unchanging string of 101001000100. Of course, a string may have many maximum local unchanging strings, and the maximum local unchanging string of an unchanging string is itself.

Lemma 4.3 *Let* $y = x_1xx_2$, $|x_1| \geq 3$, $|x_2| \geq 3$, *and x is the maximum local unchanging string of string y. Then, after two steps of evolution of y, its maximum local unchanging string is bound to become longer, i.e.* $f^2(y)$ *has x as its real substring.*

Proof Since maximum local unchanging string X must have 00 as its prefix and suffix, and considering the evolutionary rules of cellular automaton No. 164, we only need to take into account the evolution of $001ab\ldots(ab \neq 00)$. The three possible values are: 01, 10, 11, and their evolution as the follow respectively

$$\begin{array}{lll} 00101\ldots & 00110\ldots & 00111\ldots \\ 0011\ldots & 0000\ldots & 0001\ldots \\ 000\ldots & 000\ldots & 000\ldots \end{array}$$

Every of the above situation demonstrates that after two steps of evolution the unchanging string has become longer.

Note: Later when we quote Lemma 4.3, we always use its converse negative proposition.

Lemma 4.4 *Let $x \in (01 + 11)^*$, then x has at least two primary images within $(01 + 11)^*$, and one of them has 01 as its prefix, while the other has 11 as its prefix.*

Proof First note the following evolution: 0101 0111 1101 1111 11 01 01 11. For convenience, we simplify 01 to 1, and 11 to 0. Then the above evolution can be expressed as

$$\begin{array}{cccc} 11 & 10 & 01 & 00 \\ 0 & 1 & 1 & 0 \end{array}$$

If a_1, a_2 are abridged symbols, then $f(a_1a_2) = a_1 + a_2$. The addition here is modulo 2 addition.

Let the abridged form of x be $x = a_1\, a_2 \ldots a_n$, the following proof exists $y = b_1b_2\ldots b_{n+1}$ (abridged form), making $f(b_1b_2\ldots b_{n+1}) = a_1\, a_2\ldots a_n$, i.e. $b_i + b_{i+1} = a_i (i = 1, 2,\ldots, n)$. Obviously, whether b_1 is 0 or 1, linear equation set $b_i + b_{i+1} = a_i$ $(i = 1, 2,\ldots, n)$ always has one single solution. Thus there are two sets of solutions in total. Now we restore the two sets of solutions in the abridged form to the original form and get the conclusion. In fact, if string x has additional conditions, the conclusion of the Lemma can be further strengthened.

Lemma 4.5 *Let $x \in (01+11)^*$, $|x| \geq 4$, and after removing the two symbols in the front end of x, it still has a substring 01, then x has just two primary images within $(01+11)^*$, and one of them has 01 as its prefix, while the other has 11 as its prefix.*

Proof First note the following fact:

$$\left.\begin{array}{l} f^{-1}(1101) = \{010111, 111101\} \\ f^{-1}(0101) = \{010101, 110111\} \\ f^{-1}(01) = \{0010, 0111, 1101\} \\ f^{-1}(11) = \{0101, 1010, 1111\} \end{array}\right\} \qquad (4.2)$$

Expression (4.2) shows that 01 does not only have one primary image, but there is only one primary image with 01 and 11 as its prefixes, and there is only one primary image with 01 and 11 as its suffixes.

Similarly, among the primary images of 11, there is only one string which has 01 and 11 as its prefixes, and there is only one string which has 01 and 11 as its suffixes. Then it is easy to prove the conclusion about the length of x with the mathematical method of induction.

For Lemma 4.4 and Lemma 4.5, from the mirror characteristic of cellular automaton No. 164, we have the following dual conclusions:

Lemma 4.4′ *Let $x \in (10 + 11)^*$, then x has at least two primary images which are in $(01 + 11)^*$, and one of it has 10 as its suffix, the other has 11 as its suffix.*

Lemma 4.5′ *Let $x \in (01+11)^*$, $|x| \geq 4$, and after removing the two symbols from the rare end of x, it still has a substring, then x has just two primary images within $(01+11)^*$, and one of them has 01 as its prefix, while the other has 11 as its prefix.*

Lemma 4.6 *If string x has two type I elementary particles, then* $x \notin L$.

Proof Let $M_n = \{101^{2k}wl^{2l}01 |\ w = 0$ or w has 01 as its prefix and 10 as its suffix, $1 \leq |w| \leq n\}$, k and l are both positive integers. Now we use mathematical induction to prove that none of the strings in M_n is in L.

When n = 1, $M_1 = \{101^{2k}01^{2l}01\}$, we can use Lemma 4.1 to easily prove the conclusion is tenable.

When n = 2, $1 \leq |w| \leq 2$, w must be 0, i.e. $M_1 = M_2$, then the conclusion holds.

Suppose that the conclusion is tenable when $n = m - 1$, then, when $n = m + 1$, we notice that any string in M_{m+1} has type I elementary particles as its prefix and suffix. According to Lemma 4.1, the primary images of type I elementary particles are still type I elementary particles, only longer, then the primary image of any element $101^{2k}\ w1^{2l}01$ in M_{m+1} can be written as $101^{2k+2}w'1^{2l+2}01$. Here the prefix of w' is 01, and its suffix is 10, or $w' = 0$, and $|w| - 2 = w'$. It shows that $101^{2k+2}w'$ $1^{2l+2}01$ is an element in M_{m-1}, and we know from the hypothesis of induction that $101^{2k+2}w1^{2l+2}01$ is not in L, therefore, any element in M_{m+1} is not in L, and our proof is completed.

In order to extend Lemma 4.6, let us call a string which does not contain any elementary particle, i.e. $\#(x) = 0$, called standard string. Using the definition of elementary particles, all standard strings can be written with formal expression $0^*1^*(01+11)^*(1+\varepsilon)\ 0^*$. Suppose $R = \{r \mid r$ is the substring of $(01 + 11)^*\}$, then standard string x can also be written as $0^k r0^{\ l}$, in it, $k, l \geq 0, r \in R$. Obviously, the image of a standard string is also a standard string, i.e. if $\#(x) = 0$, then $\#(f(x)) = 0$.

Let $R^+ = \{r \mid r$ is the prefix of $(01 + 11)^*\}$, call $x = r0^{\ k}$ the right standard string, here $r \in R^+$, $K \geq 0$. The right standard string has the following characteristics:

Lemma 4.7 *If x is a right standard string, then it has at least two primary images, and they are both right standard strings. One of them has prefix 01, and the other has prefix 11.*

Proof Let $x = r0^k$, $r \in R^+$, $k \geq 0$. We will now discuss two different situations:

(1) If $|r|$ is an even number, then $r \in (10 + 11)^*$. From Lemma 4.4, we know that there exist $y_1, y_2 \in (01 + 11)^*$, making $f(y_1) = r$, $f(y_2) = r$, and in it, y_1 has 01 as its prefix, and y_2 has 11 as its prefix (it shows that the conclusion is tenable when $|r|$ is an even number and $k = 0$).

  ① If y_i has 01 as its suffix, $f(y_i10^{k-1}) = r0^k = x$, $i = 1$ or 2, $k \geq 1$. Here y_i10^{k-1} is the right standard string;

  ② If y_i has 11 as its suffix, $f(y_i\ 0^{k-1}) = r0^k = x$, $i = 1$ or 2, $k \geq 0$. Here y_i0^{k-1} is the right standard string. It proves that when $|r|$ is an even number, the conclusion is tenable.

(2) If $|r|$ is an odd number, then $r1 \in (01 + 11)^*$. From Lemma 4.4, we know that there exist $y_1, y_2 \in (01 + 11)^*$, making $f(y_1) = r1$, $f(y_2) = r1$, and in it, y_1 has 01 as its prefix, and y_2 has 11 as its prefix.

  ① If y_i has 01 as its suffix, expressed as $y_i = z_i01$, then $f(z_i0) = r$, and $f(z_i00^k) = r0^k = x$, $i = 1$ or 2; $k \geq 0$. Here z_i00^k is the right standard string;

② If y_i has 11 as its suffix, marked as $y_i = z_i11$, then $f(z_i1) = r$. We also notice that 21 has 1 as its suffix, therefore, $f(z_i10^k) = r0^k = x$, $i = 1$ or 2; $k \geq 0$. Here z_i10^k is the right standard string.

It shows that when $|r|$ is an odd number, the conclusion is also tenable. So far, the Lemma has been proven.

The left standard string can be defined similarly. Express $R^{-} = \{r \mid r$ is the suffix of $(10 + 11)^*\}$, we call $x = 0^k r$ the left standard string. Here $r \in R^{-}$, $k \geq 0$. The left standard string has the following similar characteristics:

Lemma 4.7′ *If x is a left standard string, then it has at least two primary images, and they are both left standard strings. One of them has suffix 10, and the other has suffix 11.*

Using the definitions of the left and right standard strings, we can naturally arrive at the following lemmas.

Lemma 4.8 *Suppose string x is not a substring of an unchanging string, and* $\#(x) = k$,

(1) *If* $k = 0$, *x can be decomposed as* $x = x_1 1 x_2$. *In it,* x_1 *is the left standard string,* x_2 *is the right standard string;*
(2) *If* $k = 1$, *x can be decomposed as* $x = x_1 0^j x_2$. *In it,* x_1 *is the left standard string,* x_2 *is the right standard string, and when x has defects, j is an odd number.*

Lemma 4.9 *If x is a standard string, then we have* $x \in L$.

Proof Obviously unchanging strings are in L, now suppose x is not a substring of an unchanging string. Also because x is a standard string, i.e. $\#(x) = 0$, let $x = x_1 1 x_2$, In it, x_1 is the left standard string, x_2 is the right standard string. We know from Lemma 4.7 and 4.7′ that there exist y_1, y_2, making $f(y_1 10) = x_1$, $f(01 y_2) = x_2$, and $y_1 10$ is the left standard string, $01 y_2$ is the right standard string. Thus, there must exist $f(y_1 101\ y_2) = x_1 1 x_2$. And $y_1 101\ y_2$ is a standard string containing 1. Similar to the above discussion, $y_1 101\ y_2$ has at least one primary image which is also a standard string, and this process can infinitely go on in order, thereby we know that x has an infinite number of primary images. Therefore, $x \in L$.

Lemma 4.10 *Suppose string x is not the substring of an unchanging string, and* $\#(x) = 1$, *x does not contain any defects, then* $x \in L$.

Proof According to Lemma 4.8, x can be written as $x = x_1 0^j x_2$. In it, x_1 is the left standard string, x_2 is the right standard string, and j is an even number.

When $j = 0$, x can be written as $x = x_1 x_2$. According to Lemma 4.7 and 4.7′ , we know that there exist y_1 as the left standard string, y_2 as the right standard string, making $f(y_1 11) = x_1$, $f(11 y_2) = x_2$. Therefore, $f(y_1 11 y_2) = x_1 x_2$. Express $y_1 11 = y_1'$ as the left standard string, for $y_1' y_2$, the above steps can be repeated similarly. There exist z_1 as the left standard string, z_2 as the right standard string, making $f(z_1 z_2) = y_1' y_2$. It goes on infinitely, so that we find $x = x_1 x_2$ has innumerable times of primary images. Therefore, $x \in L$. When $j = m$, $x = x_1 0^{m+2} x_2$, and from Lemma 4.7 and 4.7′, there exist y_1 as the left standard string, and y_2 as the right standard string, making $f(y_1 11) = x_1$, $f(11y_2) = x_2$, therefore, $f(y_1 110^m 11y_2) = x_1 0^{m+2} x_2$. From the hypothesis of induction we know that $y_1 110^m 11y_2 \in L$, therefore, $x = x_1 0^{m+2} x_2$ is in L. It shows that when $j = m + 2$, the conclusion is also tenable.

To this point, the lemma has been proven.

Lemma 4.11 *Let* $x = u10^k1$ *or* $x = 10^k1u, k \geq 2$, *and x is not a substring of an unchanging string,* $x \in L$. *Then, a certain primary image of x must contain type I elementary particles.*

Proof Since x is not a substring of an unchanging string, we can suppose that 0^k is the maximum local unchanging string of x. Otherwise, we can take any substring of x for discussion.

When $k = 2$, $x = u1001$. Since 1001 has two primary images $f^{-1}(1001) = \{101101, 010010\}$, if the primary image is 101101, then the primary image of x already has type I elementary particles, and the conclusion is already tenable; if the primary image of 1001 is 010010, then 010010 has two primary images 11011011 and 00100100. The first one, 11011011, already contains type I elementary particles, showing that the quadratic primary image of x contains type I elementary particles; the second one, 00100100, is an unchanging string, which inevitably conflicts with the fact that $0^k (k = 2)$ is the maximum unchanging string of x, therefore, when $k = 2$, the lemma has been proven.

Suppose the conclusion is tenable when $k \leq n$, then, when $k = n + 1$, let us consider the quadratic primary image of $x = u10^{n+1}1$. From Lemma 4.3 we know that, the quadratic primary image of the unchanging string 0^{n+1} of x must be shortened. If the quadratic primary image of x does not contain any unchanging string any more, it must contain type I elementary particles. Otherwise, suppose the quadratic primary image of x is $v10^m1v'$ $(2 \leq m < n + 1)$, now by induction hypothesis, we know that a certain primary image of $v10^m1$ contains type I elementary particles, thus a certain primary image of x also contains type I elementary particles. It means that when $k = n + 1$, the conclusion is tenable. The theory of induction therefore proves the lemma.

Lemma 4.12 *For string x, if it is not a substring of an unchanging string, and* $\#(x) \geq 2$, *then* $x \notin L$.

Proof Because L is a D type language, we only need to prove $\#(x) = 2$.

(1) If there are two type I elementary particles in x, from Lemma 4.6 we know that the conclusion is true;
(2) If x contains one type I elementary particle and one type II elementary particle, and suppose $x \in L$, then x has a substring which can be written as $x' = u10^k1$ or $x' = 10^k1u$. From Lemma 4.11, we know that a type I elementary particle must be added to the limited number of primary images of x'. Since the primary images of type I elementary particles are still type I elementary particles, which will not disappear, we know that a certain primary image of x must contain two types I elementary particles. According to Lemma 4.6, we know that $x \notin L$.

(3) If x contains two type II elementary particles, then from the theory of elementary particles, there must be $x \notin L$. According to Lemma 4.11, after a certain number of iterations, the primary images of x must contain at least two type I elementary particles, making $x \notin L$. Therefore, the lemma has been proven.

Lemma 4.13 *All defective particles are not in L.*

Proof According to Lemma 4.8, let us write all defective particles as 0; $D_j = \{ x_1 0^j x_2 | \ j$ is an odd number$\}$. In it, x_1 is the left standard string, and x_2 is the right standard string. Regarding D_j relative to j, we are now going to prove by using mathematical induction that any element in D_j is not in L. When $j = 1$, any defective particle can be written as $d_1 = x_1 0 x_2$, in it, x_1 is the left standard string and x_2 is the right standard string. Let there be strings y_1, y_2, and single symbols a_1, a_2, a_3, making $f(y_1 a_1 a_2) = x_1$, $f(a_2 a_3 y_2) = x_2$, and, if $f(a_1 a_2 a_3) = 0$ is tenable, there exists the following evolution:

$$\begin{array}{c} y_1 a_1 a_2 a_3 y_2 \\ x_1 \, 0 \, x_2 \end{array}$$

From Lemma 4.5 we know that $a_1 a_2 \in \{11, 10\}$; $a_2 a_3 \in \{11, 01\}$. But such a_1, a_2, a_3 do not exist. It shows that D_1 does not have any primary image. Therefore, none of the string in D_1 is in L.

Suppose the conclusion is tenable when $j = m$, (m is an odd number), then, when $j = m + 2$, the defective particle can be written as $d_{m+2} = x_1 0^{m+2} x_2$. Suppose there is a string $y = y_1^z y_2$ in L, which makes $f(y) = d_{m+2}$, or $f(y_1) = x_1$, $f(y_2) = x_2$. According to Lemma 4.5 and Lemma 4.5′, y_1 is the left standard string, and y_2 is the right standard string. Notice Lemma 4.12, $z = 0^m$. Otherwise, $\#(y) \geq 2$, then $y = y_1 0^m y_2$ is definitely not in L. Using induction, we know that such $y = y_1 0^m y_2$ is not in L, therefore, $d_{m+2} = x_1 0^{m+2} x_2$ is not in L as well. Thus, the lemma is proven. Using the language of particles, we can precisely describe the limit language L of cellular automaton No. 164:

Theorem 4.3 *The necessary and sufficient conditions of string $x \in L$ must satisfy one of the following two:*

(1) *String x is the substring of a certain unchanging string;*
(2) *String x does not contain any defective particles, and $\#(x) \leq 1$.*

Proof (1) Sufficiency. From Lemma 4.2 we know that all unchanging strings are in L. From Lemma 4.9 and 10, we know that any string which does not contain elementary particles or only has one elementary particle, and does not contain anything defective, must be in L. (2) Necessity. For all strings $x \in L$, mark $\#(x) = k$. If $k = 0$, then string x belongs to type II in Theorem 4.1; if $k = 1$, according to Lemma 4.13, string x also belongs to type II in Theorem 4.1; if $k \geq 2$, according to Lemma 4.12, we know that x must be an unchanging string belonging to type I of Theorem 4.1.

Theorem 4.4 *The limit language L of cellular automaton No. 164 is a formal language.*

Proof According to Theorem 4.3, limit language L can be written as

(1) An unchanging string and its substrings;
(2) $\{x \mid x = x_1 1 x_2\}$, in it, x_1 is the left standard string and x_2 is the right standard string;
(3) $\{x \mid x = x_1 0^j x_2\}$, in it, x_1 is the left standard string and x_2 is the right standard string, j is an even number.

Every set is a formal language. Therefore, their union set, i.e., limit language L, is also a formal language.

4.3 Measurement of the Complexity of Cellular Automata

In order to study the evolutionary behavior of cellular automata, it is not enough to only generally describe the form of their languages. Since cellular automata have been widely applied to various fields, the theory about them needs to be further improved, so as to better broaden the depth of the theory and the scope of its application. Formal languages describe the complexity of cellular automata from the perspective of speech recognition, but such a method is not suitable for large scale cellular automata. In such situations, because the corresponding computational complexity increases rapidly in a non-linear manner, it causes great difficulty for study, and it is hard to obtain an effective conclusion to guide the study of cellular automata. In this section, we are going to use the core concept of entropy to analyze the dynamic behavior and the characteristics of cellular rules of cellular automata.

4.3.1 Entropy and Information Entropy

Prigogine once said "What is entropy? There is no other concept in the history of science which has been discussed so frequently." The theory of entropy has been in discussion for about 150 years. During this period of time, scientific representatives of various schools all proposed their different ideas. There are dozens of famous names inscribed on the monument of entropy, among which, the most extraordinary are Clausius, Boltzmann, Parigogine, and Shannon.

The concept of entropy was first formally introduced by Clausius in 1855 when he quantitatively described the second law of thermodynamics. In 1877,Boltzmann gave a statistical explanation of entropy, enriched its physical connotation, and clarified the scope of its application. In 1929, Shannon discovered the relationship between entropy and information, thereby raised the meaning of entropy to a new level and further expanded its application. In 1958, Kolmogorov introduced entropy in dynamics to non-linear dynamics, making it an important tool for dealing with problems of complexity.

During the process of the continuous development of the concept of entropy, in 1854, Clausius published *Another Form of the Second Law of the Thermal Theory of Mechanics,* and gave the mathematical expression of the second law of thermodynamics during the process of a reversible cycle as $\oint \frac{\mathrm{d}Q}{T} = 0$. Thus, he introduced a new state parameter which was later named entropy. In 1865, he published a paper named "Forms of the Convenient Application of the Main Equations in the Thermal Theory of Mechanics," and formally named the new state parameter entropy. He even extended the above integral to more common cyclic processes, thereby arrived at the mathematical expression of the second law of thermodynamics, expressed as: $\oint \frac{\mathrm{d}Q}{T} \leq 0$. In the expression, the equal sign corresponds to a reversible process, while non-equal sign corresponds to an irreversible process. Therefore, entropy S is defined as

$$dS \geq \frac{dQ}{T} \tag{4.3}$$

or

$$S_a - S_b \geq \int_a^b \frac{dQ}{T} \tag{4.4}$$

Formula (4.4) express the two states at the beginning and at the end, and S_a and S_b represent the states of entropy at the beginning and the end respectively, dQ represents the heat absorbed by the system, T stands for the temperature of the source of heat. In the reversible process, T is also the temperature of the system. When the system experiences the process of thermal insulation or when it is isolated, dQ = 0. At this time we have

$$dS \geq 0 \tag{4.5}$$

Or

$$S_a - S_b \geq 0 \tag{4.6}$$

This is the Theory of The Increase of Entropy: entropy always increases within an isolated system or an insulated process. The entropy thus defined is called Clausius entropy, or entropy of thermodynamics. Such entropy is a state function and a macroscopic quantity of thermodynamics. Regarding anything happening during the heat insulation process and an isolated system, we can determine the direction and limit of the process according to the value of the entropy function.

In 1896, Boltzmann established the relationship between entropy S and the corresponding possible microscopic number W (i.e. probability of thermodynamics) which corresponds to the macroscopic state of the system: $S \propto \ln W$. In 1900, Planck introduced ratio coefficient k, which is called the Boltzmann constant, which led to Boltzmann-Planck formula

$$S = k \ln W \tag{4.7}$$

The entropy defined in formula (4.7) is called the Boltzmann entropy or statistical entropy. By this, Boltzmann proved that entropy S is related to the thermodynamic probability W. He revealed the relationship between macro and micro states, and pointed out the statistical essence of the second law of thermodynamics: the direction of the thermodynamic process in an isolated system shown in the theory of the increase of entropy corresponds to the transition of a system from a state of small thermodynamic probability to a state of great thermodynamic probability. A state of equilibrium has the greatest thermodynamic probability, which corresponds to a state with the maximum value of S. A process in which entropy is reduced automatically is not absolutely impossible, only that its probability is very small (Livi et al. 1992).

In 1948 Shanonn published *The Mathematical Theory of Telecommunication*, in which he used the method of probability and established the foundation for the modern theory of information. Shannon introduced the information entropy of the information source:

$$H(X) = -\sum_i P(a_i) \log_2 P(a_i)$$

It represents the average amount of information provided by every piece of information after the output of the information source, or the average uncertainty before the output of the information source. a_i represents information (symbol) which can be possibly obtained by the information source, $P(a_i)$ is the prior probability of the information source choosing symbol a_i as information.

In 1957, E. T. **Jaynes** introduced information entropy into statistical mechanics, and proposed the principle of maximum information entropy. His information entropy is defined as

$$S = -k \sum_i P_i \ln P_i \tag{4.8}$$

The definition in formula (4.8) has only one less ratio coefficient than Shannon's original definition of entropy. When the system being studied is a thermodynamic system, P_i in (4.8) is the probability of the appearance of micro state number i of the system, while in a general situation, P_i is the probability of the appearance of basic information element number i of the information source. Information entropy thus defined shows the uncertainty of a system (information source or a thermodynamic system, which is also an information source). Information entropy is also called general entropy.

The proposition and development of the information entropy made the basic characteristics of entropy gradually known. From the definition of entropy, we know that entropy is a measure of the degree of uncertainty of random experiments. It has the following three basic characteristics:

(1) When and only when one of P_i, $i = 1,2,3, \ldots, n$ is 1, entropy $H = 0$, in other situations, entropy is always positive;
(2) In an experiment which has n possible number of results, equal probability has the greatest entropy, and its value is lg n;
(3) If experiments α and β are independent, and their probability vectors are P and Q respectively, then

$$H(PQ) = H(P) + H(Q) \tag{4.9}$$

Now we will use the definition of information entropy as the central concept to study the related characteristics of cellular automata.

4.3.2 Cellular Automata and Entropy

The theory of entropy has become an effective tool for studying the characteristics of cellular automata. The spatial entropy of cellular automata reflects the spatial complexity of their configuration at a given moment, but it does not reflect their dynamic behavior in a temporal sense (Kari 1992). Topological entropy can describe the evolutionary behavior of cellular automata in both spatial and temporal senses, but its calculation is complicated, and its application is limited by the following three conclusions of non-existence:

(1) There is no algorithm which can determine whether the topological entropy of any cellular automaton is 0;
(2) $\forall \varepsilon > 0$, there is no rapid calculation method which can determine whether the topological entropy of any cellular automaton is greater than ε;
(3) $\forall \varepsilon > 0$, there is no algorithm which can make the deviation of the approximate value of any cellular automaton's topological entropy it calculates smaller than or equal to ε.

From this theory we can see that, by using entropy as a research tool, it is difficult to measure the complexity of cellular automata from both temporal and spatial dimensions simultaneously. Therefore, we should describe the complexity of cellular automata in the sense of a single dimension. In this book, we mainly study the evolutionary complexity of cellular automata, thus we emphasize their complex behavior in a temporal sense, and can use the evolution entropy of cells to measure the degree of complexity in cellular automata's evolution process.

According to the definitions in references, and considering the main content of this chapter, we now give the definitions of the cellular evolutionary information entropy and cellular evolutionary word entropy of the elementary cellular automata.

Definition 4.4 Cellular Automata Information Entropy, CAIE.

The cellular automata information entropy can be defined by the following formula (Duan et al. 2012):

$$CAIE = -\frac{1}{N}\sum_{i=0}^{N}\sum_{j=0}^{1} p_i(s_j) \cdot \log_2 p_i(s_j) \tag{4.10}$$

In it, $p_i(s_j)$ stands for the probability of the appearance of state s_j during the evolution of cell i. The word of cellular automata means during the process of evolution, without considering the states of the cells, if l appears as the algebraic sum of the evolution of continuous states, we call it word $-l$. The longest word in it is the total time of evolution T.

Definition 4.5 Cellular Automata Word Entropy, CAWE.

The cellular automata word entropy can be defined by the following formula (Duan et al. 2012):

$$CAWE = -\frac{1}{N}\sum_{i=1}^{N}\sum_{j=1}^{T} p_i(w_j) \cdot \log_2 p_i(w_j) \tag{4.11}$$

In it, $p_i(s_j)$ stands for the probability of the word with a length of l, i.e. w_l is among words that have already appeared (not all possible words) during the evolution of cell i, and T stands for the time of evolution calculated.

From the above definitions we know that CAIE describes the diversity of cellular automata's evolutionary behavior by calculating the probability of the appearance of cell i's state s during a cellular automaton's evolution, and CAWE describes the diversity of cellular automata's evolutionary behavior by calculating the probability of the appearance of cell i in different areas in the same state during its evolution. Both of them are collectedly called the evolution entropy of cells.

4.3.3 The Measure of the Complexity of Cellular Automata's Evolutionary Behavior

In this section, we will determine the different types of evolutionary behavior of cellular automata in different areas by establishing a CAIE-CAWE plane of the evolution process of one-dimensional cellular automata with two states.

Let the radius be 1 and the initial configuration be randomly generated with a probability of 0.5. Suppose there are 100 cells and the time of evolution is 400. We

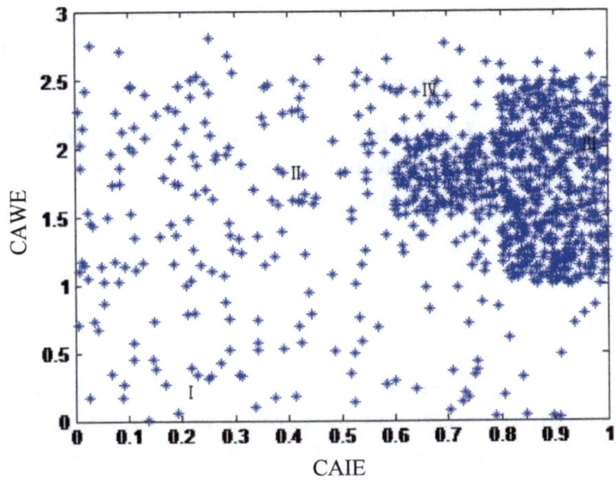

Diagram 4.4 The distribution of type domains of cellular automata

take the last 200 times of iteration to calculate, and under 256 rules, take 10 samples under every rule, thereby constructing the CAIE-CAWE plane of our experiment. Within the CAIE-CAWE plane, randomly select samples to observe their evolutionary behavior, and then classify them according to Wolfram's classification of cellular automata, so as to get the distribution of different types of them. Among them, static cellular automata are distributed in the lower left and lower right corners of the CAIE-CAWE plane, and chaotic cellular automata are distributed in the upper right corner of the CAIE-CAWE plane. The upper and lower left parts of the CAIE-CAWE plane are mainly occupied by complex cellular automata, while the rest of the plane is largely occupied by periodic or quasiperiodic cellular automata, as shown by Diagram 4.4.

In the diagram, symbols I, II, III, and IV represent four types of cellular automata separately.

If we are to further mathematically analyze the result of the measurement of cellular automata's degrees of complexity, we need to give the following two definitions:

Type domain of type i cellular automata: within the evolutionary CAIE-CAWE plane of cellular automata, if in one area, type i cellular automaton occupies the largest proportion, this area can be called the type domain of type i cellular automaton.

$$C_i = \frac{N_{ii}}{N_i} \tag{4.12}$$

In it, N_{ii} stands for the number of type i cellular automata within its type domain, and N_i stands for the total number of cellular automata within the type domain of type i cellular automata. By the result of evolution, we have calculated the different proportions of the four types of cellular automata in our samples. According to the ranges of CAIE and CAWE of different types of cellular automata in relevant

Table 4.1 CA credibility distribution in type domains

Type	I	II	III	IV
Proportion (%)	8.50	11.70	70.50	9.30
Type domain	IE = 0 or WE = 0	Reinforced area to domain I, III, IV	0.8 < IE < 1 & 1.5 < WE < 2.3	0.7 < IE < 0.8 & 2 < WE < 2.5 or 0.9 < IE < 1 & 1 < WE < 1.5
Credibility (%)	100	83	85	78

literature, we have given the different type domains in the CAIE-CAWE plane, and tested their corresponding credibility by random experiments. The result is shown in Table 4.1.

The data in Table 4.1 show: the different proportions occupied by different types of cellular automata reveal that chaotic cellular automata occupy the largest proportion, and complex cellular automata occupy the smallest proportion. From the areas of the type domains we can see that periodic cellular automata occupy the largest area, the area of the static type is 0, and the area of chaotic cellular automata is twice as large as that of the complex type. In terms of the credibility of the type domains, except for the static type, there are no clear boundaries among the other three types. This is because the evolutionary behavior of cellular automata is largely influenced by their initial configurations and is determined by the theory of the undecidability of cellular automata types. The type domains of cellular automata provide quantitative standards for the intelligent study of the rules of cellular automata and their dynamic behavioral relationships, more convenient for implementations in computer programs.

4.4 Summary

This chapter mainly describes the complexity of cellular automata from the aspect of formal languages, analyzes the complexity of both the evolution language and limit language of cellular automata, and deduces the grammatical levels of languages accepted by cellular automata. After analyzing the languages of cellular automata, we give another way of determining the complexity of them, i.e. measurement of the degree of complexity of cellular automata's evolution based on entropy. Finally we determine the complexity of elementary cellular automata by experiments, and explain such a way of measurement.

References

Boccara, N., Nasser, J., & Roger, M. (1991). Particle like structures and their interactions in spatial temporal patterns generated by one-dimensional deterministic cellular automata rules. *Physical Review A, 44*(2), 866–875.

Culik, K., Hurd, L. P., & Yu, S. (1990). Computation theoretic aspects of cellular automata. *Physica D: Nonlinear Phenomena, 45*(1–3), 357–378.

Culik, K., & Yu, S. (1988). Undecidability of CA classification schemes. *Complex System, 2*(2), 177–190.

Delorme, M., & Mazoyer, J. (1998). *Cellular automata: A parallel model* (1st ed.). Dordrecht, London: Academic Publishers.

Duan, X., Wang, C., & Liu, X. (2012). *Theoretical study of cellular automata and the applications of their simulations*. Beijing: Science Press.

Eloranta, K., & Nummelin, E. (1992). The kink of cellular automata Rule 18 performs a random walk. *Journal of Statistical Physics, 69*(5–6), 1131–1136.

Hanson, J. E., & Crutchfield, J. P. (1992). The attractor-basin portrait of a cellular automaton. *Journal of Statistical Physics, 66*(5–6), 1415–1463.

Hopcroft, J. E., & Lllman, J. D. (1979). *Introduction to automata theory languages and computation*. Reading, MA: Addison-Wesley.

Jackson, E. A. (1991). *Perspective of nonlinear dynamics* (2nd ed.). London: Cambridge University Press.

Jiang, Z. (2001). A complexity analysis of the elementary cellular automaton of Rule 122. *Chinese Science Bulletin, 46*(7), 600–603.

Kari, J. (1992). The nilpotency problem of one-dimensional cellular automata. *SIAM Journal on Computing, 21*(3), 571–586.

Livi, R., Nadal, J. P., & Packard, N. (1992). *Complex dynamics*. New York: Nova Science Publishers.

Marr, C., & Hutt, M. T (2005). Topology regulates pattern formation capacity of binary cellular automata on graphs. *Physica A: Statistical Mechanics and Its Applications, 354*(15), 641–662.

Wolfram, S. (1984a). Computation theory of cellular automata. *Communications in Mathematical Physics, 96*(1), 1–57.

Wolfram, S. (1984b). Cellular automata as models of complexity. *Nature, 311*(4), 419–424.

Wolfram, S. (1986). *Theory and application of cellular automata*. Singapore: World Scientific.

Xie, H. M. (2001). The complexity of limit languages of cellular automata: An example. *Journal of Systems Sciences and Complexity, 14*(1), 17–30.

Chapter 5
Cellular Genetic Algorithms

Introduction
In this chapter, we introduce the applications of cellular automata in genetic algorithms.

In the traditional sense, genetic algorithms (GA) originated from Darwin's evolution theory. Borrowing from the natural law of "survival of the fittest", through the genetic operations of selection, crossover and mutation, the individual's adaptability gets improved. One important feature of genetic algorithms is that the optimization process is not dependent on gradient information, which makes it especially suitable for dealing with complex and nonlinear problems which are difficult to be solved by general searching methods. But it should be pointed out that the traditional genetic algorithms are not perfect. We know that as an individual in the population, its "growth" (optimization) process is bound to be accompanied by the interaction, information exchange and energy exchange with the surrounding complex environment. This important process is precisely what the traditional genetic algorithms are not good at in simulation. In this chapter, we will put a "gene" of an individual or an "individual" in its entirety in the traditional genetic algorithms into a 2D grid of a cellular automaton, and then use the evolution rules of the cellular automaton itself to influence the genetic operations of the "individual" or the "gene". Comparing with the traditional genetic algorithms, this combination reveals many interesting results. Finally, we take stock market as an example to give the applications of cellular genetic algorithms in practical productions and in our daily lives.

X. Li et al., *Theory of Practical Cellular Automaton*,
https://doi.org/10.1007/978-981-10-7497-4_5

5.1 Traditional Genetic Algorithms

5.1.1 Overview and Basic Ideas of Genetic Algorithms

Genetic algorithms were proposed by Professor Holland of the University of Michigan in early 1970s. In 1975, Holland published the first monograph "Adaptation in Natural and Artificial System" on the genetic algorithms. In 1989, Goidberg put generic algorithms a big step forward.

"Survival of the fittest" is the central idea of the genetic algorithms. Problem solving process is actually to produce a collection of individuals and get them "PK" with each other, and then according to the requirements, select the best individual as the solution for the problem. Specifically, it is at first to encode every possible solution of the problem into a vector. We call this "vector" "chromosome". Of course, we call every element of "vector" as "gene" in analog to biology. For all the "chromosomes", we need to calculate "degree of satisfaction" (degree of fitness) in solving the problem given for a "chromosome". The greater the fitness, the more outstanding the "chromosome" is. After that, through the "selection", "crossover" and "mutation" operations on the "chromosomes", dropping out the chromosomes with low degree of adaptation, the ones with the higher degree of adaptation are kept as a new generation of individuals. In this way, each iteration makes the new individuals inherit the excellent nature of their last generation. This makes the problem continuously evolve toward the direction of the optimal solution (Holland 1992).

Unlike other search and optimization methods, the main features of the genetic algorithm are as follows.

(1) Simplification. For some complicated problems, a big obstacle in the algorithm design process is to in detail describe all the characteristics of the problem in advance, and to illustrate how the algorithms will take corresponding measures to solve the problems with different characteristics. Genetic algorithms get rid of these cumbersome procedures, directly borrow and simulate the natural phenomena of "survival of the fittest" to make an optimization.
(2) Eyeing broadly and focus on fitted few. Different from the traditional "point to point" search method, genetic algorithms start searching the solution from a "group" instead of from a single point. This determines that the genetic algorithm itself is very suitable for large-scale parallel computation, for example, to make hundreds or even thousands of computers carry out independent and evolutionary computation of their own.
(3) Search without gradient information. The algorithm only uses the adaptive value to evaluate the merits of the individual, without the need of the derivation or the help of other auxiliary information.
(4) The process of genetic algorithm has not adopted the deterministic rules, but set up the "crossover probability" and "mutation probability" to guide the search direction, which is more consistent with the "growing" process of the individual within the group in the real world.

5.1.2 The Computational Process of the Traditional Genetic Algorithm

For the convenience of comparing this section with the later context, we first use an example to illustrate the process of the traditional genetic algorithm. Without loss of generality, considering a problem of seeking maximum value, as shown below: seeking the maximum value of the function $f(x)$: $R^k \rightarrow R$ with variable as x, and x is a value within the domain $D = [a, b] \subseteq R$, and for all $x \subseteq D, f(x) > 0$. The accuracy requirement is to take n digits after decimal point for independent variable x.

1. **Encoding and decoding**

Inspired by the structure of human chromosomes, we can assume that there are only two alkali bases: "0" and "1". We use a "chain" to string them together in order and form a sufficiently long binary combination, which forms a "chromosome". A long enough chromosome can outline all the characteristics of an individual. This is the binary encoding method. The chromosome structure is shown in Fig. 5.1.

Although the above encoding method is simple and intuitive, the decoding process will be cumbersome because it needs large amount of coding (long chromosome chain) to accurately describe the individuals with complex characters, such as the translation process of DNA in biology, namely gene mapping to the phenotype. So to improve the computational complexity and operational efficiency of the genetic algorithm, here we put forward the floating-point coding method.

To meet the accuracy requirement, the domain D which the variable x belongs to should be divided into $(b - a) * 10^n$ space of the same size, here m stands for the smallest integer which makes the equation of $(b - a) \cdot 10^n \leq 2^m - 1$ holds, then for the variable x_i within the domain D, the accuracy requirement can be achieved by the binary code with a string length of m, that is, x_i can be expressed as $(c_{i1}, c_{i2}, \ldots, c_{im})$ by using a binary string.

In turn, we can transform a binary string $(c_{i1}, c_{i2}, \ldots, c_{im})$ to a real number corresponding to the interval [a, b] by the following two steps.

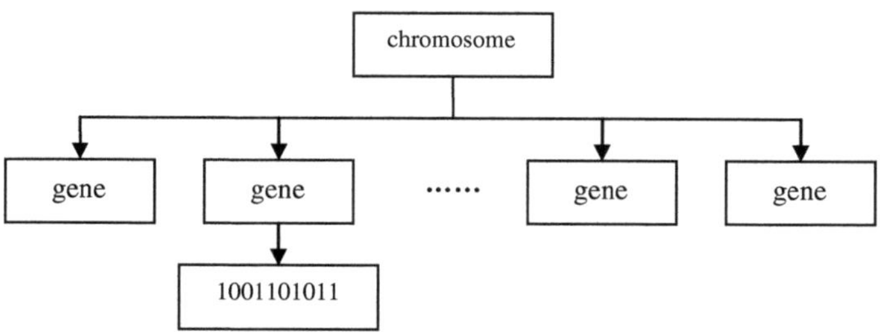

Fig. 5.1 Chromosome structure diagram

(1) Turn the binary number represented by the binary string (c_{i1}, c_{i2}, …, c_{im}) into decimal number x_i' by using the following formula

$$(c_{i1}, c_{i2}, \ldots, c_{im})_2 = \left(\sum_{j=1}^{m} c_{ij} \cdot 2^j \right)_{10} = x_i' \quad (5.1)$$

(2) Change x_i' into the real number corresponding to the interval [a, b] by using the following formula

$$x_i = a + x_i' \cdot \frac{b-a}{2^m - 1} \quad (5.2)$$

The above are the operations of encoding and decoding.

2. **Generating initial population**

Randomly select a number of individuals in the search space [a, b], and they form a biological group (encoding and decoding methods have been given above). At the beginning of the search, the solution to the problem is completely unknown, and the degree of excellence of each individual is completely unknown. Generally, the initial population is generated by using random numbers, here, N stands for the total number of the individuals, V_i(i = 1, 2, …, N) stands for each individual, and x_i can be regarded as the chromosome of V_i.

3. **Calculate the fitness of the individual**

Calculate the adaptability to the environment of the individual V_i, namely eval(V_i). Because for all $x \in D$, $f(x) > 0$, here we can directly bring the individual into $f(x)$, and use the function value obtained as a standard to evaluate the individual's fitness, and we have eval(V_i) = $f(x_i)$.

4. **Selecting operation**

(1) Calculate the fitness sum of the population

$$FIT = \sum_{i=1}^{N} eval(V_i) \quad (5.3)$$

(2) Calculate the probability that each individual V_i be selected, that is, the percentage which the fitness of the individual Vi occupies the total fitness of the population.

$$p_i = eval(V_i)/FIT \quad (5.4)$$

(3) Calculate the cumulative probability of each individual, the so-called "cumulative probability" is the sum of the probability that the individual V_i is chosen and the probability that individual $V_1 \sim V_{i-1}$ is selected

$$q_i = \frac{1}{FIT}\sum_{j=1}^{i} eval(V_j) = \sum_{j=1}^{i} p_i \tag{5.5}$$

(4) Generate a random number r in the interval [0, 1], if $r < q_1$, select the first chromosome; if not, select V_i ($2 \le i \le N$), which makes $q_{i-1} < r \le q_i$ holds.

The above operation is called "roulette wheel" method, vividly shown in Fig. 5.2.

In Fig. 5.2, the angle Θ_i of the fan sector is proportional to the fitness of the individual. Every time in making a selecting operation, the wheel is rotated for N times (that is, number of N new individuals are selected), and the individual which represented by the section where the arrow points to is selected. In this way, the population will get number of N new individuals by selecting operation.

5. **The crossover operation**

We set the crossover probability as $p_{c,}$ this probability means that the number of the individuals for cross operation is $N \cdot p_c$. We can choose individuals for a cross operation in the following ways: for each new individual selected from step (4) above, a random number r_i in the interval [0, 1] is generated. If $r_i < p_c$, the crossover operation will be conducted to the individual.

Randomly couple the selected individuals for the cross operation. For each pair of coupled individuals, generates a random number k in the interval [1, m], representing the position of the crossover point. Exchange the gene positions behind the crossover point for the two individuals in the pair, as shown in Fig. 5.3.

Figure 5.3 shows the most typical single point crossover rule for genetic algorithm. In addition to this, there are several crossover rules available such as: two-point crossover, multi-point crossover, split crossover, uniform crossover, mixed cross, et al. and they will not be covered in detail here.

6. **Mutation operation**

Set the mutation probability to p_m. For each new individual generated by the crossover operation, there is a corresponding random number r_i in the interval [0, 1].

Fig. 5.2 Roulette wheel

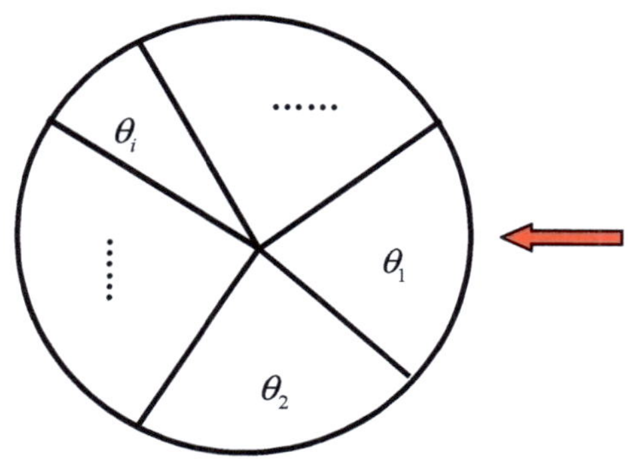

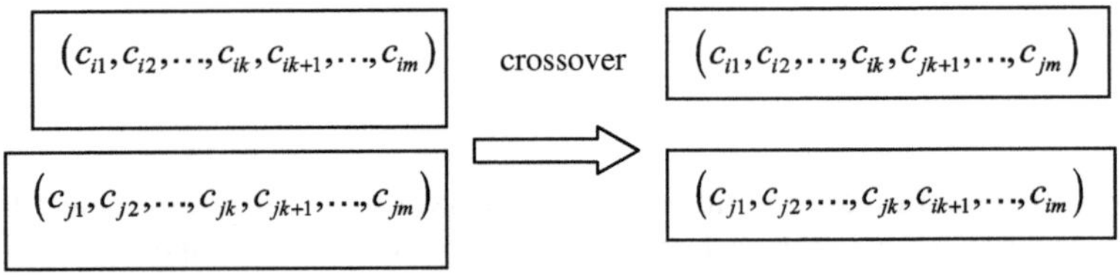

Fig. 5.3 Crossover operation

If *ri* < *pm*, a gene position is randomly selected from the individual (chromosome) for mutation operation, as shown as follows:

Before mutation: …1001100101010…

After mutation: …1001110101010…

Generally speaking, the mutation probability should not be too large, otherwise the individuals after the mutation may lose the genetic characteristics of the last generation.'

7. **Biological group evaluation**

After completion of the above operation, we need to evaluate whether the new generated population has been generated to meet the criteria for solving the problem, that is, the evaluation of biological groups. Generally speaking, after repeated implementation of the above steps 3–6, the typical ending evaluation criteria of the genetic algorithm are as follows:

(1) The maximum fitness in the population is greater than a set value;
(2) The average fitness of the population is larger than a set value;
(3) The evolution reaches a certain number of times;
(4) The increasing rate of population fitness ceases to increase with the increase of the evolutionary times.

The choice of evaluation criteria are made based on the specific characteristics of the problem.

In summary, the calculation process of traditional genetic algorithm can be expressed as in Fig. 5.4.

5.1.3 The Performance and Short Comings of the Traditional Genetic Algorithm

After describing the computational procedure of the traditional genetic algorithm, we find the following problems.

First, in traditional genetic algorithm, in selecting next generation of individuals, the possibility of an individual being selected depends on the fitness of the

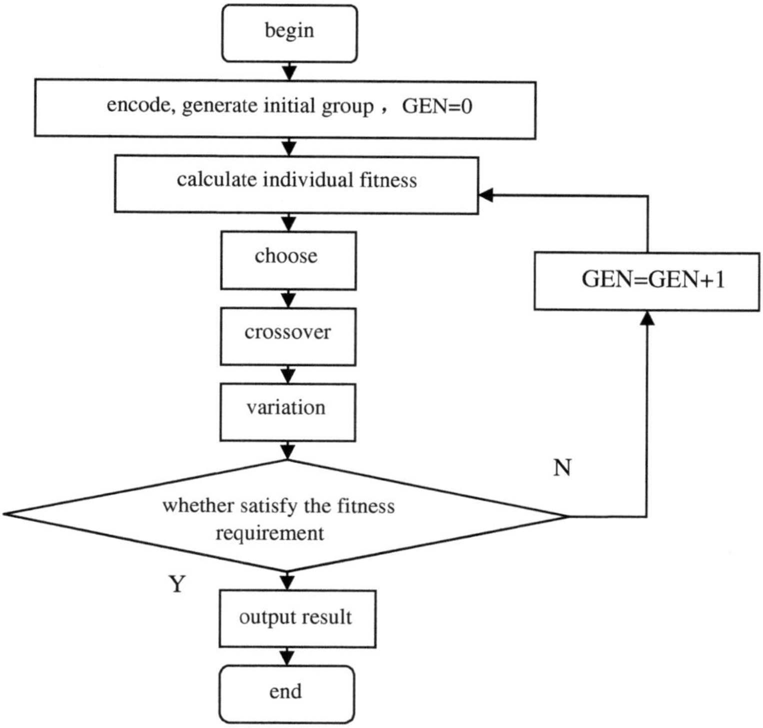

Fig. 5.4 The process of the traditional genetic algorithm

individual. However, the selection process depends on the way of Roulette wheel type, with characteristics of probability or luck.

In completely following this basic model, it may happen that individuals with greater fitness in certain generation are not selected. In contrary, because "the better ones" (individuals with higher degree of fitness) within the generation are selected in each process, the population is easily trapped in the local optimum and the "potential ones" are ignored. In view of this, some scholars successively put forward some new rules, such as Probability Elimination Method, Compulsory Preservation of Outstanding Individual, Proportional Elimination Plus Cross Value Adding method, etc. However, the existing experiments show that these methods cannot effectively solve the problem of local optimization. The elimination algorithm and increment rules of the individuals should be determined based on the actual situation of the specific problem.

Second, for dynamic problems, it is difficult to be solved by genetic algorithm, because the population may premature converge, and will no longer generate responses to the later changing data.

Third, the role of cross operation. From the point of the traditional genetic algorithm, the crossover operation can ensure not to lose some possible solutions, and prevent the population from falling into local solutions prematurely. Of course, it can be considered that the role of cross operation is only for the renewal caused by promoting the mutation process. Especially for an initial population, the crossover is almost equivalent to having a very large mutation rate. But we may change the angle in considering the problem, and we may assume that the individuals in the population have some kind of "intelligence", and the crossover operation can be understood as the "information exchange" or "mutual learning" behavior of the individuals. If we can properly guide the "cross" operation, and to make the individuals learn from each other's "excellent" components, the effect of the traditional genetic algorithm can be greatly improve.

5.1.4 Summary

In this section, we have made a detailed description of the basic ideas and calculation process of traditional genetic algorithm, and pointed out three major problems in traditional genetic algorithm. Whether these three major questions can be solved by using the cellular automaton, a tool for exploring complexity, we will try in the next section.

5.2 Cellular Genetic Algorithm

In the last section, we introduced the computational procedure of the traditional genetic algorithm, and discussed the performance and shortcomings of the traditional genetic algorithm. In recent years, there have been some improvements on genetic algorithms. Some scholars combine the genetic algorithm with cloud model and immune mechanism to form a new genetic algorithm, which achieved some effects. This series of improvements has brought us the following inspiration: the genetic algorithm is a kind of algorithm with spatial structure, when we expand our vision to the two-dimensional world, there is a continuously evolving population in this world, and the population in the process of evolution will not only be disturbed by nature, but also the individual in the population will have the phenomenon of birth, migration and death. What's more, there is a complex interaction between individuals, which is very close to the nature of the biological evolution process, and that is precisely the traditional genetic algorithm does not have. In many genetic algorithms with spatial structure, the cellular automaton is becoming a new tool for studying genetic algorithms (Chen 2005).

Cellular genetic algorithm (CGA) is a branch of genetic algorithm, which combines genetic algorithm with cellular automaton as a new computational tool, and the design idea is mainly derived from the following three perspectives. First, the time and space state of a cellular automaton is discrete, and the number of the states of each variable is limited, and the genetic algorithm has the characteristics of discrete operation. Second, in a cellular automaton, repetitive simple arithmetic rules can lead to complex system behavior, and the genetic algorithm is actually a continuous iteration of selection, crossover and mutation operations. Third, the global calculation finally can be achieved by the repeated local interactions (Kirley 2002; Li et al. 2010).

At present, the research on the genetic algorithm of cellular automata application can be broadly divided into two categories: in the first category, some genetic operations (such as cross) in the traditional genetic algorithm are replaced by the rich evolution rules of cellular automata (Lu et al. 2010), which can be considered as the representation of the genetic algorithm used in two dimensional space, with a single "cell" regarded as a "gene in the chromosome". The second category is based on the complex system theory, in which the single cell is regarded as the individual in a population, and the operation of the genetic algorithm is realized by using the neighbor structure of the cellular automaton mode, so that it can introduce the evolution rule of cellular automata to make it more consistent with the biological evolution of the real world. In the sections below, we will focus on these two types of algorithms.

5.2.1 Cellular Evolutionary Algorithm of the Genetic Algorithm (E-CGA)

1. **Theoretical basis—artificial life thoughts**

Artificial Life (AL) was proposed by Christopher Langton in 1987 at the "International Conference on the Synthesis and Simulation of Life System" held in Los Alamos National Laboratory. Artificial Life is a new inter-discipline science, which studies phenomena in the field of life sciences through simulations of life systems. The object of the study is the artificial systems with natural life characteristics and biological phenomena, and its focus is on the method of model generation, key algorithms and implementing technology, of artificial systems. In popular terms, it is the use of computer for simulation the activities or functions of organic lives.

Artificial life has following characteristics: ① as life organization, using of bottom-up modeling method; ② Local control mechanism, with the characteristics of parallel operation; ③ the behaviors of the bottom units are relatively simple, convenient for computer simulations. As a matter of fact, the idea of artificial life is quite similar with the operating principle of cellular automata. Both rely on the local simple rules to study the overall complexity. It is just that artificial life simulation stands in the bionics point of view, taking references of some characteristics of biological processes, to construct computer algorithms or simulation systems with good performance in optimization (Zhang et al. 2008).

2. **A typical rule of E-CGA–Game of Life**

For the game of life, we have described in detail in the previous chapters of this book so we will only give a brief description of the rules here.

Configuration of the cells:

(1) The cells distribute on the regular partitioned grids;
(2) The cell has two kinds of states, 0 and 1, 0 represents "dead", 1 represents "alive";
(3) The cells' neighbor form is Moore, that is, a cell is adjacent to 8 neighboring cells;
(4) The live and death of a cell at a moment is determined by the sum of the cell's own state at the moment and the states of its 8 neighbors.

Evolution rule:

(1) At the current moment, if a cellular state is "alive", and two or three cells of eight neighboring cells have the state of "alive", then at the next moment, the cell remains "alive"; otherwise the cell is "dead". The mathematical expression of the rule is:

$$if\ \ S_i^t = 1\ \ then\ \ S_i^{t+1} = \begin{cases} 1: & if \sum S_N^t = 2 \quad or \quad 3 \\ 0: & if \sum S_N^t < 2 \quad or \quad \sum S_N^t > 3 \end{cases} \tag{5.6}$$

At the current moment, if a cellular state is "dead", and three cells of eight neighboring cells have the state of "alive", then the cell's state at the next moment should be "revival"; otherwise the cell is "dead". The mathematical expression of the rule is:

$$if\ \ S_i^t = 0\ \ then\ \ S_i^{t+1} = \begin{cases} 1: & if \sum S_N^t = 3 \\ 0: & if \sum S_N^t \neq 3 \end{cases} \tag{5.7}$$

In expressions (5.6) and (5.7), S_N^t represents the state of the neighbors of the central cell i at the moment of t.

3. **A typical example of E-CGA—the cellular automaton life game algorithm of the genetic algorithm (LG-CGA)**

In the traditional genetic algorithm, we use the selection operator, crossover operator and mutation operator to operate on the individuals in the population, and the crossover operator plays an important role in entire optimization process and guarantee the diversity of the population. And in LG-CGA, we use the "life game" rule of cellular automata to replace the crossover operator, that is, to replace the crossover operations of the genetic algorithm among gene groups by using the rule of "life game" on the Moore type neighbor cells.

For the entire population space, cross operation is no longer limited to the two chromosome chains in the pair (similar to the row vector operation), the operation also include the scanning of each of the cells that is not on the boundary of the space (here, a single cell is regarded as the individual's gene), and calculate the number of its neighbors that are still "alive", and to determine the cell's state for the next moment. Figure 5.5 gives a comparison of the single point crossover operation of the traditional genetic algorithm with the crossover operation of life game.

The steps of the LG-CGA algorithm are introduced below.

(1) Population Initialization and encoding (see Sect. 5.1.2 for details).
(2) Operation selection. Calculate the fitness function of each individual, select the operation with Roulette Selection algorithm according to the size of fitness function (see Sect. 5.1.2 for details), and choose an excellent individual to enter the next generation.

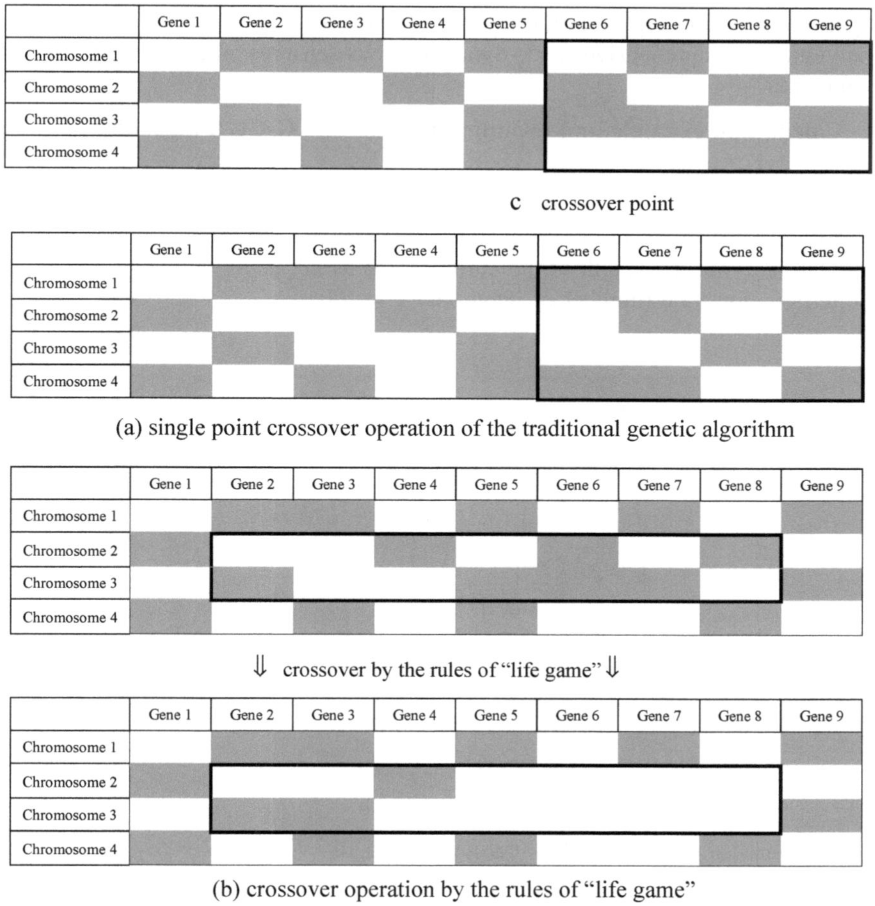

Fig. 5.5 Comparison of the single point crossover operation of the traditional genetic algorithm with the crossover operation by the rules of "life game"

(3) Cross operation. The space of the individuals is a two-dimensional matrix (see Fig. 5.5, "rows" as the individuals, "columns" as the genes). If we perform the "life game" operation on the elements in the matrix, namely the cells (except boundary matrix cell) with the crossover probability of p_c, we will get the updated matrix of next generation cells.
(4) Mutation operation. Carry out the gene position mutation operation to the individuals in the population, with mutation probability of p_m (see Sect. 5.1.2 for details).
(5) Determine whether the result meets the biological group evaluation criteria (see Sect. 5.1.2 for details), if not, return to step (2).

It is not difficult to find that the LG-CGA algorithm is somehow analogue to the traditional genetic algorithm. The difference between them is that the LG-CGA algorithm has changed the fixed pattern of crossing mode of the traditional genetic algorithm by using the evolution rules of CA, making the interaction between the individuals comprehensive and dynamic, thus ensures the diversity of the population.

4. **Calculation example and evolution process of LG-CGA algorithm**

We take the typical multimodal function $f(x) = 10\sin(5x) + 7\cos(4x)$ (see Fig. 5.6) as an example. We solve the problem of $\max\{f(x)\}$ by using the LG-CGA algorithm, and we set the independent variable as $x \in [0, 10]$, the number of the population at 50, the length of the chromosome as 20, using the binary encoding, the termination time (number of iterations) T = 100.

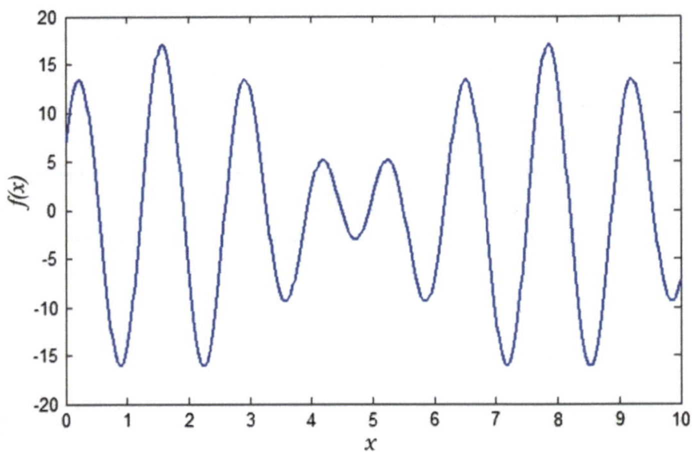

Fig. 5.6 Function $f(x) = 10\sin(5x) + 7\cos(4x)$, $x \in [0, 10]$

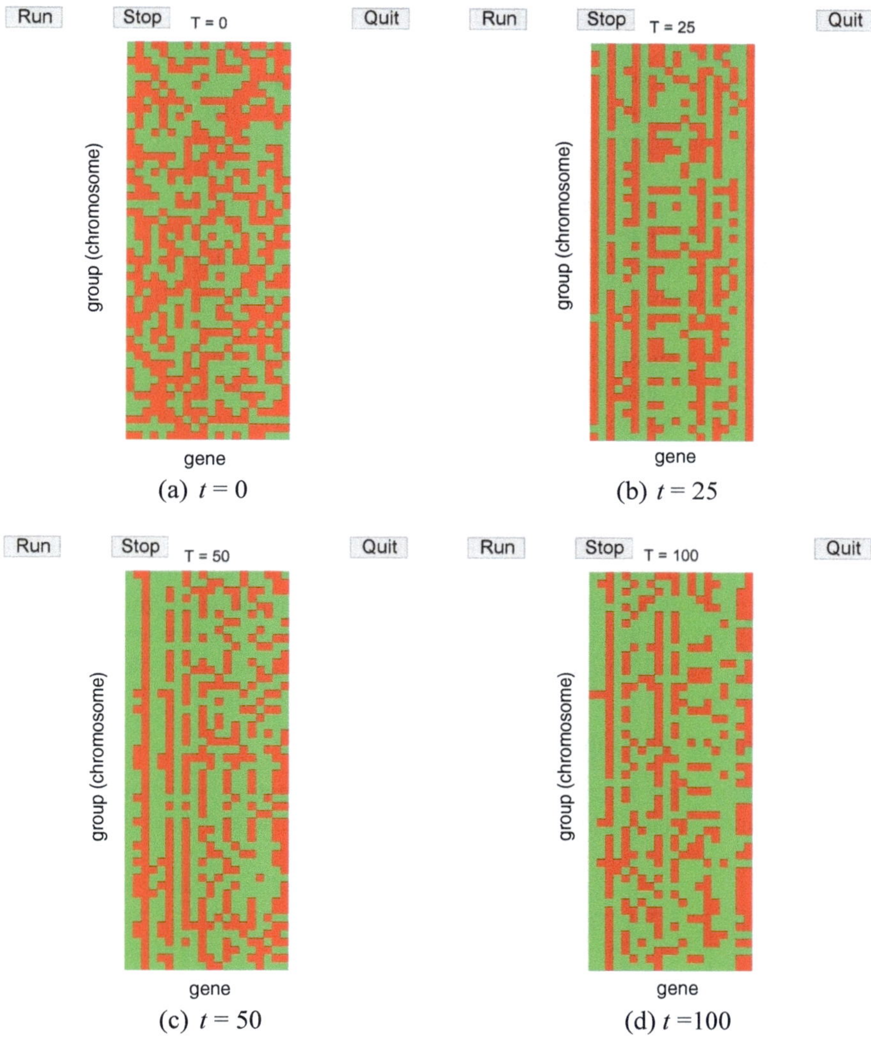

Fig. 5.7 Cellular evolution state of the LG-CGA algorithm

As shown in Fig. 5.7, in two-dimensional cell grid, each line represents an individual, each unit grid represents a gene.

It is not difficult to see that the two-dimensional world provided by cellular automata makes the encoding mode of LG-CGA algorithm more intuitive. Here, the "cross" operation is on the "genes" which represent the individual cells, so we set a relative low crossover probability of 0.1 in the evolution test in Fig. 5.7.

Figure 5.7 gives the simulation results of the evolution state of the LG-CGA algorithm at different time points after several rounds of iteration. It is not hard to see that: ① Under the action of selecting operation, the cells show a trend of regular arrangement. Under the effect of cross and mutation operations, a certain number of cells show random arrangement, guaranteeing the diversity of the population. In the same time, the evolution of the cellular states has vividly described the convergence process of the solution. ② The number of "live" cells decreases with time, which indicates that the mechanism of life game is expressed in the genetic operation (generally speaking, the survival rate of cells in life game will eventually stabilize at around 15%).

Draw the results of the solution (the maximum fitness value by 100 iterations, the crossover probability as $p_c = 0.6$, mutation probability $p_m = 0.01$), as shown in Fig. 5.8.

Figure 5.8 is a specially intercepted picture of the solution. It is not difficult to find that in running the LG-CGA algorithm, the solutions show deviation from the peak value of the function, and have difficulties in convergence. This is due to two reasons: First, the "cross (evolution)" operation is on the individual cell (gene), so that the crossover probability for chromosome cross operation is relatively large in comparison with the traditional genetic algorithm. Second, the active cross method of life game ensures the diversity of the population, and prevents the solution from converging to local optimum, and in the same time undermines the inheritance of outstanding individuals to some extent. So, in the evolutionary rule of genetic algorithm (E-CGA), the cross probability should be set at relative lower value. In the following, we will introduce several ways of applications of evolution method on cross operation.

5. **Expansion of the evaluation rules**

The "life game" rule is regarded as a typical representation of cellular automata. This rule approximately describes complex phenomena and laws in biological

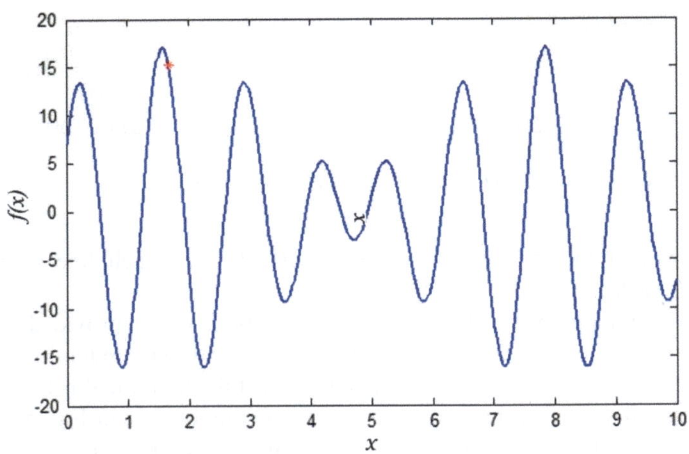

Fig. 5.8 One of the results of the LG-CGA algorithm

simulation of life activities, such as living, extinction and competition (see Fig. 5.9). However, if it is used as a crossover operator in the E-CGA algorithm, there are drawbacks in the life game rules.

According to Fig. 5.9 of the cellular evolution state distribution, such evolution rule of "life game" is relative restrictive on life requirements. After several steps of operation, the evolution movement trends stable, and eventually shows that the number of live cells become smaller and smaller and large area of cells die off, which leads to the low density of life and low probability of survival. Because of isolation and the lack of reproductive opportunities, life crisis will eventually turns up, thus ruins the succession of outstanding individuals.

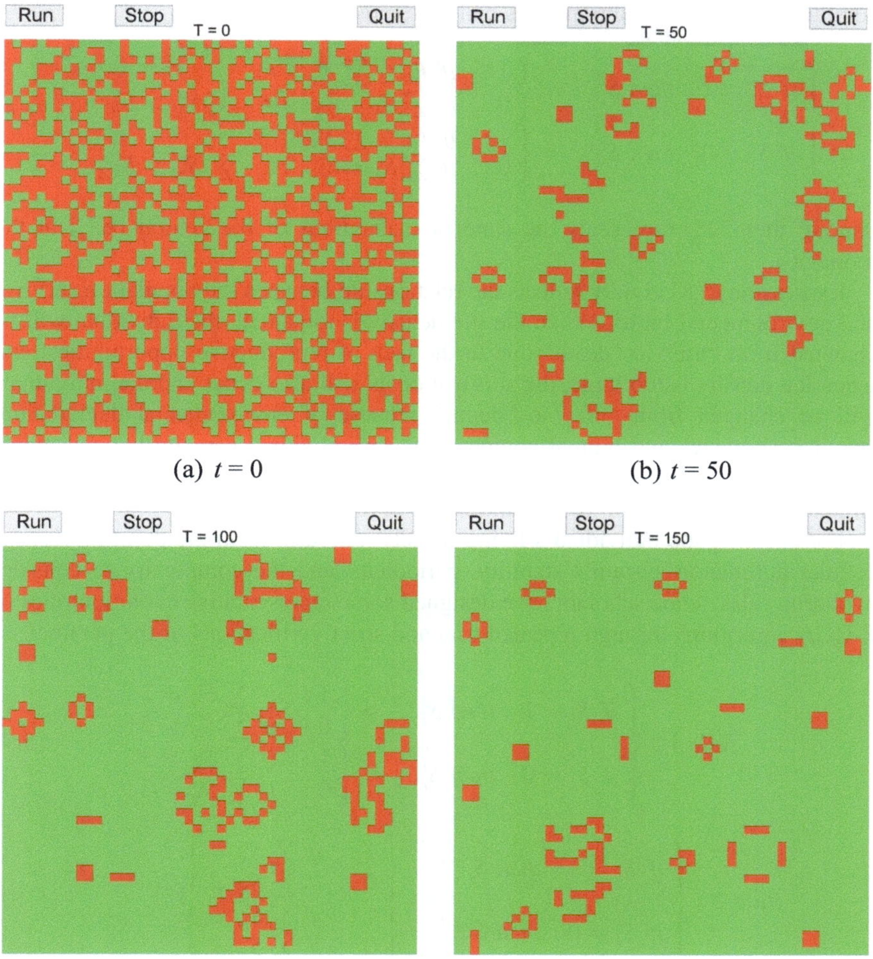

(a) $t = 0$ (b) $t = 50$

(c) $t = 100$ (d) $t = 150$

Fig. 5.9 Cellular automaton evolution of life game

It is not difficult to see that the premise of "inheritance" is "existence", the change of the cellular automaton evolution rules will have a great impact on the optimization results. In order to solve the problem of low density of life, to prevent the emergence of life crisis, a series of improved rules on the basis of the life game rules have been proposed, that is, to improve the survival probability and to increase the chance of life extension by changing the state of the neighbor cells.

A typical way of doing this is to introduce four parameters E_b, E_k, F_b, F_k to the life game rules. Among them, E_b represents the required minimum number of live neighbors for a "live" cell to keep "living" state at the next moment; E_k represents the minimum number of "live" neighbors needed by a "dead" cell to revive at the next moment; F_b and F_k are respectively the upper limit values of the above conditions, and the evolution rules can be expressed as:

$$\begin{cases} if\ S_i^t = 1 \quad then\ S_i^{t+1} = \begin{cases} 1: & if\ E_b \leq \sum S_N^t \leq F_b \\ 0: & if\ \sum S_N^t < E_b \quad or \quad \sum S_N^t > F_b \end{cases} \\ if\ S_i^t = 0 \quad then\ S_i^{t+1} = \begin{cases} 1: & if\ E_k \leq \sum S_N^t \leq F_k \\ 0: & if\ \sum S_N^t < E_k \quad or \quad \sum S_N^t > F_k \end{cases} \end{cases} \tag{5.8}$$

Among them, S_N^t represents the state of a neighbor of the central cell i at the moment t.

Expression (5.8) vividly reflects the relationship between the population survival and environmental limits. When the life density is too small, the individual will be changed from "life" to "death" due to the lack of reproductive opportunities; and when the density is too large, the survival crisis will also occur and the individuals will be changed from "life" to "death" because of environmental degradation, resource shortages and mutual competition. An individual can survive and reproduce only when the number of the individuals is at an appropriate position, so as to simulate the phenomenon of life and death in real world.

For ensuring the individual's living density, and also from the point of view of cellular automaton system's stability, periodicity and the complexity to consider evolution rules, some scholars have designed some representative evolution rules of E-CGA algorithms through repeated trial and strict verifications of the parameters:

$$Rule\ 1: \begin{cases} if\ S_i^t = 1 \quad then\ S_i^{t+1} = \begin{cases} 1: & if\ \sum S_N^t = 2 \\ 0: & if\ \sum S_N^t \neq 2 \end{cases} \\ if\ S_i^t = 0 \quad then\ S_i^{t+1} = \begin{cases} 1: & if\ \sum S_N^t = 3 \\ 0: & if\ \sum S_N^t \neq 3 \end{cases} \end{cases} \tag{5.9}$$

$$Rule\ 2: \begin{cases} if\ S_i^t = 1 \quad then\ S_i^{t+1} = \begin{cases} 1: & if\ \sum S_N^t = 1,2 \\ 0: & if\ \sum S_N^t \neq 1,2 \end{cases} \\ if\ S_i^t = 0 \quad then\ S_i^{t+1} = \begin{cases} 1: & if\ \sum S_N^t = 3 \\ 0: & if\ \sum S_N^t \neq 3 \end{cases} \end{cases} \tag{5.10}$$

$$Rule\ 3: \begin{cases} if\ S_i^t = 1 & then\ S_i^{t+1} = \begin{cases} 1: & if \sum S_N^t = 1,2,3,4 \\ 0: & if \sum S_N^t \neq 1,2,3,4 \end{cases} \\ if\ S_i^t = 0 & then\ S_i^{t+1} = \begin{cases} 1: & if \sum S_N^t = 4,5,6,7 \\ 0: & if \sum S_N^t \neq 4,5,6,7 \end{cases} \end{cases} \quad (5.11)$$

$$Rule\ 4: \begin{cases} if\ S_i^t = 1 & then\ S_i^{t+1} = \begin{cases} 1: & if \sum S_N^t = 2,4,6,8 \\ 0: & if \sum S_N^t \neq 2,4,6,8 \end{cases} \\ if\ S_i^t = 0 & then\ S_i^{t+1} = \begin{cases} 1: & if \sum S_N^t = 1,3,5,7 \\ 0: & if \sum S_N^t \neq 1,3,5,7 \end{cases} \end{cases} \quad (5.12)$$

The existing research results and the related experiments have shown that Rule 3 simulates a living condition of periodic variation, and can make the number of live cells stable at around 51%. Rule 4 uses an even-odd rule to make the biological breeding orderless, thus to make the number of living cells stabilized at around 80%. Using above rules as crossover operators for E-CGA algorithm, it will effectively solve the problem of population (gene) loss caused by the crossover rules of "life game". In the next section, E-CGA algorithm performance under different evolution rules will be illustrated and unified comparisons will be made.

6. **Comparison of performances of the algorithms**

The operation rules of the crossover operator are different, which will affect the optimization results. In this section, we draw a table which takes a typical multi-modal function f(x) = 10 sin(5*x*) + 7cos(4x) as an example. And we set the crossover probability to 0.1 (the crossover probability of traditional GA is set to 0.7), and mutation probability at 0.01, and take independent tests 100 times for each crossover rule algorithm, in order to find out the effect of "evolution rule" on optimization results. The results are as shown in Table 5.1.

Through observation of Table 5.1, it is not difficult to find out that in comparison with traditional GA, through the improvement of crossover method, E-CGA algorithms have effectively avoided trapping into local maximum in the process of optimization.

Table 5.1 Comparison of algorithms performance based on evolution rule of the genetic algorithm (100 independent tests)

Algorithm	Maximum fitness	Average fitness in evolution process	Times trapped into local maximum
Traditional GA	17.000	10.388	>50
LG-CGA	17.000	10.793	0
E-CGA based on rule 1	17.000	10.089	6
E-CGA based on rule 2	17.000	10.431	0
E-CGA based on rule 3	17.000	10.212	0
E-CGA based on rule 4	17.000	8.855	0

5.2.2 Self-adaptive Cellular Genetic Algorithm (SA-CGA)

In the previous section, the key point of evolution algorithm of genetic algorithm (E-CGA) that we introduced is to apply certain evolution rules of the cellular automaton model to the crossover operations of traditional genetic algorithm, taking reference of some characteristics of biological processes, and to use cells in the Moore Neighborhood to run rules such as "Game of Life" and others, thus to replace the crossover behavior among the chromosomes in traditional genetic algorithm. This change enriched the ways of crossover operation for traditional genetic algorithm, guaranteed population diversity, and led to better experimental results. In E-CGA algorithm, we regard an independent cell as one gene in traditional genetic algorithm. We can thus consider that the difference between the E-CGA algorithm and traditional genetic algorithm is only that they use different "operators". Although using the two-dimensional lattice of cellular automata to represent chromosomes, strictly speaking, the E-CGA algorithm itself is still confined to one dimensional space, and the algorithm does not reflect characteristics such as "intelligence" or "self-adaptive".

1. **The Theoretical Basis of Self Adaptive Cellular Genetic Algorithm-Theory of Complex Systems**

In 1973, Edgar Morin formally proposed "the complexity method" in his book *Le Paradigme Perdu: la Nature Humaine.* The core of Morin's complexity thoughts came from the principle he expressed as "order comes from noise". We can understand this principle this way: placing some small magnetic cubes in a box dispersedly, and then shake this box in a random way. At last, people see that after sufficient movement, the small cubes in the box mutually connected to form an ordered structure according to the orientation of the magnetic poles.

In this example, shaking the box randomly is a manifestation of disorder. Of course, it is certain that the ordered structure of the small cubes in the box cannot be produced by only shaking the box. The cubes themselves are magnetic, which have the potential for generating ordered structures. However, the realization of this potential relies on the disordered factor of us "shaking the box". This principle is the first to break the traditional idea that order and disorder are opposing and repelling each other, and reveals preliminarily the connection between the overall effect and local rules.

In 1984, a group of researchers in physics, economics, theoretical biology and computer science, with the support of Murray Geli-Mann and Nobel Prize winner in physics Philip Anderson, Nobel Prize winner in economics Kennet Arrow, established the Santa Fe Institute (SFI), which specializes in the research of complexity science. They tried to find a way to solve the problem of complexity by multi-disciplinary cooperation. The establishment of the Santa Fe Institute (SFI) marked the rising of complexity science. The so-called complexity science is a new interdisciplinary subject, which studies the characteristics, mechanisms, laws, and complexity of the interactions among various components in a complex system, and reveals the system's evolution, chaos, emergence, self-organization, self-adaption, self-similarity and other mechanisms and their internal laws. This subject does not depend on Newton's view of the universe, but adopts a bottom-up method to discuss the general characteristics that emerge from interactions among various small components in a complex system. These general characteristics are different from microcosmic individual characteristics. As the saying goes, "One ant hole may cause the collapse of a dyke a thousand miles long." The dyke collapse is an overall characteristic, but this result is produced by the tiny movements of the ants inside it.

Complex system and complexity are two core concepts of complexity science. Complexity, as a trait, is the space-time structure of the interacting elements or essential factors in the system. The carrier of complexity is a complex system, and the two are inseparable. Generally speaking, the definition of complexity has two meanings: (1) from the local terms, it refers to the heterogeneity, diversity and autonomy of the internal elements in a system, and the intricate interactions among the elements. This is similar to the various ants in a dyke. (2) From the overall terms, it refers to the emergence of amazing macro phenomena in a system. This is similar to the ultimate collapse of the dyke.

Comparatively speaking, a complex system is a system with relative extensive existence, and can be define as:

(1) A complex system is not a simple system, and not a random system. (2) A complex system is a nonlinear system. (3) Many subsystems exist within a complex system, which are interdependent, cooperative, and can evolve together.

At the same time, a complex system has the following characteristics:

(1) Individuals have initiative. The initiative of individuals refers to the fact that in adapting to an environment, an individual does not only passively accepts the influence of the environment, but tries to influence and change the environment in order to improve its own fitness.
(2) Individuals are learning and evolving. In order to survive in a system, individuals need to constantly collect information, sift the true from the false, update strategies, and to improve their fitness. This is like a human, he needs to keep learning and improving his abilities in order to find a foothold in a society.
(3) The characteristics of emergence. Emergence is an essential feature of a complex adaptive system. Simply put, emergence has the effect that the whole is greater than partial sum. On the basis of the evolution of microscopic subjects, a system generates changes in its characteristics and in its structure on the macroscopic level. The dyke collapses exactly because of the action of the microscopic subjects inside it—the ants.
(4) Local information without central control. In a complex system, no subject can obtain the information about the states and behavior of other subjects in the system. Each subject can only acquire information within a relatively small local range, dealing with "local information", and making corresponding decisions. This is similar to the fact that while we live in a society, it is impossible for us to know all the people in the society. The knowledge and

experiences we acquire are all through people we know (such as relatives, teachers, classmates, friends, etc.).The overall behavior of a system emerges through interactions such as competition or cooperation among individuals. For example, in a kingdom of ants, each ant does not act in unity according to "the king's" command, but adjusts its behavior according to the behavior of its peers and the environment, thereby realizes the group behavior.

Cellular automata themselves have good features such as parallelism, local rules, homogeneity, discreteness, etc., can capture the essential characteristics of the evolution of a system, and display complex evolutionary behavior of the system. Currently they have been regarded as the basic method for the research of complexity science.

As stated earlier, genetic algorithm is a kind of algorithm with a structure of spatial population, so it is easy to be mapped to the two-dimensional lattice of cellular automata. In this section, based on these characteristics, we regard a single cell as an individual in the population in genetic algorithm, give the characteristic of "intelligence" to the individual cell so that it has self-learning ability, and realize the operation of genetic algorithm with the help of the neighborhood structure of the cellular automation model and the characteristics of a series of complex systems.

2. **Cellular Space Description**

In SA-CGA algorithm, we set the cellular space as a two-dimensional lattice of $n \times n$, in which each square represents an individual in the population; the forms of the neighbors can adopt the von Neumann type, the Moore type or the extended Moore type; each individual can have 4, 8, or 24 neighbors, as shown in Fig. 5.10.

3. **Calculation Steps of SA-CGA Algorithm**

For the convenience of comparison, here we still describe the calculation steps of the algorithm using the example of solving the maximum value problem we used in Sect. 5.1.2.

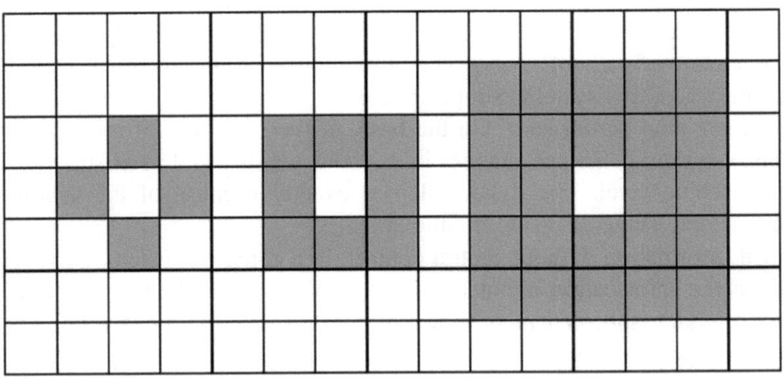

(a) VonNeumann type (b) Moore type (c) Extended Moore type

Fig. 5.10 Forms of cell neighborhoods

(1) Population Initialization: In the two-dimensional n x n grid, each square represents an individual $V_{i,j}$ (i,j = 1, … 2, n), each individual has a chromosome $x_{i,j}$,i and j represent individual coordinates, $x_{i,j} \in [a, b]$.
(2) Encoding (for details see Sect. 5.1.2): For the convenience of direct viewing and understanding, this section directly uses decimal encoding.
(3) Calculating the Degree of Fitness: Calculating the degree of fitness of individual $V_{i,j}$ in the cellular space (population) eval($V_{i,j}$), without losing generality, there is eval $(V_{i,j}) = f(x_{i,j}) - \min(f(x_{i,j}))$.
(4) Selecting Operation: In the cellular space, each individual $V_{i,j}$ makes fitness evaluations of cells (expressed as set Ω) among its surrounding neighbors (including itself, and according to the different forms of neighbors, the number can be 5 or 9 or 25) whose adaptive value is greater than or equal to itself (eval $(V_{a,b}) \geq$ eval$(V_{i,j})$)

$$p_{a,b} = \frac{eval(V_{a,b})}{\sum\limits_{a,b\in\Omega} eval(V_{a,b})} \tag{5.13}$$

The $P_{a,b}$ in the above formula, i.e. the probability that neighbor $V_{a,b}$ of individual $V_{i,j}$ is chosen (if eval $(V_{a,b})$ < eval $(V_{i,j})$), then $P_{a,b} = 0$) is the same as traditional genetic algorithm. This selection is still carried out in the form of the roulette. But unlike traditional genetic algorithm, here individuals participating in the roulette are only limited to those belonging to set Ω of individual $V_{i,j}$. Intuitively speaking, this is a process of the central cell "learning" from its neighbors, as shown in Fig. 5.11(here we use the Moore Neighborhood as an example, the central cell is $V_{i,j}$).
In Fig. 5.11, the adaptive values of the cells covered by shadows are all greater than or equal to the central cell $V_{i,j}$. According to formula (5.13), we put their probabilities in the roulette, and when the roulette turns once, the individual represented by the area the dark arrow points to is the learning object chosen by the central cell $V_{i,j}$.

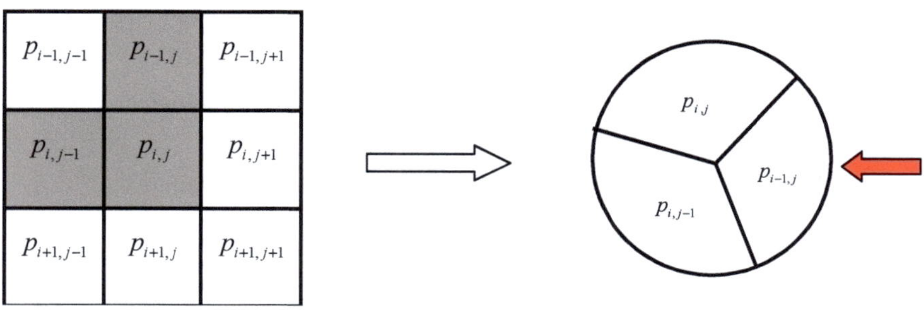

Fig. 5.11 Local roulette

(5) Crossover Operation. We still use the Moore Neighborhood as an example. Assuming that individual cell $V_{a,b}$ ($a \in [i-1, i+1]$; $b \in [j-1, j+1]$) is selected by the central cell $V_{i,j}$ in the selection process, and here we define the crossover probability as P_c, then individual $V_{i,j}$ updates the chromosomes in the following crossover way:

$$x'_{i,j} = (1 - p_c)x_{i,j} + p_c x_{a,b} \tag{5.14}$$

It is not hard to find that the difference between the two algorithms arises here. Traditional genetic algorithm makes individual crosses of the updated population according to probability after the selection operation of the "roulette." This way of cross ensures the diversity of the population to a certain extent, but at the same time it will destroy excellent individuals, In SA-CGA algorithm, however, we can consider the crossover operation as a process in which the central cell in a local area learns from individuals better than itself. "Local area" in a two-dimensional space structure ensures the diversity of the population. "Learning from individuals better than oneself" can prevent the existing excellent individuals in the population from being destroyed. Therefore, the crossover probability P_c in the SA-CGA algorithm is different from the crossover probability in traditional genetic algorithm. The crossover probability in traditional genetic algorithm expresses the possibility that an individual is chosen to participate in the crossover operation (see Sect. 5.1.2 for details), while the crossover probability in the SA-CGA algorithm can be considered as the "self-confidence level" or "learning tendency" of individual $V_{i,j}$. When $P_c = 1$, individual $V_{i,j}$ learns without reserve from those neighbors better than itself; when $P_c = 0$, individual $V_{i,j}$ is completely self-confident, and does not have any communication with its neighbors.

(6) Mutation Operation. In a way similar to that of traditional genetic algorithm, the mutation probability is defined as p_m; for each individual $V_{i,j}$ in cellular space, we select random number r from [0, 1]. If $r < p_m$, then the chromosomes of an individual are updated in the following way:

$$x''_{i,j} = x'_{i,j} + \delta_\varepsilon \varepsilon \tag{5.15}$$

Here δ_ε is a constant; $\varepsilon \sim N(0, 1)$.

(7) Judging whether it meets the evaluation standard of the biological group (for details see Sect. 5.1.2), if not, go back to step (3).

The above is the entire computing process of SA-CGA algorithm.

4. **A SA-CGA Algorithm Example and the Evolutionary Process**

This section still uses the typical multimodal function $f(x) = 10 \sin(5x) + 7 \cos(4x)$ as an example, applying SA-CGA algorithm to the problem $\max\{f(x)\}$, with independent variable $x \in [0, 10]$, decimal encoding, crossover probability 0.7, mutation probability 0.01 and end time (number of Iterations) $T = 100$.

1) **The cellular evolution process using SA-CGA algorithm based on the von Neumann Neighborhood**
   Observing Figs. 5.12 and 5.13, it is not hard to see that the fitness of the population as a whole demonstrates diffused growth along with the evolution of time and the genetic operation of self-learning of individual cells within the scope of their neighbors, which reflects the effect of local rules on entire system.

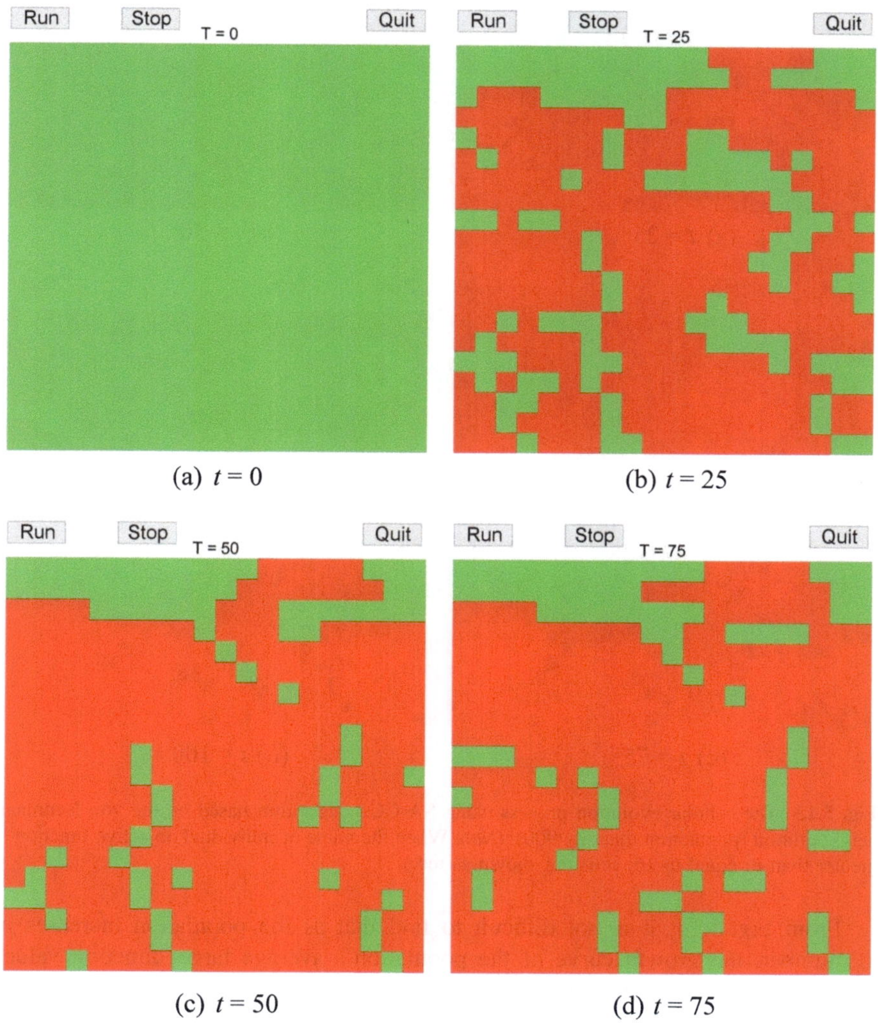

Fig. 5.12 (1) Cellular evolution process using SA-CGA algorithm based on the von Neumann neighborhood (population quantity 400). (2) The cellular evolution process using SA-CGA algorithm based on the von Neumann neighborhood (population quantity 400) (*Note* When the value of individual objective function is greater than or equal to 16, cells are shown as red.)

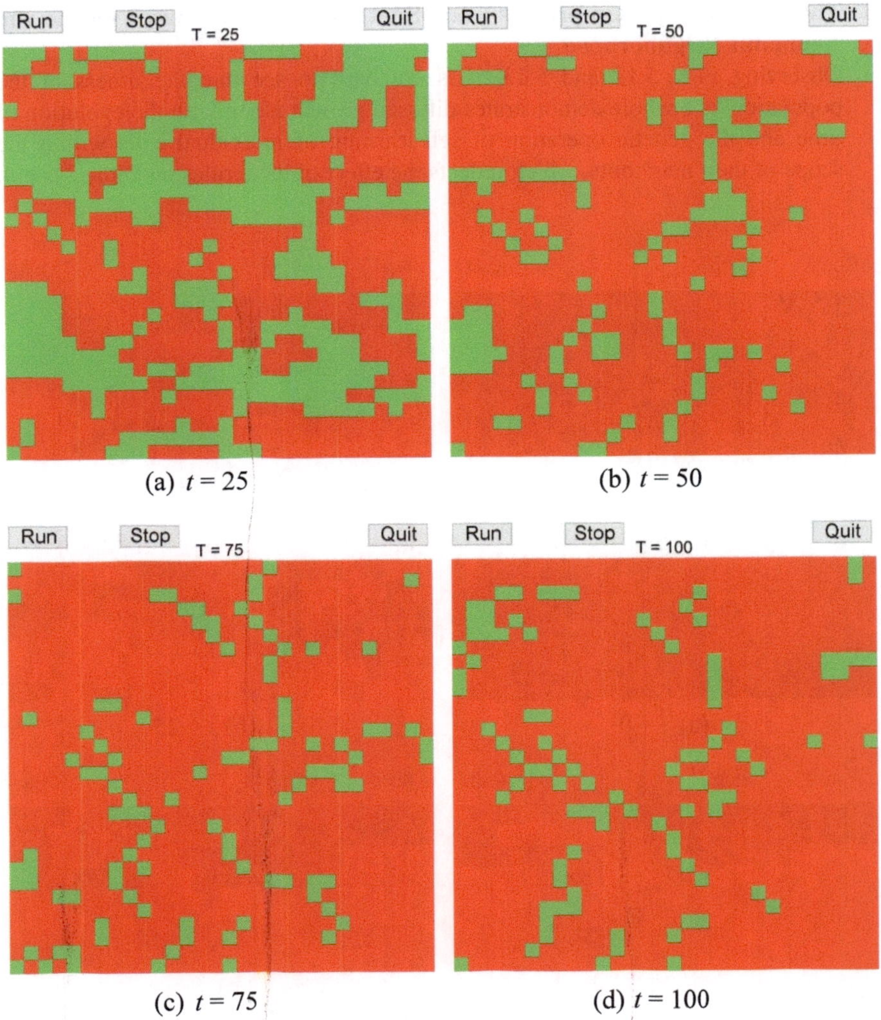

Fig. 5.13 The cellular evolution process using SA-CGA algorithm based on the von Neumann neighborhood (population quantity 900). (*Note* When the value of individual objective function is greater than or equal to 16, cells are shown as red.)

From Fig. 5.14, it is not difficult to find that as the population increases in number, the growth curve of the population's average target function values tends to become smoother, with less fluctuation. This shows that under the influence of this neighborhood structure, the population increases in number, and the uniformity of opinions among individuals in the process of optimization is improved.

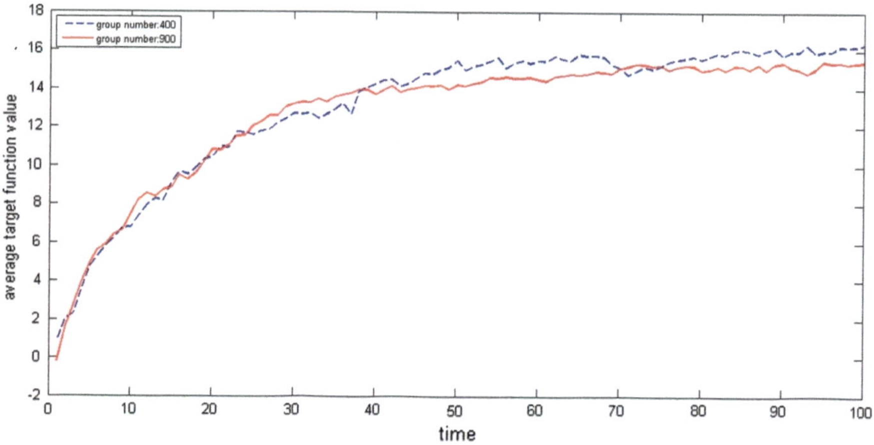

Fig. 5.14 Population's average objective function values using SA-CGA algorithm based on the von Neumann neighborhood

2) **Cellular evolution process using SA-CGA algorithm based on the Moore Neighborhood**
From Figs. 5.15 and 5.16, we can find that, just like the von Neumann Neighborhood, with the evolution of time and the genetic operation of self-learning of individual cells within the scope of their neighbors, the fitness of the population as a whole based on the Moore Neighborhood also shows diffused growth. But we can find through the statistics of the results of many experiments (see the table that follows later for experimental data) which compare individual cellular fitness under the two kinds of neighborhood structures, that at the same moment of evolution, the average cellular fitness obtained by operating under the von Neumann Neighborhood structure is in most cases higher than that under the Moore Neighborhood structure, i.e. SA-CGA algorithm based on the von Neumann Neighborhood is more efficient. We can also find this by directly observing and comparing Figs. 5.14 and 5.17.
3) **Cellular evolution process using SA-CGA algorithm based on the Extended Moore Neighborhood**
Comparing with the cellular evolution processes based on the von Neumann Neighborhood (Figs. 5.12 and 5.13) and the Moore Neighborhood (Figs. 5.15 and 5.16), the number of red cells(target function value greater than or equal to 16) has decreased significantly in the cellular evolution process based on the Extended Moore Neighborhood (Figs. 5.18 and 5.19).
We then compare Figs. 5.17 with 5.20, through statistics of many experimental results (see the table that follows later for experimental data) to compare individual cellular fitness under the two kinds of neighborhood structures, it can be found that the average cellular fitness under the Moore Neighborhood structure

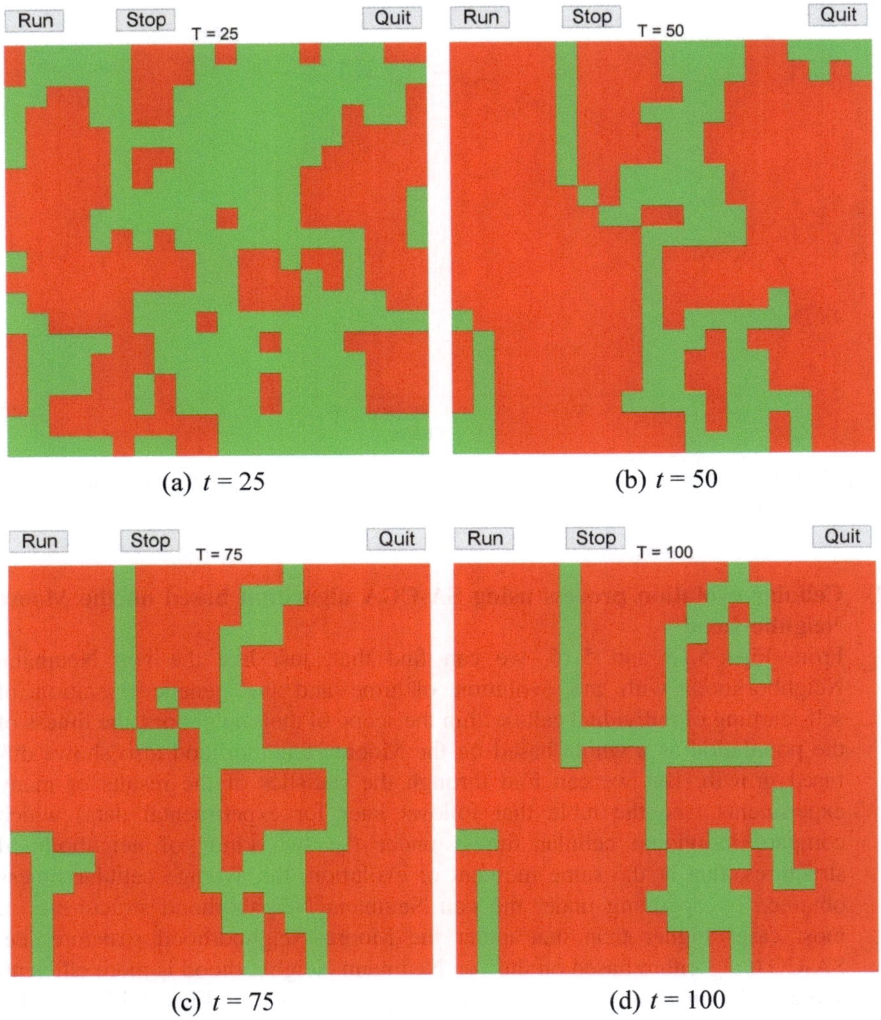

Fig. 5.15 Cellular evolution process using SA-CGA algorithm based on the Moore neighborhood (population quantity: 400) (1). Cellular evolution process using SA-CGA algorithm based on the Moore neighborhood (population quantity: 400) (2). (*Note* When the value of individual objective function is greater than or equal to 16, cells are shown as red.)

is in most cases higher than that under the Extended Moore Neighborhood structure. This indicates that SA-CGA algorithm based on the Moore Neighborhood is more efficient in two structures.

The above comparison of the cellular evolution processes based on different neighborhood structure SA-CGA algorithms demonstrates that the expansion of the neighborhood domain (the increase in the number of "learning objects"

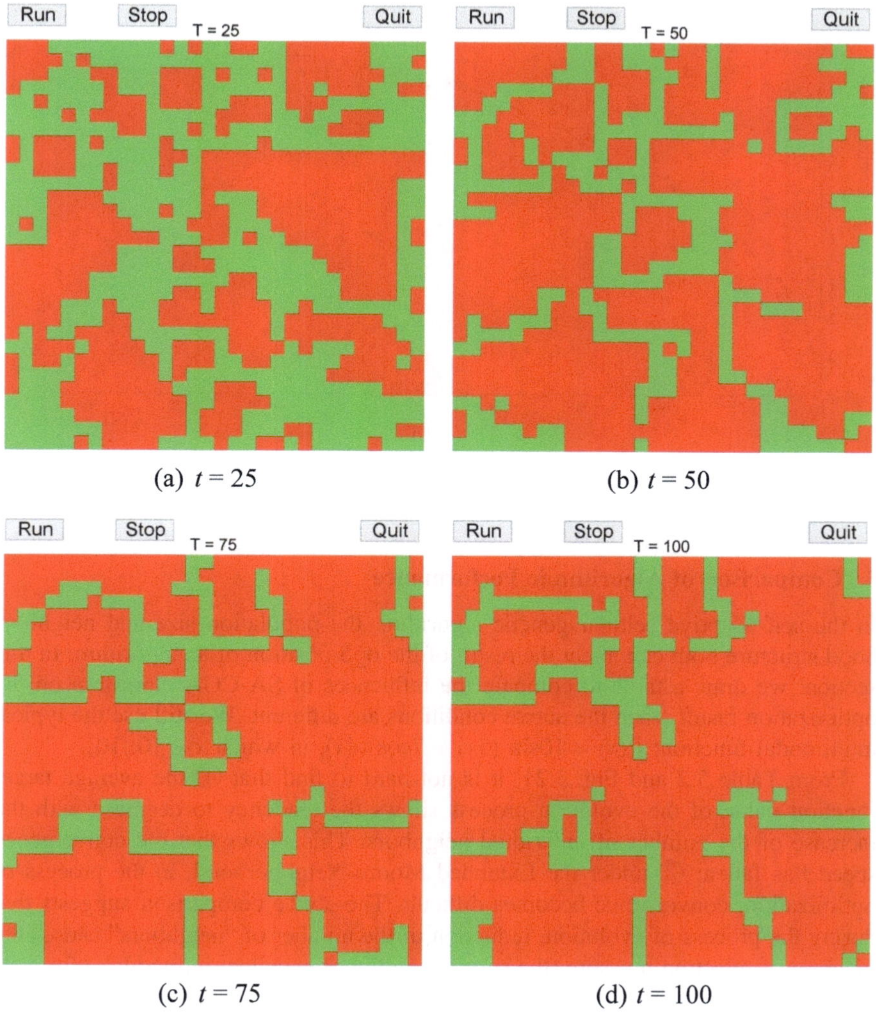

Fig. 5.16 Cellular evolution process using SA-CGA algorithm based on the Moore neighborhood (population quantity: 900). (*Note* When the value of individual objective function is greater than or equal to 16, cells are shown as red.)

which can be "referenced" by the central cell) is not beneficiary in getting a high quality solution. This point can be explained by our everyday phenomena. When we are faced with decision making, too much of referencing information often makes us hesitant, overcautious, and interferes with our judgment, thereby affects the correctness of the decision.

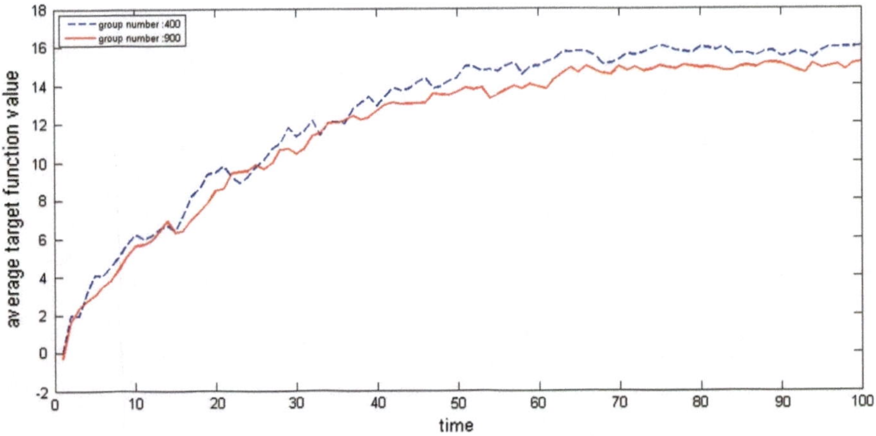

Fig. 5.17 Population average target function value variation using SA-CGA algorithm based on the Moore neighborhood

5. **Comparison of Algorithmic Performance**

In the self-adaptive cellular genetic algorithm, the population size and neighborhood structure both can affect the result of the optimization of an algorithm. In this section, we draw a table to compare the influences of SA-CGA algorithm on the optimization result when the above conditions are different .We still use the typical multimodal function: $f(x) = 10\sin(5x) + 7\cos(4x)$, in which $x \in [0, 10]$.

From Table 5.2 and Fig. 5.21, it is not hard to find that ① the average target function value of the evolution process shows the tendency to decrease with the increase of the number of individual neighbors. This shows that the convergence speed has fallen; ② under the Extended Moore Neighborhood, in the process of optimization, convergence becomes difficult. The above comparison suggests that during the process of evolution, reduction of the number of "neighbors" causes the increase of selection pressure (the survival ability of excellent individuals) for cells in local roulette, and it helps to increase the speed of optimization; ③ under different neighborhood structures, increasing or reducing the quantity of the population does not produce consistent influence on the change in fitness (under the von Neumann Neighborhood structure and the Moore Neighborhood structure, increasing the quantity of the population helps to stabilize the changing process of fitness, but it is the opposite under the Extended Moore Neighborhood structure). This shows that the quantity of the population has to be determined in specific situations.

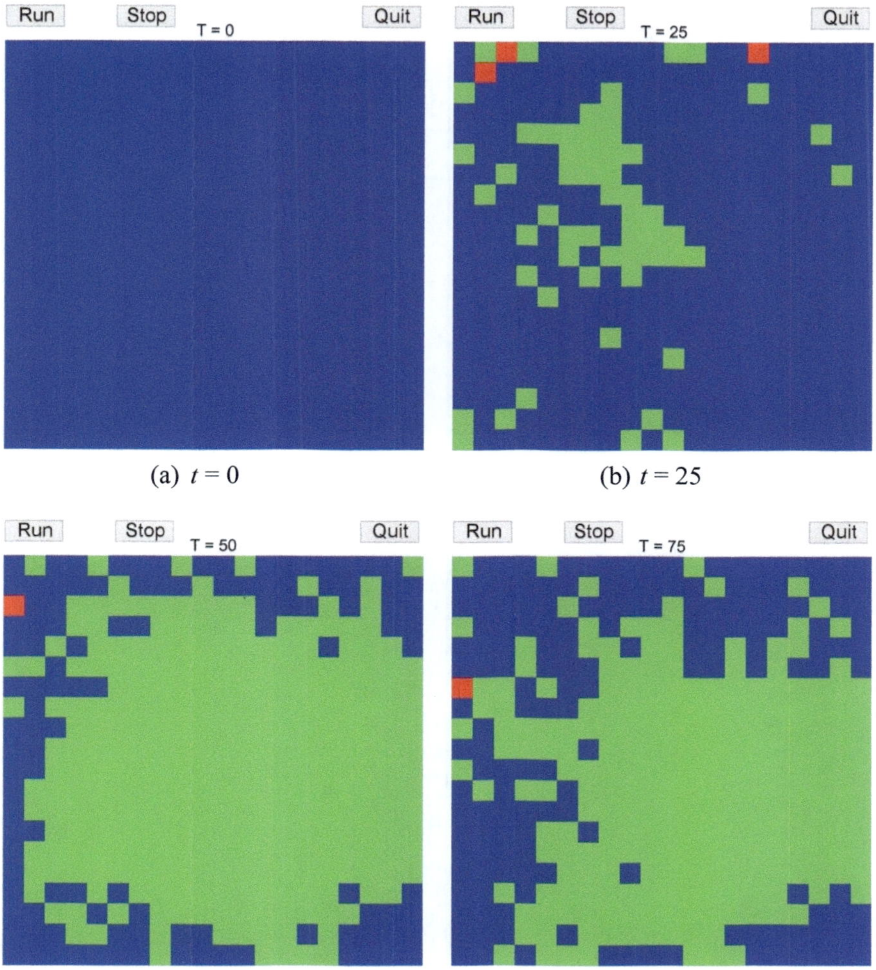

(a) $t = 0$ (b) $t = 25$

(c) $t = 50$ (d) $t = 75$

Fig. 5.18 Cellular evolution process using SA-CGA algorithm based on the Extended Moore Neighborhood (population quantity: 400). (*Note* When individual target function value is greater than or equal to 16, the cells are shown as red; when it is greater than or equal to 12 but less than 16, the cells are shown as green; when it is less than 12, the cells are shown as blue.)

5.2.3 Self-adaptive Cellular Genetic Algorithm with Evolution Rules Added (ESA-CGA)

In Sect. 5.2.1 we introduced the application of the evolution rules of cellular automata to the operational rules of genetic algorithms (the algorithm of evolution rules of genetic algorithm). Its principle is using cellular automata to simulate the

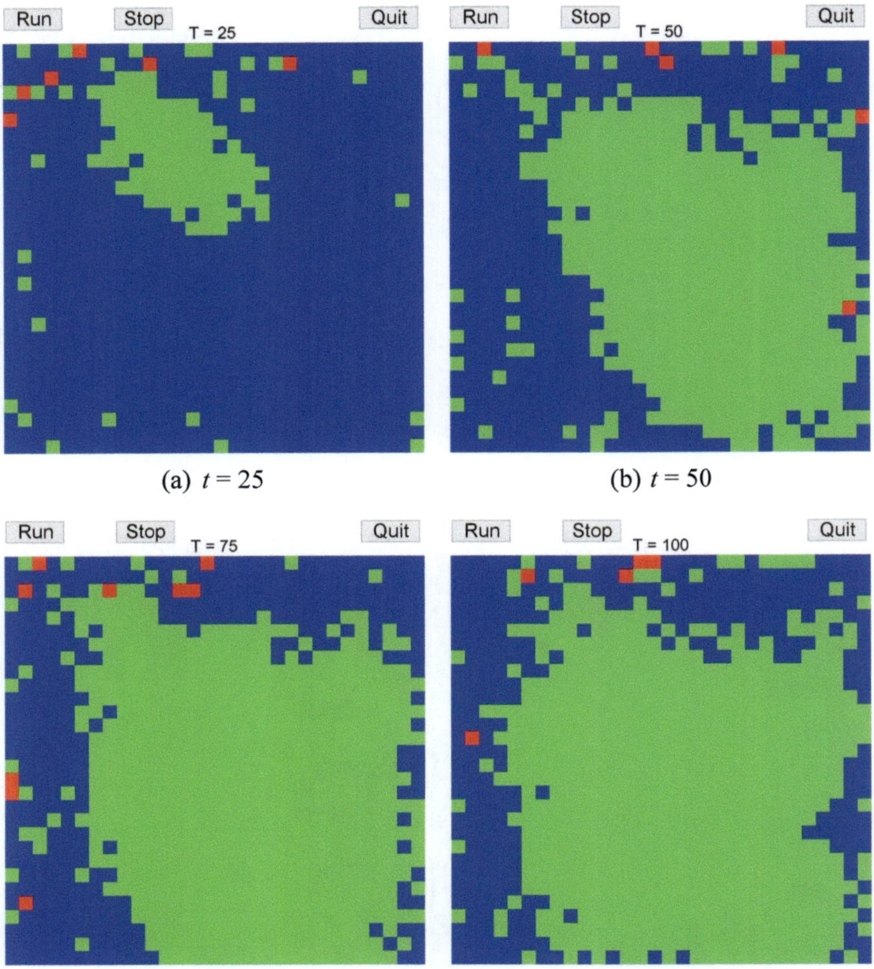

(a) $t = 25$ (b) $t = 50$

(c) $t = 75$ (d) $t = 100$

Fig. 5.19 (1) Cellular evolution process using SA-CGA algorithm based on the extended Moore neighborhood (population quantity: 900). (2) Cellular evolution process using SA-CGA algorithm based on the extended Moore neighborhood (population quantity: 900). (*Note* When individual objective function value is greater than or equal to 16, the cells are shown as red; when it is greater than or equal to 12 but less than 16, the cells are shown as green; when it is less than 12, the cells are shown as blue.)

phenomena of survival, competition, and death of natural organisms in "artificial life", and then using them to replace the crossover operator in traditional genetic algorithm. The evolution of cells is embodied in the interactions among individual genes, but ultimately E-CGA algorithm and traditional genetic algorithm are still

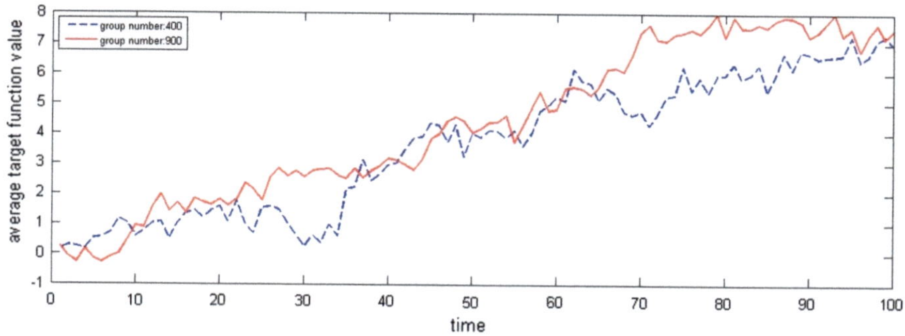

Fig. 5.20 Variation of the population's average objective function values using SA-CGA algorithm based on the extended Moore neighborhood

Table 5.2 Comparison of SA-CGA algorithm performances (independent experiments 100 times)

Neighborhood forms	Von Neumann			Moore			Extended moore		
Population quantity	100	400	900	100	400	900	100	400	900
Optimal solution	17.000	17.000	17.000	17.000	17.000	17.000	17.000	17.000	17.000
Average objective function value of the evolution process	13.248	13.242	13.050	12.342	12.103	11.867	0.549	3.738	5.315
Standard deviation of the objective function value	14.243	13.136	12.318	14.577	13.596	12.925	0.967	6.177	8.897
Difficulty of convergence	No	No	No	No	No	No	Yes	Yes	Yes

both sequential algorithms in which the use of cellular evolution rules only provides diversity for crossover operations.

But in SA-CGA algorithm, we consider a single cell as an individual with learning function, and then realize the interactions among individuals by the neighborhood structures of cellular automata, so as to complete the genetic operation. In the whole process, the cell is "alive". In real ecosystems, individual states are an ever-changing process. With the passage of time, there will be phenomena such as birth, death, etc. When we are going to study certain interactive learning behavior among individuals based on the real world, SA-CGA algorithm seems a bit too idealized. In order to simulate the survival and propagation states of individuals in nature more realistically, in this section, we introduce the evolution rules of cellular automata into self-adaptive cellular genetic algorithm (SA-CGA) to

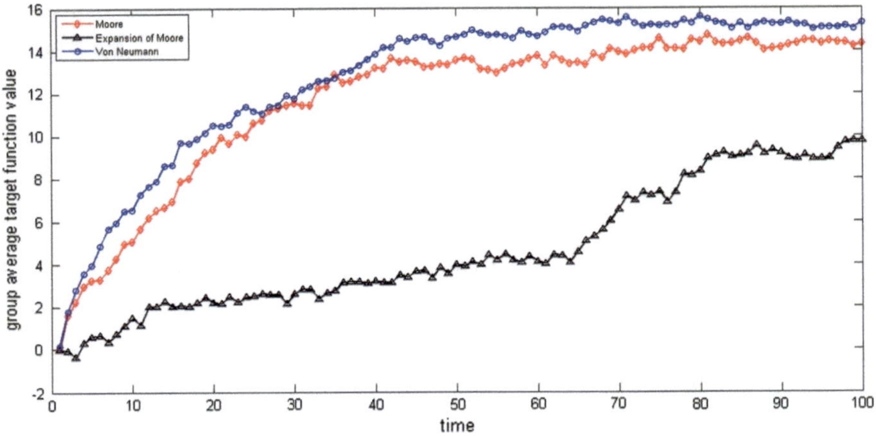

Fig. 5.21 Neighborhood structures and variations of objective function value (population: 400)

formulate self-adaptive cellular genetic algorithm with evolution rules added (ESA-CGA), which is closer to the real world.

1. **The Evolution Rules of Cells**

The individual cells are distributed in an $n \times n$ lattice, the states of the cells are live and dead, represented by "1" and "0" respectively. There are $n \times n$ randomly given individuals, with neighborhood structure the Moore type. The detailed rules to decide the cell's states of "live or dead" can be found in formulas (5.6)–(5.12) in Sect. 5.2, so we will not repeat here. The ESA-CGA algorithm in this section applies the aforementioned evolution rules to the individuals in a population, while in Sect. 5.2, the aforementioned evolution rules are applied to the crossover operator of genetic algorithm.

2. **The Computational Procedure of ESA-CGA Algorithm**

(1) Initialize $n \times n$ individuals, distribute them in an $n \times n$ lattice as the initial cells; randomly determine their states of "live" or "dead".
(2) Choose a cell of "live" state as the central cell. According to the Neighborhood type, let it conduct generic operations with its adjacent neighbors [for detailed steps, see SA-CGA algorithm steps (3)–(6)].
(3) All cell states are updated at the same time according to given evolution rules, and obtain new cell states.
(4) Judging whether this has achieved the evaluation standard of the biological group (for details see Sect. 5.1.2), if not, return to step (2).

3. **Algorithmic Example and Evolutionary Process of ESA-CGA Algorithm**

This section still uses the typical multimodal functions $f(x) = 10\sin(5x) + 7\cos(4x)$ as an example, selecting two typical cellular evolution rules, applying ESA-CGA algorithm to solve the problem $\max\{f(x)\}$ with independent variable

$x \in [0, 10]$. We use decimal encoding, with crossover probability at 0.7, mutation probability at 0.01, the population quantity at 400 and end time (the number of iterations) $T = 100$.

1) **With evolution rule as the "Game of Life"**
   From Fig. 5.22 we can see that the appearance and increase of red cells reflect the genetic operation of self-learning in the cellular space. But because of the limit of the rules themselves of the Game of Life, the population eventually displays widespread death of cells in a large area, thereby causing the loss of individuals in the process of evolution. However, certain outstanding individuals are still preserved.
2) **With the evolution rule as "Rule 4"**
   From Fig. 5.23, we find that, unlike the "Game of Life," Rule 4 adopts a kind of odd-even rule, making biological reproduction appear messy and yet stabilizes the number of living cells at about 80%. The guarantee of survival rate makes the number of red cells (excellent individuals) displays diffused growth through the genetic operation of self-learning.

It is not hard to find in Fig. 5.24, that after evolution rule adopts "Rule 4," the survival rate of cells increases, and the average fitness of the population also increases significantly.

In the process of simulation, we find that the evolution of the average target function value of the population sometimes displays the phenomenon of instant decrease when the change of "live or dead" is introduced into cellular states. This is because the evolution rules of a cell's states of live or dead at certain moments will "kill" "excellent" individuals, thereby causing the overall target function value return to a lower level again. From this point of view, the performance of ESA-CGA algorithm must not be as stable as the SA-CGA algorithm, or that the SA-CGA algorithm is an ideal state of ESA-CGA algorithm. However, the process of ESA-CGA algorithm is just closer to the interactions among individuals in the real world, thus it is more convenient to be used in our study of the microscopic processes of complex real world

4. **Comparison of Algorithm Performances**

We use a table (Table 5.3) in this section to compare the influence of ESA-CGA algorithm on the optimization results under different rules of evolution (with Moore Neighborhood, population quantity 900, crossover probability 0.7, the mutation probability 0.01).

It is not hard to find from Table 5.3 that: ① based on evolution rules 1–4, with the increase of the survival rate of cells, the average target function value of the evolution process shows a trend of steady increase; ② comparing with Tables 5.2 and 5.3, we can find that after adding the evolution rules which make a cell live or die, the average target function value of the evolution process markedly decreases due to the reason that outstanding individuals will "die" with the evolution rules. Although we can avoid prematurity and the phenomenon of local extremum, it still causes a certain degree of the difficulty of convergence (fitness is too low).

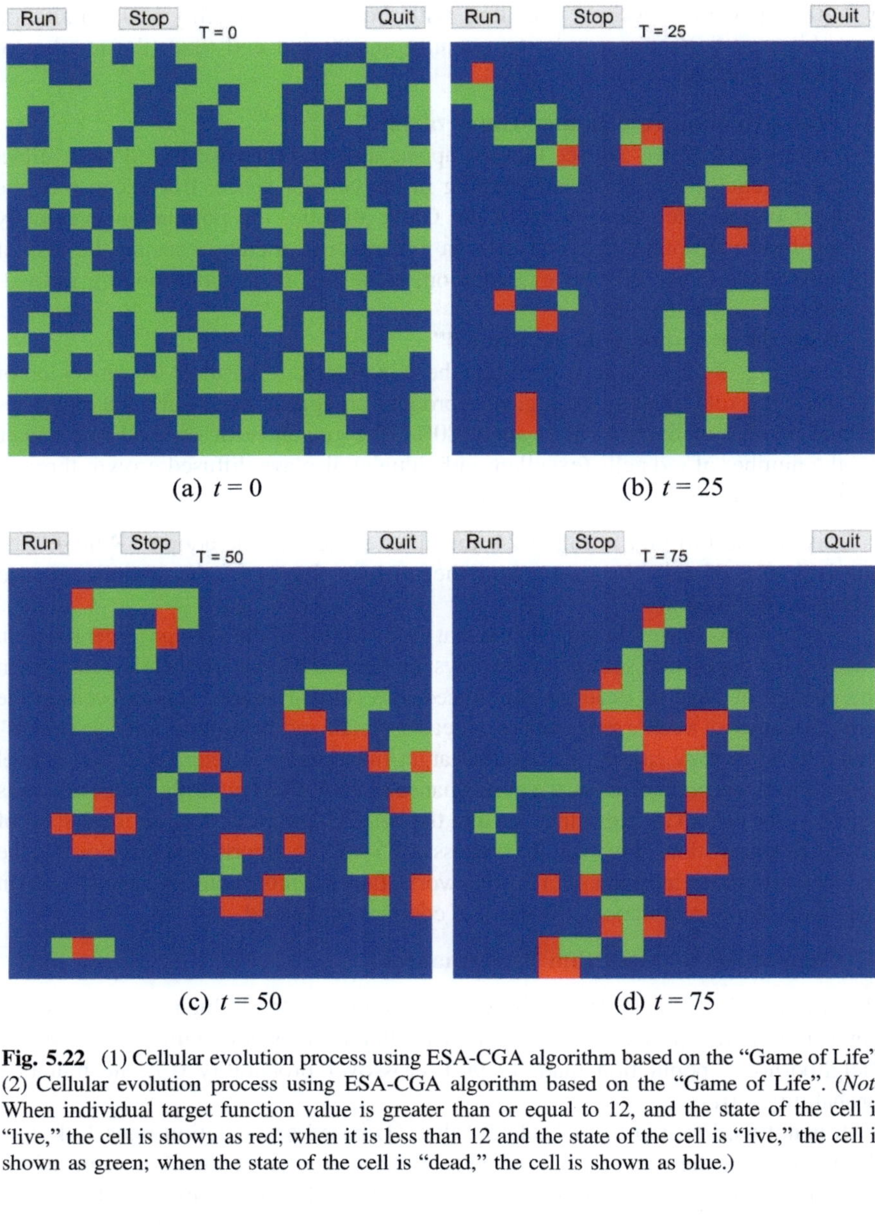

Fig. 5.22 (1) Cellular evolution process using ESA-CGA algorithm based on the "Game of Life". (2) Cellular evolution process using ESA-CGA algorithm based on the "Game of Life". (*Note* When individual target function value is greater than or equal to 12, and the state of the cell is "live," the cell is shown as red; when it is less than 12 and the state of the cell is "live," the cell is shown as green; when the state of the cell is "dead," the cell is shown as blue.)

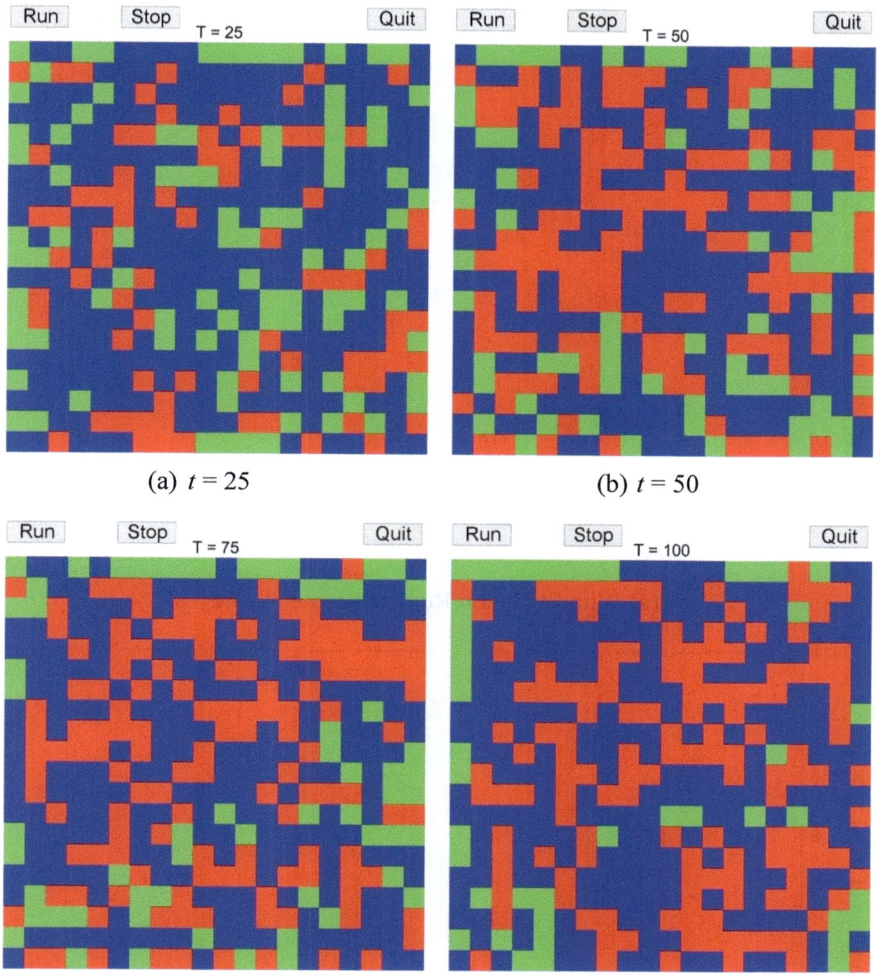

(a) $t = 25$ (b) $t = 50$

(c) $t = 75$ (d) $t = 100$

Fig. 5.23 (1) Cellular evolution process using ESA-CGA algorithm based on "Rule 4". (2) Cellular evolution process using ESA-CGA algorithm based on "Rule 4". (*Note* When individual target function value is greater than or equal to 12, and the state of the cell is "live," the cell is shown as red; when it is less than 12 and the state of the cell is "live," the cell is shown as green; when the state of the cell is "dead," the cell is shown as blue.)

5.2.4 Improvement 1: Cellular Genetic Algorithm Based on the Strategy of Elite Preservation

In the previous sections, we have introduced a few cellular genetic algorithms based on different evolution rules and neighborhood forms. We found through simulation

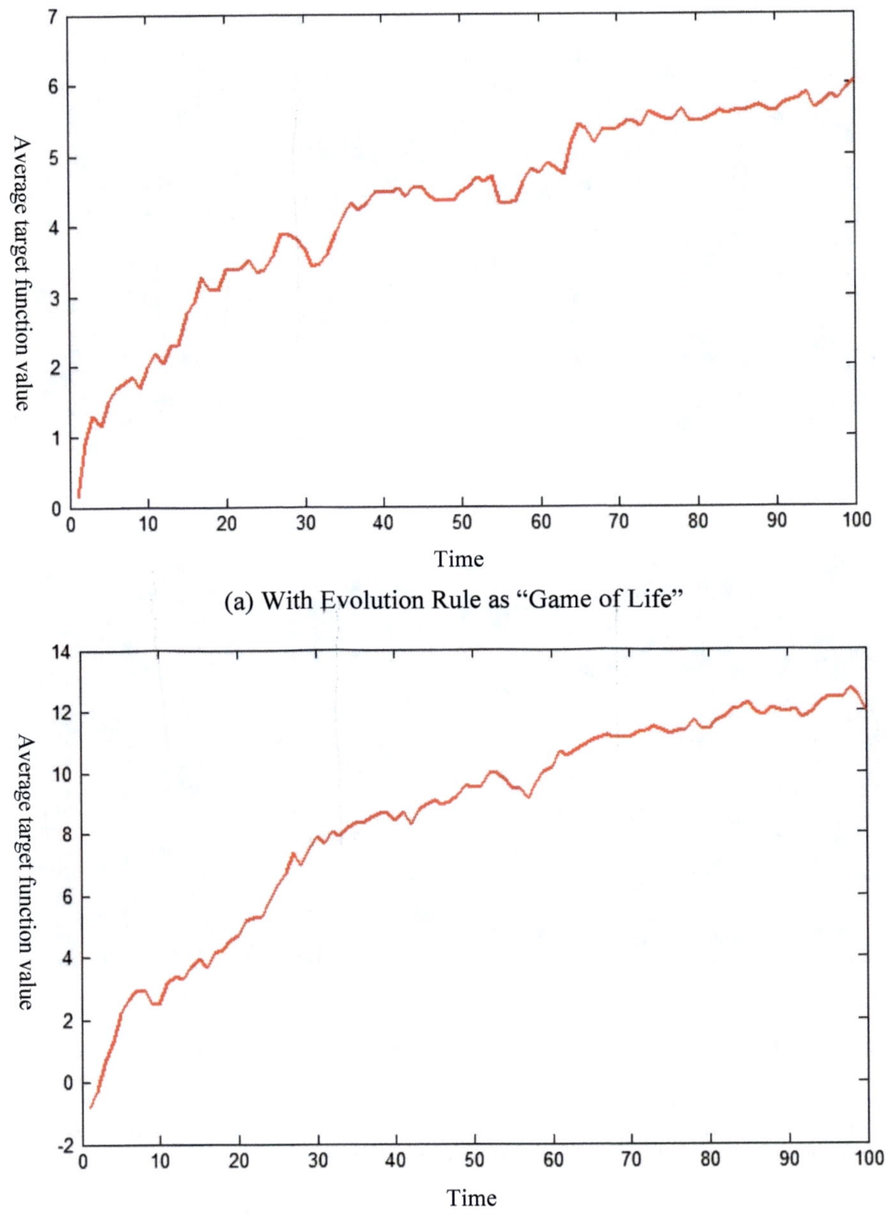

(a) With Evolution Rule as "Game of Life"

(b) With Evolution Rule as "Rule 4"

Fig. 5.24 Variations of population average target function values using ESA-CGA algorithm based on different evolution rules

Table 5.3 Comparison of ESA-CGA algorithm performances (independent experiments 100 times)

Algorithm	Optimal solution	Average objective function value of the evolution process	Number of times in local extreme value
ESA-CGA based on Rule 1	17.000	0.906	0
ESA-CGA based on Rule 2	17.000	1.730	0
ESA-CGA based on game of life	17.000	3.636	0
ESA-CGA based on Rule 3	17.000	6.504	0
ESA-CGA based on Rule 4	17.000	8.563	0

experiments that compared with traditional genetic algorithm, the introduction of cellular evolution rules makes cellular genetic algorithm effectively avoid the drawback of "local extremum." However, relative broader cellular space and limited neighborhood scope also determine that the transfer of the optimal information in the cellular space needs a certain amount of time, and this indirectly affects the convergence speed of the algorithm. Then, are there ways to solve this problem? We will introduce one method of improvement in the following context.

1. **Strategy of Elite Preservation**

It has long been proven that traditional genetic algorithm does not converge to global optimum with probability 1. In view of this, a series of improvement measures have been proposed, which improved the performance of algorithms. In the 1990s, based on the Markov chain theory, Rudolph proved that the genetic algorithm of preserved elites converged with probability 1. By "elite preservation strategy" we mean that in the selection of operators in genetic algorithm, we place the best individual in the population at the first, and preserve this individual to the next generation (the size of the population also adds one). This one does not participate in competition. It is not difficult to understand that the reason to take such an approach is to prevent the loss of outstanding individuals in each generation due to crossover and mutation operations, thus avoids falling into local extremum.

Elite preservation strategy in essence is to solve the problem of global convergence of genetic algorithm. But in using this strategy, with the addition of an individual which is closer to the optimal solution in each generation, the optimization speed of the algorithm is also accelerated. Below, we will introduce the idea of this strategy into cellular genetic algorithm, and observe the effect of calculations through the experiments of simulation.

2. **The Use of Elite Preservation Strategy in Cellular Genetic Algorithm**

In cellular genetic algorithm, a series of genetic operations such as selection, crossover and mutation are restricted to the neighborhood cells around individuals, which makes the propagation speed of the information of outstanding individuals in the population relatively slow. The formation of the global optimal solution is achieved through the mutual learning and constant renewal among the local optimal solutions. If in each generation of genetic operations, individual learning and evolution can go beyond the limit of the neighborhood, and can get the influence of the contemporary global optimal solution, then the time of optimization will be shortened. Below, we design a new crossover method to realize this influence when we introduce the elite preservation strategy into the cellular genetic algorithm. The steps of the algorithm will be shown below.

(1) Initializing the population (see Sect. 5.2.2 for details).
(2) Encoding (see Sect. 5.2.2 for details).
(3) Calculating fitness. Unlike previous cellular genetic algorithm, here, apart from calculating the fitness of every individual in the cellular space eval ($V_{i,j}$), we also need to record the maximum fitness of the population max{eval ($V_{i,j}$)} (i, j = 1, 2, …, n) and the corresponding individual $V^*_{i,j}$ by comparison.
(4) Selecting operation. For the specific operation, see the calculation steps in Sect. 5.2.2. Assuming that the individual $V_{i,j}$ selects neighbor $V_{a,b}$ ($a \in [i-1, i+1]$; $b \in [j-1, j+1]$).
(5) Crossover operation. Unlike previous cellular genetic algorithm, here, in addition to learning from outstanding individuals among their neighbors, individual cells are also under the influence of contemporary global optimal value. We define crossover probability as P_c, and have the new crossover method designed as

$$x'_{i,j} = (1 - p_c)x_{i,j} + p_c(1 - p_c)x_{a,b} + p_c^2 x^* \tag{5.16}$$

In it, x^* represents the chromosome of the individual corresponding to the maximum fitness of the contemporary population max{eval ($V_{i,j}$)} (i, j = 1, 2, …, n).
(6) Mutation operation (see Sect. 5.2.2).
(7) Judging whether the result meets the evaluation standard of the biological group, if not, return to step (3).

By now we can see that in the crossover operation of step (5), individual cell $V_{i,j}$ is influenced by both the surrounding excellent neighbors, and the best individuals in the contemporary population.

3. **Algorithmic Example of Cellular Genetic Algorithm Based on the Elite Preservation Strategy and Its Evolutionary Process**

This section still uses the multimodal function $f(x) = 10 \sin(5x) + 7 \cos(4x)$ to find the solution for max $f(x)$, with SA-CGA cellular genetic algorithm without elite preservation strategy as a contrast. Neighborhood form of Moore type is used, with population quantity of 225, independent variable $x \in [0, 20]$, decimal encoding, crossover probability of 0.5, mutation probability of 0.01, and the end time (the number of iterations) $T = 100$.

The processes of population average target function value change with the two algorithms are shown in Fig. 5.25.

We can see from Fig. 5.25 that in cellular genetic algorithm, the use of elite preservation strategy effectively improves the convergence speed of the average target function value of the population, and at the same time avoids falling into local extremum.

4. **Comparison of the performances of the two algorithms (see Table** 5.4)

It is not hard to find out from Table 5.4 that the use of cellular genetic algorithm with elite preservation strategy for the optimization of this multimodal function accelerates the global convergence speed on the basis of cellular genetic algorithm, thereby improves the overall efficiency of the algorithm.

5.2.5 Improvement 2: The Introduction of Cellular Genetic Algorithm with Self-adaptive Crossover Operator

We can see from formula (5.16) in the previous section that, after introducing the elite preservation strategy, the disturbance from contemporary global optimal individuals has been added to the crossover update of individual cells, and individuals' speed of evolution towards the direction of more excellence has accelerated. But from the perspective of crossover probability, this way of studying by crossing over is not completely self-adaptive, which is shown in the following aspects: ① All individuals use the same crossover probability P_c, and P_c is a constant value; ② The same crossover probability is adopted despite the different "degrees of excellence" of the surrounding "excellent" neighbors. Although this crossover method significantly improves the convergence speed, it will no doubt affect the diversity of the population when more complex problems arise, thus leaves the potential trouble of the prematurity of the algorithm.

1. **Self-Adaptive Crossover Operator**

In daily life, we all have had such experiences in learning from others: when the people we learn from are much better than ourselves, we tend to learn from them with great enthusiasm. When they are only a little better than us or even are the same as us, our study enthusiasm tends to recede, and sometimes we will even become "unconvinced." We introduce this phenomenon of daily life into the crossover operator in cellular genetic algorithm, and make the following improvement to step (5) as aforementioned:

$$x'_{i,j} = \left(1 - p_{c,i,j}\right)x_{i,j} + p_{c,i,j}x_{a,b} \tag{5.17}$$

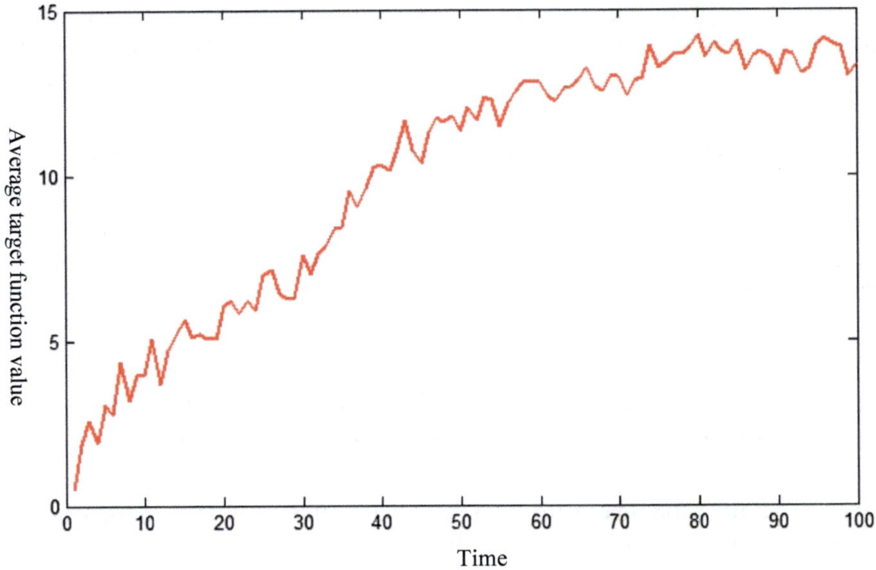

(a) SA-CGA algorithm

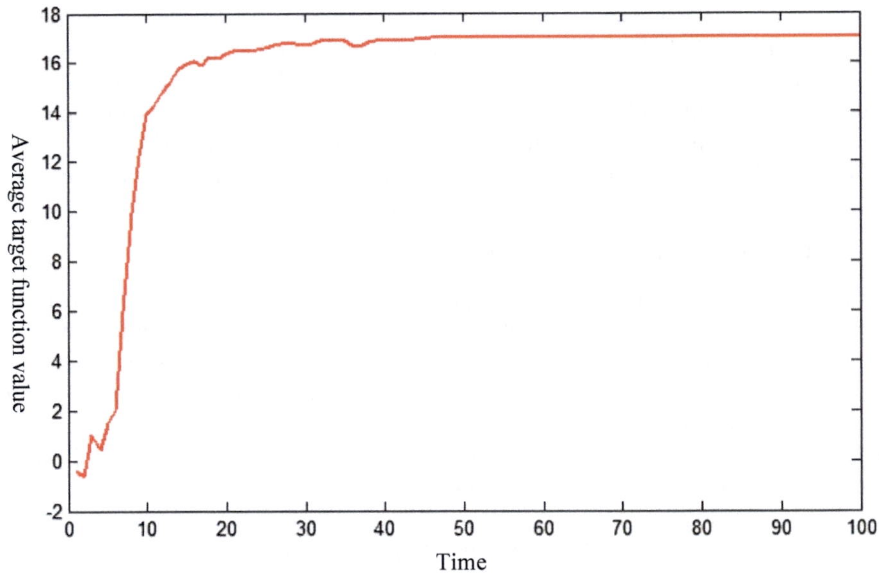

(b) cellular genetic algorithm with elite-preservation

Fig. 5.25 Changes of the target objective function value of the population

Table 5.4 Comparison of the algorithm performances (independent experiments 100 times)

Algorithm	Optimal solution	Average objective function value	Times falling into local extremum	Steps needed for objective function value > 5
SA-CGA	17.000	10.875	0	>100
Cellular genetic algorithm with elite preservation	17.000	15.600	0	<20

$$p_{c,i,j} = \begin{cases} p_c + (1 - p_c)K_1 \tanh\left\{\frac{eval\left(V^*_{a,b}\right) - eval\left(V^*_{i,j}\right)\cdot p_c}{K_2\left[eval\left(V^*_{i,j}\right) - eval\left(V^*_{a,b}\right)\right]}\right\}, \left(eval\left(V^*_{i,j}\right) \neq eval\left(V^*_{a,b}\right)\right) \\ p_c, \left(eval\left(V^*_{i,j}\right) = eval\left(V^*_{a,b}\right)\right) \end{cases} \tag{5.18}$$

In it, $P_{c,i,\ j}$ is the crossover probability of individual $V_{i,j}$ in the cellular space, that is, the intensity of its learning from its neighbors; P_c is the crossover probability of the entire population;

$V^*_{a,b}$ ($a \in [i - 1, i + 1]$; $b \in [j - 1, j + 1]$) is the optimal individual among the neighbors of individual $V_{i,j;}$ $V^*_{i,j}$ is the optimal individual in the cellular space (the population); eval ($V^*_{i,j}$) is the contemporary maximum fitness of the population; eval ($V^*_{i,j}$) = max{eval ($V_{i,j}$)}; K_1 and K_2 are adjustment coefficients.

We see that eval ($V^*_{i,j}$)·P_c in (5.18) actually provides a threshold value for the crossover process.

When the gap between adjacent excellent neighbor $V^*_{a,b}$ of an individual and the overall optimal individual $V^*_{i,j}$ is wide, the crossover probability (learning intensity) $P_{c,i,j}$ is relatively low; and vice versa. Such a design is based on the consideration of the relationship between local optimum and global optimum in the evolutionary process.

2. **Algorithmic Example and Evolution Process**

Here we test the performance of the self-adaptive crossover operator with three test functions, and use SA-CGA cellular genetic algorithm (fixed crossover operator) as a reference. The neighborhood form is the Moore type, with the population (cells) quantity at 729, decimal coding, the crossover probability at 0.7, the mutation probability of 0.01, $K_1 = 0.9$, $K_2 = 2$, end time (number of iterations) $t = 100$ and with the goal of the solution as max{$f(x_1,x_2)$}. The three test functions take the following forms.

Function No. 1: $f(x_1, x_2) = x_1 \sin(4\pi x_1) - x_2 \sin(4\pi x_2 + \pi + 1)$, $x_1, x_2 \in [0, 1.8]$

Function No. 2: $f(x_1, x_2) = 0.5 - \frac{\sin^2\sqrt{x_1^2 + x_2^2} - 0.5}{\left[1 + 0.001\left(x_1^2 + x_2^2\right)\right]^2}$, $x_1, x_2 \in [-5, 5]$

Function No. 3: $f(x_1, x_2) = x_1 \sin(2x_1 + 5) - x_2 \sin(2x_2 + 10)$, $x_1, x_2 \in [-5, 5]$

In addition, we define individual fitness eval ($V_{i,j}$) = f ($V_{i,j}$) − $f_{\min}$, in which $f_{\min} = \min\{f(V_{i,j})\}$, $(i, j = 1, 2, \ldots, n)$.

The evolution of the average solution within the cellular space is shown in Figs. 5.26 and 5.27.

3. **Comparison of the Performances of the Algorithms (see Table 5.5)**

From Fig. 5.26 and Table 5.5, it is not difficult to find out that compared with fixed crossover probability p_c, the convergence speed and quality of solution for cellular genetic algorithm have been significantly improved after introducing self-adaptive crossover operator $P_{c,i,j}$. But, in the experiment of Function No. 2, local extremum appears relatively frequently in the cellular genetic algorithm with the introduction

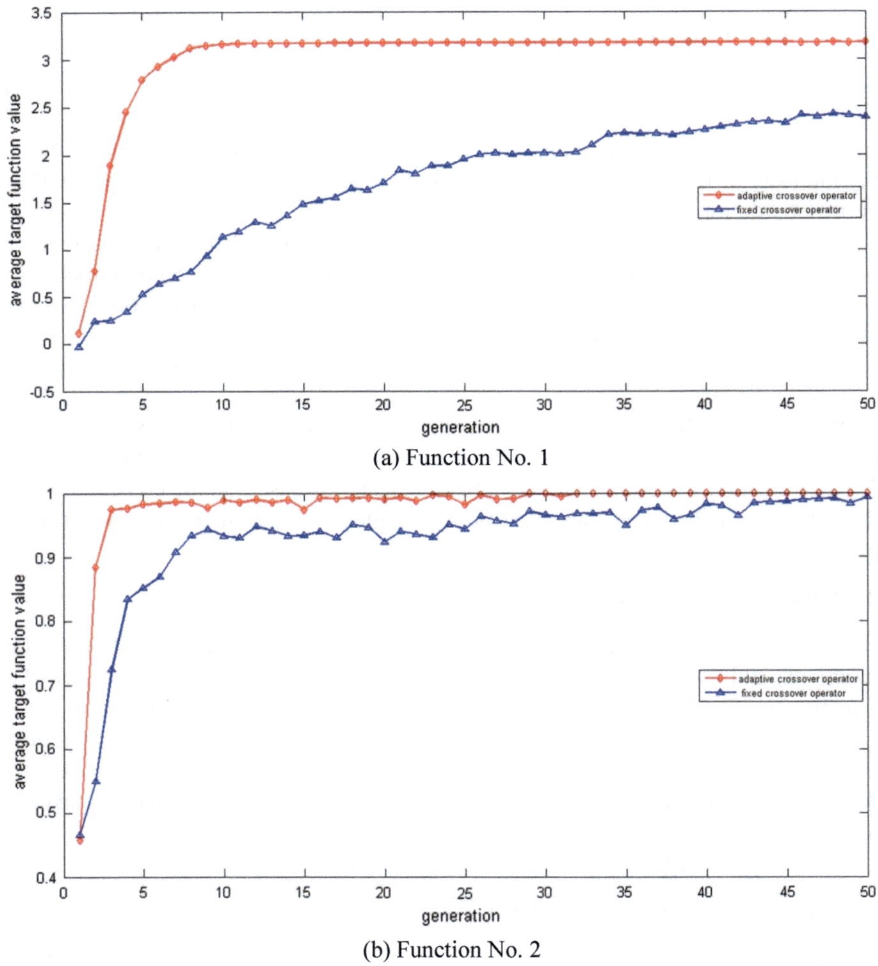

Fig. 5.26 Variations of average objective function values of the population (1), variations of average objective function values of the population (2)

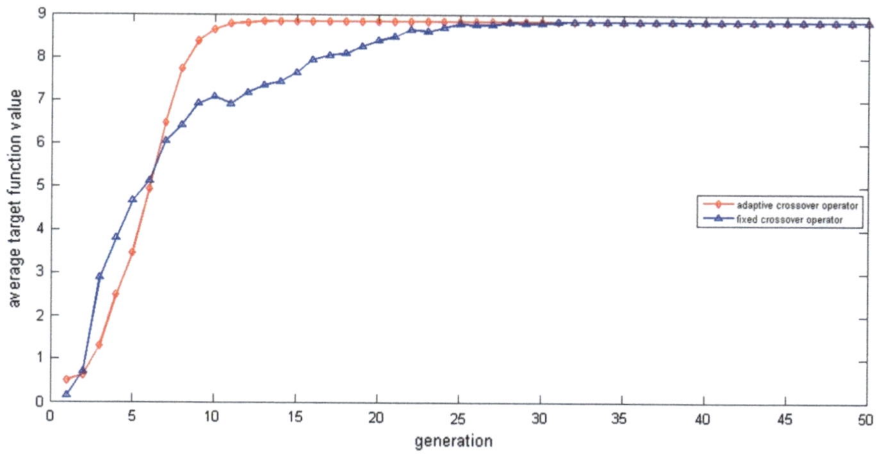

(c) Function No. 3

Fig. 5.26 (continued)

of the self-adaptive crossover operator while it significantly improves the convergence speed. Then, is there a better way to coordinate the relationship between convergence speed and the accuracy of the solution?

5.2.6 *Improvement 3: Three-Dimensional Cellular Genetic Algorithm*

In most evolutionary calculation, a common problem is how to balance the relationship between convergence speed and population diversity. They are a unity of opposites, especially for some complex optimization problems, improving convergence speed often means falling into a premature increase of probability; while expanding population diversity often means reducing calculation efficiency. In the search for the balance point between "efficiency" and "effect", plenty of scholars have conducted considerably in-depth research.

From these studies, we can sum up the following two points: first, convergence speed is often related to the searching capacity of the cell itself, and precise searching and positioning can greatly reduce the time of convergence. Second, the maintenance of healthy population diversity is often associated with the selection of the crossover operator. The richer the ways of selection and crossover, the better population diversity is maintained. In this section, we will improve the cellular genetic algorithm in two aspects at the same time.

Fig. 5.27 Test functions (1), Test functions (2)

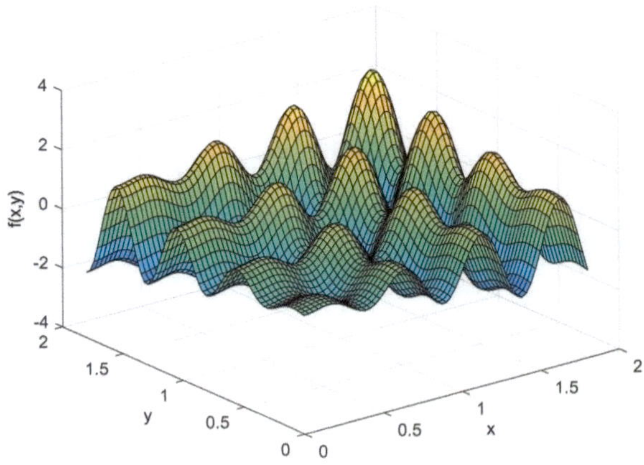

(a) Function No. 1

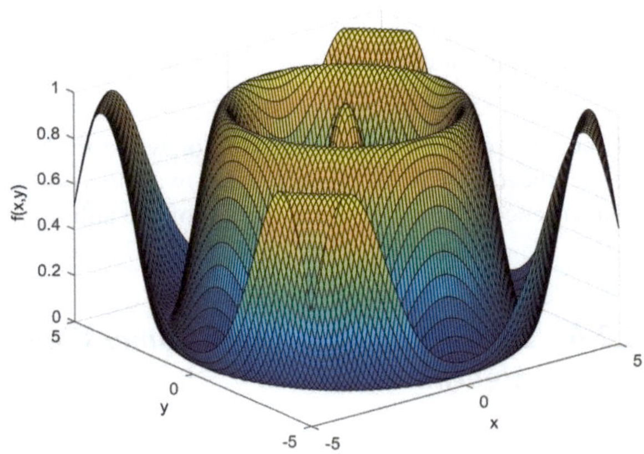

(b) Function No. 2

1. **Spatial Expansion and Neighborhood Form**

In the previous chapters, both the implementation and evolution of cellular genetic algorithm are carried out in a two-dimensional cellular space. Relative to the plane searching of two-dimensional cellular space, stereoscopic searching in a three-dimensional cellular space (see Fig. 5.28) can improve the "exploration" capabilities of the cells. This point has been explained by Asmaa Al-Naqi and others in their research (Al-Naqi et al. 2013).

In addition, neighborhood structure determines the search range of the central cell. Here, we adopt the structure of six neighbors, i.e. take the six cells which are closest to the central cell as the neighbors of the central cell, as shown in Fig. 5.29.

Fig. 5.27 (continued)

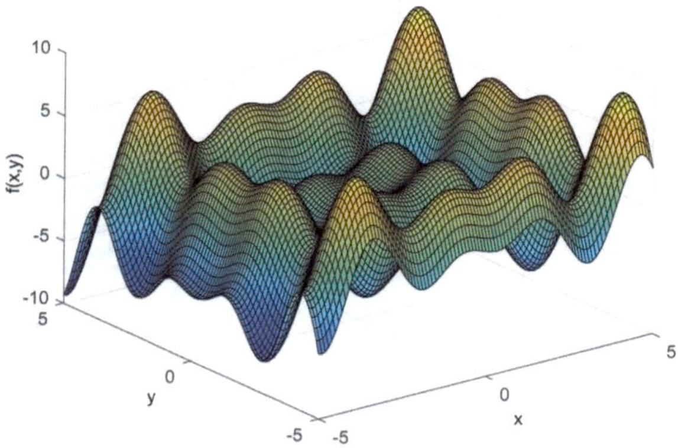

(c) Function No. 3

Table 5.5 Comparison of the algorithms performances (independent experiments 100 times)

Function	Function No. 1		Function No. 2		Function No. 3	
Crossover operator	Fixed	Self-adaptive	Fixed	Self-adaptive	Fixed	Self-adaptive
Optimal solution	3.17	3.17	1.00	1.00	8.83	8.83
Average target function value in evolution process	2.68	3.0	0.93	0.98	7.74	8.39
Times falling into local extremum	0	0	5	12	0	0
Steps needed for global convergence	21	14	>50	33	30	16

2. **Design of Selection Operator**

In the previous context, we introduced the selection operators, in the local roulette of cellular genetic algorithm within a two-dimensional space. The function of the selection operator is only to perform roulette operation on cells among the surrounding neighbors with fitness greater than the central cell itself. In the two-dimensional space with limited speed of information transmission, such selection method will undoubtedly accelerate the convergence of the algorithm.

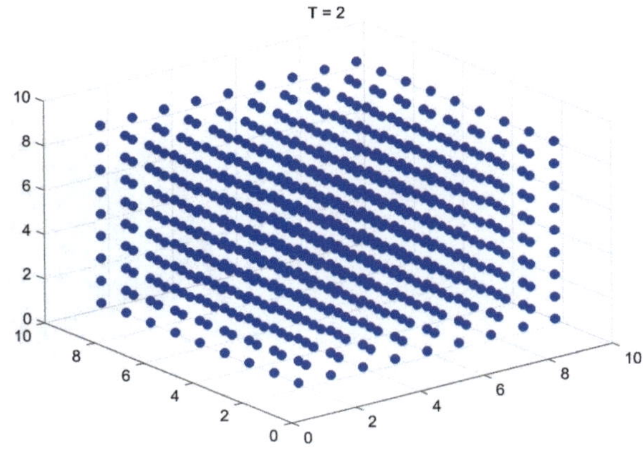

Fig. 5.28 Three-dimensional cellular space

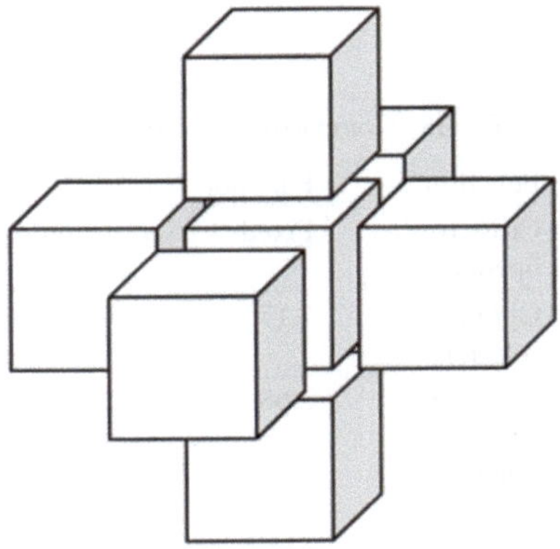

Fig. 5.29 Neighborhood structure

However, there is still room for improvement in maintaining population diversity. In order to prevent the loss of potentially outstanding individuals, in three-dimensional cellular space, we may as well make such a design: the central cell selects neighbor cells by the way of "local roulette" with a probability of p_s (including itself, for full involvement, no matter how much the fitness is). With probability $1 - ps$, it directly selects the individual with the greatest fitness among the surrounding neighbors (including itself), as shown in Fig. 5.30.

3. **A Brief Description of Algorithmic Steps**

(1) Initializing the population. In a $n \times n \times n$ three-dimensional space, $n \times n \times n$ individual cells are evenly distributed (Fig. 5.27). Each individual is expressed as $V_{i,j,k}$ $(i, j, k = 1, 2, \ldots, n)$, each individual has m chromosomes, expressed as $x_{i,j,k}^{l}$ $(l = 1, 2, \ldots, m)$.

(2) Calculating Fitness. According to the problem to be solved, calculate the fitness of each individual eval $(V_{i,j,k})$.

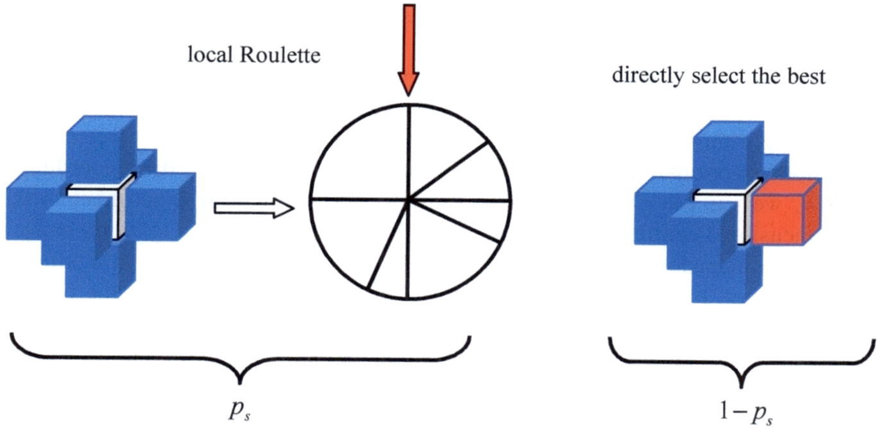

Fig. 5.30 Operator selection

(3) Selection. Aiming at the six neighbors ($V_{i-1,j,k}$, $V_{i+1,j,k}$, $V_{i,j-1,k}$, $V_{i,j+1,k}$, $V_{i,j,k-1}$, $V_{i,j,k+1}$) and its own fitness, individual $V_{i,j,k}$ performs "roulette" selection operation with probability p_s on the seven individuals including itself; and it directly selects the best individual among its neighbors and itself with probability $1 - p_s$. The selected individual is expressed as $V_{a,b,c}$.

(4) Crossing Over. Set the crossover probability as p_c, then individual $V_{i,j,k}$ updates its chromosomes in the following way

$$x'^{l}_{i,j,k} = (1 - p_c)x^{l}_{i,j,k} + p_c x^{l}_{a,b,c} \tag{5.19}$$

(5) Mutation. Set the mutation probability as p_m, and for each individual $V_{i,j,k}$ in the cellular space, select random number r from [0, 1]. If $r < p_m$, then the individual's chromosomes are updated as below

$$x''^{l}_{i,j,k} = x'^{l}_{i,j,k} + \delta_\varepsilon \varepsilon \tag{5.20}$$

In it, δ_ε is a constant; $\varepsilon \sim N(0, 1)$.

(6) Judging whether the result has met the evaluation standard of the biological group, if not, return to step (2).

4. **The Study of Selection Pressure**

Selection pressure means the survival ability of an existing individual in a population. Higher selection pressure can ensure the survival rate of excellent individuals to a certain extent, and speed up the convergence rate. Lower selection pressure is beneficial for ensuring the diversity of the population, but it may also cause the algorithm being unable to converge (Chen et al. 2011; Morales-Reyes and Erdgan 2012; Zhang et al. 2009a, b).

Enrique Alba once proposed two methods to study selection pressure: studying takeover time and growth curves. Takeover time refers to the time it takes for the most outstanding individual to reproduce and spread in the population until they eventually fill the entire population. Growth curves refer to the graphs of curves with the algorithm based algebra as the horizontal coordinate, and the percentage of contemporary optimal individuals in the entire population as the vertical coordinate.

Now, we use the growth curves method to design such an experiment in the two-dimensional cellular space (27 × 27 = 729, Moore type, 8 neighbors) as well as in three-dimensional cellular space (9 × 9×9 = 729, 6 neighbors): assigning an initial value of 1 or 2 (in equal proportions) to all the individuals in the cellular space, and then assign an individual of random location with value 3, thus there is an excellent individual existing in the entire population. Next, observing the state of diffusion of the excellent individual in cellular genetic algorithm (with "selection" operation only, no "crossover" and "mutation" operations). The experimental results are shown in Fig. 5.31.

In Fig. 5.31a, cells in both two-dimensional and three-dimensional cellular space all directly select the most outstanding individuals among their neighbors. This shows that in a situation where there are fewer neighbors, relative to the two-dimensional cellular space, the "exploration" ability of the cells in the three-dimensional cellular space is stronger, and the diffusion of information of excellent individuals is more rapid, so the selection pressure is greater. This confirms the research of Asmaa Al-Naqi et al. In Fig. 5.31b, regarding the three-dimensional cellular space, with the continuous increase of the value of p_s, population diversity is improved, and the convergence speed obviously decreases.

5. **Algorithmic Example and the Evolutionary Process**

We use the following test function

$$f(x_1, x_2) = 0.5 - \frac{\sin^2\sqrt{x_1^2 + x_2^2} - 0.5}{\left[1 + 0.001\left(x_1^2 + x_2^2\right)\right]^2}, \quad x_1, x_2 \in [-5, 5]$$

as an example to test the three-dimensional cellular genetic algorithm in this section. This function gets its maximum value at point (0, 0) (maximum value is 1), however, a circular "ridge" forms around this maximum value point, and in finding solutions, it is easy for the maximum value point to fall on this ring of "ridge" (local extremum: 0.9903). Since the gap between local extremum and global maximum is very small, we use this rather intriguing but typical function as a test function, as shown in Fig. 5.32.

Set p_s = 0.5 (indicating the probability used in using the "roulette" method for selection), crossover probability p_c = 0.7; mutation probability p_m = 0.01; population quantity as 729 (9 × 9 × 9); the evolution results of the three-dimensional cellular automaton are shown in Fig. 5.33.

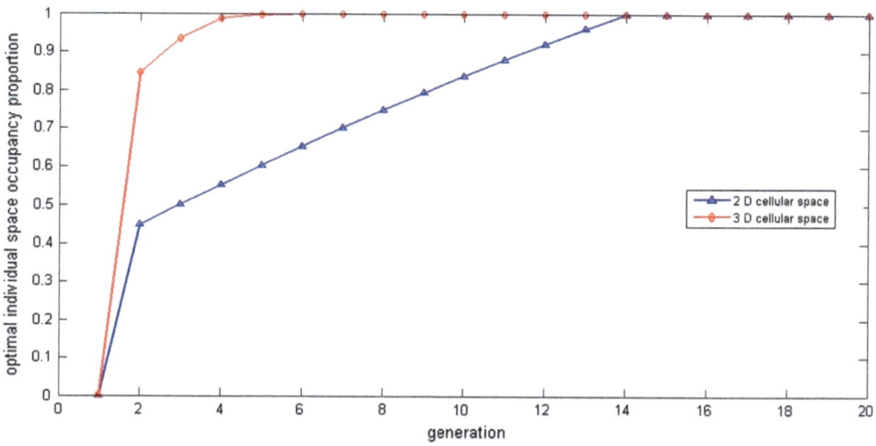

(a) State of Diffusion in Two-Dimensional Cellular Space

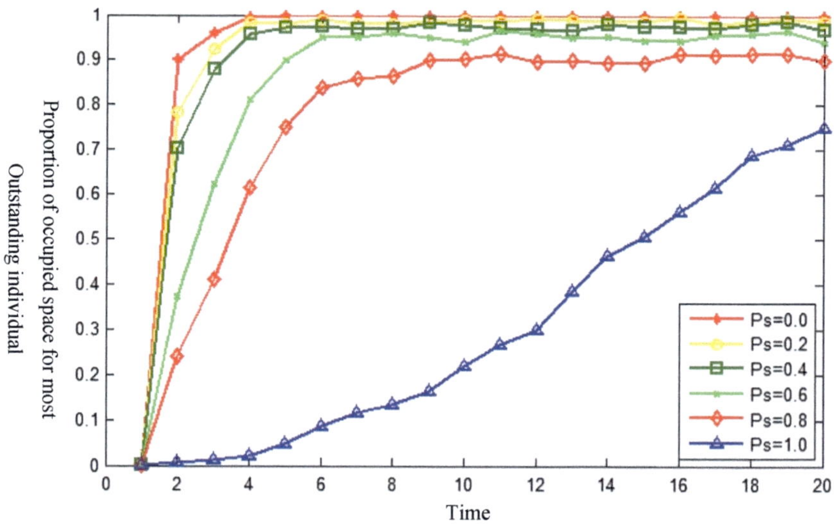

(b) State of Diffusion in Three-Dimensional Cellular Space

Fig. 5.31 Comparison of diffusion states in two-dimensional and three-dimensional cellular space

In Fig. 5.33, the red cells represent cells with individual solution function values greater than 0.9903 (i.e. cells escaping local extremum). In 100 independent experiments, the success rate of seeking convergence (escaping local extremum and converging to maximum value 1) exceeds 90%.

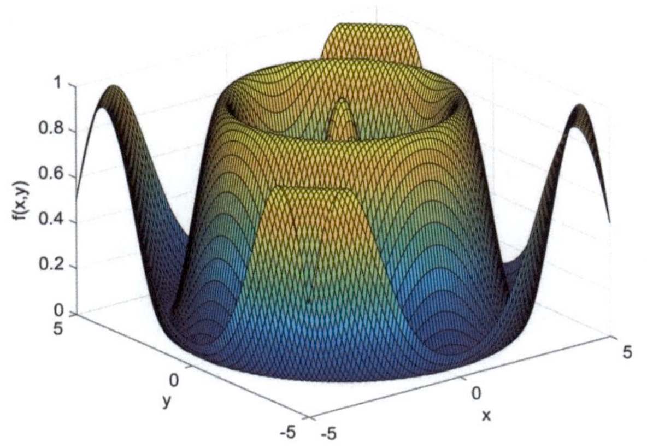

Fig. 5.32 Test function

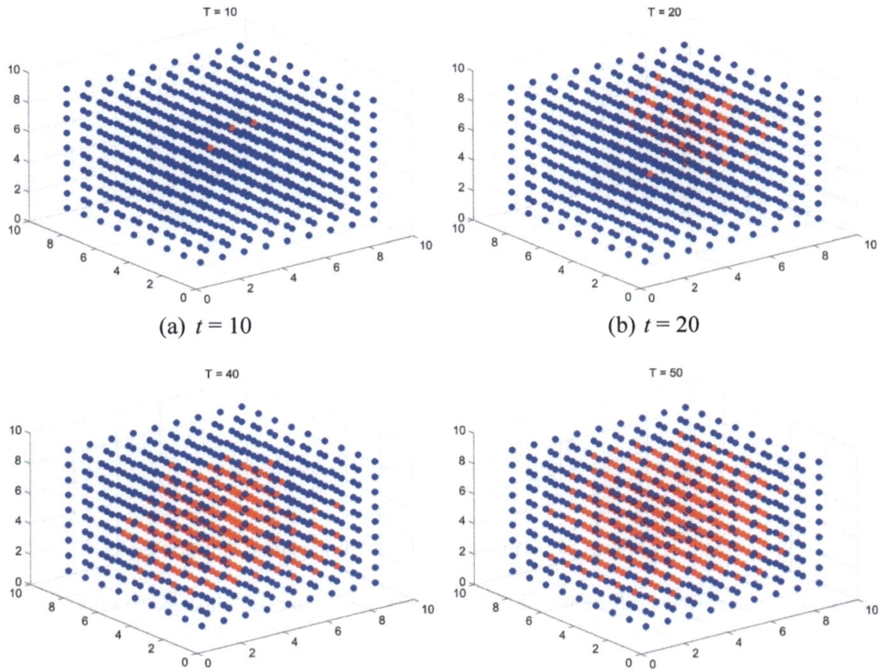

(a) $t = 10$ (b) $t = 20$

(c) $t = 40$ (d) $t = 50$

Fig. 5.33 Evolutionary process

Table 5.6 Comparison of algorithmic performances (independent experiments 100 times)

Algorithm	Optimal solution	Average target function value in evolution process	Times falling into local extremum	Steps needed for global convergence
SA-CGA	1	0.93	5	50
SA-CGA (self-adaptive crossover operator)	1	0.98	12	33
Three-dimensional cellular genetic algorithm	1	0.85	3	27

6. **Comparison of Algorithmic Performances**

We use the following function as an example:

$$f(x_1, x_2) = 0.5 - \frac{\sin^2 \sqrt{x_1^2 + x_2^2} - 0.5}{\left[1 + 0.001\left(x_1^2 + x_2^2\right)\right]^2}, \quad x_1, x_2 \in [-5, 5]$$

Set $p_s = 0.5$; crossover probability $p_c = 0.7$; mutation probability $p_m = 0.01$; population quantity as 729; evolution steps as 100. Comparing the performances of the three-dimensional cellular genetic algorithm outlined above and the two-dimensional cellular genetic algorithm as aforementioned, and we get the results as shown in Table 5.6.

Therefore, compared with two-dimensional cellular genetic algorithm, the three dimensional cellular genetic algorithm proposed in this section has good convergence effect on complex multimodal problems, and at the same time effectively avoids the premature phenomenon.

5.2.7 *Summary*

In this section, we have introduced six ways of combining genetic algorithms with cellular automata. They are: (1) cellular evolution rule algorithm based on genetic algorithm (E-CGA); (2) self-adaptive cellular genetic algorithm (SA-CGA); (3) self-adaptive cellular genetic algorithm with evolution rules and three improved algorithms; (4) cellular genetic algorithm based on elite preservation strategy; (5) cellular genetic algorithm with self-adaptive crossover degree; (6) three-dimensional cellular genetic algorithm based on improved selection operator.

Through comparative study, we discovered that compared with traditional genetic algorithm, the six algorithms that combining genetic algorithms with cellular automata all pretty well avoid the situation in which the optimal solution falls into local extremum. In particular, algorithms (2) and (3) explore neighborhood forms, population quantity, and the influence of the evolution rules on cellular genetic algorithm, and find out that the fewer the number of neighbors, the greater the population survival rate is, and the better the effect of getting the solution see. In algorithms (4), (5), (6), we discussed the dialectical relationship between convergence speed and solution quality, in which algorithms (4) and (5) accelerate the convergence speed of the population towards the optimal solution, while algorithm (6) achieves good coordination in dealing with the relationship between local extremum and the convergence speed.

5.3 The Application of Self-adaptive Cellular Genetic Algorithm in a Dynamic Environment

In the previous chapters, we have introduced several kinds of applications of cellular automata in genetic algorithm, but they are all explained with static functions as examples. In this section, we apply the most representative self-adaptive cellular genetic algorithm (SA-CGA) to an actual example of analyzing stock price behavior, and introduce to the readers the application effect of self-adaptive cellular genetic algorithm (SA-CGA) in a dynamic environment (Wan et al. 2010).

5.3.1 Decision-Making Problems in Securities Investment

In real life, if we have personally invested in the stock market, or have paid attention to it, we often found that the stock market produces certain disorder phenomena, such as abnormal fluctuations, herd behavior, price volatility, etc. These phenomena often cannot be explained by the classic "effective market theory" and some asset pricing models based on analytic paradigms. Numerous studies have found that the stock market is one of the most typical complex adaptive systems. There are a large number of investors in the market. In addition to making their own decisions, investors also learn from each other, and exchange investment experiences with each other. The eventual formation of stock prices, apart from the influence of some macro factors, is largely determined by the interactive learning among countless investors in the market. In other words, every investor has a "little calculator" of his/her own in mind. Obviously, to simulate or to explain such complexity generated stock price behavior with traditional analytic asset pricing model is not desirable (Sun et al. 2007).

As a powerful tool to explore the complexity of the stock market, the lattice squares in a cellular automaton model can be seen as individual investors, and the evolution rules of the cellular automaton model itself can be regarded as "methods" by which investors learn from the surrounding neighbors. By setting up such a scenario, changing evolution rules of a cellular automaton also changes the interactive pattern among investors in the market, thus causes the market display different pricing behavior.

In general, the applications of cellular automata to the stock market are usually divided into unconstrained or constrained stock market modeling. The so-called unconstrained stock market model is to assume in the model that the total amount of funds and the total amount of stocks circulating in the stock market are unlimited. Many scholars have systematically studied the stock market under this hypothesis by means of cellular automata. Of course, most of the results of the research of such models agree that investor mentality is an important factor for market evolution (Ying et al. 2003, 2004, 2006).

Although there exist numerous investor mental factors that influence market behavior, most of such models only consider the herd mentality, which means that the investors themselves have no ideas of their own, and overly rely on "group decision-making," and their degree of intelligence is low. To put it plainly, it means that investors follow whatever the majority around them are doing. This herd mentality will cause investors to buy or sell with no reason except to follow the trend, thereby causing great fluctuations in the market.

Some other scholars have carried out focused empirical research aiming at investors' group behavior, and found two conclusions worth referencing: (1) the learning behavior of investors in the securities market really exists; (2) different types of investors should have different investment strategies, and investors should conduct necessary self-management instead of blindly following the trend.

The goal for decision making problems in securities investment is very clear - making money. Most of normal investors will make "profits" the main purpose of their investments. Therefore, investors adopt different strategies in their buying and selling behavior in pursuing the profit. Compared with most of the existing models which only use " herd mentality" or "imitation behavior" as the evolution rules, the biggest difference of this section is the use of "self-adaptive cellular genetic algorithm", which enables investors to have judgment of a market phenomenon —"profits," improves their intelligence level by transforming them from the past "passive and blindly-following type" to the "independently learning type," and makes the system evolution closer to the real market, so that a series of interesting phenomena are discovered.

5.3.2 Raising the Question

According to the framework of the market maker model proposed by Carl Chiarella and others (Chiarella et al. 2006), we can abstract the investment decision problem in the stock market as the following model: use one single stock as the research object, with no dividend and no transaction costs. At time t, the price of the stock is P_t and the basic value is P_t^*. There are two kinds of investment strategies in the market, and they are respectively the "fundamental investment strategy" and the "technical investment strategy." Every investor will use these two strategies at the same time as the basis for placing an order, though they have different inclinations towards the two strategies. We use a weight coefficient to represent these inclinations. Here, use $W_{i,t}^{f}$ to represent the degree of inclination towards the fundamental investment strategy of investor i at moment t, $W_{i,t}^{m}$ to represent the degree of inclination towards the technical investment strategy of investor i at moment t, obviously $W_{i,t}^{f} + W_{i,t}^{m} = 1$.

Investors make trading decisions by predicting the changes of stock prices. For the fundamental investment strategy, the prediction of investor i at moment t for the changes of stock prices is represented as

$$\Delta P_{i,t}^{f} = P_t^{*} - P_t \tag{5.21}$$

In it, there is $P_{t+1}^{*} = P_t^{*}(1 + \delta_\lambda \lambda_t)$, $\lambda_t \sim \mathrm{N}(0,1)$, $\delta_\lambda \geq 0$ is a constant. This formula represents the random wandering of the basic value of stocks.

Regarding the technical investment strategy, the prediction of investor i on stock price changes is expressed as

$$\Delta P_{i,t}^{m} = P_t - \frac{\sum_{j=0}^{M_i - 1} P_{t-j}}{M_i} \tag{5.22}$$

In it, M_i represents the length of the moving average time window used by investor i, then, the quantity of orders for investor i at moment t can be expressed as

$$D_{i,t} = W_{i,t}^{f} \Delta P_{i,t}^{f} + \tanh\left(W_{i,t}^{m} \Delta P_{i,t}^{m}\right) \tag{5.23}$$

Under the market maker pricing mechanism, the price equation is expressed as

$$P_{t+1} = P_t(1 + \sigma_\varepsilon \varepsilon_t) + \mu \sum_{i=1}^{N} D_{i,t} \tag{5.24}$$

In it, $\varepsilon_t \sim$ N (0, 1); σ_ε is a constant. $\sigma_\varepsilon \varepsilon_t$ represents the noise in the pricing process, μ represents the speed of price adjustment; N represents the number of investors in the market.

The "target function" of the question is the profits which can be made by the investors, and the profit of investor i at moment t is expressed as

$$\pi_{i,t} = D_{i,t-1}\left(P_t - P_{t-1}\right) \tag{5.25}$$

The purpose of the investors is to maximize their profits with the evolution of time.

5.3.3 Using Traditional Operational Research Method for Solution

1. **Modeling**

Before using self-adaptive cellular genetic algorithm to solve this problem, we might as well first consider the traditional operational research method which does not involve complex operations by multiple agents. Investors can only make decisions on the basis of the presently known prices and order information. In aforementioned problem of investment, the important parameters determining the investment effects of the investors are $W_{i,t}^{f}$ and $W_{i,t}^{m}$, i.e. degrees of inclinations towards the two strategies.

The investors use $W_{i,t-1}^{f}$ and $W_{i,t-1}^{m}$, which can maximize profits at moment t, to guide their strategy selections, and proceed to seek the maximum profit at moment t +1. The target function and constraint conditions of the problem can be expressed as

$$\max \pi_{i,t}$$
$$\begin{cases} W_{i,t-1}^{f} + W_{i,t-1}^{m} = 1 \\ W_{i,t-1}^{f} \geq 0;\ W_{i,t-1}^{m} \geq 0 \end{cases} \tag{5.26}$$

We expand formula (5.26) without losing its generality, letting $\sigma_{\varepsilon}\varepsilon_{t} \approx 0$, then we have

$$\begin{aligned} &\max \mu\left[W_{i,t-1}^{f}\Delta P_{i,t-1}^{f} + \tanh\left(W_{i,t-1}^{m}\Delta P_{i,t-1}^{m}\right)\right] \\ &\quad \times \left[W_{i,t-1}^{f}\Delta P_{i,t-1}^{f} + \tanh\left(W_{i,t-1}^{m}\Delta P_{i,t-1}^{m}\right) + \sum D_{t-1}'\right] \\ &\begin{cases} W_{i,t-1}^{f} + W_{i,t-1}^{m} = 1 \\ W_{i,t-1}^{f} \geq 0;\ W_{i,t-1}^{m} \geq 0 \end{cases} \end{aligned} \tag{5.27}$$

In the formula, $\sum D_{t-1}'$ represents the total number of orders of others in the market besides investor i at moment $t-1$. Formula (5.27) represents the decision-making job every investor in the market needs to do within every unit time.

2. **The Drawbacks of Traditional Operational Research Method**

In last section, we built the models for traditional operational research, on the problem of stock market investment, and finally obtained the decision-making expression for every investor in the market. Observing formula (5.27) and back-tracking the entire modeling process, it is not difficult to discover the following problems.

First, what formula (5.27) reflects is the decision-making process of investors under a purely rational paradigm. Especially, the appearance of $\sum D_{t-1}'$ in (5.27) requires individual investors to know thoroughly the order information of other investors. In a real market, however, most of the investors are limited rational, with limited capacity in gathering information. Thus, an optimal decision is only an idealized status.

Second, formula (5.27) is the decision-making expression aiming for every investor, and there exists a higher order nonlinear term such as tanh (*). In computer simulation, especially when the number of investors is relatively large, the amount of computation and the time of operation are tremendous.

Third, real investors will often learn from the experiences of the surrounding people or interact with the surrounding investors in investment decision-making process. This point cannot be reflected in the modeling process under the guidance of traditional operational research method.

Fourth, as a typical complex system, one of the important reasons the stock market generate various pricing phenomena is the "heterogeneity" of the investors. The decision-making framework based on formula (5.27), on the other hand, reflects the "homogeneity" of the investors. To put it plainly, it means all people play the cards according to one routine, and this is obviously unrealistic (Wang 2004).

In view of the aforementioned problem, we may think about whether we can design a set of evolutionary learning rules, which not only can make the investors in the market evolve according to the same set of rules, but also can reflect the "heterogeneity" of their decision-making and in the same time, raise their profit levels?

5.3.4 Solution for Self-adaptive Cellular Genetic Algorithm

1. **Setting up the Cellular Automaton**

   (1) Cellular space: a two-dimensional lattice of $n \times n$; each square in the lattice represents an investor.

   (2) Neighborhood form: adopt the Moore Neighborhood type, each cell has eight neighbors.

   (3) Cell states: according to what has been discussed before, we use a set to represent cell states:

$$S_{i,t} = \left(D_{i,t}, W_{i,t}^{f}, W_{i,t}^{m}, K_i, \pi_{i,t}\right) \tag{5.28}$$

In it, $D_{i,t}$ represents the number of orders for investor i at moment t; $W_{i,t}^{f}$ and $W_{i,t}^{m}$ respectively represent the weights of the two strategies used by investor i in a certain mode of combination of strategies at moment t; K_i represents the moving average length of investor i; $\pi_{i,t}$ represents the profit of investor i at moment t.

2. **The Evolution Rules**

The investment learning process of the investors in the market can be briefly described as follows (Matsumoto 2008):

(1) Each cell (investor) determines its own investment need (number of orders) according to different strategic weight coefficients;
(2) Prices are updated;
(3) Investors calculate their respective profits on the basis of the actual prices;
(4) Investors adjust their own weight coefficients through communications with their neighbors, then enter the next round of investment in order to seek greater profits.

When we use the self-adaptive cellular genetic algorithm to represent this process, the mode of evolution can be expressed as follows:

(1) **Fitness Function**
We define the profit evaluation function as follows:

$$eval_{i,t} = \max_{j \in [1,N]} \left(\pi_{j,t}\right) - \pi_{i,t} \tag{5.29}$$

The fitness of investor i is the maximum profit among all individuals in the cellular space at moment t minus investor i's own profit. Obviously, the smaller the value of $\text{eval}_{i,t}$, the higher is the profit level of investor i. Each cell i makes fitness evaluations of on surrounding neighbors (including itself, 9 in total) whose profit level is greater than or equal to its own ($\text{eval}j \leq \text{eval}i$) (represented as a set Ω).
First, let

$$eval'_{j,t} = 1 - \frac{eval_{j,t}}{\sum_{j \in \Omega} eval_{j,t}} \tag{5.30}$$

Then, make fitness evaluation

$$fit_{j,t} = \frac{eval'_{j,t}}{\sum_{j \in \Omega} eval'_{j,t}} \tag{5.31}$$

In it, $\text{fit}_{j,t}$ is the probability that cell j which is the neighbor (including cell i itself) of cell i is chosen, then cell j becomes the learning object of cell i.
(2) **Selection**
In step (1), we have derived the probability of cell i taking individual j (whose profit level is greater than or equal to that of cell i's own) as the learning object. This probability can be understood in essence as the "roulette" operation in traditional genetic algorithm. However, unlike traditional genetic algorithm,

Table 5.7 Simulation parameter settings

Parameter symbol	Parameter meaning	Value
N	Number of investors	900
μ	Speed of price adjustment	0.01
P_1	Initial prices of stocks	10
T	Time of evolution	200
M_i	Length of moving average window	[30, 50]
p_c	Crossover probability	0.7
p_m	Mutation probability	0.01
σ_ε	Price noise	0.2

this "roulette" is an operation performed simultaneously by all individuals in the cellular space within the scope of their neighbors.

(3) **Crossover**

Define the crossover probability as p_c. After cell i learns the strategy combination weight coefficient of cell j $W_{j,t} = \left(W_{j,t}^f, W_{j,t}^m\right)$, it performs equipotential crossover operation on this weight coefficient and its own strategy combination weight coefficient $W_{i,t} = \left(W_{i,t}^f, W_{i,t}^m\right)$, to obtain a new weight coefficient. The method is as follows:

$$W_{i,t+1}^{\prime n} = (1 - p_c)W_{i,t}^n + p_c W_{j,t}^n \tag{5.32}$$

In which $n \in \{f, m\}$.

The crossover probability in formula (5.32) can also be understood as the confidence level of an individual investor: when $p_c = 0$, an investor has no exchange of information with the surrounding neighbors, while when $p_c = 1$, an investor learns without reservation the weight coefficient among neighbors whose profit level is higher than him/herself.

(4) **Mutation**

Defining mutation probability as pm; number r is randomly generated from [0, 1], if $r < pm$, the weight coefficient is updated as follows

$$W_{i,t+1}^{\prime\prime n} = W_{i,t+1}^{\prime n} + \delta_\varepsilon \varepsilon_t \tag{5.33}$$

In which $n \in \{f, m\}$; $\varepsilon_t \sim N(0, 1)$; δ_ε is a constant.

Through the above 3 steps, cell i completes the process of self-learning.

3. **Result of Simulation**

We use MATLAB 2008b to perform numerical simulation of the above-mentioned pricing system, parameter settings are shown as in Table 5.7.

The stock prices and the average profits of market investors obtained through simulation are shown in Fig. 5.34.

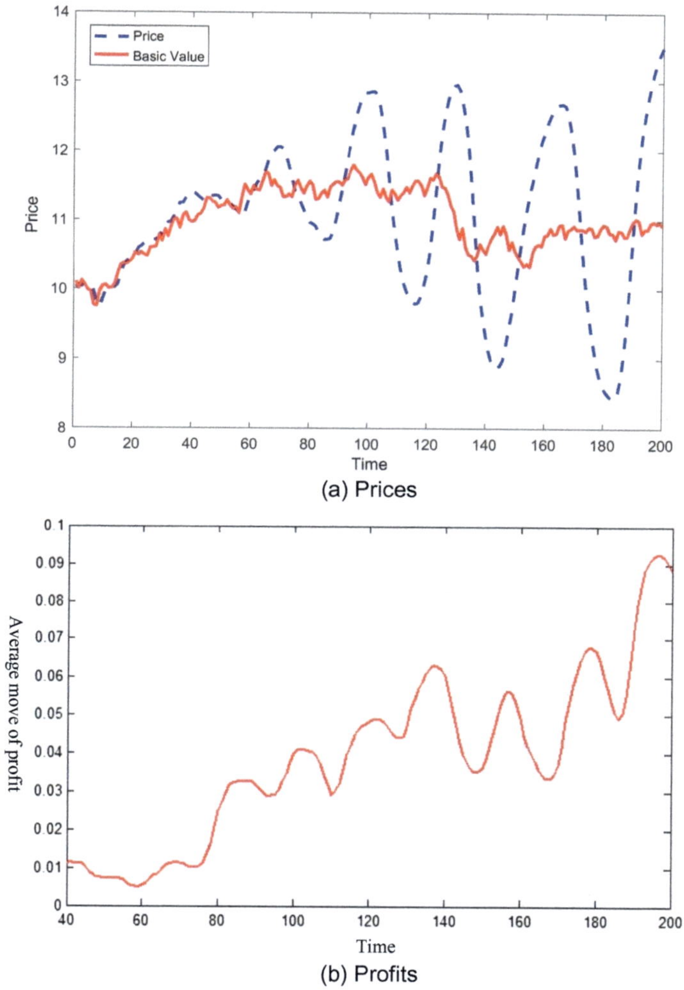

Fig. 5.34 Price and investor average profit (**a**), Price and investor average profit (**b**)

In the research conducted by Carl Chiarella et al. on the market maker pricing mechanism, it was found that compared with the fundamental investment strategy, the technical investment strategy is easier to bring excessive profit, and in the same time to cause great market fluctuation. In Fig. 5.34a, the continuous price amplitude increase around basic value just reflects the continuous increase of market investors' inclination towards the technical investment strategy through learning, while the continuous market average profit increase shown in Fig. 5.34b vividly reflects the learning effect of investors.

5.3.5 Summary

In this section, we used the stock market as an example, introduced the application of self-adaptive cellular genetic algorithm (SA-CGA) in a dynamic environment, and compared it with the solution seeking method of traditional operational research. The simulation result vividly reflects the process in which, along with the evolution of algorithmic rules, the average profits of investors in the market increase during their continuous "learning" process, and verifies the application of self-adaptive cellular genetic algorithm in complex systems.

References

Al-Naqi, A., Erdogan, A. T., & Arslan, T. (2013). Dynamic fault-tolerant three-dimensional cellular genetic algorithms. *Journal of Parallel and Distributed Computing, 73,* 122–136.

Chen, S. (2005). *Modeling theory and method of complex systems*. Nanjing: Southeast University Press.

Chen, S., Lu, Y., Yang, H., et al. (2011). Study of the selection pressure of cellular genetic algorithm under disaster mechanism. *Computer Engineering and Applications, 47*(27), 32–35.

Chiarella, C., He, X.-Z., & Hommes, C. (2006). A dynamic analysis of moving average rules. *Journal of Economic Dynamics & Control, 30*(9–10), 1729–1753.

Holland, J. H. (1992). *Adaptation in natural and artificial systems: An introductory analysis with applications to biology, control and artificial intelligence* (1st ed.). Bradford: A Bradford Book.

Kirley, M. A. (2002). Cellular genetic algorithm with disturbance: Optimization using dynamic spatial interactions. *Journal of Heuristics, 8*(3), 327–331.

Li, L., Chang, B., & Lu, Q. (2010). Multi-targets cellular genetic algorithm and its applications. *Modern Manufacturing Engineering, 7,* 46–50.

Lu, Y., Li, M., & Li, L. (2010). A cellular genetic algorithm with evolution rules. *Journal of Electronics, 38*(7), 1063–1067.

Matsumoto, K. (2008). Evaluation of an artificial market approach for GHG emissions trading analysis. *Simulation Modelling Practice and Theory, 16*(9), 1312–1322.

Morales-Reyes, A., & Erdgan, A. T. (2012). Internal lattice reconfiguration for diversity tuning in cellular genetic algorithms. *PLOS ONE, 7*(7), 1–19.

Sun, Y., Zhang, C., Gao, J., et al. (2007). Study of the modern securities pricing model. *Theory and Practice of Systems Engineering, 5,* 1–15.

Wan, C., Yang, X., & Lu, Y. (2010). Study of cellular genetic algorithm in a dynamic environment. *Applications of Electronic Devices and Components, 12*(7), 78–79.

Wang, A. (2004). *Analysis and modeling of complex systems* (2nd ed.). Shanghai: Shanghai Jiaotong University Press.

Ying, S., Fan, Y., & Wei, Y. (2006). Cellular automaton model of single-stock market and its dynamics study. *Systems Engineering, 24*(7), 31–36.

Ying, S., Fan, Y., Wei, Y., et al. (2004). Cellular automaton model of stock market evolution based on investment analysis. *Management Review, 16*(11), 4–9.

Ying, S., Wei, Y., Fan, Y., et al. (2003). Study of stock market complexity based on cellular automata: Investor mentality and market behavior. *Theory and Practice of Systems Engineering, 12,* 18–24.

Zhang, Q., Chen, G., & Yu, J. (2008). Optimization method and its applications based on artificial life. *Journal of East China University of Science and Technology, Natural Science Section, 34* (2), 273–277.

Zhang, Y., Li, M., & Lu, Y. (2009a). Study of the evolution rules of cellular genetic algorithm. *Study of Computer Applications, 26*(10), 3635–3638.

Zhang, Y., Li, M., & Lu, Y. (2009b). Cellular genetic algorithm under disaster mechanism. *Journal of Nanchang Aviation University, 23*(1), 9–12.

Chapter 6
Cellular Neural Networks

Introduction
As stated in the chapter of Cellular Genetic Algorithm, an individual cell plays the roles of both "chromosome" and "gene". Though the roles are different, they all reflect the function of "information transmission by the rules" and the intelligent form of the cells. To continue thinking along this path, may the cellular automata continue to play the role of some elements in other intelligent algorithms so as to realize some complex operations of the intelligent algorithm by using "computing by the rules" of the cells? If the answer is "yes", then what are the characteristics of such a smart algorithm? Where is the linking point? What will be the effect? If not, where are the difficulties? Will this be able to provide some ideas for the improvement of the intelligent algorithm?

Along this way of thinking, after the cellular genetic algorithm, it is very easy for us to think of another widely used intelligent information processing model—the Artificial Neural Network. In this chapter, therefore, we start with the topic of Artificial Neural Network.

6.1 Basic Principles of Artificial Neural Networks

There exist endless wonders in the vast universe. As stars moving, countless things thrive on the earth. On this blue earth, as the intelligent part of this planet, human being has a highly developed brain, the brain is the material basis of human thinking, and the thinking is the concentrated expression of human intelligence. The human brain has three basic ways of thinking: logical thinking, imaginary thinking and inspirational thinking. Logical thinking is based on concept, judgment and reasoning. Its function is to abstract the information as a concept, and then based on the rules to conduct logic reasoning. Because a concept can be represented by a symbol, and the logic reasoning can be carried out in a serial mode, the process can be written in serial orders to be completed by the machine. A computer is such a

X. Li et al., *Theory of Practical Cellular Automaton*,
https://doi.org/10.1007/978-981-10-7497-4_6

kind of artificial intelligence system which uses the machine to simulate logic thinking of human brains.

The speed of the units composing modern computer is millions of times faster than the speed of neurons in the human brain. Therefore, the computer processing speed should be much faster than processing speed of human brain in common sense. In fact, for those procedural problems which are clear in operation rules and reasoning, the computer can quickly and effectively find solution, such as playing chess. The precision and speed of computers in numerical calculations and logical operations greatly expand the human brain capacity. But in solving the problems related to imaginary thinking and inspirational thinking, the computers often seem powerless. In the issues such as face recognition (a baby can recognize its mother from the crowd, but Japan's facial recognition computers are often unable to display changed faces), cycling, swimming, and other activities of association or experience, human brain can learn from those instinctive, inexpressible intuition and experiences. It can also flexibly deal with the rules of problem solving according to the actual circumstances, so as to easily accomplish the tasks. In this regard, a computer is significantly clumsy.

As a result, the traditional computers have been seriously challenged. This made people re-evaluate the existing computer system, and to find a new way of computer development. A new neural computing which is close to the human brain and can imitate the patterns of the brain thinking is emerged—the Artificial Neural Network.

6.1.1 Biological Neuron

A neuron is the basic unit of brain. A human brain is composed of neurons of about 10^{10} orders of magnitude. Each neuron is connected with about 10^5–10^3 other neurons, forming a gigantic and complex 3D network. It is evident that this is a giant system. Biological neurons are composed of the following four parts.

(1) cell body: composed of the nucleus, cytoplasm and cell membrane, and so on.
(2) an axon, a branch stretching out of the cell body with uniform thickness and smooth surface. It is the output terminal of cell body, which is equivalent to the output cable of the cell. The end of axon has a lot of nerve endings which are the terminals for output signals and used to transmit the neural information sent from the cell body.
(3) dendrites: a lot of branches which are as thick and short as the tree branches extending from the cell body. Its function is to collect information (input) from other elements from all directions.
(4) synapse: it is the place where the two nerve cells are connected. The axon of a cell through its synapse is connected to the dendrite of another cell. If a signal transmitted through a synapse makes the cell excited, then it is called stimulating synapse, otherwise, it is called inhibiting synapse. Both types of synapses

transmitting information are in one direction. A typical neuron usually has 104–103 synapses. The information of each neuron is transmitted through the synapse. The linking strength of synapses represents the degree of coupling between two neurons in signal transmission. Such strength is changeable. This means that the signal is "weighted" when it goes through the synapse. The magnitude of the "weights", which is changeable, can be positive or negative. Positive weight means the signal is "excited" while negative the "inhibited". The summation of weighted inputs is the total effect. If the value of summation is greater or equal to neuron's threshold, this neuron is activated, or it is inactivated. Figure 6.1 is the equivalent figure of the above given structure.

As shown in Fig. 6.1, after being transported to the cell body by dendritic cells, the signals transmitted by the external stimulus signal or from other neurons are then sent to the axon. This is equivalent to an output cable, which is transmitted to the interface between the cell body and the cell body, and finally sends to the next level neuron.

In summary, biological neuron has the following basic characteristics: (1) neurons is a multi-input and single output element; (2) neurons have nonlinear characteristics of signal transfer of intensity between the input and output; (3) the intensity of signal transfer among neurons, namely the tightness of coupling, is variable and input signal can be divided into of exciting or of inhabitating effect; (4) the output response of neurons depends on the result of the superposition of all the input signal integrated. When the overall input value above a certain threshold, the neuron is "activated", otherwise it will be in the "suppression" state.

6.1.2 *Artificial Neurons*

Artificial neurons are the functional approximation to the biological neurons. It is a kind of abstract and simulation in the structure and function of the biological neurons after being greatly simplified. Of approximately more than 150 functions of a biological neuron, the artificial neuron imitates only the most basic, but also the most important three, namely:

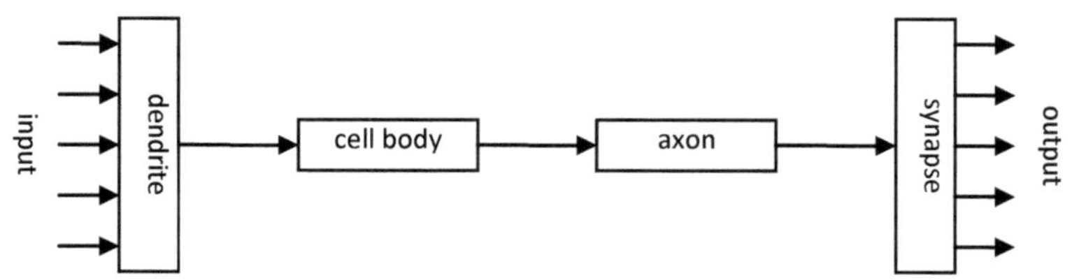

Fig. 6.1 The equivalent figure of a biological neuron

(1) A group of connections: a connection's strength is expressed by the weight of the connection. The value of the weight can be either positive or negative value. A positive weight value denotes activation while a negative weight denotes inhibition.
(2) An adder: used for getting the sum of the synaptic weights of the neuron in response to the input signal.
(3) An activation function: used to limit the output amplitude of a neuron. Activation function is also known as the suppression function, because it suppresses (limits) the input signal to a certain value within the allowable range.

The artificial neuron model is shown in Fig. 6.2.

In the figure, the input vector is:

$$X = (x_1, x_2, \ldots, x_n)$$

and its correspondent connecting weight vector is:

$$W = (w_{j1}, w_{j2}, \ldots, w_{jn})$$

so we have the net input of neuron j as:

$$S_j = \sum_{i=1}^{n} w_{ji}x_i - \theta_j \tag{6.1}$$

In formula (6.1), θ_j represents the threshold value of the neuron, also called threshold.

The net input (including the threshold θ_j) goes through the activation function $f(*)$ and we get the output of the neuron y_j

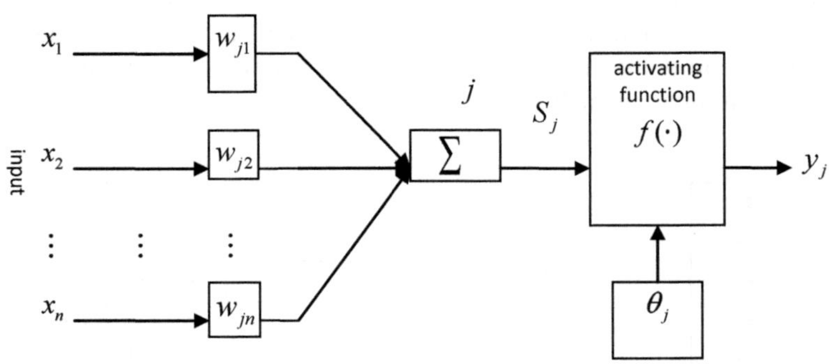

Fig. 6.2 Artificial neuron model

$$\begin{aligned} y_j &= f(S_j) \\ &= f\left(\sum_{i=1}^{n} w_{ji}x_i - \theta_j\right) \\ &= f\left(\sum_{i=0}^{n} w_{ji}x_i\right) \end{aligned} \tag{6.2}$$

The functionality of the activation function $f(*)$ is to simulate the nonlinear transfer characteristics of biological neuron. The commonly used activation functions are as shown in Fig. 6.3.

The analytic formula of each function in Fig. 6.3 is as following.

Linear function:

$$f(s) = s \tag{6.3}$$

Slope function:

$$f(s) = \begin{cases} r & \text{if } s \geq r \\ s & \text{if } |s| < r \\ -r & \text{if } s \leq -r \end{cases} \tag{6.4}$$

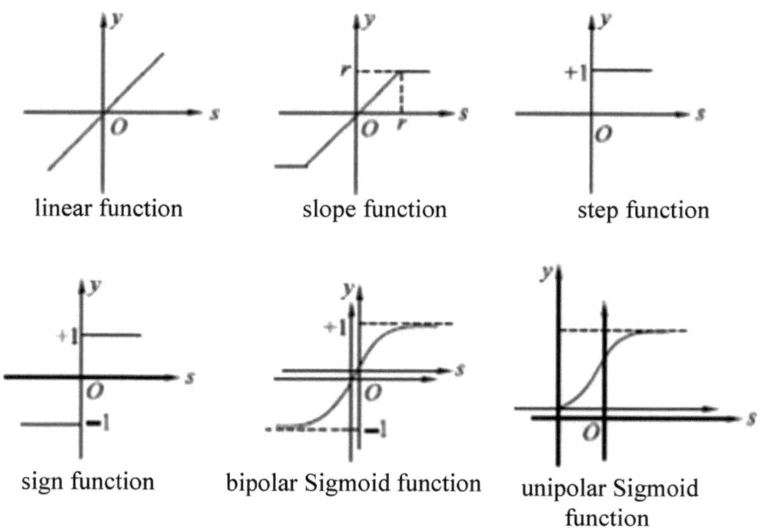

Fig. 6.3 The commonly used activation functions

Step function:

$$f(s) = \begin{cases} 1 & \text{if } s > 0 \\ 0 & \text{if } s \leq 0 \end{cases} \tag{6.5}$$

Sign function:

$$f(s) = \begin{cases} 1 & \text{if } s > 0 \\ -1 & \text{if } s \leq 0 \end{cases} \tag{6.6}$$

Sigmoid function can be simply called S type function, which is characterized by: firstly, it has the upper and lower boundaries; secondly, it is monotone increasing; finally, it is continuous and smooth. This means that it is continuous smooth and continuous differentiable. The most commonly used Sigmoid function is the Unipolar Sigmoid Function as in the formula below.

$$f(s) = \frac{1}{1 + e^{-\lambda s}} \tag{6.7}$$

It is a unipolar function with the upper boundary as 1 and lower boundary 0, that is $0 < f(s) < 1$, with $\lambda = 1$ always holds.

6.1.3 The Structure of Neural Network

In spite of the simple structure and limited function of a single biological neuron, the human brain is composed of more than 10 billion interconnected neurons which form a network to work together, and to adjust the intensity of synaptic connections among various neurons according to certain rules, thus to make the human brain possess the high level and complex functions such as memory, association, reasoning and judgment. In the same token, ANN (artificial neural network) is formed by connecting numerous artificial neurons into a network according to certain rules.

It should be pointed out that, although ANN tries to simulate BNN (Biological Neural Network) in structure and in function, there exist big differences in the aspects such as the number of neurons, the degree of complexity of topological structure of the network. Limited by the factors such as the possibility of physical realization and the simplicity of computing, ANN nowadays could only simulate BNN on a very low level on network intelligence.

Despite of variation in topological structure, the connecting methods for an ANN in general can be put in two forms: the layered type or the full connection type, as shown in Fig. 6.4.

No matter which type of the network, their common characteristics is that the learning and the operation of the network depend on dynamic evolution process of the weighted connections of various kinds of neurons (He and Liang 2000; He et al. 2001).

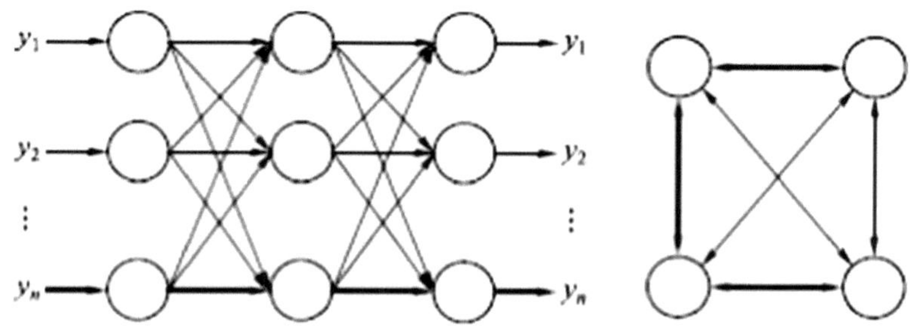

Fig. 6.4 Topological structure of ANN

6.1.4 The Learning Methods of Neural Network

To make it to possesses certain kind of intelligence, an ANN must be trained or be made to learn before it can be put into use. The so called "learning" means that we feed the network input some sample patterns (or called "training samples set"), and adjust the weight matrix of various layers of the network according to certain rules. When all the weight values of the network converge to certain points, the learning process can be called off. So we can see that the essence of learning process is to let the weight matrix of the network to make self-adjustment in accordance with the change of external stimuli.

1. Learning with a teacher
   This kind of learning method requires that in the same time of giving out the input pattern *X*, the correspondent target pattern *T* (expected output pattern or teacher's signal) should be given out. The two patterns together are called a training pair. Generally in training a network, numerous training pairs ($x1$, $t1$), ($x2$, $t2$), …, (xn, tn) are needed.
   At the training time, we put the input to concentrate on a certain input pattern and calculate out the real output pattern *Y* of the network, and then compare it with the expected pattern *T* and calculate out the error signal ε. Thereafter, based on ε obtained, we adjust the weight matrix of various layers in accordance with certain algorithm, to make the error to alter toward the direction of decreasing. By making the training to concentrate on each training pair in the training set in turn, we continuously adjust the weight value of the network. The entire training pair set will be repeatedly used on the network for many times, until the error is smaller than a pre-set tolerable value that is set before hand. Learning with a teacher process is illustrated as Fig. 6.5.
2. Learning without teachers
   Under such a learning method, the training set is composed of only input patterns and no correspondent target patterns are provided. The learning algorithm should guarantee that, the network will generate the same output patterns

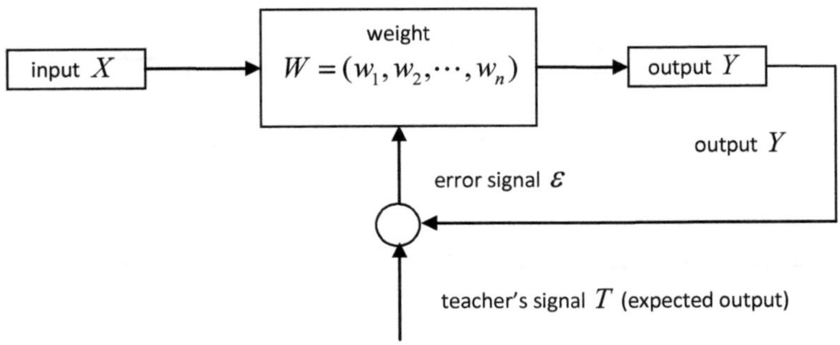

Fig. 6.5 Learning with a teacher process

when it is fed with the similar input patterns. In other words, the network is able to abstract the statistical characteristics of the training set, thus to divide the input patterns into certain subsets according to their degree of similarity. However, it cannot be known before hand, what type, or what kind of output pattern an input pattern will generate.

The network could only do correct classification on input pattern after training. This learning method is just like the human children's learning process of distinguishing the cats and dogs. There are no target patterns such as dogs or cats in the children's brain before the training. But through the repeated observations of the input patterns of cats and dogs, the children will be able to distinguish or to classify these animals. The process of Learning Without Teachers is illustrated as in Fig. 6.6.

6.1.5 The Learning Algorithm of Neural Networks

The key to the operation and the training of a neural network is to adjust the weights. Different ways of adjusting the weights will generate different algorithms of learning. Below we give the general form of the learning algorithms, as illustrated in Fig. 6.7.

Usually, the weight change w_j (incremental) is proportional to the product of three factors—the input signal vector X, learning signal $r$and learning efficiency η

Fig. 6.6 Learning without teacher process

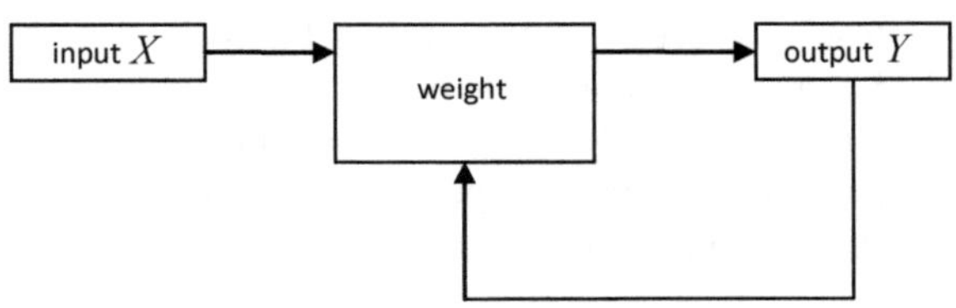

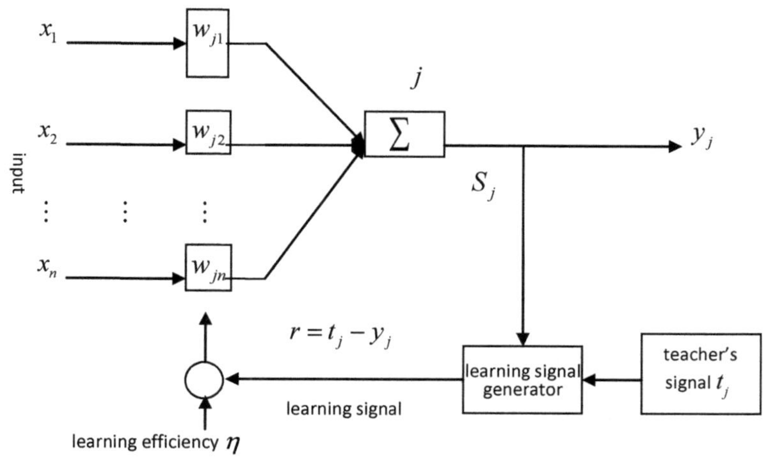

Fig. 6.7 The general form of learning algorithms

(positive), and the learning signal r is generally a function of w_j and X, and sometimes as well a function of the teacher signal t_j. That is

$$r = r(w_j, X, t_j) \tag{6.8}$$

And the general form of learning rule is

$$\Delta w_j = \eta r(w_j, X, t_j) X^T \tag{6.9}$$

so we have

$$w_j(t+1) = w_j(t) + \Delta w_j(t) \tag{6.10}$$

For discrete systems

$$w_{j,n+1} = w_{j,n} + \eta r(w_{j,n}, X_n, t_{j,n}) X_n^T \tag{6.11}$$

Taking Hebb Learning Rule as an example, taking the neural output as the learning signal, that is

$$r = y_j = f(w_j X) \tag{6.12}$$

Substituting r in the general form of learning rule (6.9) with (6.12), and we get the vector expression of Hebb Learning Rule as

$$\Delta w_j = \eta f(w_j X) X^T \tag{6.13}$$

The correspondent element expression is

$$\Delta W_j = \eta f\left(w_j X\right) X^T \tag{6.14}$$

or can be simply expressed as

$$\Delta w_{ji} = \eta y_i x_i \quad i = 1, 2, \ldots, n \tag{6.15}$$

The Hebb Rule as expressed in formula (6.15) is in line with the principle of conditioned reflex in the theory of psychology. That is, if the two neurons are excited at the same time (i.e., the outputs of the two neurons are in "1" state), the connection between them (the weight) should be enhanced; otherwise, should be weakened.

There are other common learning algorithms such as Delta Learning Algorithm, Stochastic Learning Algorithm, Competitive Learning Algorithm, etc. The difference among them lies in the different expression of neuron weight adjustment. Here we do not want to bore the readers with more of them, interested readers can go and search for more related articles or books.

6.2 The Feasibility of the Combination of Cellular Automata and Neural Networks

In Sect. 6.1, we introduced and comb through the basic principle of neural network in length. We can find two key points of the basic principle of neural network. One is the "neuron", the topological structure of which determines the input and output methods of the neural network. The other is "weight", and the adjustment of weight is the core of learning and training of the entire neural network. Associating some real examples to the understanding of above two points, it is not hard to see that the neural network algorithms are not formed completely by analytical formulas. The algorithms in the mean time have the characteristics of discrete and parallel.

Now let's move on to cellular automata again. We already knew from chapter one of this book that cellular automata (CA) have three important characteristics of discrete, parallel and computing by rules. Then it is quite natural that we come up to this consideration: whether it is possible that we can set up certain mapping, to connect neural network with cellular automata that have neighbor structure, thus to realize certain functions (Acedo 2009; Bandman 2002). The link for forming this mapping is just the computing rules of cellular automata, as illustrated in Fig. 6.8.

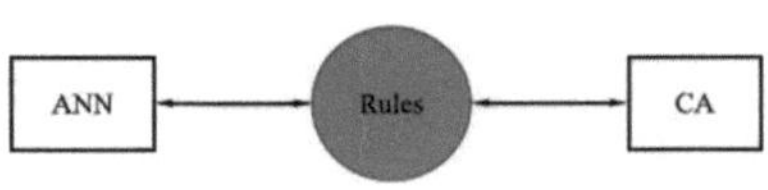

Fig. 6.8 Rules, the links connecting ANN and CA

Then, if this mapping exists and also is feasible, and what practical meanings it has, and what influences it has on neural networks and on a cellular automaton's own operation? Of course, the connecting methods that will be introduced in the remaining part of this chapter will not cover all the possible existing mappings. Interested readers can base on Fig. 6.8 to think further, to construct some rules, to design effective mappings by themselves.

6.2.1 Why the Combination?

In Chap. 5 of "Cellular Genetic Algorithms", we have used the cells to replace the genes and chromosomes in genetic algorithm, and with the help of cellular automaton rules to improve its ways of genetic operations, and ultimately improve the "local extreme value" problem. In that chapter, we started from the algorithm itself, and the idea was to optimize and redesign the algorithm.

As for neural networks, based on the available literatures to date, the results of using cellular automata to optimize or to redesign the neural network are very few. The authors of this book have designed a cellular network model that replaces the neurons in traditional artificial neural network with cells, and replaces the full connectivity of cells among the neighboring layers with local connections, and uses the rule evolution algorithm instead of the BP algorithm. In addition, the genetic algorithm is embedded to enhance the optimization. The model is rather complex. But in the experiments on red wine classification, the effect was not as good as expected (the degree of accuracy is 94.4%), lower than the degree of accuracy obtained through using pure artificial neural network (96.1%).

We could only say that, in consideration of improving the algorithms, this result was constructive. Then we might as well jump out of the algorithms themselves, and start to consider from another angle the combination of the two—"evolution". We know that the most distinctive characteristic of cellular automata is that it can simulate some complex evolutionary phenomena in real world, and the results of the overall evolution rely on simple and continuous repeated and invariable local rules (Cattaneo and Vogliotti 1997). This means that we may determine the state of a cell at the moment of $t + 1$ through the states of its neighbors at the moment of t. However, the rules directing the evolution of a cell is no longer that simple when the change of the future state of an individual cell needs to put into considerations of historical data and various comprehensive factors. Sometimes even such a "rule" itself is "not regular", thus the uncertainty in evolution is greatly increased.

However, it is the "complex system" plus the "complex rules" constitute the rich and colorful world. To this point, we may consider whether we can use artificial neural network algorithm to dig out such "irregular" "rules", to form the mapping as shown in Fig. 6.8, so as to make the evolution results of the cellular automata play a real role in forecasting.

6.2.2 *Thought on Combination: "Help" and "Replace"*

1. Help

   In the case of aforementioned complex evolutionary rules, large portions of the combinations of cellular automata and neural networks have been used to simulate the changes of land utilizations (Li and Mai 2009; Li and Ye 2005; Zhao et al. 2007), according to the domestic literatures. It is well known that the change in the land utilizations is a complex dynamic system, the intrinsic evolution rules are hard for human race to command and to describe analytically. Why cellular automata are selected to study the land utilization evolution is that cellular automata can be used to define the evolution rule of "land cell". However, such evolution rule is different from the rules as introduced in previous chapters, such as "life game", "rule number 110" etc. Although such evolution rule is also a function of cell state and a cell's relations with its neighbors, it is in fact "vague" and "dynamic" and "nonlinear" as well.

   Let us put it another way, the evolution rule for a cell between the moment t and moment t + 1 may vary. The future direction of evolution is decided by historical data, by cell state and other multiple factors. Considering how to help the cellular automata to find out and to realize such rules in real time, quite naturally we thought about neural network.

   In cellular automata, rules are functions of the relationship with neighbors. The commonly adopted model building structure is illustrated as in Fig. 6.9.

   It is not hard to find out that, in Fig. 6.9, the role of the neural network is in fact to help the formation of the evolution rule for a cellular automaton (Dohler et al. 2008; Kim and Cho 2006; Tzionas 2001).

   In aforementioned literature, based on the need of practical applications, the important feature of "interacting with neighbors" of cellular automata was often

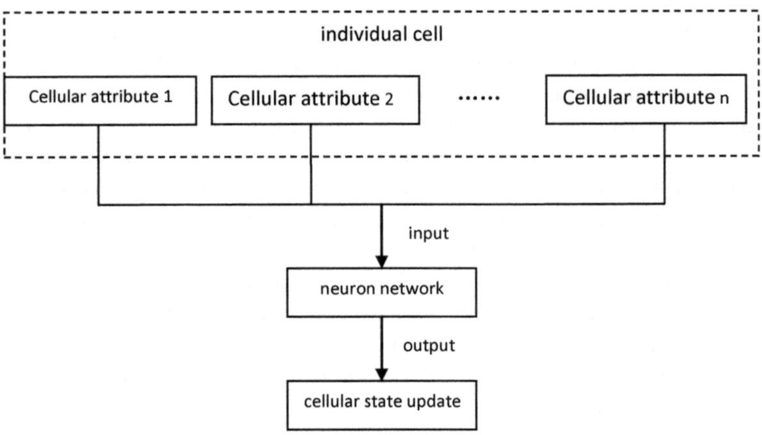

Fig. 6.9 The structure of cellular neural network model building

diluted (not abandoned). More attentions have been paid to the influence of individual cell properties on neural network output. For example, on evolution of land utilization, a piece of land can be abstracted as an individual cell. At the next moment, whether the land is to become a residential land or a commercial land, is often decided by some present properties of the land, such as the price, the planning, etc.

In Sect. 6.3, we will design a simple new model to highlight the role of the cellular automaton neighbor interaction in neural networks. The new structure in fact is a "cellular version" of neural network. Taking Moore type Neighbor Structure as an example, the center cell and neighboring cells are input neurons. The renewal of the central cell is based on the output of neural network. Here we can see that the function of the neural network is self-evident—to help the cellular automata to find out evolution rules by comprehending the neighbor states.

Some readers may consider that the aforementioned "help" is still limited to the practical applications as defined in certain literature, or is in no way different from putting new wine into old bottles. However, the aforementioned model building structure can help to solve some evolution problems with complex rules (such as forecasting of land utilization change).

2. Replacement

The aforementioned "help" refers to a neural network to help a cellular automaton on rule mining. The internal algorithm flow of the neural network is not affected by the rules of the cell automata. In the chapter of "Cellular Genetic Algorithms", we have used the evolution rules of a cellular automaton to deduce the selection and crossover operation of a genetic algorithm. Then, whether the evolution rules of the cellular automata can also be used to replace the algorithm operations in a neural network, thus to obtain the same operational results as in neural networks? In previous context, we mentioned that a neural network has two key elements, one is the neural cell and the other is the weight, and the adjustment of the weight is the core of neural network operation. In this regard, the thought of "replacement" quite naturally involves the redesign of weight renewal method. In Sects. 6.4 and 6.5, we will make such trials.

6.2.3 Brief Summary

In this section, we focused on the possibility of combining cellular automata and neural networks. The key of the combination lies in how to establish a set of rules as blue print, which can be used as a kind of mapping to link cellular automata and neural networks. The idea of building such a mapping may be used to "help" to explore the evolution rules, or may also be used to "replace" the deeply exploring the core of the algorithm.

6.3 Cellular Automata Rule Mining Based on BP Neural Networks (BP-CA)

In this section, the evolution rules of cellular automata (CA) are non-deterministic and non-local. The key for combination of CA with neural networks is on the changes of neurons and on rule mining. Below, we use the most common BP neural network algorithm to mine the rules for the evolution of the rules of CA, thus to realize forecasting of the future scenarios.

6.3.1 *BP Neural Networks and Algorithm Flow*

In 1986, scientists led by Rumelhart proposed the algorithm of Error Back-Propagation (BP) in multilayer feed-forward network. It not only increased the classification ability of the network, but also solved the problem of adjusting the weight value in a multilayered network. People generally called a multilayer feed-forward network trained by the algorithm of error back-propagation directly as a BP neural network. Its topological structure is illustrated in Fig. 6.10. The legends in the figure: n denotes the number of neurons in input layer; and p denotes the number of neurons in hidden layer.

BP algorithm flow is as follow

(1) Initialization: giving a random value between (−1, +1) to each connecting weight w_{ij}, v_{jt} and threshold value θ_j, r_t.
(2) Randomly select a pair of patterns $A_k = (a_1^k, a_2^k, \ldots, a_n^k)$, $Y_k = (y_1^k, y_2^k, \ldots, y_n^k)$ to provide to the network.

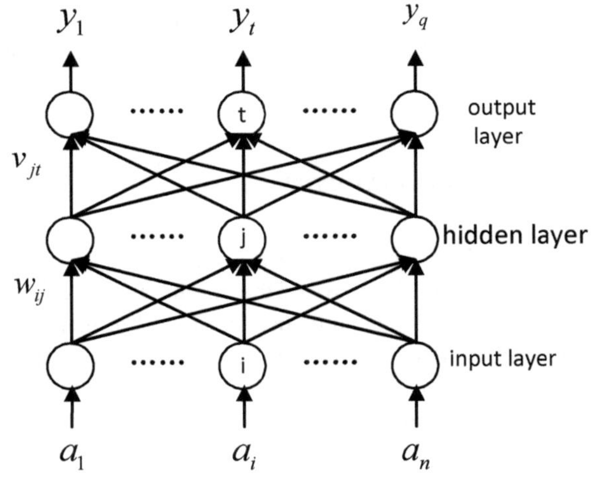

Fig. 6.10 The topological structure of a BP neural network

(3) Using input pattern A_k, connecting weight w_{ij} and threshold value θ_j to compute the input to each unit of the hidden layer s_j, then by using s_j with S function to compute the output of each unit of the hidden layer b_j, that is

$$s_j = \sum_{i=1}^{n} w_{ij} \cdot a_i - \theta_j \quad j = 1, 2, \ldots, p \tag{6.16}$$

$$b_j = f(s_j) \quad j = 1, 2, \ldots, p \tag{6.17}$$

(4) Using output of the hidden layer b_j, connecting weight v_{jt} and threshold value r_j to compute the input to each unit of the output layer L_t, then by using L_t with S function to compute the response of each unit of the output layer C_t, that is

$$L_t = \sum_{j=1}^{p} v_{jt} \cdot b_j - r_t \quad t = 1, 2, \ldots, q \tag{6.18}$$

$$c_t = f(L_t) \quad t = 1, 2, \ldots, q \tag{6.19}$$

(5) Using expected output pattern $Y_k = (y_1^k, y_2^k, \ldots, y_n^k)$ and the real network output c_t, to compute the alignment error d_t^k for each unit in output layer, that is

$$d_t^k = (y_t^k - c_t^k)c_t^k(1 - c_t^k) \quad t = 1, 2, \ldots, q \tag{6.20}$$

(6) Using connecting weight v_{jt}, the output layer alignment error d_t^k and the output of the hidden layer b_j, to compute the alignment error e_t^k for each unit in hidden layer, that is

$$e_j^k = \left(\sum_{t=1}^{q} d_t^k \cdot v_{jt} \right) b_j(1 - b_j) \quad j = 1, 2, \ldots, p \tag{6.21}$$

(7) Using the alignment error d_t^k of each unit in output layer, and the output of each unit of the hidden layer b_j, to modify the connecting weight v_{jt} and threshold value r_t, that is

$$v_{jt}(N+1) = v_{jt}(N) + \alpha d_t^k b_j \quad j = 1, 2, \ldots, p \tag{6.22}$$

$$r_t(N+1) = r_t(N) + \alpha d_t^k \quad t = 1, 2, \ldots, q \tag{6.23}$$

(8) Using the alignment error e_j^k of each unit in the hidden layer, and the input to each unit of input layer $A_k = (a_1^k, a_2^k, \ldots, a_n^k)$ to modify the connecting weight w_{ij} and threshold value θ_j, that is

$$w_{ij}(N+1) = w_{ij}(N) + \beta e_j^k a_i^k \quad i = 1, 2, \ldots, n \tag{6.24}$$

$$\theta_j(N+1) = \theta_j(N) + \beta e_j^k \quad j = 1, 2, \ldots, p \tag{6.25}$$

In above, $0 < \beta < 1$.

(9) Randomly select the next learning pattern to provide to the network and then return to step (3), until the training is finished for all the patterns.

(10) Update the learning times, that is, randomly reselect a pair of patterns from a group of learning patterns and go back to step (3), until the error E of entire network is smaller than a pre-set allowance ($E < \varepsilon$), which means that the network reaches the convergence.

(11) End the learning process.

In above learning steps, steps (3)–(6) compose forward propagation process of the input learning patterns, and steps (7)–(8) compose backward propagation process of the network error, while the steps (9)–(10) compose the process of train finishing and convergence.

6.3.2 BP-CA Algorithm

The cores of cellular automata operation are rules. In the last section, the algorithm flow of BP neural network was introduced, which can be understood as the process of rule mining for cellular automata here. The cellular automata version of the neural network is illustrated in Fig. 6.11.

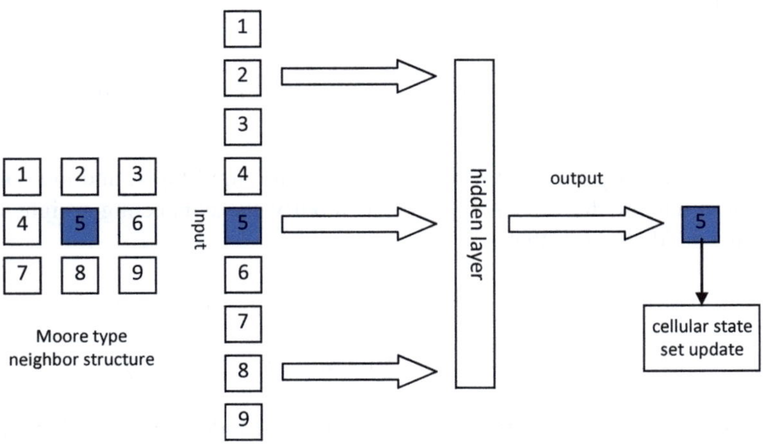

Fig. 6.11 The model building structure of cellular automata neural network

It is not difficult to find out that comparing to the BP neural network algorithm, BP-CA algorithm modifies neurons, to make them no longer groups of training data, and replace them with the states of both the cells and their neighbors. Each cell is not only part of input neuron, but also the output neuron. This kind of method of rule formation is somewhat similar to a "black box".

Next we will introduce the steps of BP-CA algorithm

(1) Training: to provide input vector and expected output for the BP neural network (cellular space $n \times n$), and train the network. The input vector can be expressed as:

$$A_k = (a_1^k, a_2^k, \ldots, a_9^k) \quad k \in [1, n^2] \tag{6.26}$$

The expected output can be expressed as:

$$Y_k = (y_1^k, y_2^k, \ldots, y_q^k) \quad k \in [1, n^2] \tag{6.27}$$

Inside the expression, $a_1^k \sim a_9^k$ denotes the states of the central cell and its eight neighbor cells, q denotes the number of the cell states, while y_{q}^k denotes the transit possibility of the cell state, which expresses the possibility of the individual cell to transit into the corresponding state at the next moment. The training will be over when the training error reaches the standard.

(2) Forecasting: put the data of the cellular state (new input vector) that needs to be forecasted as input to the trained network, forecast the state of cell at next moment of evolution.

The input vector:

$$A'_k = (a_1'^k, a_2'^k, \ldots, a_9'^k) \quad k \in [1, n^2] \tag{6.28}$$

The output vector:

$$Y'_k = (y_1'^k, y_2'^k, \ldots, y_q'^k) \quad k \in [1, n^2] \tag{6.29}$$

Expression (6.29) can be considered as the cellular evolution rule mined out by BP algorithm.

According to the above description, BP-CA process flow can be summed up as the following: extract the cell states that can reflect the overall conversion trends at the moment of t and t + 1, and input them to BP network to mine the network's transformation rules. Cellular data at moment t + 1 can also be used to predict the neural network input data at moment of t + 2.

6.3.3 Modeling Examples—Forecast Disease Transmission

Current literature in this aspect is concentrated in introducing the basic land usage. Next, we will use cellular automata to design a new model—disease transmission model. The model itself has no special meaning, with no empirical data as its validation. The purpose is just to more vividly illustrate BP-CA algorithm.

1. The set up of cellular automata
   Modeling background: There is a disease that can be transmitted within the range of Moore type neighborhood. The historical experiences in that same period showed that when entering the summer from spring season, within the range of a group of 100 people, 30% of them remained healthy, while mild infection number was 50% and severe infection number was 20%. Now we need to forecast the evolution of the group infection of the disease for this year's period from spring into the summer.
   (1) Cellular space size: $n \times n$ grid.
   (2) Cellular neighbor type: Moore type, as shown in Fig. 6.11.
   (3) Cellular state: expresses the degree of infection. It is denoted in numbers. "0" denotes healthy; "1" denotes mild infection; "2" denotes severe infection.
   (4) The rule of disease transmission: The rule we are talking here is different from any type of evolution rules we have talked about in precious chapters. Disease transmission is an event of probability, and is not decided by a certain type of deterministic rule. In the model we are going to introduce, the forecasting of a disease transmission (the formation of evolution rule) takes reference from historical data of the same period in the year, and forms an expected output pattern, to forecast the future evolution. Specifically, we are using the evolution pattern at the period of $t \sim t + 1$ to predict the evolution results for the period of $t + 2 \sim t + 3$.
2. The set up of BP neural network
   With the help of Fig. 6.11, the inputs and outputs and the flow of operating process of the neural network is shown in Fig. 6.12.
   Due to the limited space, Fig. 6.12 only shows one set of the input pattern. During BP neural network training process, each cell will provide a set of neighbor state imbedded information as the input to the network, to adjust network weights through the desired output. In the forecasting process, enter the new cellular state ("this spring"), the results obtained in the output layer can predict the probability of cellular state transition.
3. Computer simulation
   1) Setting up simulation parameters (see Table 6.1).
   2) Rule mining process (training).
      Extracting cellular automata neighbor states as a training sample inputs for BP neural network training (see Fig. 6.13), obtaining the desired output by

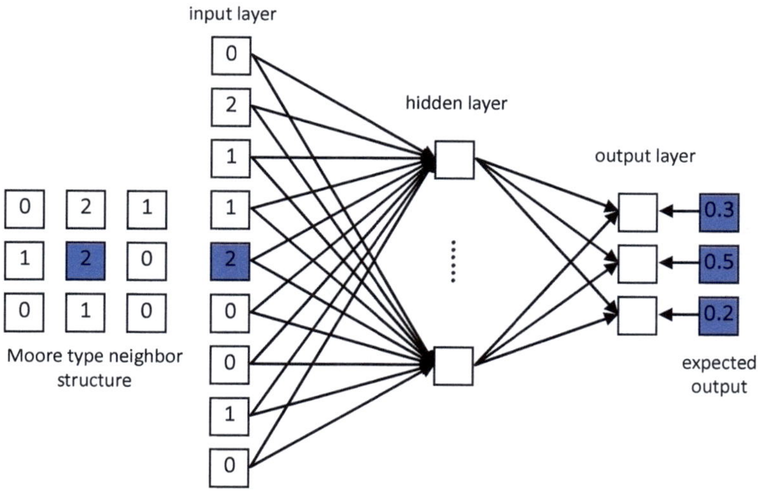

Fig. 6.12 The inputs and outputs and the flow of operating process of BP neural network

Table 6.1 Setting up simulation parameters

Parameter name	Sign	Value
Cell space size	$n \times n$	10×10
Neural cell number in input layer	–	9
Neural cell number in hidden layer	–	6
Neural cell number in output layer	–	3
Maximum training times	Epochs	2000
Training required accuracy	Goal	0.001

means of historical data with: health probability of 0.3; mild infection probability of 0.5; severe infection probability of 0.2.

3) Forecasting process (see Fig. 6.14).

In the figure, the horizontal axis represents cellular number. Three probability curves are outputs of neural network, representing at the next moment, the individual cell with its number corresponding to the horizontal axis will change into the three states with respective probability (it can be seen that changing probability of each cell is different). The simulation results are as shown in Table 6.2.

From Fig. 6.14 and Table 6.2 it can be seen that, the evolution rules can be mined out through the input patterns abstracted from cellular automata neighbor structure, and the evolution of the respective individual at next moment can be well forecasted as well. So that we can see that this evolution pattern is different from "Game of Life", etc., but a kind of "fuzzy" evolution rule formed by state transfer probability.

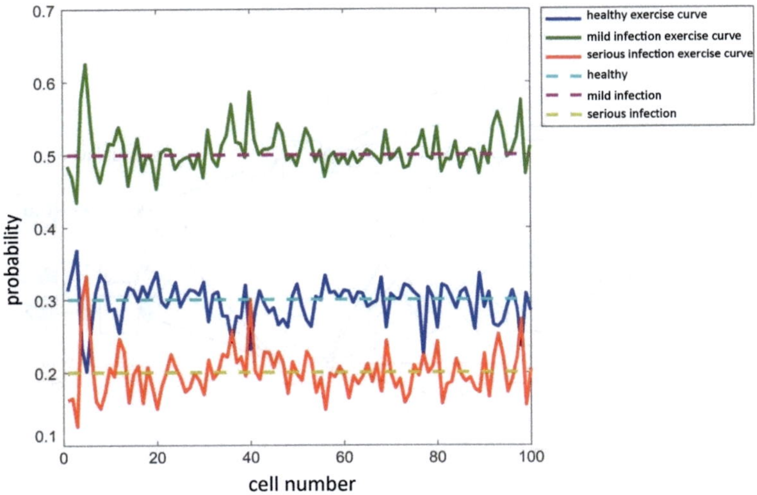

Fig. 6.13 Rule mining process (training)

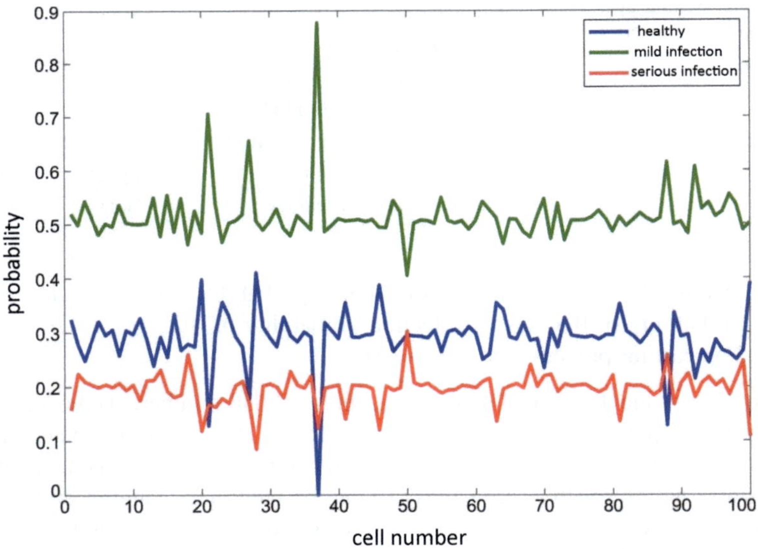

Fig. 6.14 Forecasting process

6.3.4 Summary

In this section, started from basic BP neural network algorithm, we explored how this algorithm could be combined with cellular automata, to build a cellular neural

Table 6.2 Simulation results

From spring to summer	Healthy	Mild infected	Severe infected
Historical experiences	0.3	0.5	0.2
Forecasted average evolution probability	0.289	0.516	0.196

network structure that took the states of the center cell and its neighbors as inputs, and the state renewal of the center cell as output. We also put this structure into the simulation application and obtained rather satisfactory results. However, the modeling theme in this section is to use the neural network to help the cellular automata to mine the rules. Whether the cellular automata can dig into the core of neural network algorithm and obtain good effects in realizing some functions? We leave this question to be answered in next several sections.

6.4 Self-adapting Cellular Neural Network Model (SCNN)

In the BP-CA model of previous section, the function of BP neural network is to mine the evolution rules of cellular automata. Currently, such method has been applied to the study of the evolution of land use and other related issues quite maturely. However, the combination of the two (cellular automata and neural network) has not changed or has raised the functionality of the cellular automaton itself. In this section, we will seek more in-depth combination of the two, building a "cellular neural network" model in the true sense.

6.4.1 Modeling Theme and Theory Base

In the Chap. 5 of cellular automata genetic algorithms, we discovered that local interactive operations with self-adapting feature among individual cells can reach the goal of global operation. In genetic algorithms, such interactive operations take the forms of "selection", "crossover" and "mutation". However, in artificial neural networks, local operation takes the form of parallel weight adjustment among individual neurons. The common features between the learning process of neural networks and the evolution process of cellular automata are:

(1) Parallel and distributed processing;
(2) Nonlinear processing.

The difference between the two is that a neural network has independent learning algorithms (such as Hebb Learning Algorithm, δ Learning Algorithm, Random Learning Algorithm, Competing Learning Algorithm, etc.), while a cellular automaton itself does not possess such kind of algorithms. In addition, in calculation modes, neural network algorithm and cellular automata also have large differences in operation rules. A neural network is for expression and utilization of knowledge. It converts all the problem features into numbers, and then by using preset neuron functions, to convert all the reasoning into numerical calculation. Its essence is still not out of the shackles of analytical paradigm. A cellular automaton, on the other hand, although does not have its own intelligent algorithm, it is able to generate reasoning by utilizing evolution rules, thus it is rule calculation.

From the perspective of topology, the space layout of a two-dimensional cellular automaton (CA) is pretty similar with a neural network (NN) with fully connected structure among adjacent layers of neurons.

A neural network uses "weight" to deal with the information transmission between neurons, as well as the process of activation or inhibition. On the other hand, a two-dimensional cellular automaton uses the "neighbor structure" to communicate and transfer information. The difference is that neural networks often have multiple layers of neurons, and information transmission happens between the layers. The transmission of information within the cellular space of CA does not have a hierarchy or a direction. As we all know, so far for structural design of neural network, there is no basis for systematic theories or principles, people have to depend mostly on subjective experiences for judgment or experiments. However, cellular automata are good at solving real-world complicated decision-making problems that are unstable, nonlinear, and with uncertainty. A combination of both (NN and CA), may provide a new method and a new tool for the people to understand and simulate complex phenomena in nature.

In using neural network for processing of many practical problems, the input to the system is usually a time-dependent process, such as a price, a chemical reaction, or a weather forecasting. For such problems, some scholars put forwarded the proposal of using a network model of procedural neurons to solve the time-series forecasting problems in the year as early as 2000 (He and Liang 2000; He et al. 2001; Liu et al. 2011; Xu et al. 2007). However, when the input is sampling data of discrete-time, such system input cannot be expressed accurately as a deterministic analytic function, thus limiting the use of the networks of procedural neurons. In solving this problem, based on procedural neurons, some scholars used discrete Walsh Transformation, and proposed a kind of procedural neural network model as well as learning algorithms that were based on discrete inputs, thus avoided complex integration operations.

In the same time, in real-time complex systems, it is common to encounter the issues of analyzing and simulating group decision making. Because that cellular automata have the characteristics of discrete time, discrete space and parallel computing, we can treat the individual cells in CA as individual neurons, and cellular neighbor structure as the weighted connections of neurons among neighboring layers of a neural network, and combine the feature of self adapting operation of complex system, to build a self-adapting cellular neural network, try to provide a new method for the processing of discrete data series within multiple-subjects complex systems.

6.4.2 Endogenous Time Series Forecasting Model

As everyone knows that, in a complex self-adaptive system, the complexity of the output results of system overall evolution is usually decided by individual decision results, and also decided by repeated evolution of local interactions among individuals (such as the stock market). However, from the angle of individuals within a complex system, the complexity of the overall output is usually unpredictable and with no rules to follow. A typical example is a stadium, every audience watching the game in the stadium is a maker of cheer noise. But an audience can hardly predict accurately the time and frequency of the outbreak of the cheers. In other words, the individuals within the system are contributors of overall output, but when the individuals do not have certain intelligence, such contribution is unknown.

Next, we try to build a self-adaptive cellular neural network with capacity of evolution, to study when the discrete time series are generated by the evolution of the CA itself, how a cellular neural network will simulate a time series.

1. **Network Building**
   The self-adaptive cellular neural network we will build in this section contains input-layer, hidden-layer and output-layer. Each cell within the cellular space is a cell within both the input-layer and the hidden-layer. The topological structure of the network is illustrated in Fig. 6.15, while the cellular neighbor structure of the network is illustrated in 6–16.
   The cell numbers inside Fig. 6.16 is correspondent to the cell numbers inside Fig. 6.15. Above two figures reflect the mapping between the topological structure of a cellular neural network and a cell space neighbor structure. Here we adopted Von Neumann type neighbors, that is, each cell is connected with four cells at its upper, lower, left and right. Following the evolution of neural network, the weight network between input layer and weight layer evolutes continuously, and in every unit time period, there are some connections break off, and some connections build up.
2. **Network Operation Principles and Evolution Steps**
   As discussed before, each cell in the cellular space are both an input layer cell and a hidden layer cell. In every unit of time, the cellular neural network evolves according to the following rules:

   (1) The system generates actual output by using the demand prediction information of all the cells.
   (2) Every hidden layer (central) cell collects the prediction information of itself and its four neighbors in the input layer.
   (3) Using the system's actual output as the standard, every hidden layer (central) cell processes the prediction information collected from itself and its four neighbors in the input layer.
   (4) Every hidden layer (central) cell locates the neighbor (including itself) cell in the input layer which has the minimum prediction error, establishes a

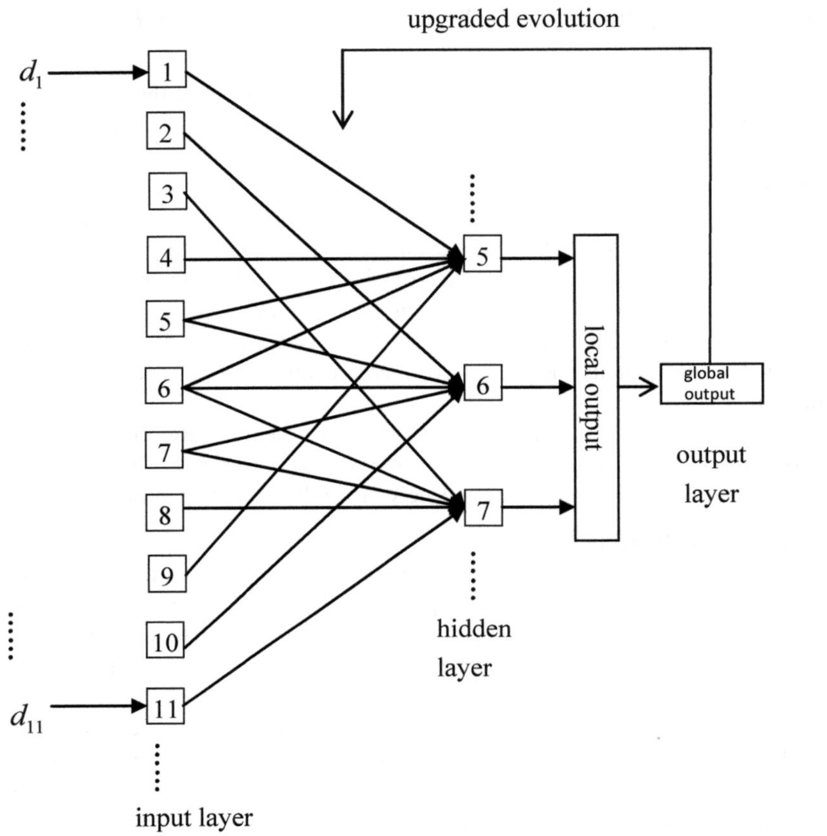

Fig. 6.15 A cellular neural network (with endogenous time series)

Fig. 6.16 The neighbor structure of local cells

	1	2	3	
4	5	6	7	8
	9	10	11	

connection with the cell's position in the input layer, and at the same time cuts off the connection with other input layer cells.

(5) Through the limited connections between the input layer and the hidden layer, the prediction information with high prediction accuracy from the input layer cells is transmitted to the hidden layer and gets preserved. At the same time, the prediction information of input layer cells is updated.

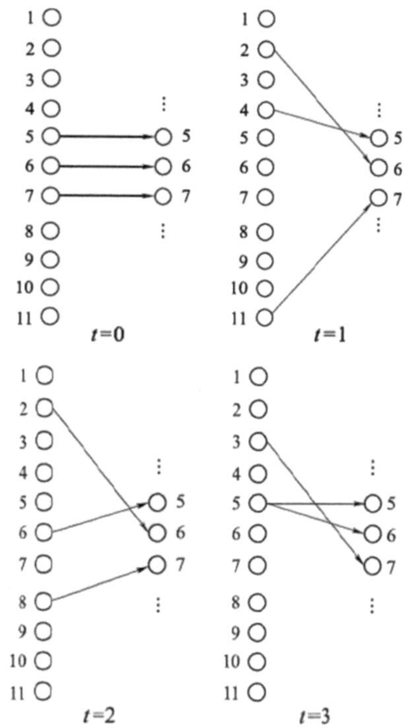

Fig. 6.17 The evolution of network connection (1). The evolution of network connection (2)

(6) Return to step (1).
It is not difficult to find that the evolution process of the network connection between input layer cells and hidden layer cells realizes the screening of the prediction information provided by input layer cells. The process of this network evolution can be shown be Fig. 6.17 (in order to avoid too many connection weights causing the result to be hard to recognize, here we use only three hidden layer cells as an example).
It can be seen that with the development of evolution, the network's state of connection is constantly being adjusted, and the prediction accuracy of the cell group will continuously improve.

3. **Computer Simulation**
Here, we use the prediction of a commodity's price-time series as an example to observe the operational effect of the cellular neural network. In this model, each cell predicts the price variation of the commodity as an independent individual, forms market demand, and then adjusts the weight connection with neighborhood cells according to the actual price output of the system, so as to obtain prediction information with higher accuracy.

1) Model Assumptions
   Cellular Space: an $n \times n$ lattice.
   Neighborhood Form: Von Neumann type neighborhood, i.e., each cell has four neighbors from the above, below, left and right.
   System Output: Here, we suppose the price of the commodity is only influenced by the overall supply and demand situation of the market, and there is a direct proportional relationship between an individual cell's demand of the commodity's quantity and its prediction of the commodity's price variation.

$$q_{i,t} = k\Delta p_{i,t} \tag{6.30}$$

   In the formula, $q_{i,t}$ represents cell i's demanded quantity of the commodity at moment t; k is the proportional coefficient; $\Delta p_{i,t}$ represents cell i's prediction of the amount of the commodity's price change at moment t. It can be seen that when an individual cell predicts a price increase, it produces positive demand quantity, and vice versa. When the demand quantities of individual cells are formed, we can update the system's output (to form the price) according to the following formula:

$$p_{t+1} = p_t + \alpha \sum_{i=1}^{n^2} q_{i,t} + \delta\sigma_t \tag{6.31}$$

   In it, α and δ represent proportional coefficients; σ_t is the random walk which conforms to normal distribution.
2) The Evolution Process of the Cellular Neural Network

   (1) Using the demand prediction information of all cells $\sum_{i=1}^{n^2} q_{i,t}$, the system generates actual output p_{t+1}.
   (2) Each hidden layer (central) cell collects the prediction information of itself and its four surrounding neighbors $\Delta p_{j,t}$ ($j \in \Omega$, Ω represents the set of neighbors).
   (3) Using the system's actual output p_{t+1} as the standard, each hidden layer (central) cell processes (compares) the prediction information of itself and its four surrounding neighbors.
   (4) Each hidden layer (central) cell locates the neighbor cell (including itself) j^* with the minimum prediction error $\min\{|p_{t+1} - (p_t + \Delta p_{j,t})|, (j \in \Omega)\}$, establishes a connection with the cell's position in the input layer, and at the same time cuts off connections with other input layer cells.
   (5) Through the limited connections between the input layer and the hidden layer, the prediction information with high prediction accuracy from the input layer cells $\Delta p_{j^*,t}$ is transmitted to the hidden layer and gets preserved. At the same time, the prediction information of input layer cells is updated.

(6) Return to step (1).

3) Setting Simulation Parameters (see Table 6.3).
4) Simulation Results (see Fig. 6.18).
Figure 6.18a represents the change image of price prediction values obtained by tracking five randomly chosen cells; Fig. 6.18b represents the average prediction error of all cells in the cellular space. It can be seen that with the evolution of weight connections among cells, the prediction values of individual cells continuously get closer to the actual values, and the average prediction error of the whole group keeps decreasing. In the prediction series generated, the maximum error is 0.4829; the minimum error is 0.002; the average error is 0.025. This is a satisfactory prediction result.

6.4.3 *Exogenous Time Series Prediction Model*

In the above "endogenous time series prediction," the "time series" is obtained by the complex evolution behavior of cellular automata. Individual cells (neurons) in a self-adaptive cellular neural network are both predictors of a time series, and contributors to its formation. The operation of a self-adaptive cellular neural network establishes a connection between the local behavior of individual cells and the complex evolution of a cellular automaton system as a whole. Next, we might as well think: if the time series used for training a cellular neural network is exogenous, and individual cells do not have the relative knowledge about the time series beforehand, then how can a self-adaptive cellular neural network predict the time series?

1. **Network Construction**
The self-adaptive cellular neural network established in this section includes an input layer, two hidden layers and an output layer. Unlike the cellular neural network constructed for studying the endogenous time series, we redesigned the network structure. Since the cells themselves are no longer contributors to the formation of the time series, cells are no longer input layer neurons, but only hidden layer neurons. The topographical structure of the network is shown in Fig. 6.19, and the local cell neighbor structure is shown in Fig. 6.20.

Table 6.3 Setting simulation parameters

Name of parameter	Symbol	Value
Size of cellular space	$n \times n$	20×20
Time of evolution	T	100
Initial price	p_0	10
Proportional coefficient	k	2
Proportional coefficient	α	0.001
Proportional coefficient	δ	0.01

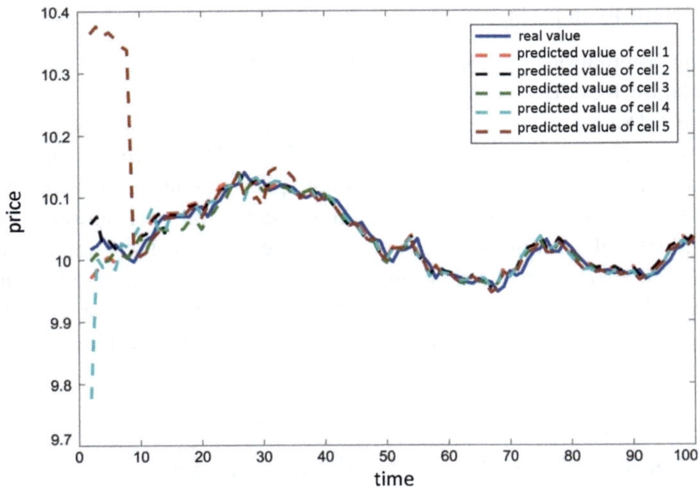

(a) Actual Price Values and Predicted Values

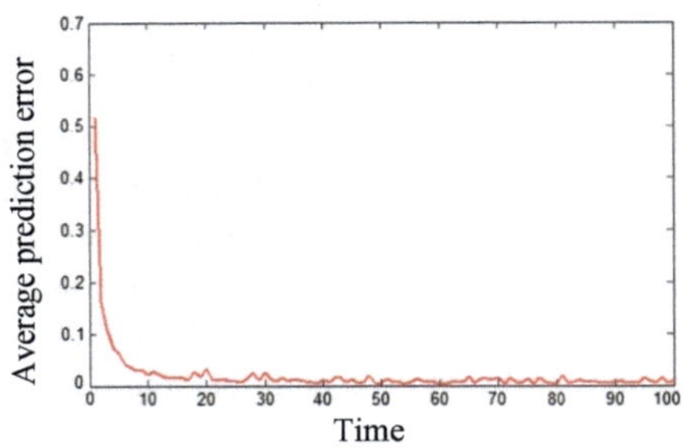

(b) Average Error

Fig. 6.18 Simulation results

The numbers of cells in Figs. 6.19 and 6.20 correspond to each other. The above two Figures reflect the mapping relationship between the topographical structure of the cellular neural network and the neighborhood structure in the cellular space. The two Figures still use the Von Neumann type of neighborhood. With the evolution of the neural network, the weight networks between the input layer and the hidden layer, as well as between the two hidden layers constantly evolve. At every unit time interval, some connections are cut off while some others are established.

2. **Network Operation Principles and Steps of Evolution**

   In a self-adaptive cellular neural network which deals with the prediction problem of exogenous time series, cells in the cellular space are all hidden layer cells. At every unit of time interval, the cellular neural network evolves according to the following rules:

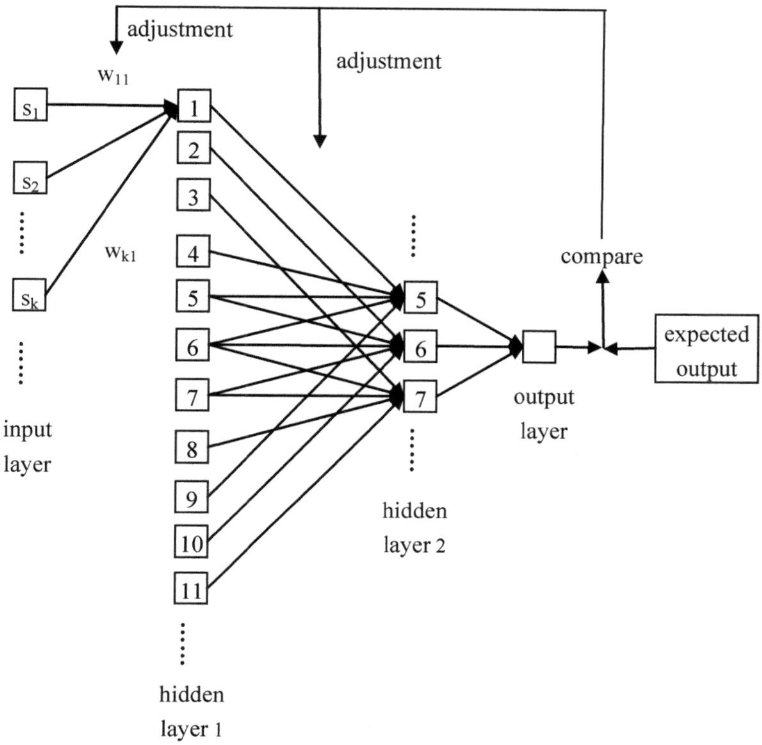

Fig. 6.19 Cellular neural network (exogenous time series)

Fig. 6.20 Local cell neighbor structure

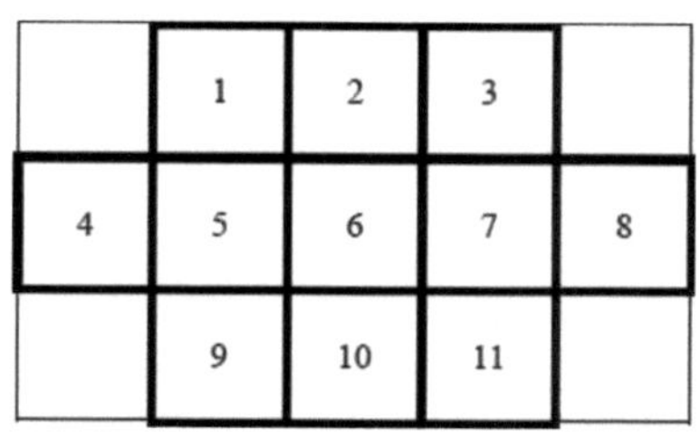

(1) The input layer accepts the historical time series change information, processes it by adding the weight coefficient and transmits it to the cells in hidden layer 1.
(2) Each cell in hidden layer 2 (central) collects the prediction information of itself and its four surrounding neighbors in hidden layer 1.

(3) Using the system's expected output as the standard, each cell in hidden layer 2 (central) processes the prediction information of itself and its four surrounding neighbors in hidden layer 1.
(4) Each cell in hidden layer 2 (central) locates the neighbor cell in hidden layer 1 (including itself) with the minimum prediction error, establishes a connection with its position in hidden layer 1, and at the same time cuts off connections with other cells in hidden layer 1.
(5) Through the limited connections established between hidden layer 1 and hidden layer 2, the prediction information with high prediction accuracy in cells in hidden layer 1, as well the weight coefficient of the connection between hidden layer 1 and the input layer are transmitted to hidden layer 2, and get preserved. At the same time, update the weight coefficient of corresponding cells in hidden layer 1 and the input layer.
(6) Return to step (1).
It can be seen that the evolution of weight connections between the input layer and hidden layer 1, as well as between the two hidden layers enables the weight connections in the cellular space which can produce relatively high prediction accuracy be preserved. The process of the network's evolution can be displayed by Fig. 6.21 (in order to avoid too many connection weights to cause the result hard to be recognized, here we only use one cell in hidden layer 2 as an example).
Thus, through the continuous adjustment of the weight connections of the network, the weights with high prediction accuracy are widely learned and preserved. By this, the prediction accuracy of the cell group will keep improving.

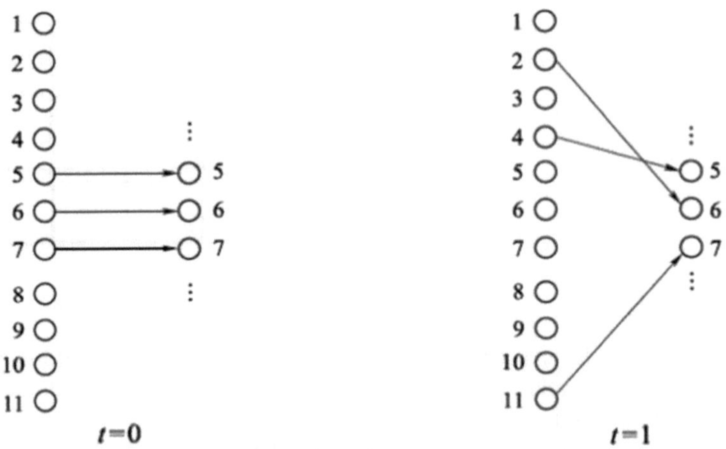

(a) cell 5 discovers that the prediction of cell 6 among its neighbors is most accurate

(b) learns from cell 6

Fig. 6.21 Evolution process of a local cellular neural network

3. **Computer Simulation**

Here, we choose the annual data of sunspots for 200 continuous years (1700–1899) as the time series of the prediction target to test the effectiveness of the self-adaptive cellular neural network in the prediction of an exogenous time series. The prediction plan is as follows: Using the data from previous s years to predict the data of the next year. For example, using data from years 1700, 1701, 1702, 1703, and 1704 to predict the number of sunspots in 1705. Here, $s = 5$.

1) Model Assumptions

Cellular space: an $n \times n$ lattice.

Neighborhood Type: Von Neumann neighborhood, i.e., each cell has four neighbors from the top, bottom, left, and right.

Cell state: expressed by the following triad:

$$S_{i,t} = \left(Q_{i,t}, W_{i,t}, L_{i,t}\right) \tag{6.32}$$

In it, $Q_{i,t}$ represents the historical data of cell i in the previous s years; $W_{i,t}$ represents the weight tendency of cell i towards the historical data in different years in the previous s years; $L_{i,t}$ represents the state of connection between cell i as a hidden layer neuron and other neurons.

2) The Evolution Process of the Cellular Neural Network

(1) The input layer accepts the historical time series change information ($q_{t-s+2} - q_{t-s+1} \sim q_t - q_{t-1}$), adds different weight coefficients $w_{1,i} \sim w_{s-1,i}$ for processing and forms the prediction of the future $E_i\ (q_t)$, which is transmitted to each cell in hidden layer 1. The input of cell i in hidden layer 1 is:

$$E_i(q_t) = q_t + \sum_{k=2}^{s} w_{k-1,i}(q_{t-k+2} - q_{t-k+1}) \tag{6.33}$$

In it, $\sum_{k=2}^{s} w_{k-1,i} = 1$.

(2) Each cell in hidden layer 2 (central) collects the prediction information of itself and its four surrounding neighbors in hidden layer 1 (represented by set Ω). For example, according to the serial numbers of cells shown in Fig. 6.20, cell 5 will collect $E1\ (qt)$, $E4\ (qt)$, $E5\ (qt)$, $E6\ (qt)$, $E9\ (qt)$.

(3) Using the system's expected output as the standard, each cell in hidden layer 2 (central) processes the prediction information of itself and its four surrounding neighbors in hidden layer 1. For example, according to the serial numbers of cells in Fig. 6.20, cell 5 will arrange $\left|q_{t+1} - E_j(q_t)\right|$ (j = 1, 4, 5, 6, 9) in order.

(4) Each cell in hidden layer 2 (central) locates the neighbor cell in hidden layer 1 (including itself) with the minimum prediction error $\left\{\left|q_{t+1} - E_j(q_t)\right|, j \in \Omega\right\}$, establishes a connection with its position in

hidden layer 1, and at the same time cuts off connections with other cells in hidden layer 1.

(5) Through the limited connections established between hidden layer 1 and hidden layer 2, the prediction information with high prediction accuracy from cells in hidden layer 1 and the weight coefficient of the connection between hidden layer 1 and the input layer $w^*_{1,i} \sim w^*_{s-1,i}$ are transmitted to hidden layer 2 and preserved. At the same time, update the weight coefficient of corresponding cells in hidden layer 1 and the input layer $w_{1,i} \sim w_{s-1,i}$.

(6) Return to step (1).

3) Setting Simulation Parameters (see Table 6.4).
4) Simulation Results
Observing Fig. 6.22, it is not difficult to see that on the whole, the average group prediction level in the cellular space simulates the real time series pretty well (since the prediction needs to use data from ten years before, the initial prediction value is 0). Errors often appear at wave crests and troughs of the series, while in other years, the prediction results are relatively ideal. In the prediction series generated, the maximum error is 15.42; the minimum error is 0.010; the average error is 4.35.

6.4.4 Summary

In this section, we established self-adaptive cellular neural network models based on both endogenous time series and exogenous time series. By combining the evolution rules of cellular automata and the learning mechanism of neural networks, we established the connection between the intelligent behavior of micro individuals and the overall output of the system, and obtained relatively satisfactory prediction results. We made the following two important improvements to traditional artificial neural network algorithm.

(1) The description of neurons: a traditional neural network only regards neurons as transfer stations relying on weighted paths to transmit information. They do not have autonomy, and are considered "death-like." In a self-adaptive cellular neural network, however, individual cells are used to replace the original

Table 6.4 Simulation parameters

Name of parameter	Symbol	Value
Size of cellular space	$n \times n$	20 × 20
Series information from previous s years which cells can use	s	10
Time of evolution	T	200
Weights of the input layer	$w_{1,i} \sim w_{s,i}$	[0, 1]

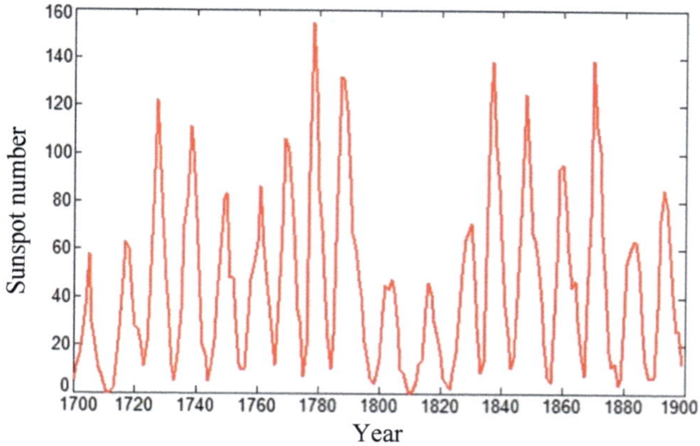

(a) Real Data (expected output)

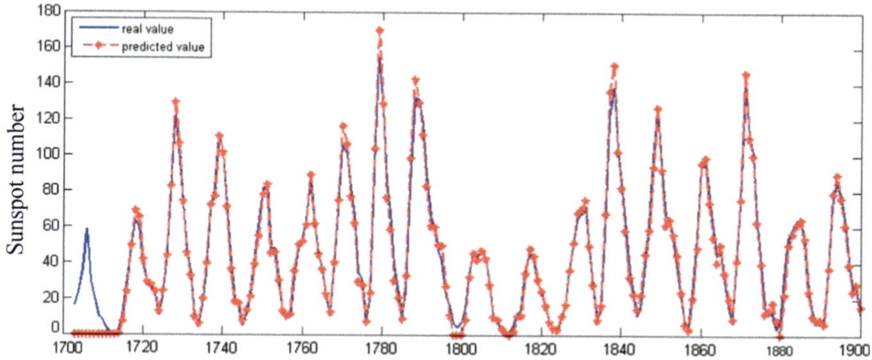

(b) Real Data and the Average Prediction Value in the Cellular Space (s=10)

Fig. 6.22 Real value and prediction value

neurons, so that neurons are given the abilities to autonomously learn and identify things. Such a design has obtained good prediction results.

(2) The "evolution" of weight: in self-adaptive cellular neural networks, the neighborhood structures of cellular automata and the weighted connections in traditional neural networks are effectively combined. Local connections are used to replace global connections, so that weighted networks which are "capable of evolving" are formed. By establishing regular networks, we enabled cellular automata to realize the function of predicting time series.

To sum up, the establishment of self-adaptive cellular neural networks provides a powerful tool for the multi-agent simulation in a complex society's economic system, as well as for group decision-making modeling.

6.5 Cellular Genetic Neural Network (CGNN)

In the previous section on cellular neural networks, we used cells to replace the original neurons, and established a kind of evolutionary weight network through cellular neighborhood structure and relationship. By establishing connections between the central cell and the excellent individuals among its neighbors, we optimized the prediction outcome and obtained relatively satisfactory result.

From the idea and the operation of "cellular genetic algorithm" as introduced in Chap. 5, it is not difficult to find that, one of the important reasons for obtaining relatively good optimization effect in combining cellular automata's evolution and evolutionary computation, is that no matter it is the chromosomes in genetic algorithm or the weights in an artificial neural network, when the information of individuals is placed in a cellular space which has neighborhood structures, the transmission effect of neighborhood structures in the process of evolution makes the information of excellent individuals well preserved, thereby raising the quality of solution or optimization.

To date, there has been plenty of literature using genetic algorithm to optimize and improve artificial neural networks. The central idea of improvement is to optimize the process of weight adjustment in neural networks by using genetic algorithm (Li et al. 2011; Yang et al. 2001). The method is to encode the combinations of weight coefficients in neural networks, regarding them as chromosomes and perform optimization of the weight coefficients through genetic operations such as selection, crossover, etc. In the following context, we will use a cellular automaton and its evolution rules to complete these operations.

6.5.1 Network Construction

In Sect. 6.4, the "weight" in the cellular neural network actually represents the evolutionary connective relationship among cells, while "neurons" are regarded as cells with self-learning abilities. In existing literature on using genetic algorithm to optimize neural networks, a frequently observed operation is to use genetic algorithm to train the weight coefficients in neural networks. Compared to classical genetic algorithm, cellular genetic algorithm possesses better problem-solving functions. Therefore, we might as well try to use the idea of cellular genetic algorithm to train weight coefficients in a neural network.

In this mode of optimization, each cell represents a encoding mode of the network weight coefficients. Through the screening and optimization of these weight coefficients with cellular genetic algorithm, the model structure of the result is shown by Fig. 6.23.

It can be seen that unlike the cellular neural network in Sect. 6.4, in a cellular genetic neural network, individual cells actually play the role of a "black box." Networks needing to be trained are stored inside the cells. The key of the algorithm

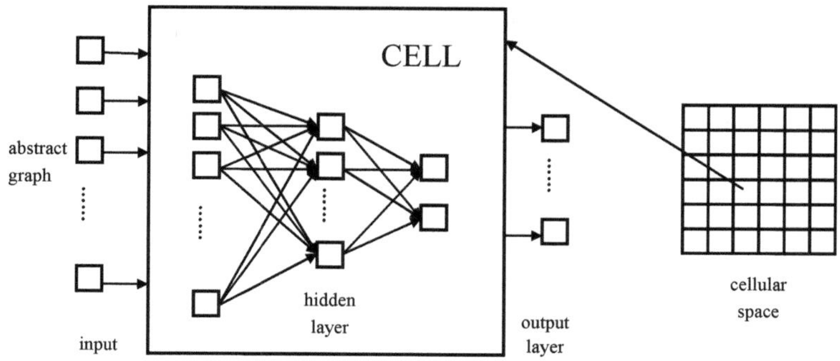

Fig. 6.23 Structure of cellular genetic neural network

is to enable networks inside individual cells to get trained by learning from each other through the neighbor relationships of cellular automata, thereby raise the overall optimization level.

6.5.2 Principles of Network Operation and Evolution Steps

Next, we will introduce the principles of operation and evolution steps of cellular genetic neural network in association with Fig. 6.23.

(1) Weight Initialization. Give each cell in the cellular space a set of its own network weight coefficients.
(2) Actual Output Calculation. Provide the same input information for each cell, use the weight network to calculate each cell's actual output. If the average actual output of the cellular space reaches the standard or completes the training steps, then end the algorithm. Otherwise, continue.
(3) Calculation of Degrees of Adaptability. Compare the expected output and each cell's actual output, and calculate the adaptability of each cell.
(4) Selection. Each cell selects the individual with the highest degree of adaptability in the neighborhood as the learning object.
(5) Duplication. Each cell performs duplication of the excellent individual neighbor which has been selected, and updates its own network weight coefficients.
(6) Return to step (2).

It is worth noticing that because each time a cellular automaton evolves, the weight coefficients are updated accordingly, i.e. the genetic operation is only performed once as CA evolves once. Unlike in simple genetic algorithm, The operations such as "crossing according to probability" and "mutation" are not performed. The purpose is to preserve excellent individuals in the process of information transmission among cells to the possibly greatest extent, but not to guarantee group diversity.

The above steps actually "embed" the weight updating operation of the artificial neural network into the cellular genetic algorithm, break away from the updating method of traditional neural network algorithm which is based on gradient information and analytic paradigm, and update network coefficients through the learning behavior among cells.

6.5.3 Computer Simulation

In this section, we still choose the annual data of sunspots for 200 consecutive years (1700–1899) as the predicting target time series, so as to test the effectiveness of the cellular genetic neural network in the prediction of time series. The prediction plan is as follows: to use data from s years before to predict the data in the next year. For example, use data from 1700, 1701, 1702, 1703, and 1704 to predict the number of sunspots in 1705. Here, $s = 5$.

1. **Model Suppositions**
   Cellular Space: an $n \times n$ lattice.
   Neighborhood Form: Moore Type Neighborhood, i.e., each cell has eight neighbors.
   Neural Network: Three-layer network structure. They are the input layer, the hidden layer and the output layer respectively. Design e number of neurons in the input layer, k number of neurons in the hidden layer, and m number of neurons in the output layer.
   Cell States: Expressed by the following two tuple:

$$S_{i,t} = \left(Q_{i,t}, WV_{i,t}\right) \tag{6.34}$$

   In it, $Q_{i,t}$ represents the historical data of cell i from s years before; $WV_{i,t}$ represents the network weight coefficients of cell i.
2. **Process of Evolution of the Cellular Genetic Neural Network**
   (1) Weight Initialization. Give each cell in the cellular space a set of its own network weight coefficients $WV_{i,t}$ (divided into $W_{i,t}$ between the input layer and the hidden layer, and $V_{i,t}$ between the hidden layer and the output layer).
   (2) Each cell accepts the historical time series change information $(q_{t-s+2} - q_{t-s+1} \sim q_t - q_{t-1})$, and uses such historical change information to make $s - 1$ different predictions $E_i(q_t)$ of real data at moment $t + 1$. The method of prediction is as follows:

$$\left.\begin{aligned} E_i(q_t)_1 &= q_t + (q_t - q_{t-1}) \\ &\vdots \\ &\vdots \\ E_i(q_t)_{s-1} &= q_t + (q_{t-s+2} - q_{t-s+1}) \end{aligned}\right\} s-1 \quad (6.35)$$

The set of $s - 1$ predictions are the input of the cell's own network ($e = s - 1$).

(3) Each cell calculates its actual output $Out_{i,t}$ through its own network weight coefficient $W_{i,t}$, as shown in Fig. 6.24.
According to the principles of neural networks, the method of calculation is as follows:

$$Out_{i,t} = \left[E_i(q_t)_1, \ldots, E_i(q_t)_{s-1}\right] \begin{pmatrix} w_{11} & \cdots & w_{1k} \\ \vdots & \ddots & \vdots \\ w_{e1} & \cdots & w_{ek} \end{pmatrix} \begin{pmatrix} v_{11} & \cdots & v_{1m} \\ \vdots & \ddots & \vdots \\ v_{k1} & \cdots & v_{km} \end{pmatrix} \quad (6.36)$$

$$In\,it, \sum_{i=1}^{e} w_{i,j} = 1 \quad (j = 1, \ldots, k); \qquad \sum_{i=1}^{k} v_{i,j} = 1 \quad (j = 1, \ldots, m)$$

(4) Each cell compares the difference between its actual output and the expected output (q_{t+1}), and calculates adaptability. The method is as follows:

$$fit_{i,t} = \frac{1}{|q_{t+1} - Out_{i,t}|} \quad (6.37)$$

(5) Each cell selects among its neighbors (including itself) the individual with maximum adaptability $\text{fit}_{\text{star},\,t} = \max\{\text{fit}_{j,t}, j\ \Omega\}$ as the learning object.

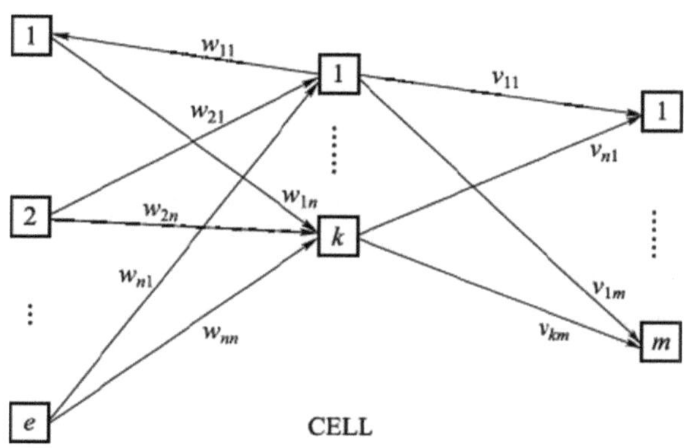

Fig. 6.24 Neurons and weights inside cells

Table 6.5 Setting simulation parameters

Name of parameter	Symbol	Value
Size of cellular space	$n \times n$	15×15
Series information from previous s years which cells can use	s	10
Time of evolution	T	200
Number of neurons in the input layer	e	9
Number of neurons in the hidden layer	k	6
Number of neurons in the output layer	m	1
Weights of the network	$w_{i,j}, v_{i,j}$	[0, 1]

(6) Each cell performs duplicate operation on the excellent individual neighbor which has been selected, and updates its own network weight coefficients.

$$\begin{aligned} W'_{i,t} &= W_{star,t} \\ V'_{i,t} &= V_{star,t} \end{aligned} \tag{6.38}$$

(7) Return to step (2).

3. **Setting Simulation Parameters (see Table** 6.5).
4. **Simulation Results**

   Regarding the sunspot data of 200 years, we use data from the first 150 years to train networks, and data from the later 50 years to perform prediction. The simulation results of training and prediction are shown in Fig. 6.25.

   From Fig. 6.25, it is not hard to discover that the group average prediction level in the cellular space simulates the real time series relatively well on the whole. Errors often appear at the series' wave crests and troughs. In other years, prediction results are relatively ideal. In the prediction series generated, the maximum error is 14.25; the minimum error is 0; the average error is 0.040. Compared to the self-adaptive cellular neural network proposed in Sect. 6.4.3, prediction accuracy has increased.

6.5.4 *Summary*

In this section, we did not change the structure of the artificial neural network itself, but blended the idea of cellular genetic algorithm into the dynamic process of updating neural network weight coefficients, thereby made predictions of time series and obtained good results. This mode of combination enriches the intelligent forms of individual cells, and provides certain reference for the modeling and simulation of group decision-making behavior in complex systems.

Combining this chapter with Chap. 5, it is not difficult to find that in the combination of cellular automata and intelligent algorithms, the points of combination

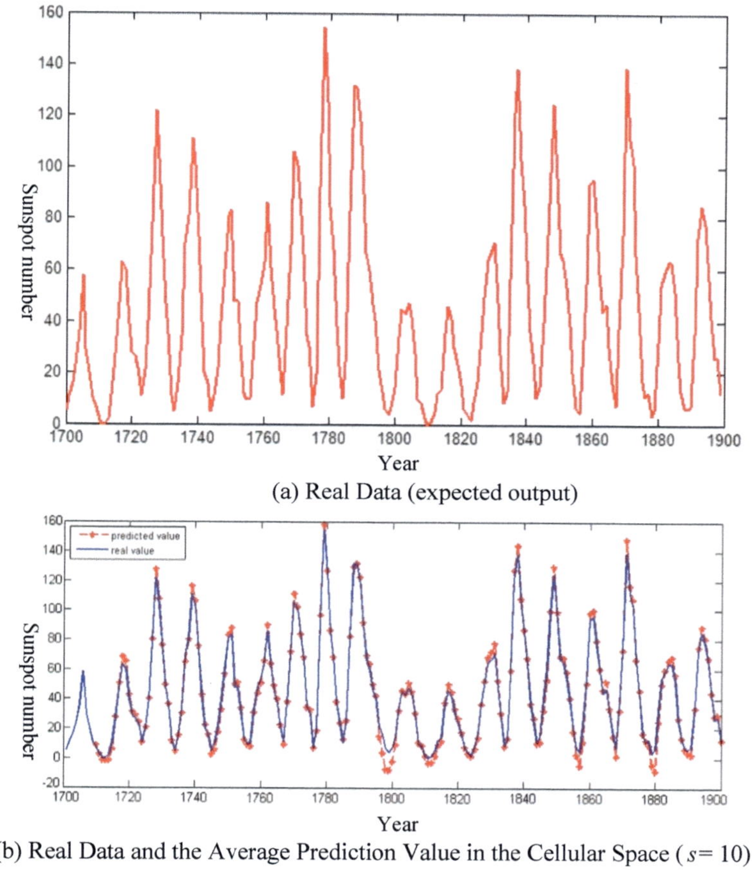

Fig. 6.25 Real value and prediction value

are often at the self-adaptive parts of intelligent algorithms (such as chromosomes, neurons, etc.). This provides insight for our future research—as more and more parts with the self-adaptive characteristic in intelligent algorithms combine with cellular automata, such a combination will become an important tool for the modeling and simulation of group decision-making behavior.

References

Acedo, L. (2009). A cellular automaton model for collective neural dynamics. *Mathematical and Computer Modelling, 50*(5–6), 717–725.

Bandman, O. (2002). Cellular-neural automaton: A hybrid model for reaction-diffusion simulation. *Future Generation Computer Systems, 18*(6), 737–745.

Cattaneo, G., & Vogliotti, C. Q. (1997). The, "magic" rule spaces of neural-like elementary cellular automata. *Theoretical Computer Science, 178*(1), 77–102.

Dohler, F., Mormanna, F., Weber, B., et al. (2008). A cellular neural network based method for classification of magnetic resonance images: Towards an automated detection of hippocampal sclerosis. *Journal of Neuroscience Methods, 170*(2), 324–331.

He, X., & Liang, J. (2000). Several theoretical issues on the process neuron networks. *China Engineering Science, 2*(12), 40–44.

He, X., Liang, J., & Xu, S. (2001). The training and applications of the process neuron networks. *China Engineering Science, 3*(4), 31–35.

Kim, K.-J., & Cho, S.-B. (2006). Evolved neural networks based on cellular automata for sensory-motor controller. *Neurocomputing, 69*(16–18), 2193–2207.

Li, L., & Mai, X. (2009). Dynamic simulation and prediction of karst rocky desertification based on CA—ANN spatial-temporal pattern. *Journal of Guangxi Normal University: Natural Science Edition, 26*(1), 84–89.

Li, X., Sun, Y., & Wu, J. (2011). A new kind of cellular network model. *Journal of Wuyi University: Natural Science Edition, 25*(4), 14–21.

Li, X., & Ye, J. (2005). Neural network based cellular automata and their applications on complex land utilization system simulations. *Geography Research, 24*(1), 19–27.

Liu, L., Li, P., Li, X., et al. (2011). The applications of discrete process neural network in time series prediction. *Computer Engineering and Applications, 47*(32), 224–227.

Tzionas, P. G. (2001). A cellular neural network modelling the behavior of reconfigurable cellular automata. *Microprocessors and Microsystems, 25*(8), 379–387.

Xu, S., He, X., & Wang, B. (2007). A study on time variation based input-output process neuron network and its learning algorithm. *Control and Decision, 22*(12), 1425–1428.

Yang, G., Cui, P., & Li, L. (2001). The applications and realizations of genetic algorithm in neural network control. *Journal of System Simulations, 13*(5), 567–570.

Zhao, J., Chen, H., & Huiping, X. (2007). Cellular automaton and neural network combined simulations on land evolution. *Journal of Tongji University: Natural Science Edition, 35*(8), 1128–1132.

Chapter 7
Agent-Cellular Automata

Introduction
In the previous two chapters (Chap. 5 "Cellular Genetic Algorithm" and Chap. 6 "Cellular Neural Networks"), we have seen that self-adaptive individuals distributed within the cellular lattice play roles of genes, chromosomes, and neurons respectively. The ability of learning among individual cells is strengthened, and at the same time the function of traditional artificial intelligence algorithm is realized. Next, we might as well consider this question—when individuals in the cellular space have different rules of evolution and learning, or they can move by themselves, or individual evolution rules change with time, can we give these individuals human characteristics such as emotions, beliefs, roles, consciousness, etc., and eventually make the space of cellular automata form a "real world" participated in by intelligent agents?

7.1 What Is an "Agent"?

Before introducing the relationship between Agent and cellular automata, let us introduce the basic concept of Agent first.

First, "agent" is an English word. Some translated it into Chinese the same as the word of "subject", while others translated it into Chinese the same as the word of "proxy". We might as well present a few examples for consideration: in news reports, we often hear that "the main (the corresponding Chinese word for "main" here has the same meaning as "subject") construction of building xx is completed"; in North Korea, there is the "Juche ('subject' and 'body,' meaning 'subjectivity' or 'agency') Idea", etc. In philosophy, "subjects" refers to persons who have the ability of cognition and practice. The opposite is "objects," i.e. objective things apart from "subjects," and which are the targets for the cognition and the practices of subjects. It is thus cleared that "subject" cannot fully reflect the original meaning of the word of "Agent".

X. Li et al., *Theory of Practical Cellular Automaton*,
https://doi.org/10.1007/978-981-10-7497-4_7

Now let us examine the other translation "proxy". "Proxy" means to fill or be responsible for a certain position on somebody's behalf. In law, "proxy" means being entrusted to conduct certain activities on the client's behalf, such as litigation, signing a contract, paying tax, etc. Thus, the meaning of "proxy" cannot express the primary meaning of Agent either.

So, what on earth is Agent?

7.1.1 The Concept of Agent

Because the word "Agent" is used widely, so far, there is no consensus on the definition of Agent among researchers. We can only find some representative descriptions of Agent in the research of different scholars:

In the book *The Society of Mind* published in 1986 by Minsky, the concept of Agent was put forward for the first time. The author considers an Agent as an individual with skills and social interactions, and a group of individuals can find methods for solving problems through mutual learning.

In describing Agent, the famous scholar of Agent theory Wooldridge and others proposed two types of definition "weak definition" and "strong definition." The weak definition of Agent refers to an individual with basic characteristics of autonomy, sociality, reactivity, initiative, etc. The strong definition of Agent adds mobility, communication capacity, rationality or other characteristics to the basic characteristics of the weak definition.

Some scholars from the field of artificial intelligence believe that apart from the basic characteristics such as autonomy, independence, and so on, an Agent must also possess certain abilities that only belong to human beings. Shoham gives Agent a strong definition on a high level: if the state of an individual includes such mental states such as knowledge, belief, commitment, desire, ability, etc., this individual is an Agent. Generally speaking, an Agent can be understood as a person who fulfills his/her wishes through his/her own efforts.

Bill Gates called an intelligent Agent as "soft software." He said: "Once a program is written, it is fixed. The soft software seems to become more and more intelligent as you use it," "you can regard the Agent as a collaborator which is directly built in the software. It will remember what you are good at, what you did in the past, and will try to predict difficult problems, and propose solutions."

Scholars Charles M. Macal and Michael J. North defined Agent as "a discrete entity with independent goals and behavior, and has the ability to control its own behavior."

As we survey these concepts of Agent given by different scholars, we might as well present the key statements which can describe Agent from the perspective of "how does complexity come into being?" We can see from the cellular automata modeling in previous chapters that the heterogeneous behavior among individuals is often the source for the overall system to produce complexity, while the degree of heterogeneity among individual cells is often restricted by local rules, different areas and levels, etc. in the cellular space, thereby restricting the generation of complexity to some extent. Therefore, we can describe Agent as follows in this book: Agent is a class of individuals which have the abilities to communicate with each other, to adapt to the environment, and to change their own behavior and the rules of operation through learning.

7.1.2 Characteristics of an Agent

From the concept of Agent, we can summarize that Agent should have the following basic characteristics.

(1) Autonomous Behavior. An agent is not directly controlled by others, and has certain control over its own behavior and internal states. Its behavior is active, spontaneous, goal-oriented and intentional. An agent can plan its short-term behavior according to the demands of its goal and the environment. One of the most basic attributes of an agent is the autonomy of its behavior.
(2) Reactivity. An agent is able to perceive its environment, and makes appropriate responses to the environment with the aid of its own behavior.
(3) Purpose. A agent does not make simple stress responses to events in the environment, instead it is able to exhibit behavior guided by a goal and to act proactively to achieve its intrinsic goals.
(4) Sociality. An agent exists in a social environment consisting of multiple agents, and exchanges information and ideas with other agents. Neither the existence nor the behavior of the agent is isolated, and we can even say that a multitude of agents form a simplified human society on a small scale.
(5) Cooperation. An agent seek to solve problems a single agent can not deal with through cooperation and coordination, thus to improve its ability of dealing with the problems. In the process of cooperation, a variety of new mechanisms and algorithms are introduced. Cooperation is one of the most important attributes of an agent, and is also a manifestation of its sociality.
(6) Operation Sustainability. Once the agent's program is started, it can maintain the state of running for quite a long time, and does not immediately halt operation with stop of the calculation.
(7) System Adaptability. An agent not only can perceive the environment and respond to it, but also can integrate the newly born agents into the system without the need to redesign the existing multi-agent system. Thus, an agent has very strong adaptability and expandability, and we may also call this characteristic as openness.
(8) Functional Intelligence. An agent emphasizes the role of rationality and can be used as the uniform model for describing machine intelligence, animal intelligence and human intelligence. An agent's function possesses comparatively high intelligence, and such intelligence is often a part of the composition of social intelligence.

7.1.3 Classification of the Structure of an Agent

The concept and characteristics of an agent can be used to abstract a most basic general model of Agent, which consists of three parts, as shown in Fig. 7.1.

Figure 7.1 is an abstract model of an agent with sensor and effector. Entities in a particular environment sense the environment through the sensor and act on the environment through the effector. Agent can use its own knowledge to solve problems, and can also carry out information exchange and cooperative work with other agents.

It is can be seen that the key of using "Agent" concept is to design a set of programs to realize the mapping function of the agent from perception to action. For this set of programs, we have to have a platform which enables them to run on it, and we call this platform "system structure." It is this platform of "system structure" that enables the designed programs not only to correctly perceive environmental changes, but also to exert correct feedback on the environment. If we consider Agent as a delicious dish, then "system structure" is the cooking utensils, and the "programs" are the ingredients. Obviously, Agent, system structure and the programs have the following relationship:

$$\text{Agent} = \text{system structure} + \text{programs}$$

Here, we start from the concept of Agent itself as introduced in Sect. 7.1.1, and divide Agent into two categories: intelligent proxy Agent and intelligent subject Agent. From the names of these two types of Agents, it is not difficult to understand that the so-called "intelligent proxy Agent" refers to Agent which can substitute human beings to finish certain work. The intelligence of this kind of Agent uses human consciousness as guidance, accepts human commands, serves people, and its

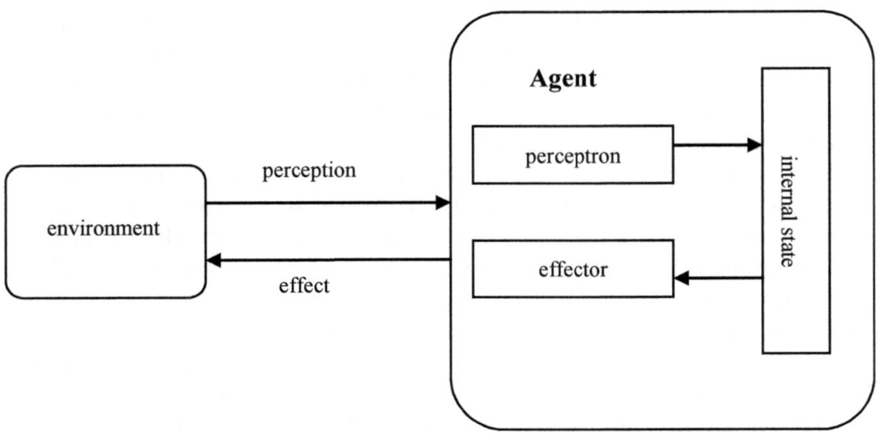

Fig. 7.1 General model of agent

behavior has excitability and follows certain procedure, such as office automation Agent and information collection Agent. The so-called "intelligent subject Agent" refers to Agent with a higher degree of intelligence and stronger autonomy. To this point, the Agent has come to have some intelligent characteristics of human beings, its action mode is no longer completing a task after accepting certain kind of instructions from people. Instead, it has high bionic intelligence and independent thinking ability to some extent, can even have emotions and personality, can independently judge the environment, and make decision for actions.

Here are two examples of "intelligent proxy Agent":

(1) Reactive Type Agent: as the name implies, this kind of Agent can only produce a response to external stimuli, but there exist no internal processes, as shown in Fig. 7.2.

The characteristics of this kind of Agent are: its level of intelligence is low and the system is not flexible, but with high speed in solving the problems.

(2) Tracking Type Agent: this kind of Agent starts the work by finding the rules internally which matches the external environment, and then performs the functions associated with the rules, as shown in Fig. 7.3.

The following are two examples of "intelligent subject Agent".

(1) Careful Thinking Type Agent: this kind of Agent keeps the tradition of classic artificial intelligence.

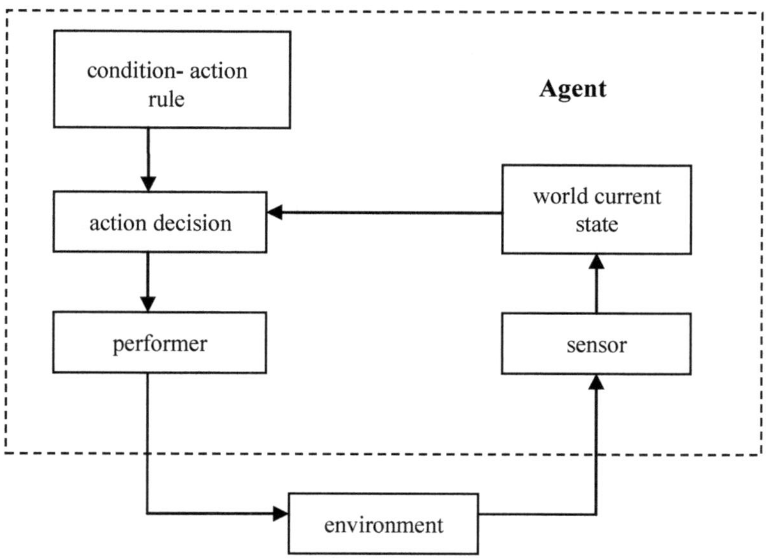

Fig. 7.2 Reactive mode agent

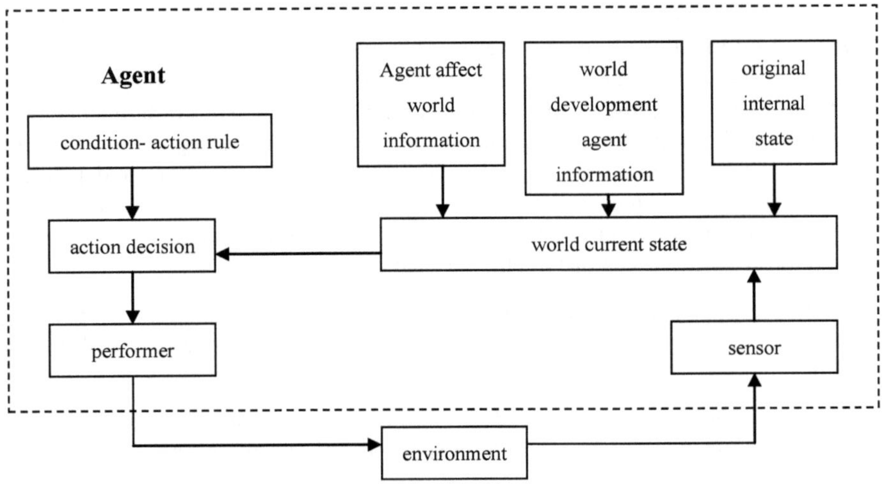

Fig. 7.3 Tracking mode agent

(2) Agent receives information from the outside environment through the sensor, and modifies its internal state, then makes action decisions through the knowledge base, and feeds back to the environment with the help of the performer, as shown in Fig. 7.4.

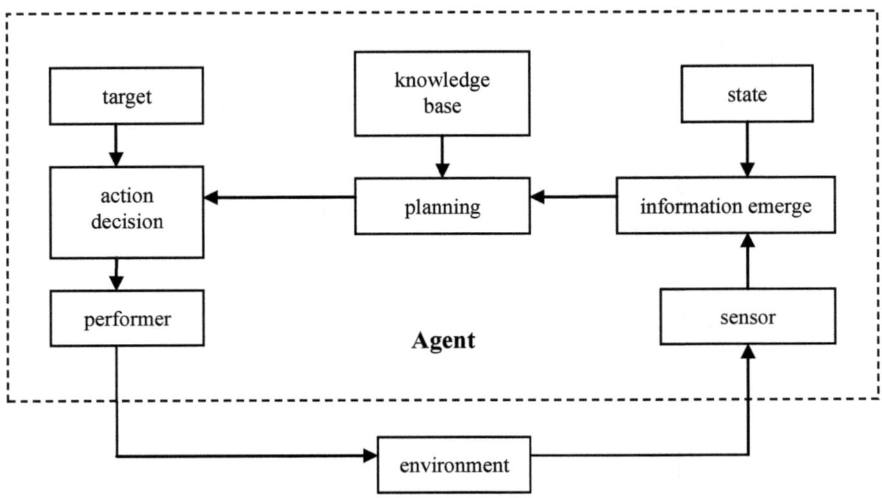

Fig. 7.4 Deliberating mode agent

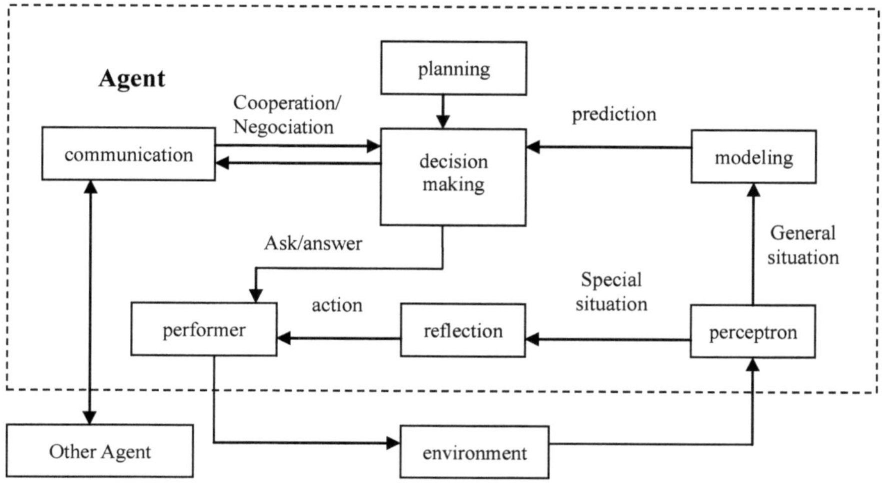

Fig. 7.5 Composite mode agent

The characteristics of this kind of Agent is that the intelligence level is high, while the speed of finding solutions is slow.

(2) Composite Type Agent: a composite Agent combines within one Agent a variety of intelligent forms which are relatively independent and are executed side by side. Its structure includes modules such as perception, action, response, modeling, planning, communication, decision-making, etc., as shown in Fig. 7.5.

In the above, we have introduced several kinds of basic classifications of Agent structures. Quite naturally that for Agent structures, different scholars will come up with different designing methods in accordance with their different backgrounds and research fields. As for complex system study, what kind of Agent structure will be used will depend on the specific situation.

7.1.4 The Internal Structure and Formal Description of Agent

1. **The Internal Structure of Agent**

After referencing a variety of Agent structure models, scholar Jianjun Ni proposed an Agent structure which is suitable for complex systems and has strong universality. Among the various studies about Agent to date, the structure Mr. Ni proposed is relatively comprehensive and coherent. We adopt the model of this structure in our book, as shown in Fig. 7.6.

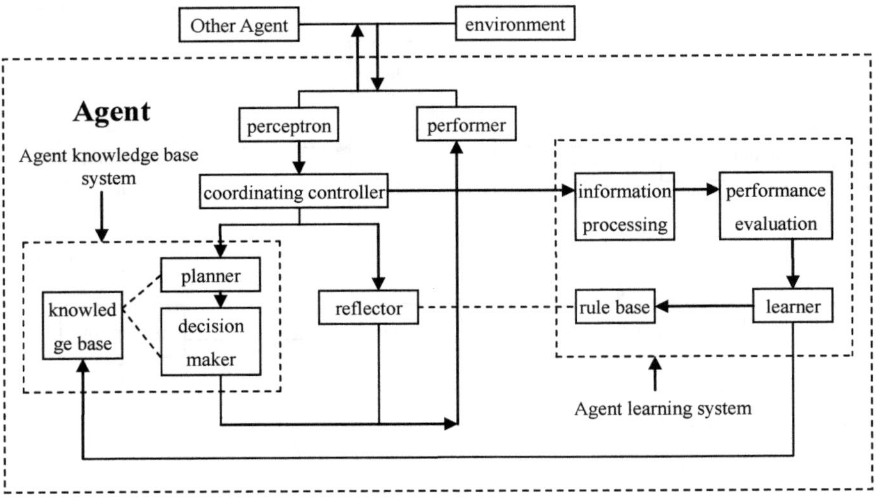

Fig. 7.6 Universal agent structure

It is not difficult to see that the structure of Agent in Fig. 7.6 is actually a synthesis of several Agent structures introduced in Sect. 7.1.3, in which the "Agent knowledge base system" and the "Agent learning system" are not only the core of the Agent's internal structure, but also the source of producing intelligence. Now we will introduce the important parts of the Agent's internal structure.

(1) The Coordination Controller: It can be seen from Fig. 7.6 that the coordination controller receives information sent from the sensor. It is responsible for classifying the information received by the sensor from the outside world. If circumstances are simple and urgent, the information is sent to the reactor; if circumstances are complex and the time for processing is sufficient, the information is sent to the planner and the decision maker for deeper processing.
(2) The Reactor: the reactor realizes the function of the "reactive type Agent" previously introduced. Its role is to let Agent make a quick response to emergent or simple events without thinking and reasoning. It has no intelligent characteristics. The rules the reactor uses can be represented by a IF statement:

IF condition perceived THEN action.

(3) The Planner: The planner within the Agent is responsible for establishing medium to short term, as well as local, action plans. The plans are "medium to short term" is because that, a complete plan for the goal is neither needed nor is possible for the Agent. The environment is constantly changing, and many

situations are unpredictable. Therefore, it is enough to just determine actions for the near term. To call the plan "local" here is due to the fact that each Agent only has limited knowledge of itself, the environment, and other Agents.

(4) The Decision maker: after the Agent has determined the goal, it will move on to select a predefined and feasible plan and hand it to the corresponding module for execution. This process is to be completed by the decision maker. Of course, these predefined plans come from the knowledge base.

(5) The Learner: The most important demonstration of an Agent's intelligence is that it has a learner. When an Agent faces a new environment and new problems, it can add mature and effective solutions to the knowledge base, or to update the rule base, so that they can be used conveniently when similar problems occur later.

(6) The Sensor: The sensor is the interface of the Agent for interactions with the external world. The Agent "sees" the real world and other Agents through the sensor, and then abstracts the things as "seen", and send them to the coordination controller.

(7) The Performer: The performer is the second interface of the Agent for interactions with the external world. It produces the agent's feedback to the external environment according to the action commands of the Agent.

2. **The Formal Description of Agent Structure Model**

For the convenience of later descriptions, we use an eight-element set to represent the structure model as shown in Fig. 7.6:

$$\text{Agent} ::= <\text{Identification}; \text{Type} ; \text{KB} ; \text{RB} ; \text{GS} ; \text{SS}; \text{AS}; \text{PS} >$$

(1) Identification:: <Agent Identification>: Identification is the Agent's number; each Agent has a unique identification.

(2) Type:: <Agent Type>: Type refers to the domain of the Agent and its knowledge and ability, or the role it plays. Agents of the same kind have the same abilities and attributes, such as are in the same school, have the same types of teachers, as well as have the same type of the students.

(3) KB:: <Knowledge Base (Agent Knowledge Base)>: Identifies the Agent's knowledge gathering. Different types of Agents have different Knowledge Bases. The difference of the Knowledge Bases is the fundamental reason for the Agent to make difference in planning and decision making.

(4) RB:: <Rule Base (Agent Rule Base)>: It refers to the rules the Agent will use when encountering an emergent or simple task. After the Agent receives the external information, it immediately matches the information with its own rule set. If the match is successful, it will perform the action specified by the rule immediately. If the Agent cannot find the matching rule, it will have to learn and add new rules to the Rule Base.

(5) GS:: <Goal Sets (Agent Goal Sets)>: They include goals which the Agent itself must achieve and the common goals the Agent must achieve for overall interests.
(6) SS:: <State Sets (Agent State Sets)>: State Sets refer to sets of some variable properties of the Agent, e.g., a student in a school, his grade ranking is a state.
(7) AS:: <Action Sets (Agent Action Sets)>: referring all the actions performed by the Agent in order to achieve a goal.
(8) PS:: <Plan Sets (Agent Plan Sets)>: referring to the plans made by the Agent to achieve a goal as it encounters complex problems or when time allows.

This structure model also reflects to a certain extent the hierarchical internal structure of the Agent.

7.1.5 Summary

In this section, we mainly introduced the concept, features, structural classification and formal description of Agent. It is important to highlight such a sentence that has summary meaning of the section—"Agent can learn to change their behavior and running rules". This sentence is also the basis of the combination of Agent and cellular automata we are going to discuss in the following context.

7.2 Cellular Automata and Agent

In the last section, we systematically introduced the concept, characteristics and structure of Agent at some length. Careful readers may now wonder whether the so-called connection between cellular automata and Agent is "placing" every Agent on every lattice square in the cellular space, then making the Agents participate in the evolution according to certain rules, and finally getting a result with some complexity. Is this connection accurate and comprehensive? This is exactly the question to be discussed in this section.

First, we begin this section with a vivid example.

7.2.1 Beginning from the Sergeant and the Soldiers

On a military training field, a sergeant is leading his squad of 10 soldiers to practice the formation drill. The sergeant can issue the following commands, and the soldiers must absolutely obey:

(1) Fall in.
(2) Right-dress.
(3) Left (Right/About) turn.
(4) Forward-march.
(5) Double time-march.
(6) Halt.
(7) Left (Right)-wheel forward (double time)-march.
(8) Dismiss.

Obviously, there are two kinds of Agents in this case: the sergeant and the soldiers. Regarding the structure of Agent, the "sergeant" here can be seen as the universal Agent in Fig. 7.6, while the "soldiers" can be seen as the simplest reactive mode Agent as shown in Fig. 7.2.

First, for clarity, we write out the formal description (Shi and Wei 2007) of the Agent structure involved in this example:

(1) Identification:: <Agent Identification>: the sergeant's number is 1, and the remaining ten soldiers are numbered from 2 to 11 sequentially.
(2) Type:: <Agent Type>: as mentioned before, there are two types of Agents in this case—"sergeant" and "soldiers."
(3) RB:: <Rule Base (Agent Rule Base)>: the sergeant Agent and soldier Agent have different Rule Bases. We can construct several rules for the Rule Base of the sergeant Agent, such as:

    ① IF the dismissal time given to the soldiers exceeds ten minutes, THEN issue the "Fall In" command.
    ② IF the training time of the soldiers exceeds forty-five minutes, THEN issue the "Dismiss" command.
    ③ IF the soldiers have assembled, THEN issue the "Right-dress" command.
    ④ IF the soldiers have assembled, THEN randomly issue the "Left (Right/About) turn" command.
    ⑤ IF the soldiers have turned left (right/about), THEN issue the "Forward (Double time)-march" command.
    ⑥ IF the soldiers have marched to the edge of the field, THEN issue the "Left (Right)-wheel forward (double time)-march" command.
    ……

Similarly, we can also construct some rules for the soldier Agents, such as:

① IF the sergeant issues the "Fall in" command, THEN forward march to the specified assembly area and search for empty space.
② IF the sergeant issues the "Dismiss" command, THEN forward march to a random position, but cannot occupy the same spot with other soldiers.
③ IF the sergeant issues the "Right-dress" command, THEN move close to the soldier on his right side; the soldier on the rightmost side moves close to the right border of the assembly area.

④ IF the sergeant issues the command of "Left (Right/About) turn," THEN change his own direction.
⑤ IF the sergeant issues the command of "Forward (Double time)-march," THEN change the speed and position of his movement.
⑥ IF the sergeant issues the command of "Left (Right)-wheel forward (double time)-march," THEN change the speed, position, and direction of his movement.
……

Of course, there are many other rules for formation drills, and interested readers can design their own rules. We are not going to go into more details here.

(4) SS:: <State Sets (Agent State Sets)>: the sergeant Agent and the soldier Agent have the same properties such as direction, speed, and position.
(5) AS:: <Action Sets (Agent Action Sets)>: on the training ground, we design the following actions:

Action 1: Forward-march—advance one square each time (in eight directions).
Action 2: Double time-march—advance two squares each time (in eight directions).
Action 3: Halt—the state of speed returns to zero.
Action 4: Left (Right/About) turn—the state of direction makes corresponding changes.
Action 5: Right-dress—all soldiers align using the right border of the assembly area as a reference.
Action 6: Left (Right)-wheel forward (double time)-march—update the states of position, speed, and direction.

……

Then, for intuitive viewing purpose, we map this 11 individual squad into the two-dimensional space of cellular automata, and describe the implementation of

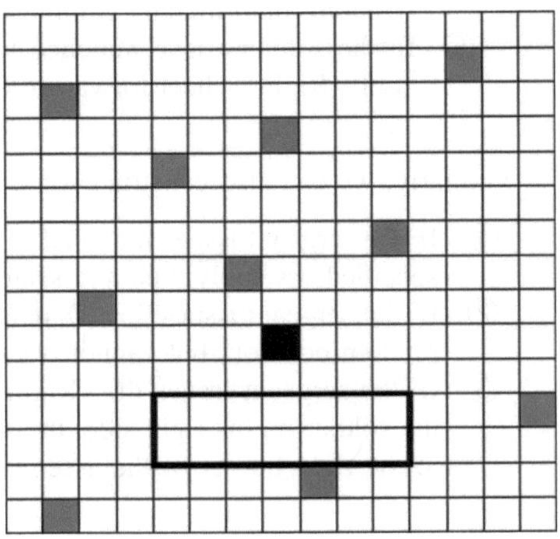

Fig. 7.7 Sergeant and soldiers in the cellular space (initial state)

these rules and actions in the cellular space by way of images. Here, we set this two-dimensional cellular space as limited (15 $\times$ 15). In reality, it represents the size of the training field, as shown in Fig. 7.7.

Figure 7.7 represents the initial state in the cellular space: the pale green squares represent the soldiers, the dark green square represents the sergeant, and the assembly area of the soldiers is outlined by the black frame. In the initial state, the soldiers are in a state of being "dismissed," and are randomly distributed in the cellular space. The properties of the cells are designed as follows:

(1) Position information (coordinates);
(2) State information ("0" represents an empty cell; "1" indicates that the cell is occupied by a soldier);
(3) Direction information (indicates the direction a soldier moves towards; there are a total of eight directions: east, south, west, north, southeast, northeast, southwest, northwest);
(4) Speed information (represents the number of squares a soldier covers within one time step).

7.2.2 *Two Sets of Rules*

Here, we focus on two commands: "Right-dress" and "Left-wheel forward-march" as examples to analyze the difference and connection between the rules in the Agent Rule Base and the rules of cellular automata.

1. **The "Right-Dress" Rule (see** Fig. 7.8)

There are many designs of the "Right-Dress" Rule. We choose one of them, and the steps are as follows.

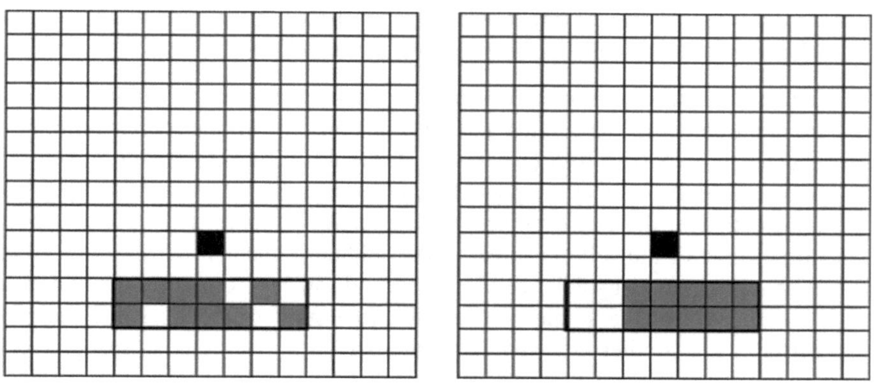

(a) The Soldiers Have Fallen In (b) Right-dress

Fig. 7.8 The "Right-Dress" Rule

(1) Search for position information (coordinates) of the soldier who is on the rightmost side of each row.
(2) Compare the cellular coordinates of the soldier on the rightmost side of each row with the right border of the assembly area: if there is no empty cell between the cell of the rightmost soldier and the right border, then it is unnecessary to update the information of the soldier cell (no movement); if there is an empty cell between the cell of the rightmost soldier and the right border, then the soldier advances one square to the right. Accordingly, the attributes of the cell need to be updated as follows:

   ① The position information of the soldier is updated from $S(i, j)$ to $S(i, j + 1)$;
   ② Because the soldier has advanced one square to the right, the state of the cell occupied by the soldier is updated to "1";
   ③ Since the soldier is moving to the right, the direction information of the cell occupied by the soldier is updated to "eastward";
   ④ The speed information of the cell occupied by the soldier is updated to "1".

(3) For every soldier in every row who is not the rightmost one, if there is no empty cell between this soldier and the first soldier searched rightward from him, then it is unnecessary to update the soldier cell information (no movement); if there is an empty cell between this soldier and the first soldier searched rightward from him, then the soldier advances one square to the right. Accordingly, the updating mode of cellular attributes is the same as in step (2).
(4) Repeat the above steps (2) and (3), until there is no empty cell on the right side of any soldier.
(5) The direction information of all the soldier cells is updated to "northward."

2. **The "Left-Wheel Forward-March" Rule (see** Fig. 7.9**)**

In Fig. 7.9, the dashed line frame indicates the area of direction change. When the soldiers enter the area of direction change as shown in the dash-line frame, the "Turn Left" rule of the cells in the two rows are as follows:

(1) For the second-row soldier cells: if the distance between the soldier cell and the right border of the cellular space is one square, then the soldier position is updated from $S\ (i, j)$ to $S\ (i - 1, j + 1)$; the direction information of the cell occupied by the soldier is updated from "eastward" to "northward"; the state information of the cell occupied by the soldier is updated to "1"; the speed information of the cell occupied by the soldier is updated to "1."
(2) When the rightmost soldier cell in the second row has completed the update in (1), the cells of the soldiers in the first row start to update: if the distance between this soldier cell and the right border of the cellular space is one square, then the soldier position is updated from $S\ (i, j)$ to $S\ (i - 1, j)$; the

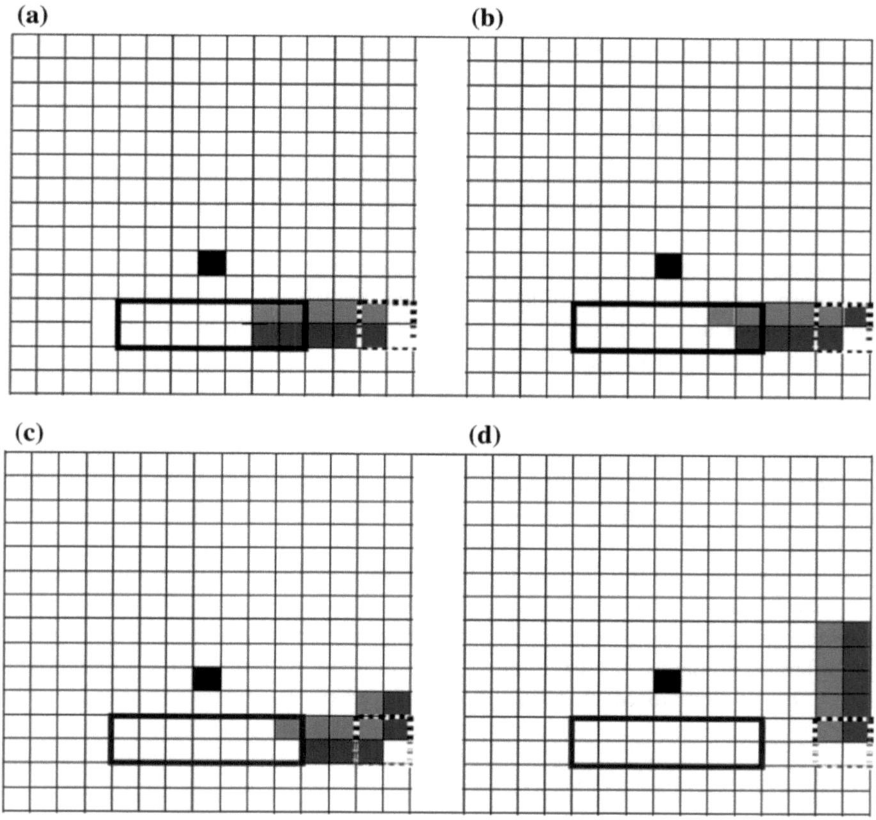

Fig. 7.9 The "Forward-wheel forward march" Rule

direction information of the cell occupied by the soldier is updated from "eastward" to "northward;" the state of the cell occupied by the soldier is updated to "1"; the speed information of the cell occupied by the soldier is updated to "1."

7.2.3 *Agent—Cellular Automata—Rules*

In Sects. 7.2.1 and 7.2.2, we use the examples of the sergeant and soldiers to design the behavioral rules for the Agent. Of course, the behavioral rules are not all the elements consisting of the Agent intelligent system. However, these rules are often the important criteria to distinguish the roles and structures of Agent, especially when we map these soldiers to a two-dimensional cellular space based on the operational rules, the "rules of action" can very intuitively reflect the connections and differences between the Agent method and the basic principles of cellular automata.

1. **The Roles of Rules**

In the case of the sergeant and soldiers, the rule bases and behavioral patterns of the "sergeant" Agent and the "soldier" Agent are quite different: in the formation drills, the sergeant issues a command and the soldiers obey. The roles are different, so the behavioral rules are also different. It is also a manifestation of agent behavior autonomy and functional intelligence. On the other hand, the components of cellular automata are uniform and homogeneous, therefore the implementation of rules has no distinction of roles.

2. **The Domains of Rules**

In the example in Chap. 5 "Cellular Genetic Algorithm", the degree of intelligence of individual cells is relatively high. They have the ability to learn from the evolution of the surrounding neighbors, and this in connection with genetic algorithm make the learning rules relatively complex, but the complexity of the rules is in a global sense, i.e., all the cells in the two-dimensional space follow the same evolutionary learning rules, and the evolution is homogeneous. When individual Agents operate in the cellular space, they may implement different operating rules in different domains, for example, in the domain within the dash-line box in Fig. 7.9 (the domain of changing direction), when the queue marches into this domain, it will start to follow the "left-wheel forward-march" rule.

3. **The Movement of Rules**

It is obvious that in the cellular space, the soldier Agents and their action rules can move. Though in the combination of Agents and cellular automata, this movement is realized by the change of cell states driven by action rules, in the final analysis, the position of an individual cellular automaton is fixed, and this point is likely to cause confusion in the process of modeling.

4. **The Hierarchy of Rules**

A cellular automaton itself is a group consisting of homogeneous cells with no hierarchy, while in the above case of soldier Agents, we designed four cellular properties (position, state, direction, and speed) for the soldier Agents, which reflect obvious Agent hierarchy. Each layer will implement the rules of its self and also will interact with other layers to realize the rules of movement of the Agents, as shown in Fig. 7.10.

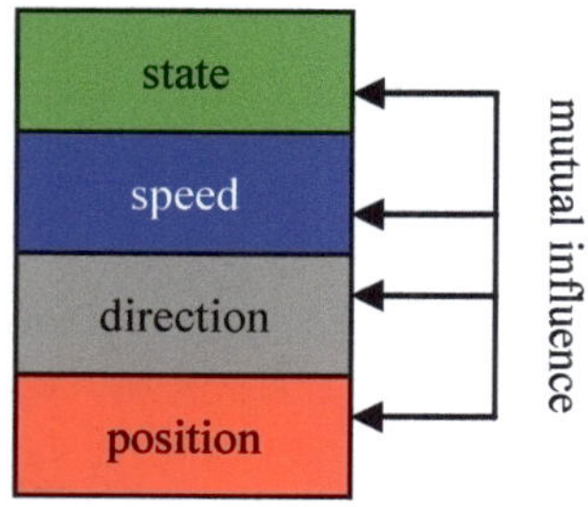

Fig. 7.10 Hierarchy of agent rules in the cellular space

7.2.4 *Communication Behavior of Agent in the Cellular Space—Cooperative Search*

Next, we let the soldiers perform another task. Such a scenario is assumed: at a certain spot in a field, there is a dangerous radioactive object and we need some soldiers to find and remove it. The search route is to be determined by the concentration of the radioactive material. The soldiers do not know the distribution of concentration of the radioactive material and the specific position of the radioactive source, but only know to advance to any one area with a high concentration of radiation. For the convenience of comparison, we design two search methods: individual search and cooperative search by two soldiers.

1. **Settings of the Cellular Automaton**
   (1) Size of the cellular space: an $n \times n$ lattice.
   (2) Form of cell neighborhood: Moore Type Neighborhood. For the soldiers that step into the cellular space, their search is only limited to be among the 8 surrounding neighbors. However, within one time step, the soldiers can move 1–3 squares, as shown in Fig. 7.11.
   (3) Cell states (attributes): concentration information of the radioactive material; of course, for the cells occupied by the soldiers, their states information also includes the position coordinates and the concentration information of the radioactive material in their surrounding neighbors.
   (4) For the concentration distribution of the cellular radioactive material, we set: the position coordinates of the radioactive source are (x^*, y^*); the radioactive density of the radioactive source is Density (x^*, y^*), (Density

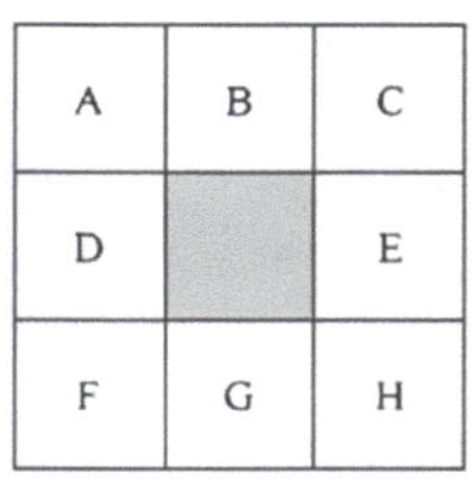

Fig. 7.11 Form of the cell neighborhood

$(x^*, y^*) > 1)$; then the concentration distribution of the radioactive material in the cellular space can be calculated by the following formula:

$$Density(x, y) = \frac{Density(x^*, y^*) - 1}{Gap(x, y)} \tag{7.1}$$

$$Gap(x, y) = \sqrt{(x - x^*)^2 + (y - y^*)^2} \tag{7.2}$$

The concentration distribution of the radioactive material is shown in Fig. 7.12.

(5) The rules of actions for the soldier Agents: when they search individually, they advance one square at a time toward any cell among the surrounding neighbors whose concentration of the radioactive material is greater than the concentration of the cells currently occupied, until the radioactive source is discovered. Specific steps are as follows.

① Soldiers obtain the concentration information of the radioactive material of the cells occupied by themselves and the surrounding neighbor cells.
② Soldiers compare the concentration information of the cells occupied by themselves with those of the surrounding neighbors, and screen out those cells of the surrounding neighbors whose concentrations are greater than the concentration of the cells occupied by themselves.
③ Soldiers advance to any one of the cells screened out.
④ Repeat step ①–③, until the discovery of the radioactive sources.

When two soldiers search with coordination, they have the same starting position. After each soldier advances a square according to the individual search rules, the two soldiers communicate, share their own respective cell positions and concentration information, and then, the soldier within the cell which has a lower concentration of the radioactive material immediately goes to the cell occupied by the other soldier (with greater concentration of radioactive material) until the discovery of the radioactive source. Specific steps are as follows.

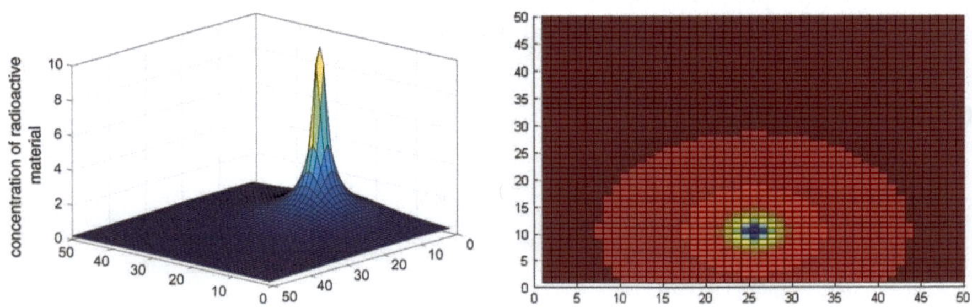

Fig. 7.12 Concentration distribution of the radioactive material (in cellular space)

① Soldier A and Soldier B both acquire the concentration information of the radioactive material in the cells occupied by themselves and the surrounding neighbor cells.
② Soldier A and soldier B both compare the concentration information of the cells occupied by themselves with the concentration information in the surrounding neighbor cells, and separately select a cell randomly among the surrounding neighbors, whose concentrations are greater than the concentrations of the cells of their own, and name them as A and B respectively.
③ Soldier A and soldier B communicate and compare the concentrations in cell A and cell B. If A > B, then Soldier A does not move, and soldier B moves to cell A, which is a new starting point; if A < B, then soldier B does not move, and soldier A moves to cell B which is a new starting point.
④ Repeat steps ①–③, until the discovery of the radioactive source.

A point worth noting is that in the cooperative search, the soldiers have an additional skill, which is the function of "closing in." On the surface, soldier A or soldier B will move several squares (1–3) within some time steps in order to meet each other. However, because of the limitation of their search scope, eventually the path the search follows is still to advance one square in one time step within the Moore Neighborhood. This is also our goal of designing the cooperative search—to study the impact of Agent communication on cellular automata rules and operating results.

2. **Soldier Agent Structure and Cellular Rule Hierarchy**

We combine the several basic structures of Agent as introduced in Sect. 7.1, to construct the soldier Agent structure in this section.

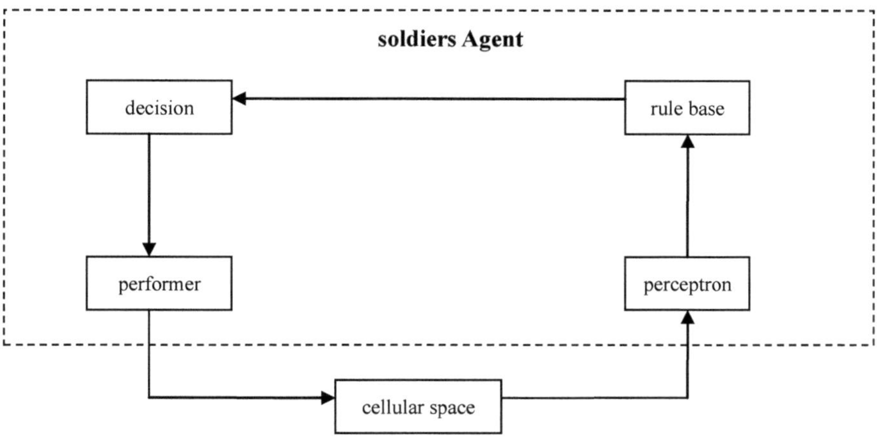

Fig. 7.13 The soldier agent structure in single soldier search

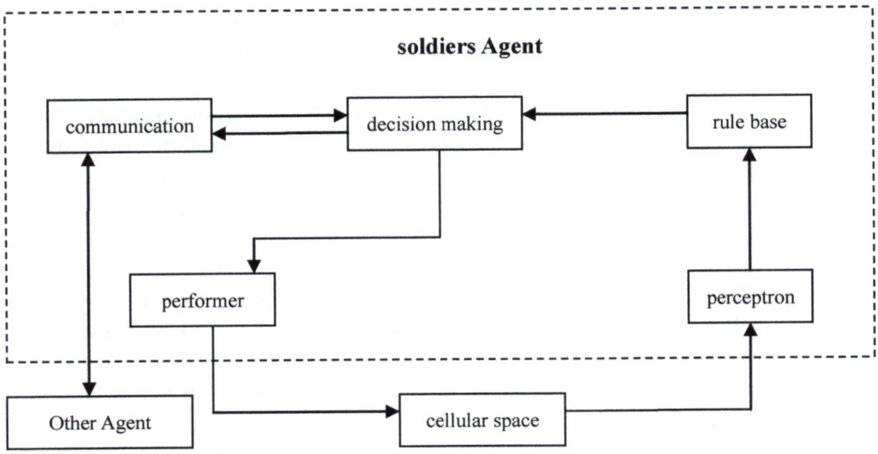

Fig. 7.14 The soldier agent structure in cooperative search

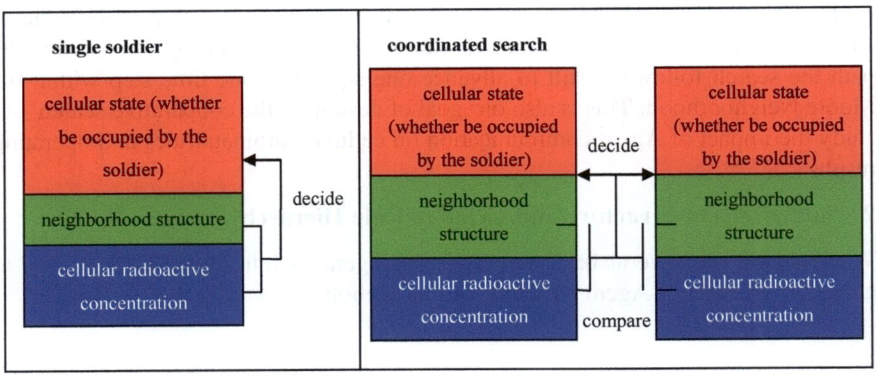

Fig. 7.15 Cellular rule hierarchy

1) Single Soldier Search (see Fig. 7.13).
2) Cooperative search (see Fig. 7.14).

The cellular rule hierarchy is shown in Fig. 7.15.

3. **Computer Simulation**

   1) Simulation Parameter Settings (see Table 7.1).
   2) Simulation Results.

In this section, we will focus on two indicators: search time and search path. By observing these two indicators, we will illustrate the effect of the communication behavior among Agents on cellular automata rules and operation results (see Figs. 7.16 and 7.17; Table 7.2).

Table 7.1 Simulation parameter settings

Parameter name	Symbol	Value
Cellular space size	$n \times n$	50×50
Radioactive density of the source	$\text{Density}(x^*, y^*)$	10
Simulation time step	T	100

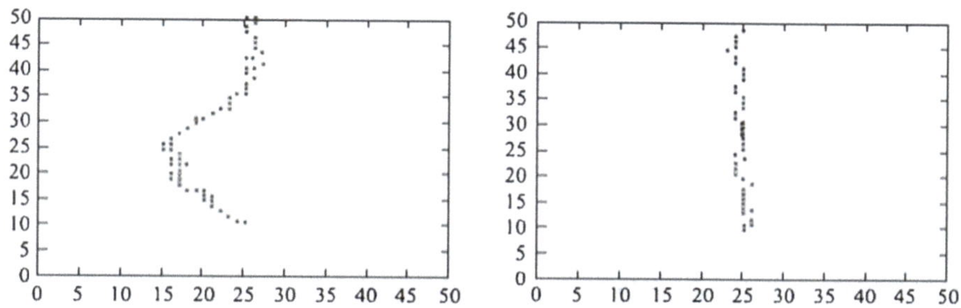

(a) Single Soldier Search (b) Cooperative search

Fig. 7.16 Search paths

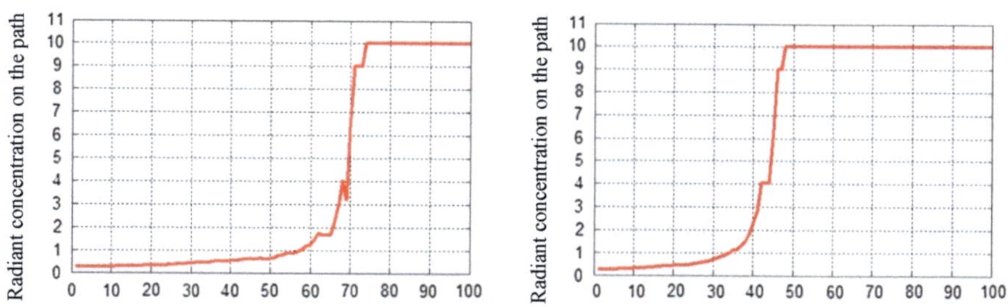

(a) Single Soldier Search (b) Cooperative Search

Fig. 7.17 Variations of radiation density of radioactive material on the search paths

From Figs. 7.16, 7.17 and Table 7.2, it is not difficult to find that compared with the single soldier search, after adding the communication mechanism among the soldier Agents so that their search is changed to a coordinated one, the action capability of the soldiers has been improved, and the search time and length of the

Table 7.2 Effect comparison of two search methods (independent experiments 100 times)

Search method	Average time	Average path length
Single soldier search	69	61
Cooperative search	45	52

search path will both be shortened (fewer detours, saving time). In other words, the communication rules among the soldier Agents have optimized the search path. This process reflects not only cellular automata's nature of "operating according to local rules," but also the Agent's characteristic of "changing one's own behavior and operation rules through learning".

7.2.5 *Agent—Cellular Automata—Interaction*

In Sect. 7.2.4, we used an example of soldiers searching radioactive material in the cellular space, and through computer simulation experiment, saw the effect of communication mechanism among Agents on the operation results of cellular automata. Through this example, we should consider such a question: we all know that in many classic rules of cellular automata (such as "Game of Life" or Langton's "Ant" rule), each square is treated as an individual with some kind of autonomy, and each can also interact with other cells. However, what are the similarities and differences between the interaction mechanism within cellular automata and that among Agents?

1. **Long Distance Communication**

In the computational process of cellular automata, most rules or interactions among individual cells are limited to a certain neighborhood type. The states of life or death of an individual cell is not affected by the states of life or death of distant cells (those outside the scope of a cell's neighborhood). For example, in the previously introduced application of "cellular genetic algorithm" in a dynamic environment (Podrouzek 2009), although the individual cells as investors have a high degree of intelligence, the communications among individuals are still limited to the neighborhood scope, and there is no remote communication behavior. In the cooperative search of soldier Agents in this chapter, however, in order to optimize the search route, the soldiers can exchange the concentration information of the radioactive material with soldiers who are outside their own search scope.

2. **Multi-Layer Interactions**

In the computational rules of cellular automata, the interactions between individual cells and their surrounding cells are mostly limited to one kind of state, e.g., the state of life or death of a cell, which is determined by the states of life or death of the surrounding cells. But in Agent modeling, because Agents have differences among themselves such as roles, positions, and so on, the interactions among them are bound to be multi-layered. In the cooperative search of soldiers in this chapter, soldier A must know not only the position information of soldier B, but also the concentration information of the cellular radioactive material at soldier B's position.

3. **"Many to One" and "One to One"**

In most regular operations based on cellular automata, a cell's state at moment $t + 1$ is often jointly determined by the neighbors around this cell at moment t. This includes some rules with higher degrees of intelligence, which are in fact also determined after an individual cell has integrated the states of its neighbors. Actually, such interactions among cells are interactions between an individual cell and the cellular group of its "neighbors", which is a relation of "many to one", while in Agent modeling, more emphasis is put on the "one to one" interaction between individuals (Bauer et al. 2009).

4. **Semantic Complexity**

As mentioned above, since the interactions among Agents are "one to one", then each type of Agent should have an independent semantic system, and this semantic system has its own syntax and communication mechanism (such as the blackboard mechanism or a message/dialog mechanism). But in the operation rules of cellular automata, such a semantic system is often simplified to a certain kind of "rules," for example, in the cooperative search of soldier Agents in this chapter, the process of two soldiers sharing and comparing the concentration of radioactive material of their own cells is the representation of regulated communication behavior.

5. **Cooperation and Coordination**

As independent computational units, Agents' purpose is to achieve a predetermined objective through mutual cooperation, and to solve a certain problem. In the course of action, individual Agents display characteristics of cooperation and coordination. But in the operation rules of cellular automata, the degree of this "cooperation and coordination" is not so obvious. This is because sometimes there will be competitions among individual cells.

6. **Focusing on Individuals or on the Whole**

One of the purposes of using cellular automata modeling is to observe the complexity of the whole system through the design of local rules. In the process of modeling, the complexity of the "whole system" or simulation of the real world is a very important reference, such as the phenomena of emergence, chaos, etc. Although Agent is also a powerful tool to explore complexity, it is often designed for solving a certain type of problems, with obvious intention, putting more attentions on individual behavioral modes and degrees of intelligence.

7.2.6 Summary

In this section, we discussed the combination of Agent and cellular automata through the example of "soldiers," and analyzed the respective characteristics of Agent and cellular automata with respect to rules and interactions. Each of them has advantages or disadvantages which the other does not have. Now, according to the content in this section, we summarize the similarities and differences between Agent and cellular automata as follows.

1. **The Similarities in Methods for the Agent and the Cellular Automata**

    (1) Same ways of modeling. Agent and cellular automata both adopt a bottom-up modeling method and a perspective of from individuals to the whole, to view the complexity of the system as the emergence of individual states (Mitchell Waldrop 1997; Ni 2011).
    (2) Strong openness. Agent and cellular automata both have good openness, which enables them to be flexibly applied to different fields, to be combined with other technologies and thus achieve mutual improvement.
    (3) Parallel operation. Both Agent and cellular automata divide work into discrete parts, which can help solve large scale and complex computational problems.
    (4) They both have the characteristic of being rule-driven. No matter the intelligent behavior in Agent modeling, or the operations of cellular automata, both in fact can be seen as being driven by certain rules (Li et al. 1990; Liu and Sun 2010).

2. **Differences in Methods for the Agent and the Cellular Automata**

    (1) Different system structures. The system formed by Agent individuals has distinct hierarchy, while the cellular automata system is a group of homogeneous cells without hierarchy.
    (2) Difference on whether to have roles. Agent individuals can be divided into many roles, such as "sergeant" Agent, "soldier" Agent, etc., and they have autonomy. Cellular automata, on the other hand, are relatively simple and homogeneous (Yin 2011).
    (3) Different evolution rules. First, the evolution rules of cellular automata are uniformed, while different Agents have different evolution rules due to the difference in their roles. Further, Agents may implement different evolution rules at different spatial positions. Finally, the evolution rules of cellular automata is single layered, while the action rules of Agent are multi-layered and can influence each other.
    (4) Different factors of influence for individuals. In the evolution process of cellular automata, individual cells are usually only influenced by local cells and their own states, while the mutual influences of Agents are not limited to a certain range of neighbors, and also have to take into account the interactions between an individual and the environment (Wu and Bin 2009).
    (5) Difference in mobility. The individual positions in cellular automata are not changeable, while Agent individuals can move in space.

7.3 Example of Cellular Automata and Multi-agent Modeling: Road Traffic

In Sect. 7.2, we designed a simulation example of solders' cooperative search for the radioactive source. The example itself does not have any practical significance, and the assumption is also ideal. Its main purpose is to conveniently explain the change of cellular automata's evolutionary result brought by the communication behavior of Agent in the cellular space. In this section, we will use the example of road traffic flow to comprehensively introduce the integral modeling of Agent and cellular automata.

After 1950s, with the rapid increase of road traffic, the randomness of traffic phenomena decreased, and a variety of new theoretical models emerged. Since 1990s, the applications of cellular automata models in traffic flow suddenly arise. Applying cellular automata to the traffic system was first proposed by Cremer and Ludwig in 1986. After cellular automata were introduced into the field of transportation, they gained rapid development. Some of the classic models and their improved versions were proposed successively. Referencing relevant literature, it is not difficult to find that because of the complexity of the traffic system, it is inevitable that we need to include modules such as perception, action, response, planning, communication, decision-making and others in the modeling process. Therefore, whether it is a real simulation of actual road traffic conditions or improvement of such conditions, more or less infiltrated by the idea of multi-Agent (intelligent body) modeling.

7.3.1 *NaSch Model*

In 1992, German scholars Nagel and Schreckenberg proposed the famous NaSch model, which was extended from Wolfram's No. 184 model. In this model, time, space and speed are all discrete. Even though the form of the model is simple, it can describe some actual traffic phenomena (Bin et al. 2007; Binghan and Bingham 2007; Wu et al. 2008).

1. **Settings of the Cellular Automaton**

   (1) **Size of the Cellular Space**: $1 \times n$ discrete squares, which represent a road, as shown in Fig. 7.18.

   (2) **Cellular Neighbor Form**: because there are $1 \times n$ squares, each individual cell has only two neighbors in the front and back respectively. Since each cell represents a car, rear-end collision between the cars in the front and back must be avoided.

Fig. 7.18 Cellular space

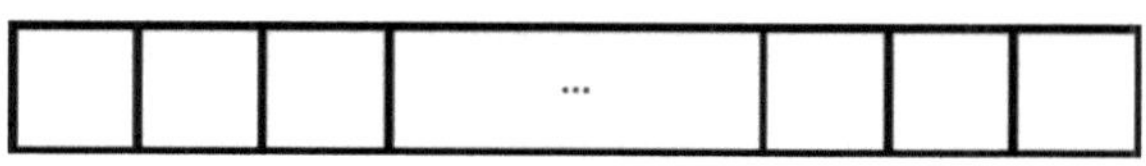

(3) **Cell State**: each cell is either empty or occupied by a car. When a cell is occupied by a car, the speed of the car can take 0, 1, 2 …v_{max}.

(4) **Action Rules of the "Car Agent"**:

① Acceleration: $v_n \rightarrow \min\{v_n + 1, v_{max}\}$: this step describes the characteristic that drivers always expect to drive at the maximum speed.

② Slowing down: $v_n \rightarrow \min\{v_n, d_n\}$: this step describes the measures drivers take to avoid collision with the car in the front.

③ Random deceleration: with probability p, $v_n \rightarrow \min\{v_n - 1, 0\}$: it describes a car's deceleration due to various uncertainties, such as poor road conditions, or when a driver encounters some problems, etc.

④ Movement: $x_n \rightarrow x_n + v_n$: meaning the car moves forward according to the adjusted speed. In the formula, $x_{n,}$ v_n respectively represent the position and speed of car n; $d_n = x_{n+1} - x_n - l$ represent the numbers of empty cells between car n and car $n + 1$, and l represents the length of the car.

(5) **Boundary Conditions**: here we use open boundary conditions. Suppose the cell at the leftmost of the road corresponds to $x = 1$, and the entrance to the road contains v_{max} cells, then the car enter the road can be from cells (1, 2, …, v_{max}). At moment $t \rightarrow t + 1$, after the cars on the road have all been updated, we search the positions of the first car x_{first} and the last car x_{last}, if $x_{last}> v_{max}$, then a car with speed v_{max} will enter cell $\min\{x_{last} - v_{max}, v_{max}\}$ with probability α. At the exit of the road, if $x_{first}> L_{road}$ (L_{road} represents the length of the road), then the first car on the road will exit it with probability β, and the car following immediately behind it will become the new leading car.

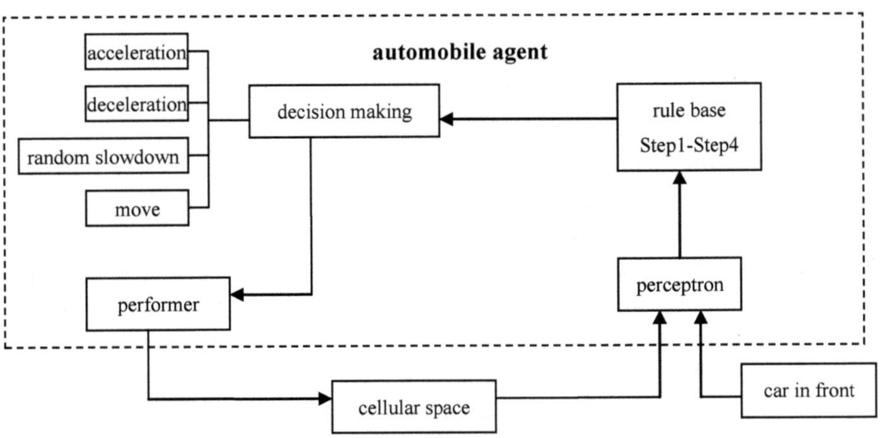

Fig. 7.19 Car agent structure

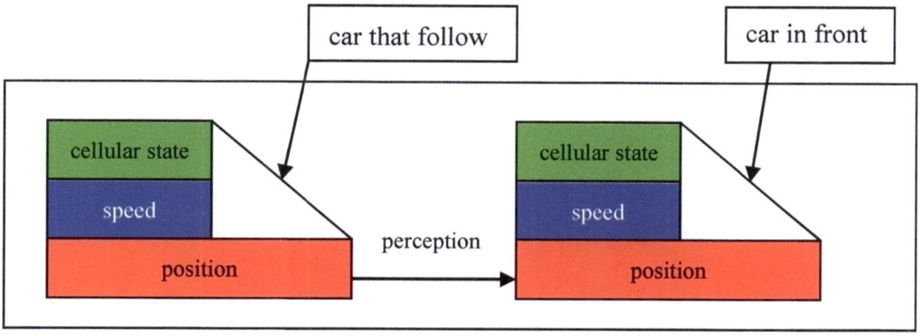

Fig. 7.20 Nasch model cellular rule hierarchy

Table 7.3 Setting of simulation parameters

Parameter name	Symbol	Value
Road length	L_{road}	100
Maximum speed	v_{max}	3
Random slow down probability	p	0.4
Probability having a car at road starting point	p_c	0.5
Initial number of cars on road	m	7
Simulation time step	T	150

Fig. 7.21 Traffic flow

2. **Car Agent Structure and Cellular Rule Hierarchy**
   1) Car Agent Structure (see Figs. 7.19 and 7.20).
3. **Computer Simulation**
   1) Settings of Simulation Parameters (see Table 7.3):
   2) Simulation Results:

      ① Traffic flow (see Fig. 7.21).

The (a) and (b) in Fig. 7.21 respectively represent the road conditions at the initial stage and after a number of steps of evolution. The white squares represent the “Car Agent,” and it is easy to see that after a relatively large number of vehicles join the traffic, obviously traffic jam occurs.

② Space-time diagram of traffic flow (see Fig. 7.22).

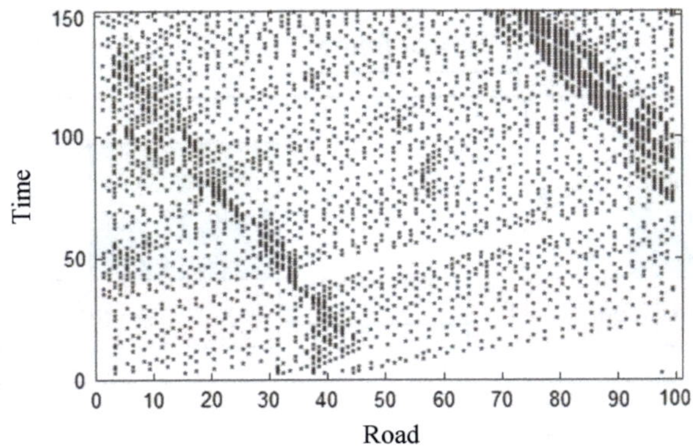

Fig. 7.22 Time-space diagram of traffic flow

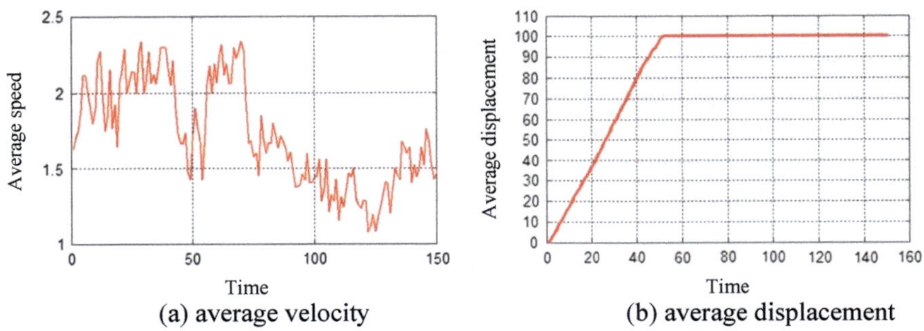

Fig. 7.23 Average velocity and average displacement

Figure 7.22 is a space-time traffic flow diagram: the horizontal axis represents the road and the vertical axis represents time evolution; the "black spots" represent a car's corresponding positions on the road at a certain time. The concentration of the black spots means a traffic jam.

③ Average velocity and average displacement (see Fig. 7.23).

Figure 7.23a, b are images of average velocity and average displacement respectively, which represent the average velocity and average displacement of all vehicles entering the road at any time. When the average displacement exceeds the length of the road, our recording will stop. The point is that when the average displacement is more than the length of the road, we stop recording so it is easy for us to observe how long it takes on average for a vehicle to drive from one end of the road to the other end.

7.3.2 *Improvement of the NaSch Model—The Brake Lights (BL) Model*

In Sect. 7.3.1, we described and simulated the NaSch model. It is not difficult to find that although in the deceleration rules for the car Agent, we clearly designed the function of "driver's perception of distance from the car in the front", when a certain number of cars enter the road, traffic jam still occurs. Therefore, we consider whether there is an improvement method to relieve such a jam, so that traffic flow will be smoother. As for the reason of traffic jam occurs in the NaSch model, we have the following considerations.

(1) Determination of the random deceleration probability. In the NaSch model, the random deceleration probability is designed as a constant p, which means that regardless of the number of empty cells (the distance from the car in the front) in front of a car, the car will decelerate with the same probability. This obviously does not reflect the real situation. In addition, when a car travels at different velocities, the random deceleration probability should not remain the same, but should be related to the velocity of the car.
(2) Updating car velocity. An obvious feature of the NaSch model is that within time steps $t \rightarrow t + 1$, the acceleration or the deceleration of a car only consider the distance between two cars at moment t without considering the fact that the car in the front will continue to move forward. The updating of velocity is in fact static, resulting in wasted velocity. Thus, in deciding a car whether to accelerate or to decelerate, the real-time velocity information of the car in front of it should be considered.

In 2000, Knospe and others proposed a model which can make drivers drive smoothly and comfortably, making traffic flow smoother. This model adds the "brake lights" to the design of the cars, so that the function of the car Agent is further strengthened.

1. **Setting of the Cellular Automaton**

In this model, cellular space, neighborhood form and states are the same as in the NaSch model, so we will not repeat them. Here we focus on the parallel action rules of the car Agent.

(1) **Determination of the random deceleration probability *p***

$$p = p[v_n(t), b_{n+1}(t), t_h, t_s] \tag{7.3}$$

$$p[v_n(t), b_{n+1}(t), t_h, t_s] = \begin{cases} p_b & \text{if } b_{n+1} = 1 \text{ and } t_h < t_s \\ p_0 & \text{if } v_n = 0 \\ p_d & \text{if all other cases} \end{cases} \tag{7.4}$$

$$b_n(t+1) = 0 \tag{7.5}$$

Here, b_n is the state of the brake lights of car n, b_n = 1 (0) represents the on (off) of the brake lights, $t_h = d_n/v_n(t)$ is the time headway of cars, $t_s = \min\{v_n(t), h\}$ represents the safe time interval, h is the impact area of the brake lights. Formula (7.4) represents that the car Agent determines the random deceleration probability based on its own velocity, the brake lights state of the car in front of it and the safety distance from the car in the front.

(2) **Acceleration**

$$\begin{aligned} & if\{[b_{n+1}(t) = 0 \; and \; b_n(t) = 0] \; or \; (t_h \geq t_s)\} \\ & \quad v_n(t+1) = \min(v_n(t) + 1, v_{\max}) \\ & else \\ & \quad v_n(t+1) = v_n(t) \end{aligned} \tag{7.6}$$

Formula (7.6) shows that the acceleration effect of the car Agent is determined according to the brake lights state of the car in front of it and the safety distance from it.

(3) **Deceleration**

$$\begin{aligned} & v_n(t+1) = \min[d_n^{eff}, v_n(t+1)] \\ & if \; [v_n(t+1) < v_n(t)] \\ & then: b_n(t+1) = 1 \end{aligned} \tag{7.7}$$

In this formula, d_n^{eff} represents the effective distance between the car Agent and the car in front of it, the expression is as follows:

$$d_n^{eff} = d_n + \max\{v_{\exp} - gap_{saft}, 0\} \tag{7.8}$$

Here, $v_{\exp} = \min\{d_{n+1}, v_{n+1}\}$represents the expected speed of the car in the front; gap_{saft} is the control parameter.

Formula (7.7) represents that when the car Agent decelerates, it should make real-time consideration of the effective distance between it and the car in front of it, and update the state of the brake lights.

(4) **Random Slow Down**

$$if[rand < p]then : \begin{cases} v_n(t+1) = \max[v_n(t+1) - 1, 0] \\ if\ (p = p_b)\ then : b_n(t+1) = 1 \end{cases} \tag{7.9}$$

(5) **Position Update**

$$x_n(t+1) = x_n(t) + v_n(t+1) \tag{7.10}$$

From aforementioned driving rules, it is not difficult to find that the biggest improvement of the brake lights (BL) model as compared with the NaSch model is that it further coordinates the relationship between acceleration (or deceleration) behavior and the distance with the car in front of it, so that the driving behavior of the car Agent fits more with the actual situation.

2. **Cellular Rules Hierarchy**

The Agent structure of the brake lights model is similar to that of the NaSch model, so we will not repeat. Figure 7.24 shows the cellular rule hierarchy of the car Agent.

3. **Computer Simulation**

   1) Setting of simulation parameters (see Table 7.4)
   2) Simulation result.

(1) Car Flow (see Fig. 7.25)

Comparing Figs. 7.25 with 7.21, it is not difficult to see that with the influx of a considerable number of cars, the overall distance between cars in the car flow of the brake lights model is more equal, and local congestion phenomenon rarely appears.

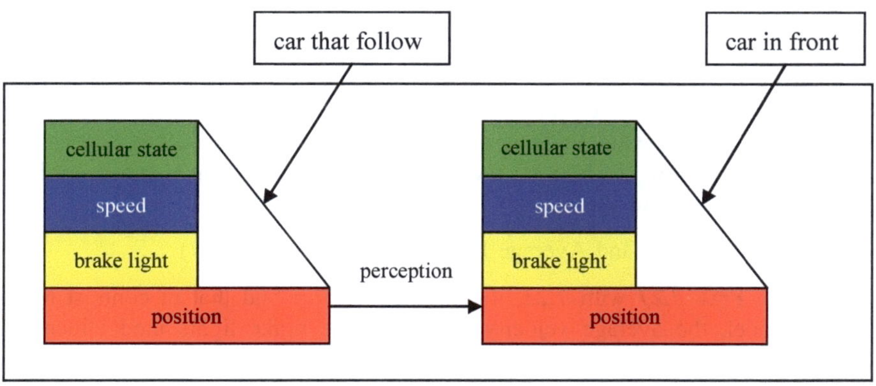

Fig. 7.24 Cellular rule hierarchy of the brake lights (BL) model

Table 7.4 Setting of simulation

Parameter name	Symbol	Value
Road length	L_{road}	100
Maximum speed	v_{max}	3
Effective range of brake light	h	6
Control parameter	gap_{saft}	2
Probability of car at road starting point	p_c	0.5
Parameters determining the probability of random slow down	p_b	0.94
	p_0	0.5
	p_d	0.1
Initial number of cars on road	m	7
Simulation time step	T	150

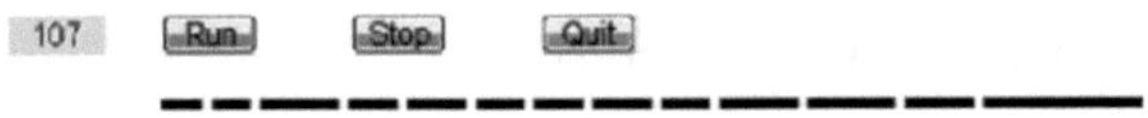

Fig. 7.25 Car flow

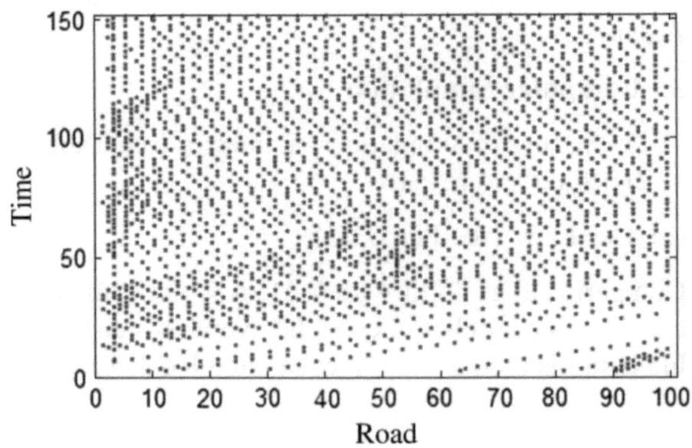

Fig. 7.26 Space-time diagram of car flow

(2) Space-Time Diagram of the Car Flow (see Fig. 7.26)

Comparing Figs. 7.26 with 7.22, it is not difficult to find that in the space-time diagram of the car flow of the brake lights model, the congestion phenomenon basically disappears, which indicates that after improving acceleration, deceleration and the random slow down rules, the reaction of the car Agent is more sensitive, and its driving is more smooth.

(3) Average Velocity and Average Displacement (see Fig. 7.27)

Comparing Figs. 7.27 with 7.23, it is not difficult to find that in contrast to the NaSch model, the average velocity of cars in the brake lights model increases significantly. Therefore, cars can travel from one end of the road to the other end in a shorter time (the average displacement of cars reaches 100 earlier).

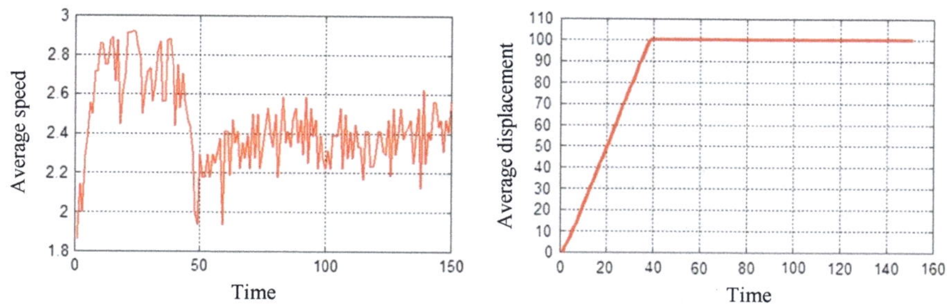

(a) average velocity (b) average displacement

Fig. 7.27 Average velocity and average displacement

7.3.3 Summary

In this section, we use two simple traffic models as examples to introduce the typical application of multi-Agents and cellular automata modeling. In the brake lights model, acceleration, deceleration and random slow down rules of the car Agent are improved, making traffic flow more orderly and smooth, and traffic jam relieved. The construction of these two models shows that the optimization of Agent rules and enhancement of the degree of its intelligence can also improve the operation effect of cellular automata. The solution optimization process for a problem is also a process of the organic combination of cellular automata and individual Agent operating rules.

7.4 Example of Cellular Automata and Multi-agent Modeling—Industrial Cluster

In 1990, American scholar Michael Porter first proposed the concept of industry cluster in his book *The Competitive Advantage of Nations* (Porter 2007). The so-called industrial cluster refers to the phenomenon that in a particular field (usually led by a dominant industry), great amount of enterprises with close industrial ties, as well as related supporting institutions concentrate in a space, and form strong and lasting competitive advantage. Therefore, it is not only a special economic entity, but also a typical complex system with obvious complex characteristics. The study on industry clusters mostly uses the deductive method, namely, to analyze the essence of the phenomenon from top to bottom in a formalized manner.

From the perspective of enterprises operations, the importance of industrial cluster lies in the realization of scale efficiency through enterprise resource sharing, so as to reduce the costs of information and logistics, to increase profits, and form regional competitiveness. Then, in real situations, how is this effect reflected? Here, we adopt the reduction method, using cellular automata combined with Agent to build a simple model of industry cluster.

7.4.1 *Settings of a Cellular Automaton, Agent Structure and Hierarchy*

1. **Settings of a Cellular Automaton**

   (1) Cellular space: a lattice of $n \times n$.
   (2) Neighborhood structure: Moore type neighborhood, each cell has eight neighbors, and at every time step, the business Agent can move within the scope of the neighborhood.
   (3) Cell state: whether a cell is occupied by an enterprise Agent, attraction of the industrial cluster region to the cell, and profit levels.
   (4) Evolution rule briefing: the enterprise within the cellular space learn from their neighbors through methods of "forming an industry cluster" or "not forming an industrial cluster," in order to enhance their own profit levels.

2. **Structure of the Enterprise Agent (see** Fig. 7.28)

We can see that when enterprises form an industrial cluster, the function of interacting with the cellular space is added to the Agent structure, which determines the movement and learning of the enterprise Agent. We can approximately understand it as: when the enterprise Agents do not form a cluster, the way of learning is passive; otherwise, learning is active.

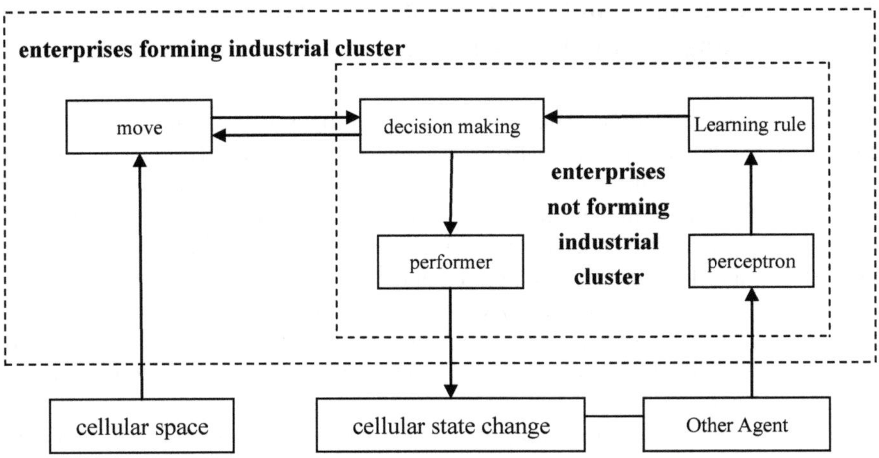

Fig. 7.28 Structure of the enterprise agent

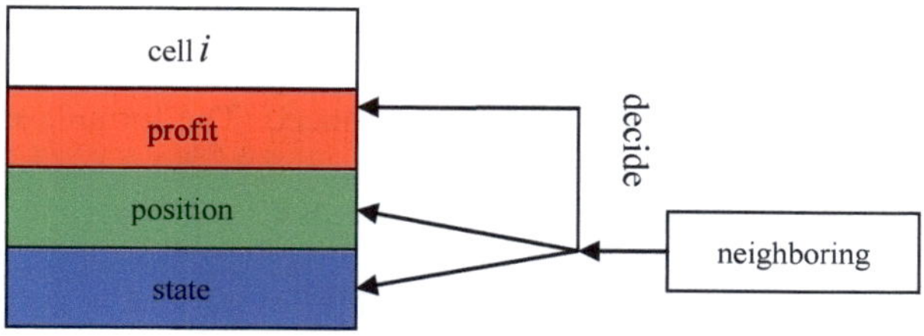

(a) Enterprise do not form an industrial cluster

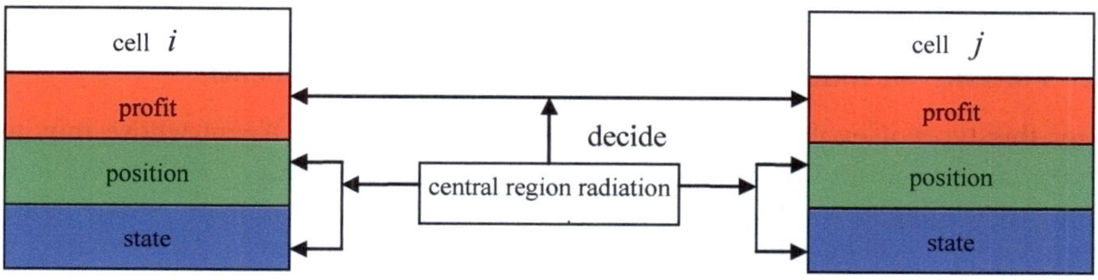

(b) Enterprise form an industrial cluster

Fig. 7.29 Layers of the business agent

3. **Enterprise Agent Hierarchy (see** Fig. 7.29)

The attraction of a regional center to the enterprise Agent is the driving force for an enterprise to learn independently, and is also the driving force for the ultimate occurrence of clustering phenomenon. Figures 7.28 and 7.29 reveal the reason for the formation of industrial clusters from both inside and outside an enterprise. Then, in the process of the formation of an industrial cluster, how do the profitability and resource sharing of a business evolve? What are the characteristics of this kind of evolution? We might as well further observe these through a simulation experiment.

7.4.2 Evolution Rules

1. **No Formation of an Industrial Cluster (an enterprise does not move)**

With this kind of evolution, an enterprise exists in a static environment and has no mobility. Its learning behavior is only limited to the neighborhood, specifically:

(1) Enterprise initialization: in a two-dimensional lattice of $n \times n$, produce a number of enterprise cells randomly with a certain probability.
(2) Each enterprise cell records the profitability of all the cells in the neighborhood (if a cell is not occupied by a enterprise, then the profit probability is 0).

(3) Each enterprise cell selects another enterprise cell among its neighbors whose profit situation is better than its own, to exchange with and learn from. After such learning, its own profit level is enhanced. The formula is as follows:

$$R_{t+1}(i,j) = R_t(i,j) + \delta\left[R_t^* - R_t(i,j)\right] \tag{7.11}$$

In it, $R_t(i, j)$ represents the profit probability of the cell at position (i, j) and at moment t; δ is the rate of resource sharing between enterprises; R_t^* is the profit probability of the learning target of cell (i, j) at moment t.

(4) Return to step (2).

2. **Forming an Industrial Cluster (with enterprise movement)**

For this type of evolution, an enterprise is an independent Agent whose moving motive comes from the radiation attraction of industrial cluster forming region to the surrounding areas. The effects here are abstracted as the radiation attraction and policy support of the cellular space center to the surrounding areas. The attraction of the cellular space center to the positions of the surrounding cells can be expressed as the following formula:

$$att(i,j) = \frac{rad}{\sqrt{(x^* - i)^2 + (y^* - j)^2}} \tag{7.12}$$

In it, x^* represents the x-coordinate of the cellular space center, y^* represents the y-coordinate, rad represents the radiation intensity of the cellular space center, which can be understood as the radiation attraction of the industrial cluster region to the surrounding areas. In reality, such attraction can be produced by factors such as policy, environment, personnel and others. It can be seen that the motive of an enterprise's movement is a function associated with distance. The greater the distance is from the center, the less the moving motive and the smaller the influence of the industrial cluster region on the enterprise. Specifically:

(1) Enterprise initialization: in a two-dimensional lattice of $n \times n$, produce a number of enterprise cells randomly with a certain probability at initial stage.

(2) Movement of an enterprise: The enterprises in the surrounding region will move towards the central region due to policy, environment and other factors, ultimately forming an industrial cluster. This moving behavior is determined by the following rules: each enterprise cell records the attraction of the surrounding neighbors. The greater the attraction value, the better policy support and investment environment the neighbor cell obtains. If there is a neighbor whose attraction value is greater than the attraction value of the enterprise cell itself, and the neighbor cell is not occupied by other enterprises, then this enterprise cell moves to this spot. If there is no neighbor cell whose attraction value is greater than the attraction value of the enterprise cell itself, or if the neighbor is occupied by another enterprise, then this enterprise cell does not move.

(3) Information collection of enterprise. Each enterprise cell records the profit probability of all the surrounding neighbor cells (if a cell is not occupied by an enterprise, then the profit probability is 0).

(4) Learning behavior of an enterprise. Each enterprise cell selects an enterprise cell among its neighbors whose profit probability is greater than its own to learn from. After such learning, its own profit probability is increased. The formula is as follows:

$$R_{t+1}(i,j) = R_t(i,j) + \delta\left[R_t^* - R_t(i,j)\right] \quad (7.13)$$

(5) Return to step (2).

7.4.3 Computer Simulation

1. **Setting of simulation parameters (see Table** 7.5)
2. **Evolutionary Process of Industrial Cluster Formation (see** Fig. 7.30)

Obviously, under the radiation attraction effect of the central region on the surrounding areas, enterprises continuously move towards the central region, forming an industrial cluster.

3. **Changes of Profit Status (the sum of the profit status of all the enterprise Agents in the cellular space, see** Fig. 7.31)

Figure 7.31 shows the overall profitability of the enterprises in the region. It is clear that in the process of the formation of an industrial cluster, profitability increases progressively. This is because after enterprises "gather together", as the number of individual cell neighbors increases, interactions with surrounding neighbors are strengthened, and the level of learning from enterprises with high profitability increases, while when enterprises do not form an industrial cluster, the profit level tends to remain stable and no longer rises after a short time of increase.

Table 7.5 Setting of simulation parameters

Parameter expression	Meaning	Value
$n \times n$	Cellular space size	50×50
rad	Cellular space center radiation rate	2
T	Evolution step	50
p	Probability of having initial enterprises	0.1
$R(i,j)$	Profit status of initialization	rand $\in [0, 1]$
δ	Rate of resource sharing	0.7

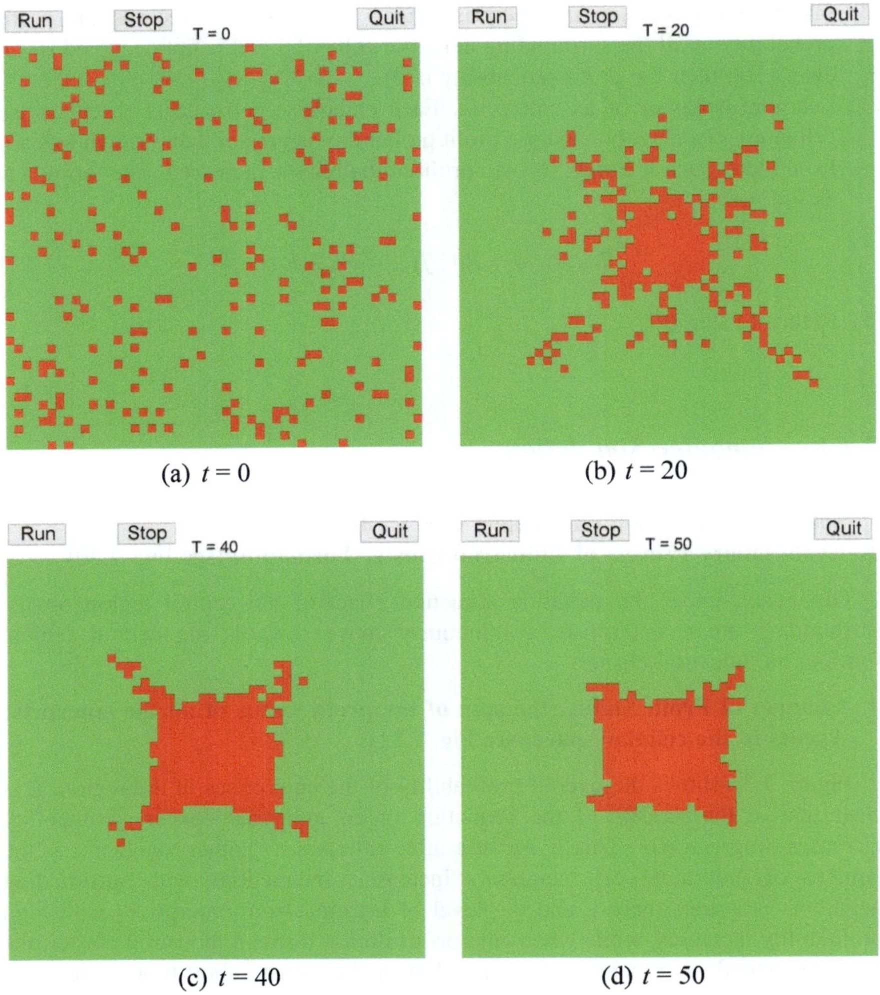

Fig. 7.30 Evolutionary process of industrial cluster formation

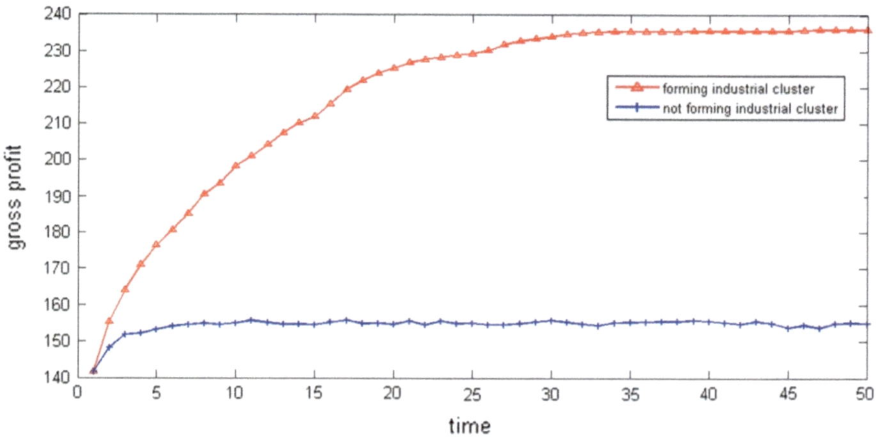

Fig. 7.31 Overall profit status in two evolution modes

7.4.4 Summary

In this chapter, we designed a simple model of enterprise cluster based on the combination of the theories of cellular automata and Agent. For the process of enterprises learning to cluster, not only the neighborhood rules of cellular automata are applied, but also the characteristics of self-organization, self-learning, and self-adaptation of Agent theory are combined. This reflects the idea of the complementary modeling of cellular automata and Agent.

References

Bauer, A., Beauchemin, C. A., et al. (2009). Agent-based modeling of host-pathogen systems: The successes and challenges. *Information Sciences, 179*(10), 1379–1389.

Bin, J., Gao, Z., Li, K., et al. (2007). *Modeling and simulation of traffic system based on cellular automata*. Beijing: Science Press.

Binghan, J., & Bingham, B. (2007). Hybrid one-dimensional reversible cellular automata are regular. *Discrete Applied Mathematics,155*(18), 2555–2566.

Li, W., Packard, N. H., & Langton, C. (1990). Transition phenomena in cellular automata rule space. *Physica D: Nonlinear Phenomena, 45*(1–3), 77–94.

Liu, C., & Sun, S. (2010). Comparative study of agent and CA method, with agent simulating the system behaviors. *Practice and Understanding of Mathematics, 40*(2), 164–169.

Mitchell Waldrop, M. (1997). *Complexity: The emerging science at the edge of order and chaos* (C. Ling, Trans). Beijing: SDX Joint Publishing Company.

Ni, J. (2011). *Theory and application of complex system multi-agent modeling and control*. Beijing: Electronic Industry Press.

Podrouzek, J. (2009). Stochastic cellular automata in dynamic environmental modeling: Practical applications. *Electronic notes in Theoretical Computer Science, 252*(1), 143–156.

Porter, M. E. (2007). *The competitive advantage of nations* (M. Li & R. Qiu, Trans). Beijing: CITIC Press.

Shi, C., & Wei, Z. (2007). *Agent based computing*. Beijing: Tsinghua University Press.

Wu, J., & Bin, Hu. (2009). Simulation of multi-agent entities with interactions between informationization and group behavior. *System Engineering Journal, 24*(2), 218–225.

Wu, X., Yuan, Z., Li, Y., et al. (2008). A single-lane double probability cellular automaton model. *Beijing Jiaotong University Journal, 32*(6), 42–46.

Yin, F. (2011). Study of the theoretical model and development method of agent. *Electronic Design Engineering, 19*(10), 63–66.

Chapter 8
The Application Fields of Cellular Automata

Introduction

Cellular automata theory is a kind of new ideas, different from the traditional thoughts and methods on treating system problems. For many problems that were difficult for traditional methods to find a solution, cellular automaton has made new progresses. For more than 20 years to date, a variety of applications based on the idea of cellular automaton has been booming, they can be roughly summarized as follows: ① Simulation of phenomena in the fields of physics and chemistry; ② modeling of biological organisms; ③ high speed computing; ④ image processing and pattern recognition; ⑤ military combat simulation; ⑥ simulation of the transportation, epidemics and stock investors' behavior; ⑦ applications in geographical and ecological areas such as land use scenarios, waste water, exhaust gas diffusion, as well as the dynamic changes of biological species.

In this chapter, we use the examples dealing with the problems just in the fields of economy, urban transportation and disease transmission, to introduce the simulation and exploration of cellular automata to practical issues. In these three fields, individual cells play different roles and render different evolutionary effects. However, all the aforementioned issues have a common characteristic, that is, the relationships among individuals can be described by very simple rules, and their state change depends on their surrounding environment. Using cellular automata to study this kind of problem, we may define the interactions among individuals from micro-level, which is hard to be accomplished by using macro-level study methods.

8.1 The Application of Cellular Automata in Economic Fields

A economic system is a complex evolution system. It contains many subsystems and many variables of perplexing relations, thus rendering multi-layer, nonlinear, open, uncertain, dynamic characteristics. These characteristics influence each other,

X. Li et al., *Theory of Practical Cellular Automaton*,
https://doi.org/10.1007/978-981-10-7497-4_8

and this determines the specific evolution processes of the economic system. At present, the researches on the economic system generally start from the macroscopic angle, using the theory of economics to establish a macro econometric model and a general equilibrium model. In present market, macro variables not only are numerous in quantity, but also have complex relationship among each other. In building an economic model, we must perform variable abstraction and simplified handling, ignoring secondary factors. Economists generally adopt two methods for simplification of their research objects. One method is behavior analysis in completely ignorance of the microscopic subjects; the other method is to ignore differences between individuals but to use typical individuals instead of using whole groups. Although these two methods can simplify the modeling process, they have many disadvantages that lead to great deviation in research. The separation of macroeconomic analysis and microeconomic analysis may lead to the ignorance of important economic phenomenon in the research processes.

Since 1980s, more and more scholars began to explore the methods using the combination of macroeconomics and microeconomics to study the economic system. The agent-based micro evolutionary simulation model built on the complex adaptive theory was one of such effective methods. Comparing with the micro simulation models that were based on the method of data analysis, the agent-based micro evolutionary simulation model not only emphasizes the complexity and the adaptability of the economic system, but also emphasizes the agent-based intelligence issues and the simulation of the learning behavior. Its core idea is through the establishment of an economic system based on computer simulations, to study various complex economic phenomena with great deal of experiments in evolutionary simulations. Since 1990s, scholars from many different fields have participated in the agent-based computational economics study, and have brought continuous development and perfection to the field.

8.1.1 Cellular Automata and Evolutionary Economics

In economics, agent-based evolutionary computation was emerged since the 1940s. At first in 1940s, John Von Neumann put forward the theory of cellular automata. The theory gained wide applications in natural science and in social science, in the issues such as the evolution and the outbreak of economic crisis, the social attribute of the personal behavior. Later in the 1950s, MIT professor J. W. Forrester proposed a simulation method based on system dynamics. Through system analysis, the method first built up causality figure among the key elements of the system, and then transformed the causality figure into the structural equation recognized by a computer, and performed simulation on the equation.

The application of system dynamics in the field of economy mainly includes the market growth model, the stock market model. In 1990s, under the proposal of some world-class masters of science including Nobel Prize winner M. Gell-Mann,

K. J. arrow, P. W. Anderson, a group of young scientists in the United States from various fields founded the Santa Fe Research Institute, put forward "complex adaptive systems" concept. They considered that all the complex system, including the life system, immune system, ecosystem, human brain system, economic system, all had a kind of ability, could make the order and chaos to achieve a special balance. On this so called "the edge of chaos" balance point, the breaking of the system was not really locked in a position, but also never broke down, into chaos.

The application of complex adaptive theory in economics mainly includes the evolution of social norms, the bottom-up modeling of the market process, the road map and economic organization of the economic network. In recent years, using network theory and methods to study economic phenomena has been called a direction for new development based on agent-based evolutionary computation. The application of this theory in economics is mainly concerned with various economic relations and social relations, and with the study of various networks, such as supply chain network, transportation network, relational network, etc.

The applications of agent-based evolutionary computation in economics are classified into the field of evolutionary economics. The concept of evolutionary economics was put forward by Nelson and Winter as early as in 1980s, in the study of evolution of industrial organizations. Evolutionary economics in the narrow sense is an economics sub field that is based on computer simulations, taking the micro individual or microcosmic law as the starting point, taking the entire evolution process or the ending of complex economic system as the purpose of study. According to the classification of Mr. Jia Genliang, the evolutionary economics can be divided into the old school system, the new Schumpeter school, the Austria school, the complex system theory school and the evolutionary game theory school.

The evolutionary economics has had an impact on the theoretical basis and methodology of traditional economics. One of the theoretical foundations of the traditional economics was the "economic man" hypothesis, which assumed that the participants of the economic system took maximizing the benefits as the goal, and they could get the information that would maximize their benefits. This hypothesis has been questioned in recent years. The methodology of traditional economics originated from reduction theory. This methodology starts building the model based on various participants in the economic system, and then getting the sum by addition, taking the whole as the sum of the individuals. This research method is not suitable for the study of the complex behavior of the economic system in its entirety. Evolutionary economics, however, especially the application of the automata in economics, utilizes the characteristics such as "bounded rationality" and "systematic evolution emergence" to build the models for the study of economic systems. It can overcome the shortcomings of the traditional economic theory and methodology.

8.1.2 *Examples of Cellular Automata Applications in Economic Fields*

1. **The applications of cellular automata theory in new products marketing**

1) The factors affect the new product marketing

The key factors that affect the marketing of new products are the following.

(1) The leading edge of new products. The extent the new product is leading the competitors' products determines the degree of competition in the introduction stage of the new products. The leading edge of a new product is mainly reflected in two aspects of the innovation and the difficulty in imitation. The more innovative a new product is, the more difficult to imitate, and it is more difficult for competitors to close up to the new product in a short time, the more obvious leading edge the new product has, thus more conducive to the promotion of the new products, easier to achieve sales target and market share objectives, making it possible to sell at higher prices with higher profit margins.
(2) Sales channels for new products. There are two channels in market expansion process of a new product: the first is the existing enterprise channel. Using the existing sales channels has the benefits of low cost and the familiarity of the enterprises to the entire process, as well as the ease to control market risk. But it is difficult to demonstrate the advantages of new products to the market, resulting in the difficulty in affecting the consumers to favor the new product. The second is to create a new sales channel for the new product. A tailored new channel has the advantages of high pertinence, strong adaptability, and easier to be discovered by consumers thus with higher marketability. But a new channel also has the disadvantages such as high cost of marketing, difficult to control the channel and higher market risk.
(3) The cost performance of the new product. There are two aspects that affect the new product cost performance: one is the price factor, which is a very important factor to the promotion of a new product to the market. Under the same conditions, the higher the new product price, the greater the purchase cost, the smaller the probability of being chosen by consumers. Such products lack market competitiveness. The other is the non price factor. In the situation of the same price, the non price factor is the key to a new product promotion. The more obvious is the non price advantage (such as the product quality), the greater value the product means for the consumer (functional value, the sensory value, etc.), the higher probability the product be chosen by consumers, the more competitive the product is.
(4) Consumer factor. The social development, the popularization of the Internet and the guidance of the legal systems of the society make consumers more and more mature. Consumers' ability in product appreciation is enhanced. This has a big impact on a new product's marketing performance. This is because for rational consumers, factors are considered more comprehensively in choosing a

product. On the one hand, they will carefully observe the functionality, quality and cost performance of the new product. On the other hand, the consumers may get to know the new product through the media, especially through the consumers who have used the new product. The consumers will make the decision for purchase after going through the above process. The rationalization trend of the consumers forces manufacturers to accelerate the development of more effective marketing strategies, to survive in the competition.

2) Details of cellular automata modeling

Using cellular automata to build the marketing model for a new product, one needs to set up the rules and perform the simulation on the observed economic phenomena. The concrete details for building up a cellular automaton are as following:

(1) The parameters of the cellular automaton

The new product marketing model based on a cellular automaton has the following parameters:

① Price index $P(x) = \ln(1 + x)$, reflects the level of product pricing, x represents the price of the new product, the larger P(x), the more consumers are inclined to not buy this new product;
② Advertising index $A(y) = 1/(1 + 5e - y)$, reflects the influence of the product advertising through the mass media such as TV and Internet, y represents the advertising investment, the bigger the $A(y)$, the more consumers incline to buy such product.
③ Product quality index $Q(z) = 1/(1 + 5e - z)$, is a comprehensive reflection of the product's quality, innovation and service level after sales. Z represents the comprehensive quality of the product, the larger the Q(z), the more consumers incline to buy such product.

(2) Cellular automaton model building

Assuming that each cell in a cellular automaton model represents a consumer in the market, cellular space is a two dimensional lattice space, and the cellular neighbors are Moore—type elements. In the market, there are three kinds of products, A, B, C, and B is a substitute product of A and, C is the complimentary product of A.

$C_{i,j}^t$ represents the consumer state at the time of t, on the position of (i, j). The consumer state is influenced by its eight neighbors. $C_{i,j}^t = \{00, 10, 11, 12, 20, 21, 22\}$ represents the cellular state space, in which, 00 represents the potential consumers not in the use of any products yet; 10(20) represent the consumers that are using the product A(B). These consumers are the showcases of the product for the surrounding consumers. 11(21) represent the consumers that have used the product A (B), and have given the positive reviews for the product and continue to use the product. These consumers have been generating positive effects on the surrounding consumers for the product. 12(22) represent the consumers that have used the product A(B), and have given the negative reviews for the product and have stopped using the product A(B), and have changed to use product B(A). These consumers have been generating negative effects on the surrounding consumers for the product.

(3) Evolution Rule

When $C_{i,j}^t = 00$, taking into account that the potential consumers are not very familiar with products A and B, or do not have preference for any one of the two, thus the potential consumers are only influenced by joint external effect and advertising effect. The potential consumers may buy product A or B at the next moment, or may choose not to buy any. That is to say that at the next moment, the cellular state of $C_{i,j}^t = 00$ may be 00, 10, 20. Assuming $P_{00,00}$, $P_{00,10}$ and $P_{00,20}$ are the probability of conversion to the next state, the formula for calculation of the conversion probability is as follow:

$$
\begin{aligned}
P_{00,00} &= 1 - P_{00,10} - P_{00,20} \\
P_{00,10} &= \left[\frac{n_{10} - n_{20} + n_{11} - n_{12} + n_{22} - n_{21}}{8} + (A_1 + a_1 A_3 - a_2 A_2)\right]\beta \\
P_{00,20} &= \left[\frac{n_{20} - n_{10} + n_{12} - n_{11} + n_{21} - n_{22}}{8} + (A_2 + a_3 A_1 - a_4 A_3)\right]\beta
\end{aligned}
\tag{8.1}
$$

In the formula, n_{10}, n_{11}, n_{12}, n_{20}, n_{21}, n_{22} represent the neighbor numbers of the cells that had the cellular state as 10, 11, 12, 20, 21, 22 respectively at the last moment. α_1, α_2 are adjustment coefficients of the advertising index A_3, A_2 respectively, that affect the cellular state change from 00 to 10. α_3, α_4 are adjustment coefficients of the advertising index A_1, A_3 respectively, that affect the cellular state change from 10 to 20.

When $C_{i,j}^t = 10\left(C_{i,j}^t = 20\right)$, considering that consumers have used the product A(B), the impact of the joint external effects and the advertising effect has been reduced, the comprehensive quality and the price of the product play a major role to the consumer's decision. After the consumers have used the product A(B) for a period of time and start to evaluate the product, the results may be high praises, bad comments or no comment. So after a period of time, the cellular state of $C_{i,j}^t = 10\left(C_{i,j}^t = 20\right)$ may be 11, 12, 00. Assuming that $P_{10,00}$ $P_{10,11}$ and $P_{10,12}$ are the probabilities of conversion to the next state, the formula for calculation of the conversion probability is as follow:

$$
\begin{aligned}
P_{10,00} &= 1 - P_{10,11} - P_{10,12} \\
P_{10,11} &= 0.3P_{00,10} + Q_1 + q_1 Q_3 - q_2 Q_2 - P_1 + p_1 P_3 - p_2 P_2 \\
P_{10,12} &= 0.3P_{00,20} + Q_2 - q_3 Q_1 - q_4 Q_3 - P_2 - p_3 P_1 - p_4 P_3
\end{aligned}
\tag{8.2}
$$

In the formula, q_1, q_2 and p_1, p_2 are adjustment coefficients of the comprehensive index Q_3, Q_2 and price index P_3, P_2 respectively, that affect the cellular state change from 10 to 11. q_3, q_4 and p_3, p_4 are adjustment coefficients of the comprehensive index Q_1, Q_3 and price index P_3, P_4 respectively, that affect the cellular state change from 10 to 12.

After the establishment of the new product marketing model based on cellular automata, we can analyze the market share of the new product under different business strategies. When the initial state of all cells is 00 and the initial states of all parameters are the same, we can obtain the computer simulation figure of the amount of market diffusion of the products A and B over time, as shown in Fig. 8.1. There is little difference in the amount of market diffusion between the products A and B. It can be considered that both occupy equal market share, the market reached a temporary equilibrium. But this equilibrium is not stable. The changes of the various aforementioned products in price index, the advertising index, the comprehensive quality will make the amounts of market diffusion of products A and B reach a new equilibrium.

Assuming that manufacturer A, at the moment of t = 10, in order to seize market share, lower the price of product A, the price index is reduced to P(0.18). If the manufacturer B does not respond, the price index of its own product (product B) is still P(0.20), the simulation results are shown in Fig. 8.2. The diffusion amount of product A is significantly more than product B.

At the same time, advertising investment and quality differences can also change the market share of the products. Figure 8.3a shows the result of market diffusions of product A and B, after only the product A increased its advertising investment, and the 8.3b shows the result of market diffusions of product A and B after only the product A improve its quality.

The new product marketing model obtained by using cellular automata can lead us to such conclusion that the manufacturer can improve the competitiveness of their products by lowering the price, improving the intensity of advertising,

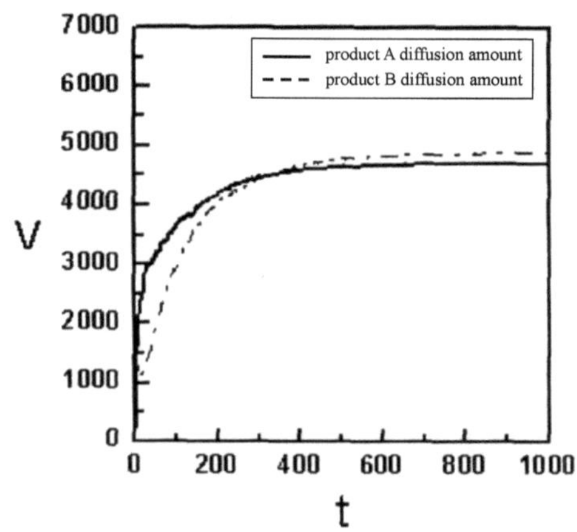

Fig. 8.1 New product diffusion with initial parameters

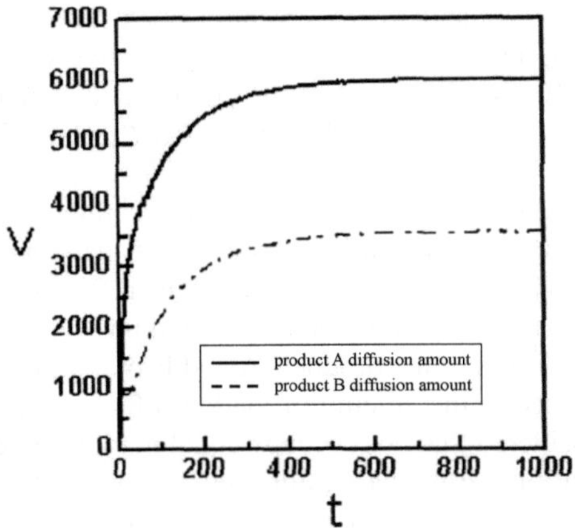

Fig. 8.2 New product diffusion when only product A lowered the price

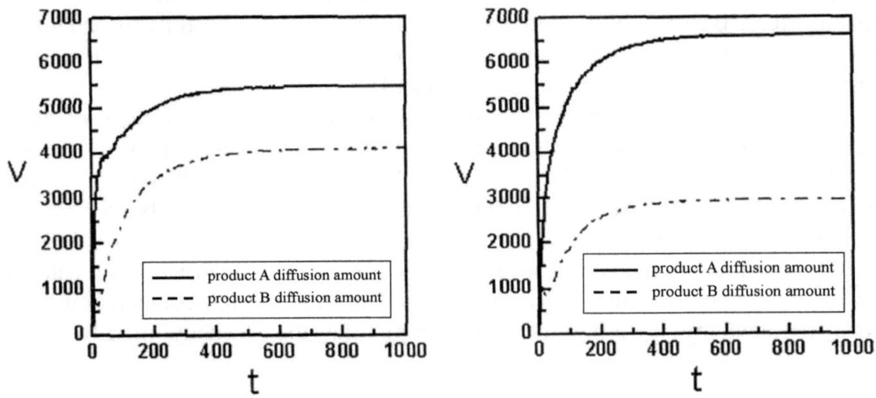

Fig. 8.3 Market diffusion affected by the increase in advertising investment (**a**) and the improvement in product quality (**b**)

improving the product quality and so on. This conclusion shows that cellular automata can well simulate the economic phenomenon of the new product market diffusion.

2. **Cellular Automata based stock market model**

In building a cellular automata based stock market model, the cells can be classified according to the market behaviors of the traders. Past research showed that in an open stock market, the traders can be classified into four categories based on their market behaviors. The four categories are the basic traders, the technical traders, the moderate traders and the following the crowd traders respectively (Li 2011, 2012).

1) Fundamental traders

Fundamental traders consider that in stock market, stock price changes will be reflected quickly in stock market information. They think that only the current information in stock market will affect the current stock prices, and they will not be influenced by the past stock prices. In addition, fundamental traders can understand and master more accurately the basic values of the stocks. The basic value of a stock is the value of the company assets taking into account the expected profit margin in the future. Fundamental traders consider that even though the stock price may fluctuate around the basic value of a stock at this stage, it is only temporary. They believe that with the passage of time, stock investors will get more and more stock information, the price of the stock will eventually be settled into its basic value. Therefore, we can say that the state of a Fundamental trader, either to buy or to sell a stock, is determined by the stock price and the difference of the stock price to the basic price. If we use t (i, j, t) to represent the investment state of a cell at position (i, j) and at moment of t. Then we have:

① If the market price is lower than the basic value of the stock, the state of a fundamental trader should be buying the stock, and at the moment τ $(i, j, t + 1) = +1$;
② If the market price is higher than the basic value of the stock, the state of a fundamental trader should be selling the stock, and at the moment τ $(i, j, t + 1) = -1$;
③ If the market price is equal to the basic value of the stock, the state of a fundamental trader should be hold, and at the moment τ $(i, j, t + 1) = 0$;

Assuming $p*(t)$ to represent the basic value of the stock at the moment of t, $p(t)$ is used to represent the price of the stock at the t moment. The evolution rules of fundamental traders are:

① if $p*(t) > p(t)$, then a basic trader is willing to buy the stock at the moment and the quantity of buying is $a(i, j, t)$;
② if $p*(t) < p(t)$, then a basic trader is willing to sell the stock at the moment and the quantity of selling is $b(i, j, t)$;
③ if $p*(t) = p(t)$, then a basic trader is holding the stock at the moment and is not doing nay buying or selling.

2) Technical traders

Different from fundamental traders, technical traders believe that the current price of a stock is closely related to its previous prices. They are usually used to predict the current or future stock price at a certain time through the stock's past prices. As with all the forecasting methods, although the technology analysis method can not accurately predict the future price of a stock at a certain moment or in a time period, technical traders can roughly have the knowledge of the future price of a stock at a certain moment or in a time period, so as to provide the basis for them to sell or buy a stock, as well as to decide the trading volume.

Technical traders can determine the time of selling or buying, according to the stock moving trend and its position with the moving average. The closer the stock price to the moving average, the lower probability the investors buy or sell a stock. The farther away the stock price moves from the moving average, the higher probability the investors buy or sell a stock. Through the analysis, we can see that the probability for a technical trader to trade a stock is in positive correlation with the stock price deviation from the moving average.

When a stock price moves below moving average, there is an upward trend for the stock. This kind of upward move will make the stock price move above the moving average and then keep upward moving. With certain probability, a technical trader will sell the stock during this kind of upward move. On the contrary, in the situation that a stock's upward move leads the price to fluctuate around the moving average, a technical trader will start to consider buying. When the price of a stock in downward move is moving below the moving average, and the price continues moving downward further and further from the average, a technical trader tends to buy stocks. On the contrary, in the situation that a stock's downward move leads the price to fluctuate around the moving average, with certain probability, a technical trader will sell the stock. In general, one should buy a stock when it moves above the moving average and keep moving upward. On the contrary, one should sell a stock when it move moves below the moving average and keep moving downward.

Assuming that we use five day moving average and the moving average curve can be expressed as the following formula:

$$B(5) = \frac{p(t-5)+p(t-4)+p(t-3)+p(t-2)-p(t-1)}{p(t-1)} \tag{8.3}$$

Using $D(t)$ to represent the stock price deviation from the moving average as in the formula below:

$$D(t) = p(t) - B(5) \tag{8.4}$$

If $D(t) > 0$, then $p(t)$ is above the moving average
if $D(t) < 0$, then $p(t)$ is below the moving average
if $D(t) = 0$, then $p(t)$ converge on the moving average curve.

Assuming $\eta_2(t)$ represent the probability a technical trader will conduct a stock trade at moment of t, then the probability that a technical trader will conduct a stock trade at moment of $t + 1$ can be expressed as:

$$\begin{cases} \eta_2(t+1) = e^{\frac{-2}{|D(t)|}} & D(t) \neq 0 \\ \eta_2(t+1) = 0 & D(t) = 0 \end{cases} \tag{8.5}$$

Assuming the number of stocks a technical trader trades at the moment of $t + 1$ as $c(i, j, t + 1) \times \eta_2(i, j, t + 1)$ and variable $\theta(i, j, t + 1)$ represents the probability a technical trader will conduct a trade at the moment of $t + 1$, then we have:

$$\theta(i,j,t+1) = \frac{p(t)}{B(5)} \tag{8.6}$$

If $0.5 < \theta < 1$, then we assume that a investor only conducts the trade activities of buying, that is $\tau(i, j, t + 1) = +1$; if $0 < \theta < 0.5$, then we assume that the investor only conducts the trade activities of selling, that is $\tau(i, j, t + 1) = -1$; if $\theta = 0.5$, then we assume that the investor will hold and will not conducts any trades, that is $\tau(i, j, t + 1) = 0$.

3) Moderate Traders

Comparing to fundamental traders and technical traders, moderate traders lack the ability of fundamental analysis and technical analysis. Their decisions for trade are influenced by two factors: the first, they are under the influences of the investment behavior of the surrounding neighbors. Namely, in the present model, the moderate traders are affected by the investment behavior of the investors on his left and right, above and below. Here we use the degree of self confidence of a security investor to represent the degree of influence of his neighbors on him. The so called "self confidence" of a security investor means the degree of self dependence of the investor in making the decision for stock trades. The second factor is that a moderate investor's trading behaviors are influenced by the investor's own investment psychology. Here we take an investor's risk appetite as a criterion. The risk appetite of an investor refers to the attitude of the investor in holding, or buying, or selling stocks when facing the risks. We divide the risk appetite of investors into risk loving, risk averse and risk neutral. Risk loving investors love to take risks; risk averse investors' attitude toward risks is "avoidance"; while the risk neutral investors have an "indifferent" attitude toward risks.

We use $V(t)$ to express the risk coefficient of a stock at the moment of t, when $0 < V(t) < 1$, the investor wants to sell the stock to avoid the risk. This investor is risk averse at this moment. When $-1 < V(t) < 0$, the investor wants to buy the stock to obtain more return. The investor is risk loving at the moment. When $V(t) = 0$, the investor wants to hold the stock for better return, and the investor is risk neutral at the moment. The risk appetites of investors are determined by the return of the stocks. The better return the investors obtain through trading of a stock, the more the investors hate to take risk, the greater probability they will sell the stock for avoiding the risks. On the contrary, the more investors have lost through trading of a stock, the more the investors want to buy the stock for more future returns, thus the greater probability they will buy the stock. Assuming the return of the stock $v(t) = p(t + 1) - p(t)$,because $V(t)$ and $v(t)$ belongs to the same function, therefore we assume that the degree of the stock's return is equal to the degree of investor risk appetite, and we have $V(t) = v(t)$.

Using $\eta_3(t)$ to express the probability of trading for a moderate trader at the moment of t, then we can express the probability of trading for this moderate trader at the moment of t + 1 as:

$$\begin{cases} \eta_3(i,j,t+1) = \frac{1}{e^{\frac{3}{v(t)}}-1} & v(t) \neq 0 \\ \eta_3(i,j,t+1) = 0 & v(t) = 0 \end{cases} \tag{8.7}$$

The number of stocks the moderate trader trades at moment of t + 1 can be expressed as:

$$c(i,j,t+1) \times \eta_3(i,j,t+1) \tag{8.8}$$

4) Herd traders

Herd investors do not have enough self confidence so that they like to follow the herd in making investment decisions. Therefore, it can be said that a trade decision made by a herd trader is only influenced by the investment behaviors of his neighbors. For a herd trader, when he is surrounded by positive news about a stock, for example, three of the herd trader's neighbors are buying a stock at moment of t, then it is likely that the herd trader at the moment of t is buying the stock $a(i, j, t)$. On the contrary, if the herd trader is surrounded by negative news about a stock, for example, three of the herd trader's neighbors are selling a stock at moment of t, then it is likely that the herd trader at the moment of t is selling the stock $b(i, j, t)$. If two of his neighbors are buying or selling a stock at moment of t, the herd trader will not buy or sell, and will continue to hold the stock. In stock market, the price of a stock is decided by the demand and supply relationship. When the supply is larger than the demand, the stock price will show a downward trend; while when the supply is smaller than the demand, the stock price will show an upward trend. In this book, we use $d(t)$ and $z(t)$ to express the supply and the demand at moment of t, and we can express them as:

$$\left.\begin{aligned} d(t) &= \sum_{i,j,t>0} \tau(i,j,t) \\ z(t) &= \sum_{i,j,t<0} \tau(i,j,t) \end{aligned}\right\} \tag{8.9}$$

The stock price is proportional to the demand and supply relationship. Based on this, we may express the stock price at moment of t + 1 as:

$$p(t+1) = p(t)\frac{d(t)}{z(t)} \tag{8.10}$$

The next figure gives out the evolution pattern generated by a cellular automaton based stock market model. In Fig. 8.4, a gray cell represents a cell with the value of 0, that is, the stock trader represented by the cell is not buying or selling a stock,

Fig. 8.4 Evolution pattern of stock market model

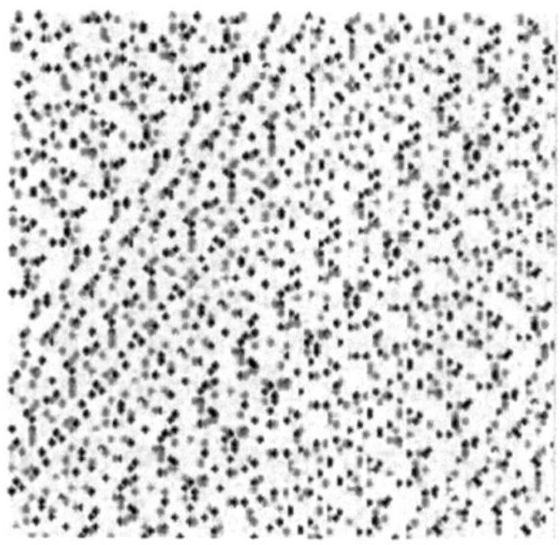

and is holding the stock instead. A white cell represents a cell with the value of 1, that is, the stock trader represented by the cell is buying the stock. A black cell represents a cell with the value of −1, that is, the stock trader represented by the cell is selling the stock.

Analyzing above model, we can get the following conclusions:

Firstly, if there exist moderate traders and herd traders in stock market, the trading volume of a stock will have the characteristics of volatility clustering. On the contrary, if there exist no moderate traders and herd traders in stock market and only fundamental traders and technical traders exist in the stock market, the trading volume of a stock will not have the characteristics of volatility clustering as described by the statistical experiences. The volatility of the trading volume will not change with the change of time *t*, and will not show a continuous higher or lower pattern during a certain period of time. When fundamental traders and technical traders have larger proportion and moderate traders and herd traders have relative smaller proportion in the market, the trading volume volatility of stocks will be relatively small. When only moderate traders and herd traders exist in stock market, the volatility clustering of stock trading volumes can be obviously observed. Therefore, we can say that volatility and clustering of stock trading volumes will grow with the growth of the proportion of moderate traders and herd traders in the market. When moderate traders and herd traders disappear from stock market, volatility and clustering of stock trading volumes will disappear completely.

Secondly, with the increase of the proportion of moderate traders and herd traders, the stock market starts to show instability, and when the stock market only exist fundamental traders and herd traders, the trading volumes of the stocks do not have the characteristics of volatility clustering as described by the statistical experiences. The volatility of the stock trading volumes is not large and stock market is relatively stable.

On the contrary, when the stock market only exist moderate traders and herd traders, we can obviously observe the volatility clustering of the stock trading volumes, and the fluctuation of stock trading volumes is relatively large, so that the stock market appears more volatile. Similarly, the blindness of investors leads to the irrational investment behavior, such as blindly chase the winners and cut the losers, tracking the "stock makers", and investment speculation on a variety of hot plates in the market. This will lead to instability of the stock market, even threaten the security of national economy.

Thirdly, fundamental investors and technical investors have the "leader" role in stock market. The investment public tend to sincerely trust the mainstream views of the stock market makers spread through the media, which bring huge shocks to the securities market, resulting in the market cycles of irregularity, and will make the stock market be easily manipulated and used by the market makers.

3. **Industrial cluster study based on cellular automata**

An industrial cluster is a typical complex system. From the microscopic point of view, an industry cluster is an individual behavior that a group of enterprises of the same location, shares a certain size of the market, shares resources, transportation and other related service facilities. From the macro point of view, an industrial cluster is formed by the different industries in the same location in order to obtain the external economic agglomeration, thus obtaining the competitive advantage that cannot be obtained through simple gathering of individual enterprises. These companies gather together thus appear systematic. At the same time, an industrial cluster also shows the characteristics of a complex system such as dynamic, open, nonlinear, far-from-equilibrium, self-organization and emergency of entirety.

1) Key elements in forming an industrial cluster

To build a cellular automata based industrial cluster model, first we need to conduct economical analysis on such an industrial cluster. For an industrial cluster, the formation of which mainly have the following elements:

Firstly, an industrial cluster can reduce the composite cost of an enterprise. The composite cost generally includes production cost, transaction cost and sales cost. Enterprises can gather together to use basic channels, including transportation, communications, urban pipe network, power and other public facilities (infrastructure environment) that are of supporting roles, thereby reduce the cost of productions and operations of the enterprises. The network connections between clustered enterprises reduce the cost of information search in business transaction processes. The gathering of enterprises from various related industries in one place makes it easier for these enterprises to maintain the long-term business interactions. All these plus the personal connections insides the cluster that are based on family ties and friendly relations promote the formation of mutual trust among the enterprises in the cluster. This kind of trust culture greatly reduces the opportunistic behavior and moral hazard, reduces the transaction cost. The clustered enterprises can reduce the sales cost through the joint marketing, joint promotion and joint market expansion.

Secondly, industrial agglomeration can improve the production efficiency and enhance the marketing power of these enterprises. The geographical concentration of enterprises of related industries promotes the specialized division of labor among the enterprises. This in turn improves the efficiency in utilizing specialized personnel and special equipments, so that makes the enterprises operate to their most competitive advantages, achieving high production efficiency. The geographical proximity reduces the transaction cost among the enterprises, this makes the specialized enterprises collaborate with low cost, thus improves the production efficiency and the ability of quick adaptation to market changes for the whole cluster.

Thirdly, industrial agglomeration can improve the innovation capacity. Enterprises located in the cluster can make more innovation, and the agglomeration of enterprises is conducive to the rapid spread of innovation. Industrial cluster can provide enterprises with a good atmosphere for innovation, can provide the enterprises with a variety of resources for innovation, and also can promote knowledge dissemination and application.

2) The negative effects of excessive enterprise clustering

Excessive clustering of enterprises, in the mean time, will generate some negative effects as expressed in the following:

First, the excessive enterprise clustering causes the increase in business costs. With the increase in enterprise density within the cluster, the land, the infrastructure and other resources become increasingly scarce. In the mean time, excessive demand for professional skills of the workforce also makes labor prices to rise. In addition, some negative externalities, such as pollution and other effects are also growing. These have become the negative effect of clustering, and have become the centrifugal force driving the enterprise to leave the cluster.

Secondly, the excessive enterprise clustering causes the emergence of vicious competitions. Appropriate competition has a positive effect on maintaining the vitality of the clusters and facilitating enterprises innovation in the clusters. On the other hand, competition also brings adverse effects. Excessive price competition will reduce corporate profits, and even make the enterprise to cut corners to reduce costs, resulting in the deterioration in the quality of the products. With the increase of enterprises in the cluster, if attention is not paid to fostering products diversity among the enterprises, the products in the cluster will appear homogeneous, and this will cause vicious competition with price as main means.

Thirdly, excessive enterprise clustering causes knowledge leak. Knowledge spillover is one of the important advantages of enterprise clustering, which can promote the spread of knowledge in the cluster, thus forming an innovative environment, to improve the innovation capacity of the whole cluster. However, it is undeniable that excessive knowledge spillover causes the leak of enterprise technology secrets. Especially in the regions where intellectual property rights cannot be effective protected, enterprise patents and business secrets do not get effective protection, this causes the emergence of great amount of imitators in a short time for innovation of any enterprise in the cluster. Innovative enterprises can only get the profits brought by innovation in a very short period of time, and a lot of innovation profit will be lost due to the imitational competition from other enterprises in the cluster.

3) Models based on cellular automata

Based on a cellular automaton's enterprise cluster model, a cluster is divided into a set of square grids, each containing an enterprise, and is expressed as a unit cell of the automaton. There are two states of 0 and 1 for each cell, where the cells with the state of 0 represents no enterprise entered, or have already exited from the area; the state of 1 represents that an enterprise has been attracted to enter. Neumann Von type neighbor is adopted for the cellular neighborhood. The rules of the enterprise cluster model based on cellular automaton are as follows:

① With the cell state as 0, when the number of neighboring cells with state of 1 is between [1, 3], the state of the cell changes to 1.
② With the cell state as 1, when the number of neighboring cells with state of 1 is larger than 4, the state of the cell changes to 0.

The results from evolution of such a cellular automaton model can lead to several conclusions as follows:

First, there exist complex nonlinear effects among enterprises in the cluster. In a certain time period, the cluster is far from equilibrium state; and after a period of evolution, the disordered state is transformed into a relatively ordered state of time, space and function. From the development of enterprise clusters, a cluster itself is an open system, which is influenced by competitions of the enterprises inside, the growth of cooperative association and the external policies. The overall economic benefits start to rise, and this will drive the regional economic development, thus the enterprise layout, division of labor and cooperation inside the cluster start to show an ordered structure. Once the external environment changes, for example, the great changes in the market, policy, economic environment, etc. occur, the cluster starts to move away from equilibrium, after the exchanges with the internal and external energy to achieve a new equilibrium state, entering the new orderly structure.

Secondly, there exists logistic growth model in the enterprise cluster that is similar to the ones in biological species. Ecology considers that, in the limited environment, the natural species population is not likely to grow exponentially in the long term. When the population grows in a limited space, with the increase of the density, under the limitation of space resource and the limitation in utilizations of other living conditions, the increase of competition within the population will inevitably affect the birth rate and death rate of the population. Under the limited environmental conditions, the continuous growth of population shows a S type curve.

Figure 8.5 shows the increase with time of the number of enterprises in the cluster during model evolution, which is similar to the growth of the biological species population. The shape of the curve shows that the enterprises in a region are influenced by market capacity, competition, environment and other factors. The growth cannot be long-term exponential, and will eventually become stable in the absence of the influences of new factors.

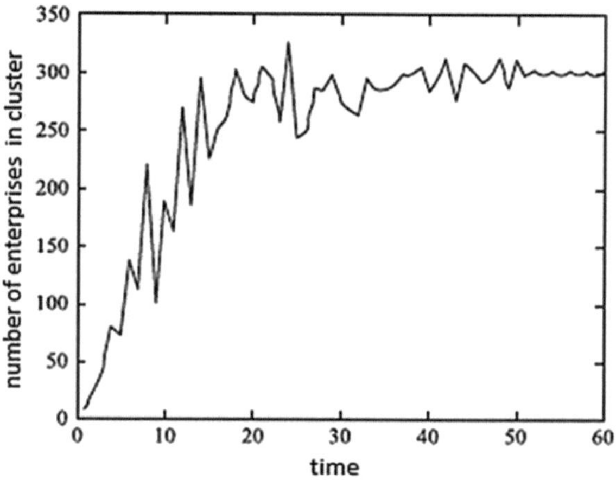

Fig. 8.5 Change of the number of enterprises inside a cluster

8.1.3 Characteristics of Cellular Automata Application in Economical Fields

From aforementioned three examples we can see that the applications of cellular automata in economical fields have the following characteristics:

First, the economic models based on cellular automata are built on the simulations of the phenomena in the micro economy. For example, the new product marketing model is the simulation of the micro factors in the diffusion of new products. The model of the stock market is based on the simulation of different traders' behaviors in the stock market. The building of enterprise cluster model is based on the simulation of enterprises entering and exiting in the enterprise clusters. This is a prominent feature of the applications of cellular automata in economic fields.

Second, the applications of cellular automats in economical fields generally complement various mathematical tools. Cellular automata usually are used in combination with mathematical analysis to compensate each other, such as in the description of the utility function of the micro participants. In the automaton, the number of relationships cannot be found, the need for strict mathematical derivation. For example, the changes of various parameters in the system are not simple linear but rather nonlinear relationship. There may also be complex probability analysis, such as the new product marketing model and the calculation of the conversion probability in the stock market model.

Thirdly, modeling based on cellular automata is closely related to both economics and management. The aforementioned various economic models can all be used to analyze the evolution of the economic market and the influence of micro behavior on macro behavior, so as to put forward the suggestions in economics and management. From the achievements made by various evolutionary computational tools aforementioned and papers published, we see that their applications and achievements in economics and management are the richest.

Fourthly, modeling based on cellular automata is also closely related to other social sciences, it takes its origin from the fields such as social sciences, psychology etc. Some economic research subjects also belong to social research subjects, such as the formation of social customs, the evolution of social relationships, the psychological inducement of the behavior of economical participants, etc. They can all be studied by the way of combing the cellular automata method and sociology as well as psychology.

8.1.4 The Development Direction of Cellular Automata Theory in the Field of Economics

With the rapid development of the theory and tools of complex systems, researchers should pay attention to development of cellular automata in the following aspects.

1. **The Mutual Integration of the Cellular Automata Method and Other Computational Tools, Especially Intelligent Algorithms**

In recent years, new computational methods for studying complex systems have been constantly emerging, such as neural networks, genetic algorithms, the "ant" algorithm, etc. The creation of these intelligent algorithms mainly depends on the constant development of computer science and its crossing with other fields of study. The integration of cellular automata and these new computational methods is the new direction of development for cellular automata. For example, Zarandi and others combine cellular automata, genetic algorithms and neural networks to study the Bullwhip Effect in economics. At the same time, the combination of various simulation methods is also a direction of development for cellular automata. For example, Chatfield and others used many simulation methods to conduct simulation study of the supply chain; He and others used the method of integrating cellular automata and system dynamics to study the development of cities.

2. **Further Discussion of Evolution Rules**

There has always been such a dispute in the field of evolutionary economics, that is, whether the evolution of economic systems follows the rules of self-organization or the rules of natural selection, or both? This is a profound philosophical question, and it has great influence on how to explain economic phenomena as well as establishing evolutionary economic models. If the evolution of systems follows the rules of self-organization, an evolutionary computational model should use a bottom-up modeling method. If the evolution of systems follows the rules of natural selection, an evolutionary computational model should simulate the "elimination" process in nature. If both kinds of rules are followed, system modeling should use both the bottom-up method and simulate the "elimination" process.

Currently, the research of cellular automata is mainly guided by the theory of self-organization, which believes that the macro phenomena of economic systems are obtained through the emergence of micro individual behavior and interactions. But how to add the rules of natural selection into the evolution rules of cellular automata is another direction of the development of cellular automata which should be paid attention to.

3. **Comparison and Integration with Traditional Economics**

Evolutionary economics as represented by cellular automata provides a new perspective for studying the complex system of economics, and challenges traditional economics' method of understanding economic systems and solving economic problems from the level of methodology. And yet these two methods will still coexist and learn from each other for a long time. The clash of these two methodologies will provide new momentum for the development of evolutionary economics represented by cellular automata.

8.1.5 Summary

This section explains the relationship between cellular automata and evolutionary economics, gives several practical examples of the application of cellular automata in the field of economics, summarizes the characteristics of the application of cellular automata theory in economics. Finally, we provide an outlook of the development of cellular automata in economics. In essence, the development of evolutionary economics, with cellular automata as its representative, is a result of the dissemination and development of the idea of complex systems in economics. The research of complexity greatly enhances people's understanding of both natural and social sciences. Parigogine has the following comments on the research of complexity: "We are at the beginning of a new scientific era. We are witnessing the birth of a science which is not limited by idealized and simplified situations, but reflects the complexity of the real world." Evolutionary economics which is represented by cellular automata will no doubt provides powerful and new momentum for obtaining greater achievements in the research of complex economic systems and the development of economics.

8.2 The Application of Cellular Automata in City Traffic Systems

8.2.1 *Analysis of City Traffic Systems Based on Cellular Automata*

1. The Engineering of City Traffic Systems and Social Complexity

A traffic system is an important component in people's lives and social economic activities. A good traffic system is an indispensable basic condition for people's everyday lives and the normal operations of businesses and institutions. It is also a stimulation of the rapid development of economy. However, traffic jams typical in cities have become a serious problem which hinders the development of a city and affects life quality. It has become the major bottleneck that restricts a city's continuous development and is a social problem which needs to be solved urgently at present (Jia et al. 2007; Gou et al. 2012; Kong et al. 2006; Zhu 2012).

A city traffic system is a typical, open and complex enormous system composed of road system, traffic flow system and management system. Reasons for the complexity of a city traffic system are: ① vehicles, road sections, crossroads, and traffic engineering constructions in a city's road network are numerous, and they are closely connected to form a complex network. ② The human-vehicle traffic flow of a traffic system is intelligent. It can respond to the surrounding environment and has abilities of self-organization, self-adaptation and self-driven. ③ The moving vehicles in a road network have non-linear interactions. At the same time, a traffic system has its hierarchies and integrity, and the system is also dynamic and random. It is undergone constant development and changes. ④ A city traffic system can be in an unbalanced state. The accumulation effect, strange attractiveness and openness further enhance the degree of complexity of a traffic system.

The complexity of city traffic and its non-linear system characteristic have been a common understanding in scientific circles. Using complexity science to study city traffic systems, not only a description of the system is needed, but also the revealing of the evolution rules of city traffic systems should be paid more attention. The hierarchical characteristic of city traffic system has decided that the levels of the research on the system have a great difference. For example, on the macro level, we may study problems of the planning of a city traffic system and its relationship with a city's development, while on the mid-micro level, we may study the complexity of a traffic system network, or the self-organization of a traffic system, etc.

From engineering perspective, a traffic network is composed of crossroads and roads that connect them. Vehicles run in the network, while city traffic infrastructure and city traffic framework have the function of traffic supply. The efficiency of the city traffic system can be enhanced through improving the passing capacity of city traffic infrastructure, improving the road network configuration, adjusting the city traffic structure. Although grand-scale, high-intensity and high-standard traffic infrastructure construction improves traffic conditions, traffic jams still happen often.

Let us consider the reason: from the perspective of social engineering, most modern urban traffic problems are social problems which center around people's transportation activities. Thus, they are more social, subjective and complex. A transportation system is not only an engineering system, but also a huge system of human activities. The core of a system of human activities is "people," and all the activities in the system are planned, carried out, changed and perfected by "people." The subjectivity of people in this system is more obvious than in several other systems, which includes a great deal of social, political, man-made activity factors and complex situations.

Compared with the features of the motor-vehicle-only traffic flow in other countries, China's mixed traffic flow differs a great deal in characteristics, especially in situations of mixed traffic flow at intersections, where vehicles, bicycles and pedestrians interfere with each other, causing traffic passing capacity to seriously decrease. Many traffic control measures which are quite effective in other countries are not practically effective as expected in our country.

2. **Evolution of Cellular Automata Models in Urban Road Network Traffic Flow**

City roads (except for loop roads) are usually criss-crossing and have many intersections, forming a certain road network structure. Compared with highways, this kind of structure is much more complex, and its traffic flow is also much more difficult to simulate. It is very difficult to directly use a one-dimensional cellular automaton traffic flow model to simulate the traffic flow of a city's road network. Therefore, more suitable two-dimensional cellular automata traffic flow models emerged.

1) The BML Model

In 1992, Biham, Middleton and Levine proposed the first two-dimensional traffic flow cellular automaton model (the BML model). In the BML model, vehicles are not allowed to change directions. Therefore, the total number of vehicles on each road is determined by the initial condition. Also, since it uses periodical boundary conditions, the total number of vehicles does not change with time. The mutual interference between east-west traffic and south-north traffic at different intersections will cause traffic jams.

2) The Expanded and Derivative BML Model

Usually, the numbers of vehicles east bound and north bound are not completely equal. Nagatani studied the asymmetric distribution of vehicles. Also, in the BML model, vehicles, no matter north or east bound, can move forward one cell position at most in one time-step. By introducing high-speed vehicles, Fukui and others expanded the BML model. In the expanded model, vehicles east bound still follow the same updating rule as in the BML model.

Nagatani and others used the expanded BML model to examine the situation of the vertical crossing of the roads (i.e. overpasses). Their method was to randomly choose a certain proportion of cells and define them as an overpass based on the BML model. The introduction of overpasses reduces the probability of the appearance of a network lock in the BML model, and obviously improves the passing state of the road network traffic flow. By modifying the BML model, Chung and others studied the influence of traffic lights which became ineffective on the traffic system. Based on the BML model, people proposed a green wave (GW) model to study GW synchronization (under usual conditions, traffic lights on a city's main roads are controlled synchronously to enable vehicles to pass more smoothly). Unlike the parallel updating of the BML model, the GW model uses partial backward sequence updating.

3) The Coupling Model Combining NaSch and BML

Although the BML model can describe certain basic characteristics of a city's road network traffic, it is too simple and cannot simulate certain finer traffic characteristics. The initial motive for establishing a coupling model was to catch certain basic characteristics displayed by the NaSch model and the BML model on the one hand, and on the other hand, try to keep the model as easily operable as possible. This requires the further refinement of a road section between two adjacent intersections into $D - 1(D > 1)$ cells. In this way, traffic on the road section between the intersections can be described according to the NaSch model's rules of updating positions, acceleration or deceleration introduced before, and then we can also take into consideration the interactions among vehicles running on the same road. In addition, people need to change the colors of the traffic lights regularly and periodically according to certain time interval $T(T \geq 1)$.

4) The Cellular Transmission Model

Daganzo used the concept of cellular automata and established a cellular transmission model (simplified as CTM) to study the problem of dynamic traffic in a network. CTM is a discrete approximation of the macro dynamic model LWR, and is a model which is consistent with the "model simulating hydrodynamics." It can catch the phenomenon of discontinuous changes in a network traffic flow, while the LWR model cannot. Moreover, it can clearly describe the physical effect of lining up, and can simulate characteristics of traffic dynamics such as shock wave, formation of lining up, dissipation of lining up, interactions among multi-road sections, etc. relatively well.

5) The Double-Lane Cellular Automaton Model

Nagtani first used a completely definitive rule to study a double-lane system $V\max = 1$. In this system, vehicles drive forward or change lane within one time step. Rickert et al. and Chowdhury et al. in 1996 and 1997, separately expanded the single-lane NaSch model to a double-lane system by introducing the one-lane lane change rule. Jianping Meng, Shiqiang Dai and others proposed a mixed traffic flow double-lane cellular automaton model which included motorcycles. In operational process of the double-lane cellular automaton model, each time step is usually divided into two sub-time steps: in the first sub-step, vehicles change lanes according to lane changing rules; in the second sub-step, vehicles on both lanes update according to the single-lane updating rule.

8.2.2 *Humanistic Intersection Simulation Based on Cellular Automata*

1. **Background of the Modeling of Humanistic Intersections**

Road intersections, as a typical representative of city traffic problems, are a social engineering system centering on human activities. It is an enormous complex system with multi factors, multi levels, multi goals, multi functions, multi stages and multi changes. It not only involves transportation facilities and traffic control, but also is closely related to society, economy, culture, and so on. It is both a problem in the system of human activities, and a soft system problem which lays particular emphasis on society but with yet unclear mechanism.

Since real traffic flow is a comprehensive and complex behavior on the whole, which emerges from the respective individual entities in execution of simple behavioral rules, using traditional mathematical modeling method to simulate traffic flow has its inherent insufficiency. Cellular automata have temporal, spatial and state discreteness, and evolve on the discrete temporal dimension according to certain local rules. They can easily duplicate complex phenomena or the force of attraction, self-organization and the phenomenon of chaos in the process of dynamic evolution. Therefore, the dynamic model of traffic flow based on cellular automata has become an important branch of theoretical models of traffic flow, and has been taken seriously more and more by scholars at home and abroad.

Nonetheless, existing traffic flow models based on cellular automata treat vehicles over- simply and abstractly, and we rarely see studies of models which include vehicles, roads, traffic lights and pedestrians at the same time. Also, vehicles in these models lack intelligence and autonomy, thus causing the difficulty that different entities at intersections such as road facilities, transportation tools, participants, etc. must all be abstracted as discrete cells with limited states. Various traffic rules, the mechanism of social traffic behaviors and their impacts can only be mapped as local evolution rules of cells. Cells are simple themselves and cannot reflect a subject's intelligent characteristics such as self-adaptation.

Modern city transportation system is an enormous complex system with multi factors, multi levels, multi goals, multi functions, multi stages and multi variations. Relatively simple cellular automata models still have plenty of problems in simulating the social complexity of road intersections. For this reason, it is necessary to construct cellular automata models of different levels based on the analysis of the complexity of intersections, and to conduct multi-level integration in cellular automata modeling, as well as in computer realization.

2. **Analysis of the System of Intersections**

First of all, the system of city road intersections is not a completely self-organizing system. This is because during the process of the system's operation and evolution, the system is influenced by behavioral psychology of each traffic participant, and this plays an important role in the formation of the system's complexity.

Second, the system of city road intersections is a typical dynamic system, and the states of each traffic participant are rich and changing at different times and in different traffic situations.

Third, the distribution of traffic participants in the system of city road intersections can be vividly mapped onto a two-dimensional cellular automaton.

3. **Cellular Automata Multi-Layer Modeling Impacted by Traffic Participants Behavior**

1) The Construction of an Ideal Cellular Automaton Model Based on the Analysis of a Micro Simulation Model

(1) **The Definition of Cells**

We use an example of a one-way triple-lane model, and define the vehicles and the pedestrians both at 8 m of length and 4 m of width. In this model, the characteristics of cells include the state of occupation, the time of occupation, the state of movement, the traffic signal, etc. The state of occupation indicates whether a cell is occupied. When a cell is occupied, there will be time of occupation. The time of occupation stands for the stop of the vehicles or the halt of walking for pedestrians. The state of movement refers to whether a cell is moving or static. The traffic signal displays the signals for traffic at the intersection where a cell is being controlled.

(2) **Cellular Space**

There are two kinds of cellular space in this model, respectively are the cellular space of roads outside the intersection and the cellular space of the intersection area.

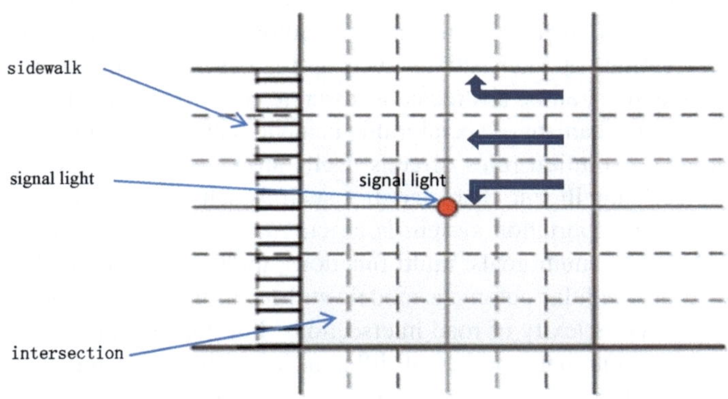

Fig. 8.6 Intersection cellular space

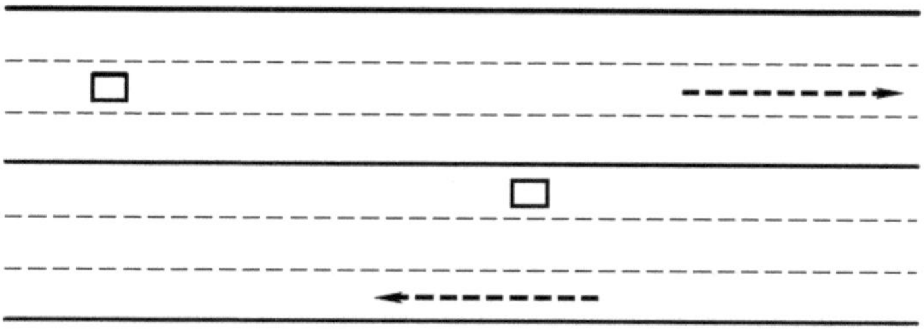

Fig. 8.7 Traffic lane cellular space

Figure 8.6 shows an intersection cellular space of 6 × 6, and Fig. 8.7 shows a cellular space of traffic lanes.

(3) **The Definition of Neighbors**

Define the value of every cell's maximum velocity as the length of two cells, i.e. $V_{\max} = 16$ m/s, and the radius of the neighbors is $r = V_{\max}$.

(4) **Rules**

Define one time step equals unit 1, i.e. 1s, cell's velocity at moment t as $r = V_t$, the cell's maximum velocity as $V_{\max}$, the probability of slowing down as P_{slow}.

Rule of Acceleration: If $V_t < V_{\max}$, then $V_{t+1} = \min\{V_{\max}, V_{t+1}\}$
Rule of Deceleration: If $V_t >$ gap, then $V_{t+1} =$ gap
Rule of Randomness: With probability P_{slow}, $V_{t+1} = \max\{V_{t+1} - 1, 0\}$
Position Update: $X_{t+1} = X_t + V_{t+1}$.

2) Model of Participants' Characteristics

The design of a humanistic intersection needs to respect the right-of-way of various kinds of participants,and to effectively incorporate the social factors of various traffic behaviors. In this model, we use one of the major types of participants in traffic behavior—pedestrians, as an example for analysis. The rules pedestrians must follow while crossing streets are defined as follows: within one update cycle, each cell selects its desired movement according to the "transfer probability"—p_{ij}, in which subscript ij stands for the cell's position. The transfer probability is composed of a static part and a dynamic part. The static part of a cell's transfer probability includes:

(1) Weight of choice of direction D_{ij}, with forward direction as the primary choice and a weight of 0.5; choices of left and right directions both have a weight of 0.25.
(2) Weight of geography effect G_{ij}, with the weight of 0 representing fixed barriers on pedestrian crossings, and the weight for others is 1.
(3) Effect of pedestrians coming from the opposite direction: the average delay time for a pedestrian to walk around another pedestrian coming from the opposite direction is 0.25; if the delay time is converted to a decrease of a

pedestrian's forward moving velocity, then the pedestrian's displacement will be reduced by the length of one cell.

The dynamic part of a cell's transfer probability includes:

(1) Weight of effect of traffic light TL*ij*. When the traffic light for pedestrians turns to red, for pedestrians who are going to walk onto the zebra crossing, the TL*ij* of cells at the boundary of the crossing is 0, in other cases it is 1, i.e., pedestrians who are already on the crossing can move forward.
(2) Weight of occupancy marking of the target cell *nij*. Only when the target cell (*i*, *j*) is empty and there is no obstruction between the source position and the target position, can the target cell be occupied. Otherwise, the pedestrian cannot move to the target cell, i.e.

$$\left.\begin{array}{l}\text{if}\quad (i,j)\quad \text{is allowed}\\ \text{then}\quad (n_{ij}=1)\\ \text{else}\quad (n_{ij}=0)\end{array}\right\} \tag{8.11}$$

3) Model of Participant Interactions

At the peak time of pedestrian street crossing, conflicts between the pedestrian flow and the vehicle flow at road intersections often happen. Moreover, in real situations, many pedestrians do not use crossings, causing vehicle flows that move forward or change directions to conflict with multiple pedestrian flows. The increase of conflict points and frequent braking by vehicles not only reduce passage efficiency at intersections, but also easily cause traffic accidents.

(1) **Pedestrian's Street-Crossing Rules**

Pedestrians' decision of whether to cross a street is mainly based on the distance between themselves and the vehicles approaching, i.e., the psychologically safe distance. This model here uses young people as an example: suppose that the probability of a young person running the red light is 0.5, and also suppose: when the vehicle speed is between 30 and 39 km/h, the average distance between pedestrians who begin to cross the street and an approaching vehicle should be 45 m, and a young person crosses the street with a probability of 0.6. When the vehicle speed is between 40 and 49 km/, the average distance between pedestrians who begin to cross the street and an approaching vehicle should be 50 m, and under the situation, a young person crosses the street with a probability of 0.8.

(2) **Driver's Driving Rules**

Let $X_{i,n}$ and $V_{i,n}$ respectively stand for the position and driving velocity of driver n in traffic lane i, $d_{i,n} = X_{i,n+1} - X_{i,n}$ represents the distance between vehicle n and the vehicle ahead of it in lane i, $d_{n,\text{ other}}$ represents the number of empty cells between vehicle n and the vehicle ahead of it which is in the target lane, *dn*, back represents the number of empty cells between vehicle n and the vehicle in the back of it which is in the target lane, $d$safe represents the safe distance to avoid collisions in lane-changing, and we set $d$safe = Vmax +1. The driver's characteristics are reflected by $V_{i,n}$, Vmax and reaction time. The driver's driving rules are as follows:

① Slow Start: for $0 \rightarrow V1$, with probability of $1 - p_s$ ($0 \leq p_s \leq 1$), that is, sometimes a vehicle will not immediately start after it stops.
② Random Deceleration: with probability of p_r ($0 \leq p_r \leq 1$) for $V_n \rightarrow \max(V_n - 1, 0)$. This refers to the deceleration of vehicles caused by various uncertain factors.
③ Lane-Changing: $d_n < \min(V_n + 1, V\max)$, $d_{n,\text{ other}} > d_n$, and dn, back $> d_{\text{safe}}$. During the vehicle driving process, when lane-changing conditions are met, drivers will change lanes with probability p_{change} ($0 \leq p$ change ≤ 1).
④ Position Update: $x_n \rightarrow x_n + V_n$, that is, vehicles will go forward at the adjusted speed.

4) Conflict Resolving Rules

According to the *Road Traffic Safety Law of The People's Republic of China*, pedestrians have the right-of-way to cross an intersection when the pedestrian crossing signal turns green. Motor vehicles turning right must wait for pedestrians to cross first, and drive through the pedestrian crossing as well as the intersection when a gap in the pedestrian flow allows it. In the actual operation of intersections, however, traffic participants are not all completely law-abiding rational persons. Not only may drivers behave against the law or regulations, but also the pedestrians sometimes cross intersections at improper places or run red lights. Therefore, conflicts between motor vehicles and non-motor vehicles such as bicycles or pedestrians are widespread in actual traffic situations. In our discussion here, we assume that drivers are rational, but pedestrians may violate law and regulations, to cross a street with the probability of p at running a red light. In this situation, a driver makes a decision to either slow down or stop the vehicle to avoid a collision according to a comprehensive judgment of vehicle velocity and safety distance. Let d_{safe} represent the safety distance between a motor vehicle and pedestrians, $d_{\text{safe max}} = V_{\max} + 1$, and let d represent the actual distance between the motor vehicle and pedestrians. The specific rules are as follows:

① Avoidance by deceleration: if $2\,d_{\text{safe}} > d > d_{\text{safe}}$, the driver must decelerate to guarantee that pedestrians will safely cross the street first, i.e.

$$\left.\begin{array}{ll}\text{If} & 2d_{\text{safe}} > d > d_{\text{safe}} \\ \text{then} & -V\end{array}\right\} \tag{8.12}$$

② Avoidance by stopping the vehicle: if $d \leq d_{\text{safe}}$, the driver must stop the vehicle, i.e.

$$\left.\begin{array}{ll}\text{If} & d \leq d_{safe} \\ \text{then} & V = 0\end{array}\right\} \tag{8.13}$$

4. **Simulation Result and Analysis**

For the convenience of analysis, here we set the condition as that the pedestrians would violate traffic regulations to cross streets on red light (i.e. pedestrians who run red lights), and we will limit our study to the influence of such condition on the motor vehicle flow at the relevant intersection. Modifying the parameters of the model to that, the pedestrian crossing signal is always red, the probability of pedestrians appearance at the crossing is constant, the probability of pedestrians crossing the street in violation of regulations is *Pd*, and *Pd* is not zero.

The output of the operational model is the temporal-spatial distribution figure of the road traffic flow, as shown in Fig. 8.8, with 500–1500 time steps (seconds). The data is obtained through observing the number of vehicle flow within 1200–4800 time steps (seconds). In our discussion here, *Pd* represents the probability of pedestrians crossing the street in violation of regulations, and *p*peo in the following context represents the probability of an individual running a red light at a certain moment. For example, *p*peo = 0.1 indicates that the probability of a pedestrian running a red light at an intersection at moment *t* is 0.1. This means that 10% out of pedestrians on average will run a red light to cross the street. *P*peo = 0.2 indicates that the probability of a pedestrian running a red light at an intersection at a certain moment is 0.2, i.e., there will be 20% of pedestrians on average who will cross the street by running a red light. Let us set the probability of pedestrian appearance at this place as 1, the speed of pedestrian crossing as 1.5 m/s, vehicle appearance probability at the crossing as 0.4, and vehicle velocity as 3.75 m/s.

For spatial-temporal distribution figure of Fig. 8.8a, motor vehicle appearance probability is 0.4, random deceleration probability is 0.2, slow-start probability is 0.3, vehicle lane-changing probability is 1.0, and the probability that a pedestrian running a red light within a unit time (second) is 0.1. Compared with Fig. 8.8a, b displays the temporal-spatial distribution of a pedestrian running a red light within a unit time with probabilities 0.2 and 0.3 respectively.

Compared with Fig. 8.8a–c, is a temporal-spatial distribution figure of pedestrians running red lights with a probability of 0.1. Figure 8.8a displays that, although there are phenomena of vehicles slowing down and stopping at certain road sections, only a few traffic jams appear at pedestrian crossings. This is because that the probability of pedestrians running red lights is relatively low, and the number of violators is relatively small. Therefore, vehicles can basically all pass through pedestrian crossings.

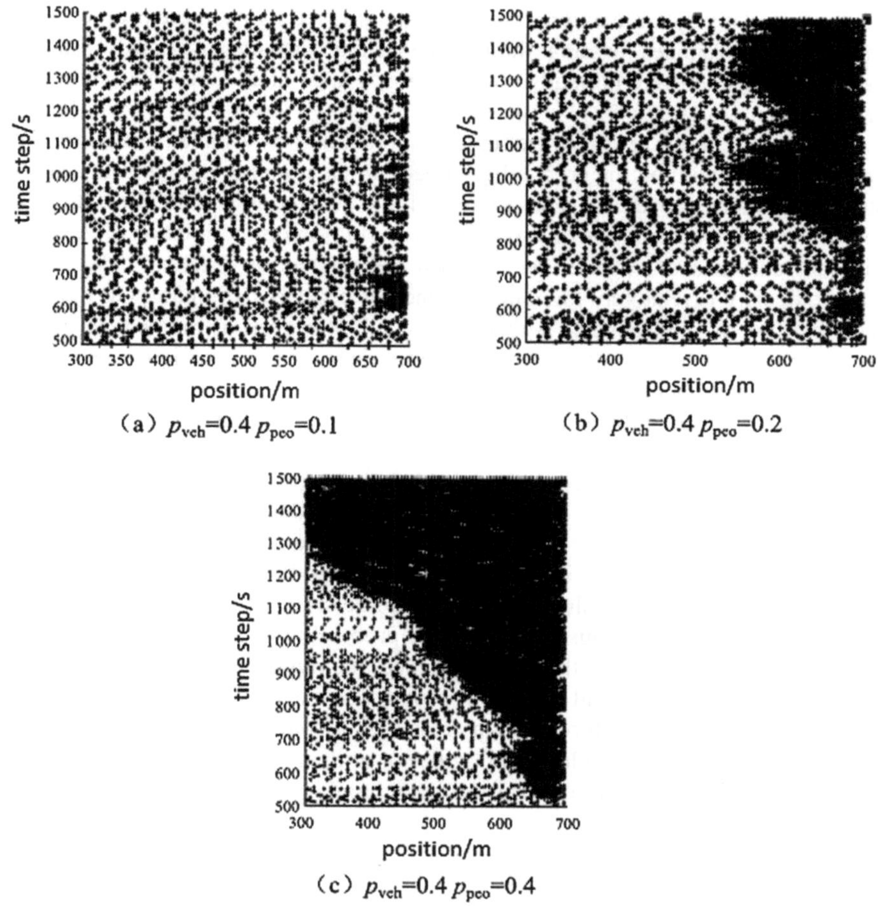

Fig. 8.8 Temporal-spatial distribution figure with the same *p*veh and different p_{peo}

Figure 8.8b, c show that, under the same conditions, with the increase of the probability of pedestrians running red lights, serious traffic jams start to appear at pedestrian crossings, causing subsequent vehicles unable to go through, and leading to large-area, long-time traffic congestion. Moreover, with the increase of time, the length of road sections having traffic jams increases as well. The reason for the appearance of such serious traffic jams is that the probability of pedestrians running red lights is too high, and there are too many people running red lights, causing vehicles at pedestrian crossings almost unable to go forward, and thus leading to chain reactions and causing serious traffic jams.

If we compare Fig. 8.8a, b, it is clear that when the vehicle appearance probability is relatively high, i.e., vehicle density is relatively high, a few pedestrians running red lights will not affect the normal operation of vehicles. However, when there are a relatively large number of people running red lights, these people start to influence the vehicles passing through pedestrian crossings seriously, causing vehicles unable to drive normally, and leading to large-area, long-time traffic jams at pedestrian crossings.

In addition, in our research, we limit the probability of vehicle appearance. We can also choose to limit the probability of pedestrians running red lights, in order to study the passing capacities under different traffic generation probabilities. It can be seen that with same situation of pedestrians crossing streets in violation of the rules, different densities of vehicles on the road are influenced differently. When the vehicle density is relatively low, the influence of pedestrians running red lights on the whole on driving vehicles is relatively small. However, as the vehicle density increases, the influence on the whole, of pedestrians who run red lights on passing vehicles starts to increase dramatically.

Figure 8.9 is an influence tendency figure of the probability of pedestrians running red lights on vehicle flow volume, with vehicle appearance probability as 0.4, random deceleration probability as 0.2, slow-starting probability as 0.5, and lane-changing probability as 1.0. As the figure shows that, when the probability of pedestrians running red lights is below 0.2, the decrease in total flow of traffic is not very obvious. However, when the probability of pedestrians running red lights exceeds 0.2, vehicle flow volume starts to decrease dramatically. The occurrence of such a phenomenon is because that when the probability of pedestrians running red lights is relatively low, even though it influences the running of vehicles to a certain extent, with a relatively small number of people who run red lights, vehicles coming behind can still get through pedestrian crossings smoothly within the allowance of corresponding operation rules, and will not influence the traffic flow much. However, when the probability of pedestrians running red lights is relatively high,

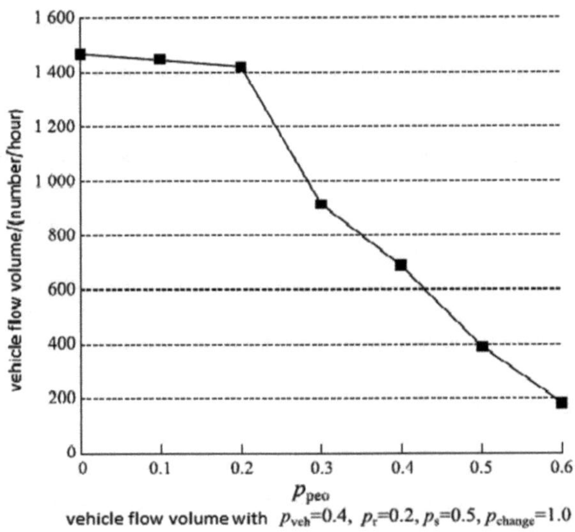

Fig. 8.9 Vehicle flow in different P_{peo} situations

i.e., when the number of people running red lights is relatively large, it will influence the vehicles at intersections seriously, causing large volume of vehicles to decelerate at pedestrian crossings, even having to stop and wait for pedestrians to go through. Long-time traffic jams will appear and the traffic flow volume on the road will decrease dramatically.

8.2.3 *The Application of Cellular Automata in Calculating Urban Traffic Jam Costs*

1. **Modeling Background of Urban Traffic Jam Costs Calculation**

Urban traffic jams usually have temporal and spatial characteristics, and generally happen in a relative limited temporal period and a relative limited spatial range. Traffic jam is a phenomenon showing that normal running of urban traffic has been interrupted.

1) Characteristics of Traffic Jams

From the perspective of traffic flow, traffic jams mean that vehicle speed will decrease with the continuous increase of traffic volume density, thus causing time delays. The relationship between velocity and volume density is the most basic model for describing traffic flow. As Fig. 8.10 shows, at the initial stage, the traffic flow volume is 0, and the vehicle velocity has maximum value of *VA*. As traffic flow density increases, the impact on vehicles increases, causing vehicle velocities to continuously decrease. While the traffic flow volume gradually increases to maximum value *Q*, and roads capacity eventually reaches saturation. After that, as the number of vehicles on road continues to increase, traffic density becomes

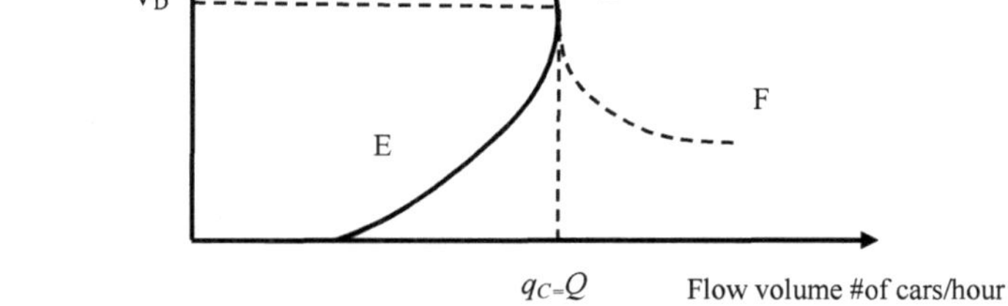

Fig. 8.10 The relationship between vehicle velocity and traffic flow volume

higher. The phenomenon that vehicle velocity and traffic passing volume decrease at the same time appears. This leads to the gradual decrease of the efficiency of road utilization. If this kind of situation persists, traffic jam will be intensified until the traffic flow volume becomes 0, and traffic flow is interrupted.

From the perspective of travelers, an urban resident generally has certain psychological expectation about the time needed for his trip, or he is prepared for the traffic to be interrupted for certain times and for the time spent on interruptions. When traffic jam occurs, the actual situation exceeds the traveler's expectation. Under such situation, the relationship among traffic jam *C*, travel time *t*all, the number of times of traffic flow interruption *d,* and the time span of traffic flow interruption t_{delay} can be expressed by the following function:

$$C = f(t_{all}, d, t_{delay}) \tag{8.14}$$

From Fig. 8.11 we can see that when the number of traffic interruptions or the interruption time span in traveling process is within a tolerable range, traffic jam can be regarded as non-existent. With the increase of the number of traffic interruptions or the increase of the interruption time span, travelers' psychological anxiety level increases slowly. When the traffic jam starts to seriously affects the traveler's trip, the travelers' anxiety about this trip rapidly increases, the sense of traffic congestion thus gradually increases.

From economical sense, traffic jams are caused by the conflict between transportation supply and demand. Transportation demand derives from social economic activities, and is affected by multiple factors such as a city's society, economy, politics and traffic culture, as well as the convenience and safety and the time needed for travel in the city, etc. Traffic jams can be studied according to different OD points, different modes of transportation or different time periods. Transportation supply is the transportation capacity provided by the construction of transportation facilities which are in turn brought by a city's social and economic

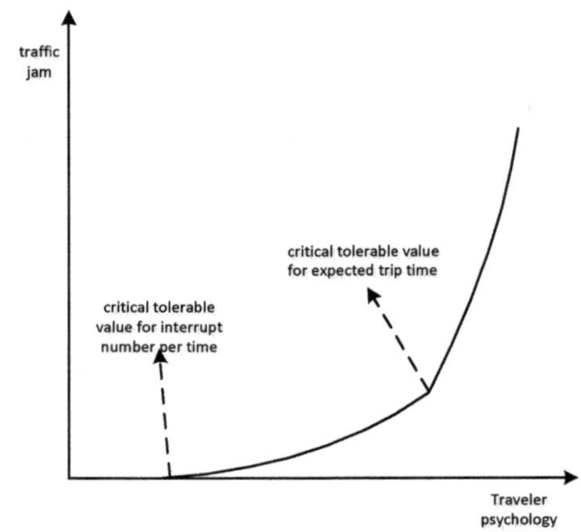

Fig. 8.11 The relationship between traffic congestion and travel mentality

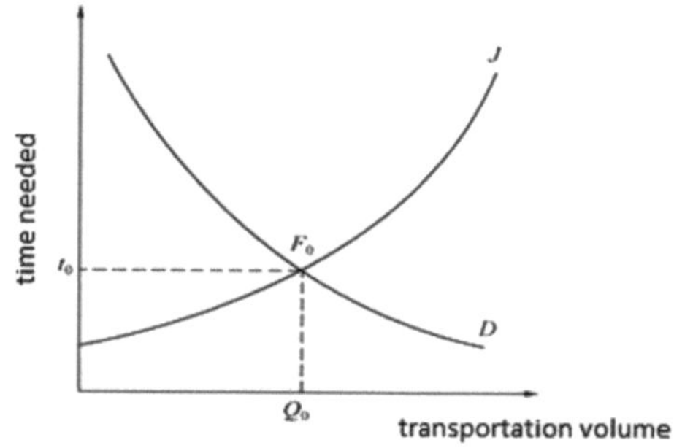

Fig. 8.12 Supply-demand relationship

development level, city configuration, land-utilization mode, and industrial structure. It also involves resource consumption, urban planning, regional planning and other factors.

Under certain social economic conditions, the curve representing relationship between transportation supply function J and transportation demand function D can be shown by Fig. 8.12. In the figure, F_0 represents the supply-demand balance point of transportation. That is, a balance is reached under the interaction of transportation demand and supply. But when supply is less than demand, the transportation balance will be broken and cause traffic congestion.

2) Characteristics of Traffic Jams

The occurrence of urban traffic jams has the characteristic of temporal-spatial variations, and has unique features in time, space and types.

(1) Temporal Characteristic: The main goals of travel for urban residents are work and study, therefore, during work days, traffic jams appear at morning and evening rush hours. Traffic flow suddenly starts to increase continuously within a certain period of time. According to traffic statistics, the peak hours during work days are between 7:00 and 9:00 a.m. and 17:00 and 19:00 p.m., which will cause frequent traffic jams all over the city. In particular, with the development of modern urbanization, heavy traffic jams appear obviously during the peak hours of Monday mornings and Friday evenings both city-bound and out-of-city directions.
(2) Spatial Characteristic: Since urban transportation roads are divided into different levels, with corresponding primary and secondary traffic capacities, traffic jams usually happen at intersections of arterial roads, expressways, sub-arterial roads, and branch roads, i.e., at a point where a road with large traffic capacity transits to a road with smaller traffic capacity. At the same time, as affected by vehicles turning left and the traffic lights at intersections, the traffic capacity at intersections will decrease, thus forming points of traffic congestion, which will cause serious congestion on a road section rapidly.
(3) Frequent Occurrence and Occasional Occurrence: According to the causes that generate the jams, traffic jams can be divided into frequent ones and occasional

ones. Frequent traffic jams are periodic, and are regular and predictable in time and space. They happen because a sudden increase of traffic flow exceeds normal traffic capacity. Occasional traffic jams are unexpected, and have no regularity in time and space. They are very difficult to predict, and are usually caused by unusual events (traffic accidents, large-scale events, inclement weather, etc.).

3) Traffic Congestion Time

The function of transportation products is to realize the spatial displacement of the transported objects. Transportation time is the most important factor of product quality. For passenger transport, the shortening of travel time can help passengers save time, and to convert this into the time value for each passenger, the gain of each passenger from this can be estimated. For cargo transport, the shortening of time of cargos in transit means the increase of the turnover speed of social products, which in turn influences the efficiency of social production.

Traffic congestion increases the traveling time of urban residents to a great degree. Residents' travel time consists of time en route, time spent getting on and off board, and transfer time.

First, the obstructions caused by traffic jams greatly increase passengers' time en route.

Second, traffic congestions decreases the travel efficiency of urban public transportation, making residents unable to go whenever they want to, hereby increasing the uncontrollability and unpredictability of travel time.

Third, although the development of urban subway systems can sufficiently relieve traffic congestion, redirecting urban ground passenger flow to underground, due to the inconvenience of the transfer between ground transportation and the subway transit system, usually passengers using both modes of transportation cannot make the transfer seamlessly. The existence of various transfer problems causes transfer time to greatly increase for passengers. Often the result is that the decrease of travel time cannot make up for the increase of transfer time.

The occurrence as well as the spreading of traffic congestion increase passengers' time en route, time for getting on and off board, and transfer time, so much so that urban residents' travel time and travel cost are greatly increased.

2. Analysis of the System of Urban Traffic Congestion Costs

First, the system of urban traffic congestion costs is not a complete self-organizing system. This is because that during the process of operation and evolution, the system is influenced by various traffic costs, which play an important role in the formation of the system's complexity.

Second, an urban traffic congestion cost system is a typical dynamic system, which includes the cost of vehicle driving and the cost of traffic congestion. If we analyze it on a deeper level, the system should also include the influence of traffic congestion on the environment, the cost of passengers' waiting, economic losses caused by traffic congestion, the externalities of vehicle driving, etc.

Third, the distribution of the various costs of urban traffic congestion cost system can be intuitively mapped onto a two-dimensional cellular automaton.

3. The Modeling of the Cellular Automaton of Urban Traffic Congestion Costs

1) Parameters of the Cellular Automaton

The main indicators of the model's output are the running time of vehicles in a given road traffic network, and the cost for vehicles to run in this network, i.e., how much social economical resources a vehicle consumes during one trip.

In the model, one cell represents one vehicle driving in the network. Such a cell is largely different from cells in a common cellular automaton. Here the cell is not only the smallest unit in a system and needs to interact with others, but also it should be a recorder and decision-maker, recording the vehicle operating status in the traffic network and determining the routes for completion of the trip. In a traffic network, there is not only one route from the starting point to the destination, the time and money spent for the trip are quite different with different driving routes. Studying the routes of vehicles in a traffic network can help to optimize the network and to channel the traffic flow.

We now introduce some basic parameters in the model:

First, vehicles run in a road network. The model assumes that the cost for vehicles to drive normally is 1 for each time step, and the cost of each time step in a traffic jam is 0.5.

Second, passengers who choose to go from road 1 to road 2 needs to add 4 for public transportation cost.

Third, since parking lot A is relatively small, the parking fee is set at 10. Last, by using public transportation, the time needed to go from parking lot B to the urban central district is set at a fixed value of 10.

In the model, all time and cost variables do not have measurement units, i.e., they are dimensionless. Since the cellular automaton will evolve step by step on track of time steps, in the model, the measurement unit of time is one time step, and this unit is abstracted by the discretization of actual time. It can be seen from the rules that trip cost is the function of the discrete time step, and the parameters of this function are determined according to a cell's state at this time step. In this one time step, if the cell is in a moving state, then the parameter of the function is 1; if the cell is in a state of being in congestion, then the parameter is 0.5. The parameter indicates that the trip cost of a running vehicle is not the same as the one that is stuck in congestion.

2) The Construction of the Cellular Automaton Model

The cellular automaton model has four components: cellular space, cell neighbors, cell states and evolution rules. We will now construct the cellular automaton model of traffic trip costs from these four aspects.

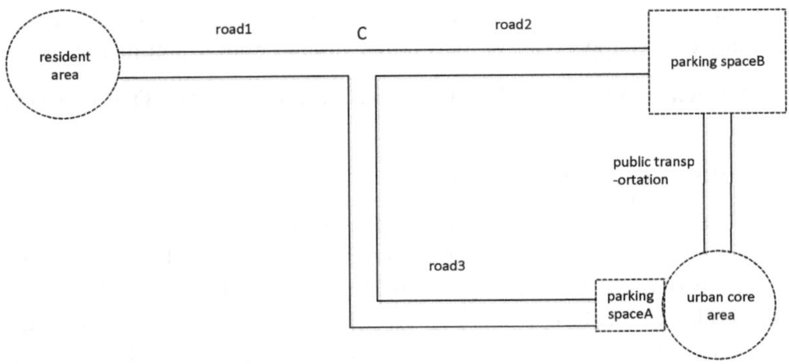

Fig. 8.13 Simulated urban traffic network

(1) Cellular Space

The cellular space in the cellular automaton model of traffic trip costs is an abstraction of a road network. Suppose there is a traffic network as shown in Fig. 8.13. There are two choices to go from the residential area to the urban core area: one can go through road 1 and road 3 to arrive at the relatively small parking lot *A*, and then walk a little distance to reach the destination. The alternative is to go through road 1 and road 2 to arrive at a big parking lot *B*, and then take commuter public transportation to reach the destination.

There is a trade-off here: since the number of travelers is relatively large, and the number of vehicles parking lot *A* can accommodate is relatively small, there is a high probability that travelers who choose to take the first route to drive to the urban core area will have to wait to enter parking lot *A* for parking. But the advantage of choosing the first route is that, when traffic flow is smooth, the travel time is shorter than using the second route.

Such a traffic network can be abstracted as the following cellular spaces: from the residential area to point *C* can be abstracted as a cellular space of 50 cells, i.e., when traffic flow is smooth, it only takes 50 time steps to go from the residential area to point *C*. To go from point *C* to the urban core area by road 3 can also be abstracted as a cellular space of 50 cells; to go from point *C* to the urban core area by road 2 can be abstracted as a cellular space of 70 cells. By now, the model's cellular space has been constructed.

(2) Cell Neighbors

What the model simulates is the running states of vehicles in a traffic road network. Since at this time only the cell in front of it can influence its state, each cell in the model has only one neighbor, which is the cell in front of it.

(3) Cell States

① Vehicles drive on road R, and since in the traffic network under discussion, vehicles' driving routes are only from road 1 to road 2 or from road 1 to road 3, R's value space is {1, 2, 3}.
② A vehicle's driving time is M.
③ A vehicle's waiting time is W. M and W both are integers with values greater than 1. Here, time is discretized and is replaced with the evolution time steps of the cellular automaton.
④ A cell's position i in the cellular space is also the position of the vehicle in the cellular space.
⑤ Each cell's state is $C(i)$, and when the cell is occupied by a vehicle, $C(i) = 1$, otherwise, $C(i) = 0$.

(4) Evolution Rules

A cell in the model follows the rules as expressed below:

① For R, when $i = 50$ and there is no vehicle in the first cellular space on road 2 and road 3, jump towards road 2 and road 3 randomly with a probability of 50%;
② For M, if $C(i + 1) = 0$ then $M = M + 1$, $C(i) = 0$, $C(i + 1) = 1$;
③ For W, if $C(i + 1) = 0$ then $W = W + 1$.

4. **Evolution Results and Analysis**

After establishing the cellular automaton model of traffic trip costs, we used MATLAB for programming and simulation, and obtained the following results.

Figure 8.14 displays the result after running the model for 1000 time steps. In this simulation, the entire traffic system has a total number of 434 vehicles passing

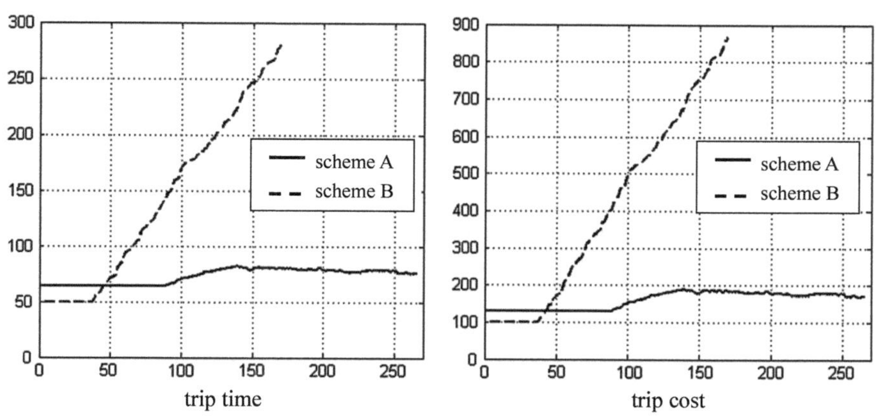

Fig. 8.14 Simulation of travel time and trip costs (The horizontal coordinate represents evolution time steps, and the vertical coordinate represents travel time and trip costs)

through. Among those, 265 vehicles pass through road 1 and road 2, and 169 vehicles pass through road 1 and road 3.

In this system, the cause for congestion comes from the very low capacity of parking lot *A*, and travelers have to wait for parking space. Such wait causes congestion on road 3, which then passes along road 3 until it eventually causes the congestion of the entire system. Therefore, in this section, we discuss two measures to improve the system's conditions of congestion: enlarging the accommodation capacity of parking lot *A* or putting up a sign to indicate the remaining capacity of the parking lot at the moment.

(1) Increasing Supply (expanding the capacity of parking lot *A*)

With all other conditions remain unchanged, expanding the capacity of parking lot *A* from 10 to 20. Then the evolution of the system in 1000 time steps is shown in Fig. 8.15.

In 1000 time steps, there are 468 vehicles which pass through the traffic system, raising the passage percentage by 7.83%. Among these vehicles, 259 in total pass through road 1 and road 2, and 209 vehicles pass through road 1 and road 3.

(2) Information Update (Putting up an indicator Sign)

With all other conditions remain unchanged, putting up a sign at intersection *C*, specifying how much empty parking space is available in parking lot *A* at the moment, so as to guide the distribution of traffic flow on road 1 and road 2. Suppose that the sign shows that there are fewer than 3 empty parking spaces in parking lot *A*, vehicles passing through point *C* would choose road 2 with a probability of 90%, and choose road 3 with a probability of 10%, then the evolution of the system can be shown by Fig. 8.16.

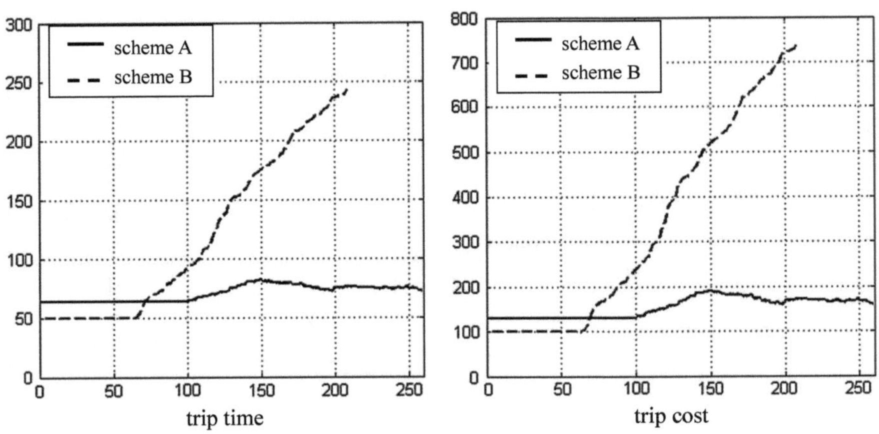

Fig. 8.15 Travel time with expanded parking lot capacity

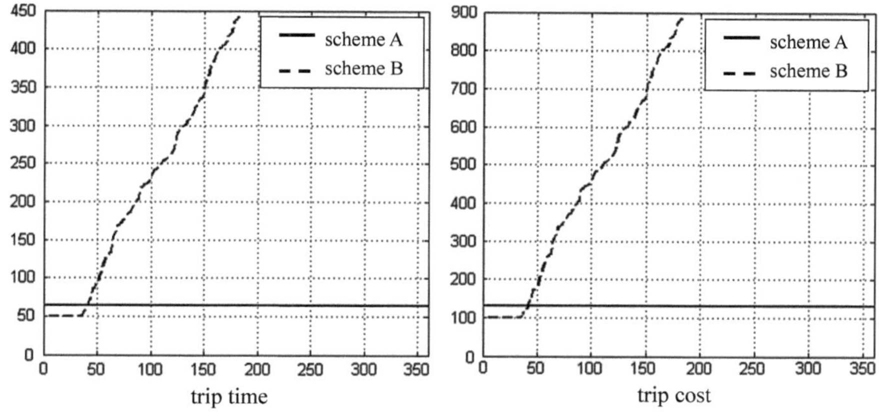

Fig. 8.16 Trip costs with an established sign

In 1000 time steps, there are 542 vehicles which pass through the traffic system, raising the passage percentage by 24.88%. Among these vehicles, 360 in total pass through road 1 and road 2, and yet only 182 vehicles pass through road 1 and road 3.

The modeling results basically accords with the economic analysis of urban traffic congestion. The operation of the entire traffic system has a threshold value. When the number of vehicles in the system is below the threshold value, the vehicles in the traffic system run smoothly. The travel time is relatively short and trip costs are relatively low. Under such conditions, the system is in a good operating state. Once the number of vehicles in the system exceeds the threshold value, traffic congestion starts to occur (the threshold value is 65 in the first situation, 125 in the second situation, and 129 in the third situation). Once beyond threshold, as the number of vehicles in the system continuously increases, so does the road congestion, causing the efficiency of the system to continuously decrease. By this comparison, we can see that the threshold value and the allowable number of vehicles in the system, i.e., traffic supply, have an obvious positive correlation. It can be seen from the figure that with the increase of traffic supply, the system's congestion time becomes apparently shorter.

8.2.4 Summary

In this chapter, we first started from a micro aspect to introduce the application of cellular automata in urban traffic systems, designed and simulated humanistic intersections. Then we approached the question from a macro angle and analyzed the economic characteristics of urban traffic congestion, introduced the cellular automata modeling method from a social economic aspect, and used a simple intersection as an example to explain how cellular automata are used in the research of the economic costs of urban traffic congestion.

8.3 The Application of Cellular Automata in the Study of the Disease Spreading Process

In real world, the spread of infectious diseases among people is influenced by various inevitable or occasional factors. The process is obviously a complex phenomenon. The local effect of interactions and contacts among people, as the most basic carrier for disease dispersion, will bring about emergent behavior of social groups, and their ways of behavior also have relatively great influence on the spread and dispersion of the diseases (Chneckenreither et al. 2008; Hoya White et al. 2007; Slimi et al. 2009; Yang 2009).

How to take measures for control and intervention of an epidemic outbreak? Which control strategy has the best effect? At what stages should we take what kinds of strategies? These questions are no doubt very important for the control and prevention of the diseases.

From the mid-20th century, deterministic models dominated by differential equations started to gain attention, and it still has high academic value even today. Among these models, a very influential one is the SIR model, which can often give operational results quite close to the actual computational results. However, the form of the differential dynamic system on the other hand brings such models some disadvantages. Such models involve complex calculation, in addition, they cannot really be assimilated into the various contact behaviors among people in real world. Moreover, these dynamic models which are based on an analytic paradigm cannot deal with random and sudden events in actual processes very well.

In real life, the occurrence, spread and decay of infectious diseases take the form of spatial dispersion. This is consistent with the principle of cellular automata dealing with complex parallel problems. What is more, cellular automata which have neighborhood structures and are based on local rules are also similar to the disease spreading process among people, thus can eliminate the complex calculation process of common differential equation models, and can be more intuitive.

Currently, there has been a lot of literature using cellular automata to study the spreading and control of diseases, and the simulation effects of these studies have strong similarities to the actual disease spreading patterns. Therefore, as one of the important application fields of cellular automata, in this chapter, we are going to conduct cellular automata modeling and simulation of disease spreading in complex situations, and thereby observe the influence of control strategies in a cellular space on the spreading of diseases.

8.3.1 Assumptions

1 **Assumption of State Transfer**

According to descriptions in common literature of disease spreading models, the state transfer process and evolution process of diseases can be described as in Fig. 8.17.

Figure 8.17 provides a flow chart of the transfer of the various states of diseases. From the perspective of disease development we can see that, after a susceptible individual is infected, it enters a state of incubation. When the incubation period is over, it enters the state of infection. Individuals in the incubation period and infected individuals can all receive treatment, while during infection or treatment, death will occur among them. After being cured and the immunity period passes, the individual will lose immunity again and become a susceptible individual.

Considering certain actual situations in real life, in the model introduced in this section, individuals in incubation state, individuals receiving treatment (not being quarantined) and infected individuals all have infectivity. However, there is be difference on the degree of infectiousness.

2. **Cellular Automata Assumption**

(1) Cellular Space: a square area of $n \times n$;
(2) Neighborhood Form: here we adopt the Von Neumann neighborhood form, i.e., each individual has four neighbors from above, below, left, and right, as shown in Fig. 8.18.
(3) Cell States: as expressed by the following quadruple form

$$S = (STA, INF, INC, IMM) \tag{8.15}$$

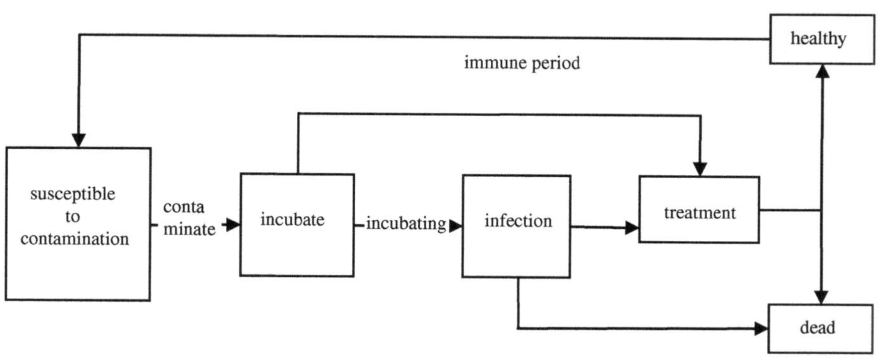

Fig. 8.17 State transfer of diseases

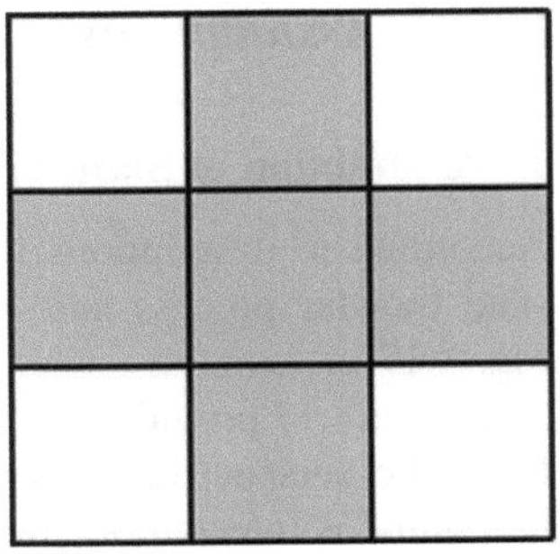

Fig. 8.18 Neighborhood form

STA(i, j) indicates whether the cell in position (i, j) is occupied. STA(i, j) = 0 represents cell (i, j) is not occupied, while STA(i, j) = 1 represents cell (i, j) is occupied.

INF(i, j) indicates the health state of the individual in position (i, j). INF(i, j) = 1 represents a healthy individual; INF(i, j) = 2 represents a susceptible individual; INF(i, j) = 3 represents an individual in the incubation period; INF(i, j) = 4 represents an individual participating in treatment; INF(i, j) = 5 represents an infected individual.

For individuals in the incubation period, INC(i, j) is used to record the time of incubation of the individual in position (i, j). When this time exceeds the incubation period, the individual in incubation period becomes an infected individual.

For healthy individuals, IMM(i, j) is used to record the immunity time of the individual in position (i, j). When the time of immunity exceeds the immunity period, the healthy individual becomes a susceptible individual.

(4) Movement: at each moment, each individual in the cellular space moves to any unoccupied position among the positions of its eight neighbors with a probability of p move, as shown in Fig. 8.19.

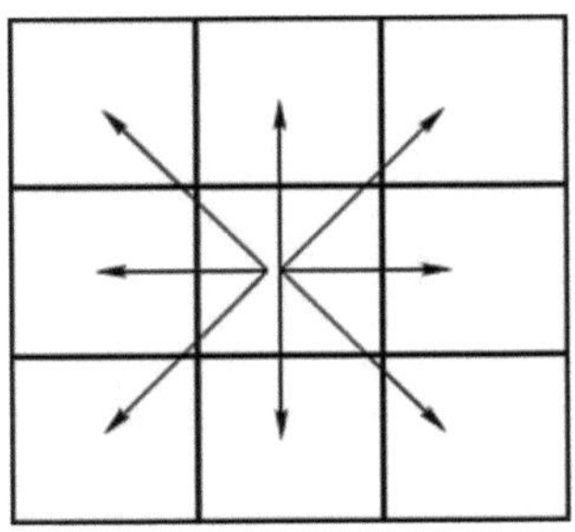

Fig. 8.19 Individual movement

8.3.2 *The Evolution Rules of the Cellular Automata*

1. **Disease Infection Rules**

Rule 1: Individuals in the incubation period, during treatment, and infected individuals all have infectivity, and can all turn susceptible individuals into individuals in the incubation period. Among them, infected individuals have the greatest infectivity, next are individuals in treatment, while individuals in the incubation period have the lowest infectivity. At each moment, regarding each susceptible individual in position (i, j), we first calculate the overall illness condition of its four surrounding neighbors (here expressed by ILL (i, j)):

$$ILL(i,j) = INF(i-1,j) + INF(i,j-1) + INF(i,j+1) + INF(i+1,j) \quad (8.16)$$

Obviously, ILL$(i, j) \in [0,20]$. We hereby design the following rules: if $16 <$ ILL $(i, j) \leq 20$, a susceptible individual enters the incubation period with a probability of $\beta 5$; if $12 <$ ILL$(i, j) \leq 16$, a susceptible individual enters the incubation period with a probability of $\beta 4$; if $8 <$ ILL$(i, j) \leq 12$, a susceptible individual enters the incubation period with a probability of $\beta 3$. Here, $\beta 5 > \beta 4 > \beta 3$. We can see that this rule indicates that the difference in infectivity among three kinds of patients: infected individuals, those participating in treatment, and those in the incubation period.

Rule 2: A disease has a period of incubation $t$inc, and when an individual enters the incubation period at moment t (INF$(i, j) = 3$), then at moment $t + t$inc, the individual becomes an infected one (INF$(i, j) = 5$).
Rule 3: A disease has a period of immunity $t$imm, and when an individual enters a healthy state at moment t (INF$(i, j) = 1$), then at moment $t + t$imm, the individual loses immunity with probability σ, and becomes a susceptible individual (INF$(i, j) = 2$).

2. **Treatment Rules**

Rule 1: At each moment, an infected individual participates in treatment with probability ε, and becomes an individual in the treatment period.
Rule 2: At each moment, an individual in the incubation period participates in treatment with probability ε', and becomes an individual in the treatment period.
Rule 3: The cure rate of a disease is γ, i.e., at each moment, individuals in the treatment period become healthy individuals with probability γ.

3. **Rules of Birth and Death for Individuals**

Rule 1: Natural death. At each moment, individuals in the cellular space die with probability d.

Rule 2: Natural birth. At each moment, the cellular space produces new individuals with probability b, and these new individuals are all susceptible individuals. Here, we suppose $b = d$.

Rule 3: Death caused by illnesses. At each moment, infected individuals die with probability $\overline{d}$.

4. **Disease Control Strategies**

From the above evolution rules we can see that, in order to control diseases, we can take measures from three aspects:

(1) Raising the treatment participation rate ε' of individuals in the incubation period i.e., conducting treatment among people who are suspected to be infected (people who display characteristics of being in the incubation period, or people who show slight symptoms of infection).
(2) Raising the treatment participation rate ε of infected individuals by increasing the intensity of inspection, because to include more infected individuals in the scope of treatment can effectively slow down the transmission speed of diseases;
(3) Raising the cure rate γ, i.e., raising the probability of turning ill individuals into healthy ones among those who participate in treatment.

The following simulation study will be centered on these three strategies, so as to observe the effects of control strategies in reality.

8.3.3 *Simulation of the Spreading of Diseases in a Cellular Space*

1. **Setting Simulation Parameters**

Unless noted in particular, the values of all parameters are set as in Table 8.1.

2. **No Treatment or Prevention Measures Are Taken** (see Figs. 8.20 and 8.21)

In these figures, the green cells represent healthy individuals; the blue cells represent susceptible individuals; individuals in the incubation period, during treatment, or infected individuals are all represented by red cells. The black area means there is no patient there.

From Fig. 8.21 we can see that, if no treatment measure is taken, the number of infected individuals will first increase greatly with time, and then, with such increase of infected individuals, the death number will increase accordingly, causing a decrease of the total population. Figure 8.21b demonstrates the daily data statistics in Beijing in 2003 during the SARS epidemic. Thus we can see that the rising trend of the number of infected people in the simulation result is similar to what was reflected by actual data.

Table 8.1 Setting of simulation parameters

Important parameters			System parameters		
Name	Symbol	Value	Identification	Symbol	Value
Infection probability	β_3	0.4	Cellular space size	$n \times n$	50×50
Infection probability	β_4	0.8	Time of evolution	T	100
Infection probability	β_5	1	Total number of initial patients	N_0	Generate in an $n \times n$ cellular space with a probability of 0.5
Incubation period	t_{inc}	4	Total number of initially susceptible people	S_0	Generate in N_0 with a probability of 0.3
Immunity period	t_{imm}	8	Total number of initially infected people	I_{50}	Generate in N_0 with a probability of 0.2
Individual movement probability	p_{move}	1	Total number of initially healthy people	R_0	Generate in N_0 with a probability of 0.5
Group natural birth rate	b	0.001	Infected people's rate of participation in treatment	ε	0.1
Group natural death rate	d	0.001	Rate of participation in treatment of people in the incubation period	ε'	0.1
Death rate of infected individual	$\bar{d}$	0.01	Rate of losing immunity for healthy individuals	σ	0.1
Cure rate	γ	0.1			

3. **Under Disease Control Measures**

First, when all the parameters operate completely according to Table 8.1, we get a figure of disease evolution as shown in Fig. 8.22.

Strategy 1: Raise the cure rate to $\gamma = 0.6$,and we obtain the evolution result as shown in Fig. 8.23.
Strategy 2: Raise the treatment participation rate of infected individuals from $\varepsilon = 0.1$ to $\varepsilon = 0.6$, and we obtain the evolution result as shown in Fig. 8.24.
Strategy 3: Raise the treatment participation rate of individuals in the incubation period from $\varepsilon' = 0.1$ to $\varepsilon' = 0.6$, and we obtain the evolution result as shown in Fig. 8.25.

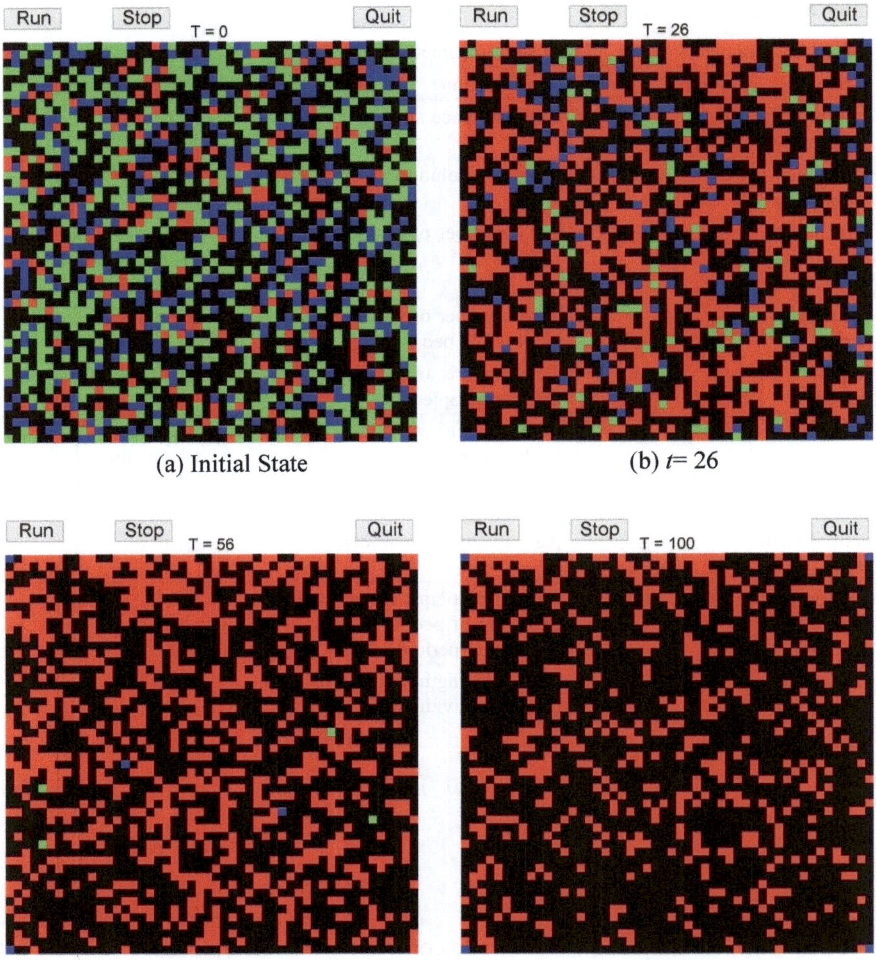

(a) Initial State

(b) t= 26

(b) t= 56

(b) t= 100

Fig. 8.20 The process of the evolution of infection (1) and infection (2)

From the simulation data we can see that, raising the disease cure rate is no doubt the most effective strategy to control the spreading of epidemics. Although raising the treatment rate of infected individuals effectively reduces the number of patients, its effect is not as good as raising the treatment participation rate of individuals in the incubation period. From the model simulation results in this chapter we can also get a conclusion: to increase the intensity of study and inspection of diseases in the incubation period, and timely urge individuals in the incubation period to get treatment can effectively control the spreading of the diseases.

Fig. 8.21 Population variation during an infection

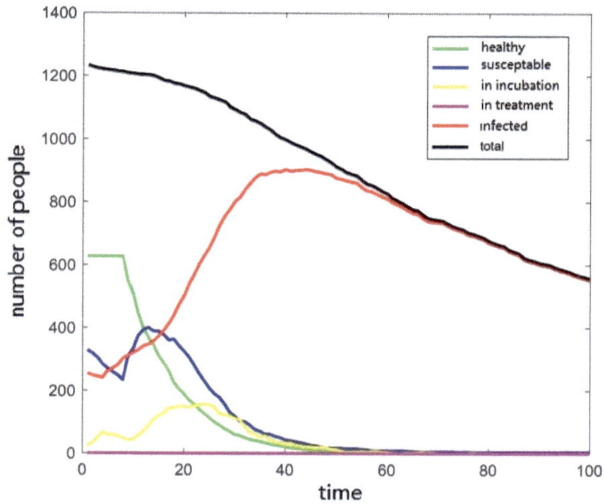

(a) Simulation Results

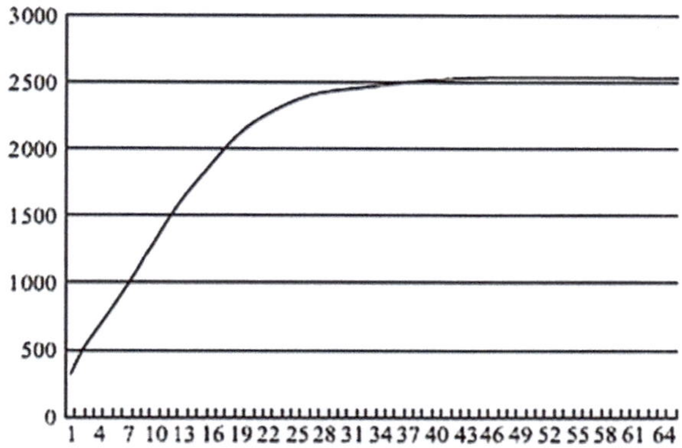

(b) Number of People Infected by SARS in 2003 in Beijing (from April 20- June 12)

8.3.4 Summary

In this chapter, we applied cellular automata to a dynamic model of disease transmission which is closely related to daily life. We also discussed the transmission process of epidemics, and the modeling of a cellular automaton focusing on epidemics. Cellular automata simulation avoids the complex solutions and calculation analysis of differential equations, objectively reflects the dynamic process of disease transmission. Thus the results obtained from the simulation are similar to the real data, and verify the effective strategies for disease infection control.

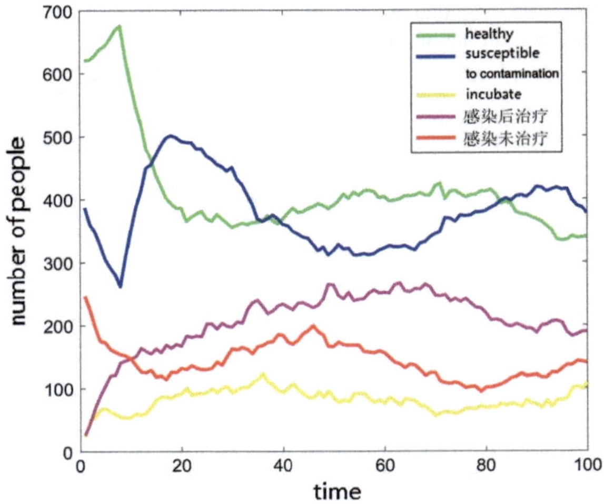

Fig. 8.22 $\gamma = 0.1$, $\varepsilon = 0.1$, $\acute{\varepsilon} = 0.1$

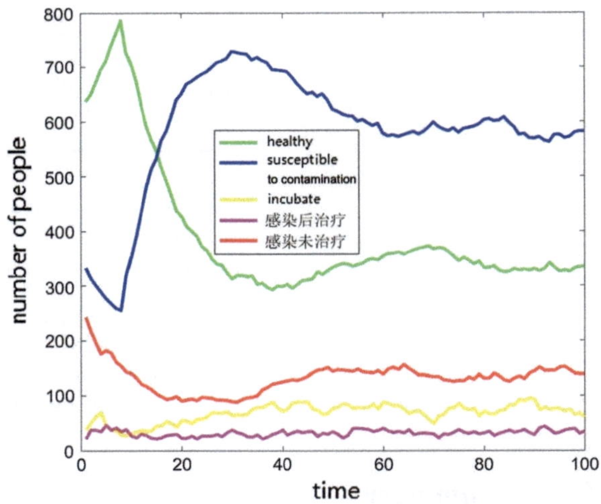

Fig. 8.23 $\gamma = 0.6$, $\varepsilon = 0.1$, $\acute{\varepsilon} = 0.1$

Fig. 8.24 $\gamma = 0.1$, $\varepsilon = 0.6$, $\acute{\varepsilon} = 0.1$

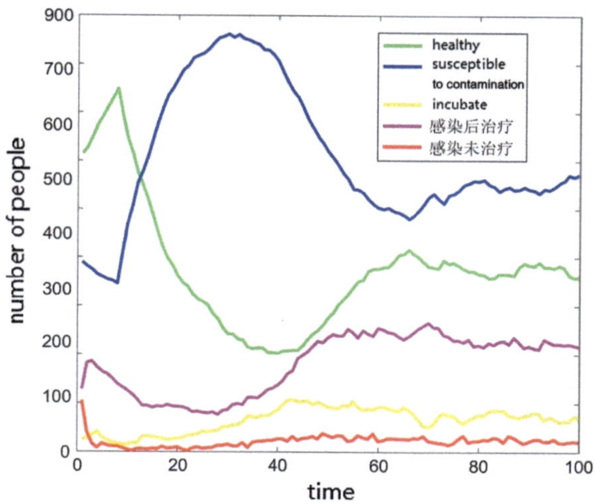

Fig. 8.25 $\gamma = 0.1$, $\varepsilon = 0.1$, $\acute{\varepsilon} = 0.6$

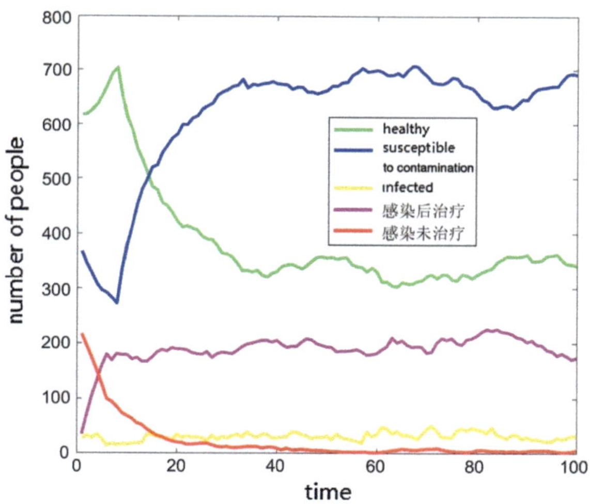

References

Chneckenreither, G, Popper, N., & Zauner, G. (2008). Modeling SIR-type epidemics by ODEs, PDEs, difference equations and cellular automata–A comparative study. *Simulation Modeling Practice and Theory*, *16*(8), 1014–1023.

Gou, J., Zou, Q., & Wang, L. (2012). Analysis of teenagers' traffic violation behavior based on behavioral theory for improvement plans. *Journal of Beijing Jiaotong University, 11*(3), 85–90.

Hoya White, S., Martin Del Rey, A., & Rodri´guez Sa´nchez, G. (2007). Modeling epidemics using cellular automata. *Applied Mathematics and Computation, 186*(1), 193–202.

Jia, B., Gao, Z., Li, K., et al. (2007). *Traffic system modeling and simulation based on cellular automata*. Beijing: Science Press.

Kong, X., Gao, Z., Li, K., et al. (2006). Single-lane cellular automata model considering the influences of the nearest neighboring vehicles and next to the nearest neighboring vehicles. *Journal of Beijing Jiaotong University, Natural Science Section, 30*(6), 11–15.

Li, J. (2011). Option pricing model based on cellular automata. *Journal of Wuyi University, 25*(4), 50–56.

Li, J. (2012). Study of the modeling of the financial market based on cellular automata. Beijing: Beijing Jiaotong University.

Slimi, R., El Yacoubi, S., & Dumonteil, E. (2009). A cellular automata model forchagas disease. *Applied Mathematical Modelling, 33*(2), 1072–1085.

Yang, G. (2009). Quarantine control of the mathematical model of epidemic SIR. *Journal of Biological Mathematics, 24*(3), 479–483.

Zhu, M. (2012). Analysis of the social economic influences of traffic congestion. Beijing: Beijing Jiaotong University.

Chapter 9
Concluding Remarks—Looking to the Future

9.1 Rule Based Modeling of Complex Systems

In the process of modeling the real world, an important question is: should the model be as abstract as possible or as realistic as possible? Should it describes as generally as possible, or depicts as specifically as possible? One thought is that the prerequisite of grasping the overall functionality of a system is to analyze in-depth the units which comprise the system; another thought believes that the so called "individuals" have relatively strong disorderliness and randomness, thus cannot completely represent the overall behavior of the system. Constant occurrence of complexity, on the other hand, will make it difficult to discover new laws. For the first thought, the mode of construction of its system analysis is from top to bottom. The framework is basically composed of mathematical equations with relatively fewer parameters and environmental changes. It is a highly linear modeling method. For the second thought, its mode of construction of system analysis is from bottom up; the framework of the model is composed of adaptive agents, with relative more parameters and environmental uncertainty. It is a highly nonlinear modeling method. Then, what role do the research and application of cellular automata play in the clash of the two different thoughts of modeling?

Let us revisit the simplest "Game of Life." As we all know from the content of previous chapters that, its basic rule is that the state of the central cell is determined by the collective states of its surrounding neighbor cells. Thus, "the states of neighbor cells" and "the state of the central cell" form a causal relationship. This causal relationship with time difference is exactly the kind of problems for which the top-to-bottom tradition research method is good at handling. And yet for each cell in the cellular space, the change of its state is in sync with each time step. In other words, if a cell was a person, he is able to know the rules his neighbors follow in changing the states, but will not be sure what states his neighbors will change into at the next moment. This synchronous relationship is also an important mechanism for producing complexity. The description and display of such

X. Li et al., *Theory of Practical Cellular Automaton*,
https://doi.org/10.1007/978-981-10-7497-4_9

synchronous relationship is exactly cellular automata's forte. A model's depiction of the real world should be the combined action of the "causal relationship" and the "synchronous relationship."

The traditional top-to-bottom modeling method often uses a set of analytic equations as the starting point. These analytic equations abstract system-level observable characteristics from elements in the real world. The operation of the model is just the computing of the equations. Along with the computing of the equations, the observable characteristics are continuously evolving. On the other hand, in the bottom up multi-agent modeling method, the starting point of modeling is often the direct or indirect interactive behavior among individuals. During the model's operational process, observable characteristics emerge. The complementarity of the two modeling ideas can be shown as in Fig. 9.1.

It can be seen that from the perspective of real application, multi-agent models are easier to construct, while for traditional models defined by a set of mathematical equations, their solutions and computing processes require a great deal of complex mathematical techniques. In the situation that some behavior in real world cannot be analyzed, the computer simulation result is the solution of the model, as long as the attributes such as multi-agent behavioral rules can be defined. Yet cellular automata can just provide an intuitive image of the framework for the definition of the behavioral rules of multi-agents. It can thus be considered that cellular automata can greatly facilitate the embodiment of observable attributes into intuitive images of the individual behaviors.

Next, we will use examples to explain this based-on-rules modeling idea.

9.1.1 The Combination of Modeling Methods of Bottom-Up and Top-Down

There has always been the debate that in order to grasp the functionality of a system, whether we should start our research from the whole or from individuals. For half a century, with the constant change of people's way of thinking, complexity science has been continuously on the rise. Even though it is revolutionary, it is not meant to replace something, not to mention complexity purely for complexity's sake. The combination of bottom-up and top-down methods is the

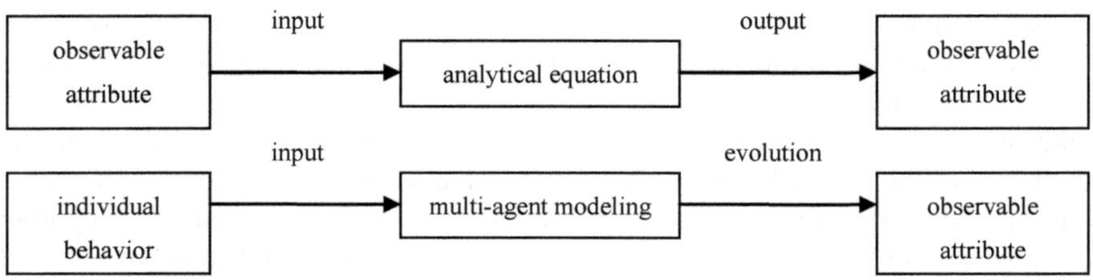

Fig. 9.1 Two ideas of modeling

inevitable trend of future development. In Sect. 8.3, we constructed a disease transmission model by using cellular automata, defined the nature of a disease and cell states, designed the transfer rules of cell states by using causal relationships, and in the computer simulation afterwards, observed in the form of figures the simultaneous processes of the emergence and evolution of disease transmission in cellular space. In fact, such definition of the transfer rules of cell states can also be a mathematical equation model or a certain attribute that can be expressed as the function of a mathematical equation, the characteristics of which can be observed. Next, we will examine the nine evolution rules of cellular automata designed in Sect. 8.3.2. From these rules, it is not hard to see that at every moment, the change in the number of susceptible individuals is caused by the factors such as being infected by latent individuals, infected by individuals who participate in treatment, and by already infected individuals, as well as by the newly born population and originally healthy population who have lost immunity. The change in the number of latent individuals is caused by the increase of newly infected individuals, by individuals whose latent period has ended, and by individuals who participate in treatment, and individuals who die naturally. The change in number of individuals who participate in treatment is caused by the total number of people who participate in treatment, by the number of people who are cured, and by the number of individuals who die naturally. The change in number of people who are infected is caused by the number of people whose latent period has ended, by people who participate in treatment, by people who die of diseases, and by people who die naturally. The change in number of healthy individuals is caused by the number of people who are cured, by people who die naturally and by the number of people who have lost their immunity.

Therefore, we can abstract these nine rules as a differential dynamic system:

$$
\begin{cases}
\frac{dS}{dt} = Nb + \sigma R - \alpha_3 I_3 S - \alpha_4 I_4 S - \alpha_5 I_5 S - dS \\
\frac{dI_3}{dt} = \alpha_3 I_3 S + \alpha_4 I_4 S + \alpha_5 I_5 S - (\mu + \varepsilon' + d) I_3 \\
\frac{dI_4}{dt} = \varepsilon' I_3 - (\gamma + d) I_4 + \varepsilon I_5 \\
\frac{dI_5}{dt} = \mu I_3 - (\varepsilon + d + \bar{d}) I_5 \\
\frac{dR}{dt} = \gamma I_4 - (\sigma + d) R
\end{cases}
$$

In this system, N represents the total number of individuals in the cellular space, $N = S + I_3 + I_4 + I_5 + R$; S represents the number of susceptible individuals; R represents the number of healthy individuals; I_3 represents the number of individuals in the latent period; I_4 represents the number of individuals participating in treatment; I_5 represents the number of infected individuals; σ represents the rate at which the healthy group loses immunity; α_3 represents the infection coefficient of susceptible individuals being infected by individuals in the latent period; α_4 represents the infection coefficient of susceptible individuals being infected by individuals participating in treatment; α_5 represents the infection coefficient of susceptible individuals being infected by already infected individuals. Then $\alpha k\ Ik$ (k = 3, 4, 5) represents the rate of infection; d represents the rate of natural death in cellular space; b represents the rate of natural birth in cellular space; μ represents the proportion of people whose latent period has ended and who become infected individuals; ε' represents the rate of participation in treatment of people in the latent period; ε represents the rate of participation in treatment of infected individuals; γ represents the cure rate of a disease; $\overline{d}$ represents the fatality rate of a disease.

Thus, what the above analytic model describes is the state changes of a group. The infection coefficients α_3, α_4, α_5 in a differential dynamic system show the state changes among different groups, but do not involve the chain behavior among individuals within a system, while the infection probabilities β_3, β_4, β_5 which are based on neighborhood structures in the construction of cellular automata in Sect. 8.3 start from individuals and show the state changes among different individuals.

Next, we use the analytic method to determine the control strategies for diseases. Let

$$\frac{dS}{dt} = \frac{dI_3}{dt} = \frac{dI_4}{dt} = \frac{dI_5}{dt} = \frac{dR}{dt} = 0$$

and suppose it is at an equilibrium point with no disease, then there is $I_3 = I_4 = I_5 = 0$, and $\overline{d} = 0$, then it is easy to obtain the equilibrium point with no disease, which is $P^* = (N_0, 0, 0, 0, 0)$.

The Jacobian matrix of the above analytic model at equilibrium point P^* is:

$$J(P^*) = \begin{pmatrix} -d & -\alpha_3 N_0 & -\alpha_4 N_0 & -\alpha_5 N_0 & \sigma \\ 0 & \alpha_3 N_0 - \mu - \varepsilon' - d & \alpha_4 N_0 & \alpha_5 N_0 & 0 \\ 0 & \varepsilon' & -\gamma - d & \varepsilon & 0 \\ 0 & \mu & 0 & -\varepsilon - d - \bar{d} & 0 \\ 0 & 0 & \gamma & 0 & -\sigma - d \end{pmatrix}$$

It is easy to see that $-d$ and $-\sigma - d$ are both the negative characteristic roots of $J(P^*)$, while the other three characteristic roots are determined by

$$K(P^*) = \begin{pmatrix} \alpha_3 N_0 - \mu - \varepsilon' - d & \alpha_4 N_0 & \alpha_5 N_0 \\ \varepsilon' & -\gamma - d & \varepsilon \\ \mu & 0 & -\varepsilon - d - \bar{d} \end{pmatrix}$$

From the conditions for the local asymptotic stability of the model's equilibrium point (Jacobian matrix odd order principal minor <0, even order principal minor >0):

$$tr(K(P^*)) = \alpha_3 N_0 - \mu - \varepsilon' - \gamma - \varepsilon - \bar{d} - 3d < 0$$

$$\begin{aligned} \det(K(P^*)) = {} & (\alpha_3 N_0 - \mu - \varepsilon' - d)(\gamma + d)(\varepsilon + d + \bar{d}) \\ & + \alpha_5 N_0 \mu(\gamma + d) + \alpha_4 N_0[\varepsilon'(\varepsilon + d + \bar{d}) + \varepsilon\mu] < 0 \end{aligned}$$

We know:

$$\begin{aligned} &\alpha_3 N_0(\gamma+d)(\varepsilon+d+\bar{d})+\alpha_5 N_0\mu(\gamma+d)+\alpha_4 N_0[\varepsilon'(\varepsilon+d+\bar{d})+\varepsilon\mu] \\ &<(\mu+\varepsilon'+d)(\gamma+d)(\varepsilon+d+\bar{d}) \end{aligned} \tag{9.1}$$

From the perspective of analytic formulas, in order to control epidemics, it is necessary to try to make the system reach the equilibrium point of no disease, i.e. make formula (9.1) true. By analyzing the formulas, it is not hard to obtain the following control strategies:

(1) Raising the rate of participation in treatment ε' of individuals in the latent period;
(2) Raising the rate of participation in treatment ε of infected individuals;
(3) Raising the cure rate γ.

These strategies comply with common sense, and are also consistent with the control strategies obtained after analyzing the rules of cellular automata in Sect. 8.3. However, which of the three strategies is the most effective? Which affects the entire system more? How about their sensitivity? It would be a headache and tedious to answer these questions by pure analytic analysis and mathematical calculation. However, with the help of computers, by designing the evolution rules of cellular automata, to give individuals in reality the analytic model's illustration of a group, the system-level characteristics represented by the analytic model will emerge.

At the end of Sect. 8.3, the evolution results were obtained through cellular automata simulations. We discovered that obviously, raising disease cure rate is the most effective control strategy, while raising the rate of treatment participation of infected individuals can effectively reduce the number of patients, yet its effect is not as good as raising the rate of treatment participation of individuals in the latent period.

Therefore, under certain specific conditions, bottom-up, local, dispersive, and discrete information processing and top-down, concentrated, rule-oriented information processing can interchange. The evolution of cellular automata also objectively reflects the conclusion as reflected by the mathematical model. Moreover, the traditional analytic paradigm can provide system-level information of attribute transformation for cellular automata modeling (i.e. providing the theoretical basis for the state transition of cells), while the discrete unit processing (rule) of cellular automata can uncover the complex characteristics of the solution difficulty of analytic models, and the two complement each other.

9.1.2 Complex Problems and Simple Rules

After various modifications, combinations, and modeling of cellular automata, let us go back to the beginning of the book. There we mentioned that Newton unifies the complex laws of the motions of heaven and earth with the concise three main laws of mechanics and the law of gravity. In this framework, many scientific theorems and laws can be deduced step by step from a couple of simple axioms, and these different layers of deductions have strict logic and rigorous proofs. When the research on complexity and rule computing has been continuously recognized, people discovered repeatedly that some quite simple rules can often generate very complex results (Mitchell 2011; Tian et al. 2007). As we all know, "Game of Life" is one of the simplest evolution rules of cellular automata, and yet this evolution rule which simulates life bodies gives us quite valuable and profound thinking: if such simulation of the evolution of life which is based on two most basic information codes—"0" and "1", can generate such complex results, then is it possible that many complex and mysterious phenomena in the world each corresponds to a simplest rule? Similarly, there exist in reality many complex phenomena which are generated by simple rules, such as:

① The "Butterfly Effect"—the occasional flapping of its wings of a butterfly in the rain forest of the Amazon River Basin in South American can cause a tornado two weeks later in the state of Texas in the U.S.

② The "Broken Window Effect"—if one of the windows in a house is broken and no one fixes it, soon, other windows will strangely be broken by someone. If some graffiti on a wall is not washed off, soon, the wall will be covered by a mess of things.

③ The "Bullwhip Effect"—when the information flow on the supply chain is transmitted from the end customer to the original supplier, because effective information sharing cannot be realized, minute information distortion at the starting point will be gradually enlarged, causing the information of demand to fluctuate more and more. This directly increases the risks of the supplier on supply and stocks, and can even disturb the manufacturer's plan and the order of marketing and management, and in turn can cause a chaos of manufacturing, supplying and marketing.

④ The "Catfish Effect"—in the past, the survival rate of sardines during transportation is quite low. Later, someone discovered that if a catfish is put into the sardines, the situation will be improved and the survival rate will greatly increase. Why? Because when the catfish is put into an unfamiliar environment, it will become agitated and swim everywhere. For the sardines which prefer to be quiet, it undoubtedly creates a disturbance. At the same time, when the sardines discover that a "stranger" is among them, they will also become nervous and swim faster. This easily solves the problem of a lack of oxygen for the sardines, and they will not die.

⑤ The "250 Law"—do not offend any customer, because there are 250 customers behind every customer, including their friends and relatives. If you drive away one customer, it equals driving away 250 potential customers.

The charm of modeling with cellular automata, on the other hand, is exactly to obtain rich evolutionary results by using rules of relatively low costs. When faced with complex phenomena in the real world, once some rules hidden behind them are mined, it will facilitate people to understand laws in the objective world. Currently, in the rule mining of cellular automata, the geographic cellular automaton is a typical example. As a cellular automaton system, transformation rules are at its core. As for the evolution of geographic phenomena, it is often complicated to define these rules, which are loaded with trivial details, while traditional methods such as the heuristic method are greatly influenced by subjective factors, and mathematical formulas have limitations when reflecting complex relationships. Nowadays data mining and neural networks have been widely used to obtain evolution rules. The basic flow chart is shown in Fig. 9.2. When evolution rules such as shown in Fig. 9.2 are mined, the parameters of the model are thus obtained. By using these rules, we can predict future changes of the land use situation, under the condition that there have not been dramatic changes in the natural, social, and economic conditions in the area (He et al. 2005; Li and Ye 2004; Liu and Li 2006, 2007; Liu et al. 2007; Wu 1998).

Therefore, using rules to explain changes avoids complex mathematical formulas and can intuitively describe complex relationships in nature, with stronger expressive capacity. In future research, complex problems will inevitably have many non-linear and none-equilibrium states. For these problems, the simplification of hypotheses should be reduced in the modeling process, and the mining of simple rules should be strengthened.

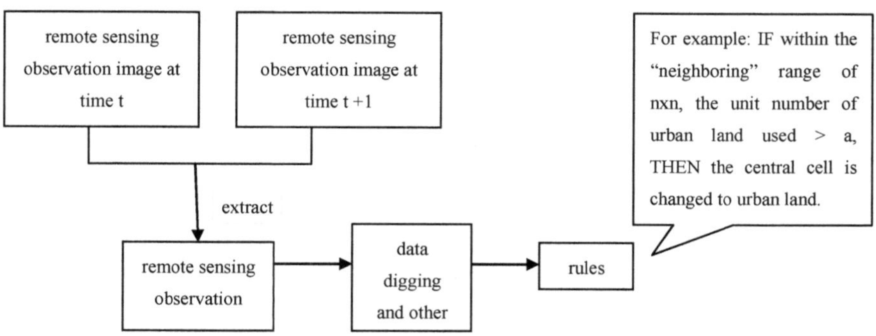

Fig. 9.2 Data mining of geographical cellular automata

9.2 Cellular Automata's Rule Mining

The research on cellular automata rules mainly starts from two angles: first, if a cellular automaton's rules are given, how to study its characteristics and behavior; second, search for cellular automata rules which have certain specified functions. In the real applications of cellular automata, it is the second kind of problems which demands prompt solution, i.e., cellular automata's inverse problem research.

A basic characteristic of cellular automata is that the overall dynamic behavior can evolve from local rules. But in real life often the phenomenon of evolution is first observed, i.e. the reverse problem of cellular automata needs to start from overall behavior to deduce local rules. Since the specific evolution rules of common things are hidden and are often difficult to summarize, during the application process of cellular automata, using evolution phenomena to mine the corresponding rules is a problem which must be solved.

Simple rules can sometimes analyze, explain or verify complex multi systems such as various kinds of evolution in nature, the development of social sciences, the intelligence system in human society, etc. In the process of using cellular automata for modeling to simulate and solve actual problems, the main difficult research problem is to abstract real objects as codes of 0 and 1. The real agents and the laws of interaction among themselves form the key content of cellular automata models. The rules of cellular automata start from the simplest 256 kinds of there-digit one-dimensional combination rules to high-dimensional multi-neighbor mixed rules, and different rules can evolve out highly different systems. Although we have already studied the complexity of some cellular automata in previous chapters, however, they are only a very small portion of cellular rules, while the majority of the rules need to be induced in-depth from mathematics and logic aspects. From the perspective of computer science, the fields of expansion and application of cellular automata have already involved natural science systems, humanities and social sciences systems, economics and management systems, medical science and natural ecosystems, etc. The analytic framework based on evolutionary computation is being used to explain more and more things, yet in the study of these systems, the most important thing is the discovery and induction of rules.

The definition of transformation rules is the core of cellular automata models. It expresses the logical relationship of the simulation process and determines the result of spatial variation. Currently, there are certain defects in the methods for defining the transformation rules of cellular automata. Clarke and others proposed the method of judging by naked eye to obtain the parameter values of a model. But this method is largely affected by subjective factors, thus has limited reliability. When spatial variables exist with relatively large quantity, there will be quite many parameter value combination plans. Once Mr. Wu proposed using analytic hierarchy process (AHP) to determine model parameter values, and later, he proposed to use the method of linear logistic regression to extract transformation rules. This method was very simple and practical, and therefore it was applied quite widely. However, using the linear method to extract complex phenomenal rules seemed too simple. Li and Yeh proposed using the method of neural network training to automatically obtain transformation rules. The limitation of this method is, however, neural networks have problems such as over-learning, local minimum value and slow convergence speed, thus belonging to the black box structure. Xia Li and others later proposed the method of using See 5.0 decision tree to obtain cellular automata's parameter values. But See 5.0 tends to fall into local optimum. Xiaoping Liu and Xia Li proposed the method of using the nuclear learning machine to obtain cellular automata's nonlinear transformation rules in space with high dimension characteristics, and yet this method also has problems of unclear physical significance of transformation rules and large operating volume. In the process of discovering and inducing cellular automata's transformation rules, the methods for obtaining rules mainly come from two frameworks. One is the mining of cellular automata's transformation rules led by rules of local variation, and another is global-phenomena-oriented cellular automata rule fitting.

9.2.1 Rule Mining Based on Local Evolutionary Phenomena

We know from the definition of cellular automata that a cellular automaton model consists of four parts, i.e., cells, cellular space, cell neighbors and cellular rules. To understand this from another aspect, a cellular automaton can be seen as composed of a cellular space and the transformation function defined in this space, and the mining of a cellular automaton's rules is the optimization of this transformation function. As in real life, cellular spaces and transformation functions of different cellular automata are quite different. From the simplest one-dimensional elementary cellular automata to Von Neumann's 29-state cellular automaton which can simulate the reproduction of life. The determination of cellular transformation functions is always the major component in the construction of cellular automata models. Generally, the independent variable of a cellular transformation function is the original states of the target cell and its neighbors, and the domain and the range are the same discrete set. Therefore, in simple cellular automata (uniform cellular automata), cellular transformation functions are exhaustive. For example, elementary cellular automata have 256 transformation rules. Wolfram did the job of analyzing the evolutionary characteristics of every transformation function in detail, and classified them. Base on these prior studies of cellular transformation rules, we can reasonably choose cellular transformation rules in modeling problems in reality, and simulate realistic situations.

Under the condition that cells have simple characteristics, i.e., states are concentrated and there are relatively fewer elements, we can directly abstract the basic rules of real things as cellular rules to construct cellular automata's simulation models, such as during the construction process of Conway's "Game of Life," he abstracted three simple survival and reproduction rules of a biotic community as cellular automata's transformation rules, and simulated complex life phenomena such as survival, competition, extinction, etc. in life activities, which are quite close to the evolution of life in reality. This is a typical modeling process which abstracts and mines cellular rules from already familiar or grasped laws in reality.

Also, in one-dimensional cellular automata models, since there are relatively fewer kinds of cellular rules, we can utilize the laws of change for realistic things to directly choose corresponding transformation functions from already known cellular rules. For example in the simulation of traffic flow, German scholars Nagel and Schreckenberg, during the construction of the NS traffic flow model, abstracted the basic rules for vehicle driving as: a black cell represents it is occupied by one car; a white cell represents there is no car; if there is a car in the front square, then stop; and if the square in the front is empty, then move forward one square. This is to construct cellular automata based on Rule 184 (see Fig. 9.3) of elementary cellular automata. In the process of rule mining, they combined the abstraction of rules in reality and already known cellular rules, which both realized situation simulation and guaranteed computability.

In the construction process of cellular automata for physical system simulation, Hardy, Pomeau and Pazzis established in the 1970s the so-called HPP lattice gas model, which actually was a cellular automaton. This model is composed of particles with simple and fully-discrete dynamic characteristics. Particles, by way of maintaining momentum conservation and particle number conservation, move and collide on two-dimensional square lattice. This model originally was used as a theoretical model to study the basic statistic characteristics of interacting gas particles.

Historically speaking, people have already used the idea of discrete system to simulate real phenomena. The spinning Ising model is a very good example. In the field of fluid study, as early as by the end of the 19th century, Maxwell proposed a discrete velocity system of interacting particles as a gas model. In fact, discrete velocity models such as lattice gas have been developing independent of cellular automata theory. However, cellular automata have proposed a new framework based on new concepts and have provided an effective numerical tool, and preserved the important ideas of micro laws of physics, such as the simultaneity of movement, the locality of interactions and the reversibility of time, etc. Cellular automata rules can be seen as another form of micro reality, with predictable macro behavior. At the end of the 1980s, people predicted from a numerical perspective that fully discrete computer models could replace wind tunnel tests. The first cellular automaton model which convinced people of this possibility was the famous FHP model, almost simultaneously proposed by U. Frisch, B. Hasslacher, Y. Pomeau and S. Wofram in 1986. These authors proved that, although their models

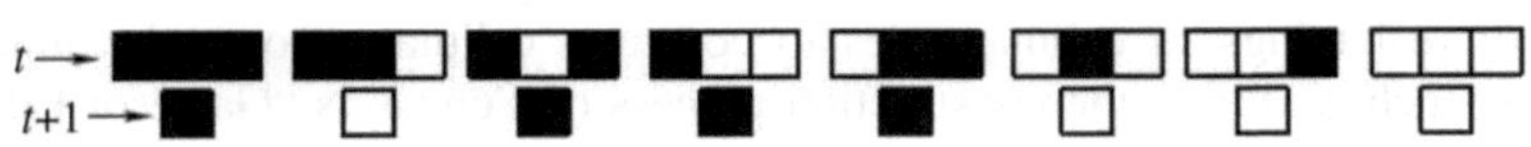

Fig. 9.3 Rule No. 184

belonged to fully discrete dynamics, they all in certain scopes conformed to the characteristics described by the Navier-Stokes equation in mechanics. When the micro rules are already known, the key point for cellular automata simulation is to catch the basic characteristics of designated phenomena, and transform them into appropriate forms to obtain effective numerical models.

This way of inducing the transformation rules of cellular automata by abstraction, using the local laws of other disciplines as background, played an important role in the process of cellular automata's coming into being and development, and enabled cellular automata to maintain strong vitality. However, as the individual under study gradually became more complex and its relationships to its neighbors also became more complex, the induction of cellular automata rules became quite difficult.

In particular, since cellular automata developed into the age of hybrid cellular automata, a cellular rule set has developed from a finite set to a countable infinite set, and the original uniformed cellular automata cannot realize the accurate simulation of real things in many cases (Chopard and Droz 2003; Crutchfield and Hanson 1993). Especially, after cellular automata were introduced into economic management, simple cellular automata rules could not completely and effectively solve corresponding problems of evolution. At the same time, the rule space of hybrid cellular automata is far larger than the rule space of uniformed cellular automata, therefore, rule mining must be carried out in another way. In some of the recent studies from various disciplines, scientists separately designed many effective intelligent algorithms in solving the problem of cellular automata's rule searching, mining the concrete forms of rules.

9.2.2 Rule Mining Based on Intelligent Algorithms

In the 1980th, with the deepening of the research theory of cellular automata, the application and theoretical research of cellular automata in various disciplines developed by leaps and bounds, most remarkably in geography, biology, traffic management, etc. Our research reveals that, before cellular automata were introduced into these disciplines, the local change laws of respective systems were complex non-linear problems, and thus difficult for system simulation. With the development of computer technology and intelligent algorithms, however, cellular automata's evolution rules can be selected by various intelligent algorithms to realize a system's simulation modeling. In the following, we will use cellular automata models in several specific disciplines to analyze the applications of various intelligent algorithms.

1. **Genetic Algorithm**

Genetic algorithm is a searching algorithm based on global probability of biological evolution mechanisms such as natural selection, genetic variation, etc. Similar to the analytic method based on derivatives and other heuristic search methods (such as the hill climbing method, the simulated annealing algorithm, the Monte Carlo method), genetic algorithm is an iterative method in form. It starts from a chosen initial solution, and gradually improves the current solution through continuous iterations, until the optimum solution or satisfactory solution is obtained by the final search. In genetic algorithm, the process of iterative computation adopts the evolution mechanism which simulates living organisms. It starts from a set (a group) of solutions, using a method similar to natural selection and sexual reproduction, and on the basis of inheriting the original good genes, generates a set of next generation solutions which have better performance index.

Genetic algorithm uses coding space to replace the parametric space of a problem, uses the fitness function as the basis for evaluation and the coding group as the basis of evolution, so as to realize the selection and genetic mechanism for genetic operation on individual bit strings in a group, and thus establishes an iterative process. In this process, the random reorganization of important genes in the coded bit strings will make the new generation bit string set superior to the old generation bit string set. The individuals in the group continuously evolve to gradually reach the optimum solution, and eventually the purpose of solving the problem is achieved.

Using genetic algorithm to seek the rules of cellular automata is feasible. Since the chromosome structures of genetic algorithm are consistent with cellular automata rules in defining form, we only need to take cellular automata's binary rules as chromosomes to establish corresponding fitness functions and then effectively solve a problem.

(1) **The Ant Colony Algorithm**

The ant colony algorithm is a bionic artificial intelligent algorithm originating from the biological world in nature. Rule mining based on the ant colony algorithm was first proposed by the Brazilian scholar Parpinelli and others in 2002, which mainly uses the foraging principle of ant colonies to search the optimum rules in the data base. The rule mining based on the ant colony principle is divided into three stages. First, starting from an empty path, repeatedly chose path nodes to add to the path, until a complete path is obtained, i.e. rule construction. Second, prune the rules. Finally, update the external hormone concentration on all the paths to exert influence on the next ant's rule formation.

We define the ant colony's search path as a line connecting attribute nodes and class nodes. Any attribute node appears only once at most and there must be class nodes. As shown by Fig. 9.4, every path corresponds to a classifying rule, and the mining of classifying rules can be regarded as the search for the optimum path.

At the beginning, a rule is randomly generated, and its form is as follows:

IF <term1 AND term2 AND …> THEN <class>

In the formula, term1 is a condition term, the grouping of condition terms is expressed as <attribute, operator, value>, and the rule conclusion (the THEN part) defines the forecasting class of the sample.

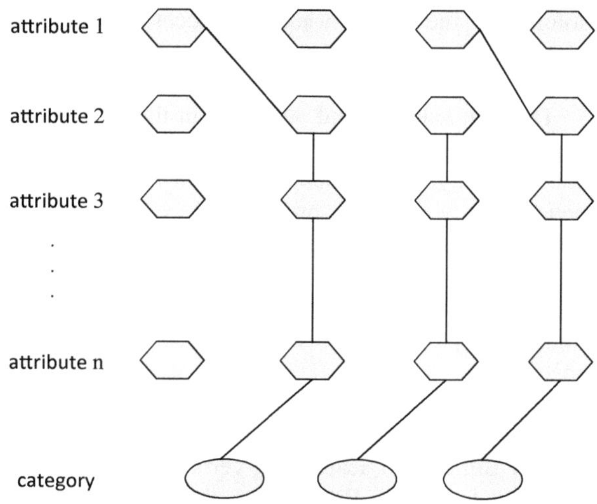

Fig. 9.4 Paths corresponding to the classifying rules in ant colony algorithm

The construction of the rule simulates the foraging behavior of ants, and it is actually a process of selecting attribute nodes. First, selecting a node from all the nodes in the first attribute according to certain standard, i.e., selecting one of the nodes among the nodes in attribute 1 as shown in Fig. 9.4, and then select a node from among all the nodes in attribute 2, and so on, until all the attributes are covered by an ant, i.e., the ant has selected a node in each attributes. Among these attributes, class attributes are a special type, but an ant will also select one class among all classes just like it selects other attributes. Thus, a rule is generated.

The transformation rules extracted by this algorithm do not need to be expressed by a mathematical formula. It can describe complex relationships in nature more conveniently and accurately. Also, these rules are easier for people to understand than mathematical formulas. In ant colony algorithm, since the information elements are updated continuously, the positive feedback information thus provided enables an ant to update its own knowledge base according to the change of environment and the result of its past behavior, thus leads to stronger self-adaptive ability for artificial ants. When ant colony algorithm is used for the extraction of cellular automata transformation rules, such positive feedback mechanism can increase the self-adaptive ability of transformation rules, thus lead to greater extension adaptability of the simulation (Tero et al. 2010).

2. **Discrete Particle Swarm Algorithm**

Particle Swarm Optimization Algorithm (PSO algorithm) is a random search algorithm based on group cooperation, which was proposed by Kennedy and Eberhart according to the foraging behavior of biotic communities such as flocks of birds, schools of fish, etc. The location of the solution, through the communications among individuals, guides the whole group to move towards the direction of a possible solution, and thus gradually increases the possibility of discovering a better solution in the problem solving process. In PSO algorithm, each individual in a biotic population can be regarded as a particle with neither mass nor volume in the space of optimization, and flies with certain velocity in the searching space.

Through learning and adjusting in the environment, the individual dynamically adjusts its flying velocity according to comprehensive analyzing result of individual and group flying experiences, so that members of the group gradually move to a better area within the problem space. The position of a particle represents a potential solution of the problem being optimized in the searching space. All of the particles have a fitness value each, which is determined by the optimized function. Moreover, every particle has a velocity determining the direction and distance of its flight, and particles follow the current optimal particle to search in the solution space.

Since rules in the rule space of two-valued cellular automata are represented by binary symbol strings, and the number of cellular rules in the space is quite large, it is very difficult to search out certain cellular rules which can realize previously specified functions. Referencing the features of binary particle swarm algorithm, each cellular rule can be regarded as a particle, and the algorithm based on the cellular rules of discrete particle swarm evolution was proposed. The steps of such algorithm are as follows:

(1) Assuming that the number of cellular rules is m, the radius is R, the evolution time of the cellular automaton is T, and the evolution of the biotic population is represented by E;
(2) Generating random number $U(0, 1)$, which is evenly distributed in interval (0, 1). If $U(0, 1) > 0.5$, then the value in dimension j corresponding to cellular rule i is $r_{ij}^0 = 1$, otherwise it is

$$r_{ij}^0 = 0 \quad (i = 0, 1, \ldots, m; j = 0, 1, \ldots, d);$$

(3) Limiting the velocity of the cellular rule v_i^t to $[v_{\min}, v_{\max}]$, in it, $-v_{\min} = v_{\max} = 4$. The velocity of the initial rule is

$$v_{ij}^0 = v_{\min} + (v_{\max} - v_{\min}) * rand()$$

In it, rand() is a random number between 0 and 1

(4) Evolving each rule in the population T steps, computing its fitness value $f(r_i^0)$ $(i = 0, 1, \ldots, m)$. Computing the individual optimal rule $pb_i = r_i^0$, i.e. $pb_i = [r_{i1}^0, r_{i2}^0, r_{i3}^0, \ldots, r_{id}^0]$ and the optimal value of the rule $fpb_i = f(r_i^0)$; computing the global optimal value $fpb = \max\{fpb_i\}$ and global optimal rule $gb = [r_{k1}^0, r_{k2}^0, \ldots, r_{kd}^0]$;

(5) Updating the velocity of cellular rules as:

$$v_{id}^{t} = h(wv_{id}^{t-1} + c_1 r_1 (pb_{id} - r_{id}^{k-1}) + c_2 r_2 (gb_d - r_{id}^{k-1}))$$

In it, w is the inertia weight; c_1, c_2 are the cognitive parameter and the social parameter respectively, and are both positive constants; r_1, r_2 are random numbers evenly distributed in (0, 1);

$h(*)$ is the velocity compression function, which satisfies

$$h(v_{id}^{k}) = \begin{cases} v_{\max}, v_{id}^{k} > v_{\max} \\ v_{id}^{k}, \left|v_{id}^{k}\right| \le v_{\max} \\ v_{\min}, v_{id}^{k} < v_{\min} \end{cases}$$

(6) Updating cellular rules

$$r_{id}^{t} = \begin{cases} 1, & U(0,1) < \mathrm{sigmoid}(v_{id}^{t}) \\ 0, & \text{otherwise} \end{cases}$$

In it, sigmoid $(v_{id}^{t}) = 1/(1 + e^{-v_{id}^{t}})$;

(7) Updating the cellular rule of the optimal individual: if $fpb_i < f(r_i^t)$, then $fpb_i = f(r_i^t)$, $pb_i = r_i^{t;}$ otherwise, fpb_i and pb_i remain unchanged;
(8) Updating the global optimal rule: if $\max\{fpb_i, i = 1, \ldots, m\} > fgb$, then $\max\{fpb_i, i = 1, \ldots, m\} = fgb$, and gb = rmlebal; otherwise fpb_i and gb remain unchanged. In it, mlebal refers to i which satisfies $\max\{fpb_i\}$;
(9) If the iteration termination condition is met, the algorithm will stop running; otherwise, returning to step (4).

In the process of using the discrete particle swarm algorithm to solve cellular automata's rules, since the structure of the particles is quite suited for the construction of cellular rules, its searching speed for cellular automata's rules is much faster than that of common genetic algorithm.

3. **Nonlinear Kernel Learning Machine Algorithm**

The process of studying the laws of complex geographical phenomena often involves a great amount of spatial data. Different spatial data have complex relationships, and using the kernel learning machine to automatically obtain the transformation rules of geographical cellular automata can conveniently and accurately reflect the complex relationships of different spatial data. The Kernel learning machine uses linear technology to design nonlinear information process algorithm in an implicit high-dimensional feature space generated by a kernel function. It provides a simple and effective method for solving complex nonlinear problems.

Currently, methods based on the principle of nucleation have become research focuses in machine learning, and have been applied successfully in many fields. And yet research in this aspect has just started in China. The kernel learning machine mainly includes kernel Fisher nonlinear discriminant, support vector machine, and kernel principal component analysis. Many studies show that the performance of kernel Fisher discriminant is superior to support vector machine and kernel principal component analysis.

In cellular automaton model for urban development, the kernel Fisher discriminant maps series of space variables from low-dimensional feature space to high-dimensional feature space, and projects the series of space variables in the high-dimensional feature space to a certain direction, so that in the changed data, points of the same class converge as much as possible, while points of different classes are separated as much as possible. Whether a city is developing is determined according to the decision rule that the ratio of inter class mean to the sum of intra class variance is maximum. Since the feature information included in the high-dimensional feature space is rich enough, it will to a great extent enhance the ability of recognizing whether a city is developing. Moreover, transformation rules can also fully reflect the complexity of urban development.

Therefore, the practical significance represented by the transformation rules is to map linearly inseparable complex geographical phenomena (such as urban development) in low-dimensional feature space to high-dimensional feature space, so as to achieve the goal of making these phenomena linearly separable. Frequently used kernel functions include polynomial inner product kernel function, radial basis inner product kernel function, Sigmoid inner product kernel function, etc. Since the system involves a large amount of spatial data, and complex relationships exist among different spatial data, using kernel learning machine to automatically obtain geographical cellular automata's transformation rules can conveniently and accurately reflect the complex relationships of different spatial data.

Using the kernel Fisher discriminant to automatically obtain geographical cellular automata's transformation rules can better reflect the complexity of urban development as compared to general linear cellular automata models. This method uses kernel functions to generate a hidden high-dimensional feature space, and transforms complex nonlinear problems into simple linear problems. It provides a very effective way for solving complex nonlinear problems. Using the method proposed here to automatically obtain geographical cellular automata's transformation rules not only greatly reduces the time needed for modeling, but also better reflects the complex characteristics of geographical phenomena, hereby improves cellular automata's simulation effect.

From different methods of cellular automata's rule mining, we can discover that no matter it is abstracting cellular rules from local evolution phenomena, or inducing cellular rules from global evolution phenomena, the purposes are both to simulate and to explain the system's evolutionary process, and yet the mechanism of how local rules generate global phenomena by evolution is not logically explained. Theoretically speaking, the rule mining of cellular automata is for the purpose of revealing the mechanism of how cellular automata generate evolutionary phenomena. Currently, cellular automata's rule mining still mostly aims at simulation computing, and yet only when the problem of semantic representation of cellular automata's rules is solved in theory, can the liberation of cellular automata's rules be realized, so that cellular automata can be applied in more fields.

9.3 Cellular Automata's Emergence Computing

The mode of traditional calculation is usually serial and centrally controlled. A computer can only complete one step of computing at each moment. Computer theory has proven that such serial computers can theoretically simulate all computing, but the premise is that we do not have any requirement for computing efficiency. And yet calculation efficiency has great significance in reality. As we know, computing is a physical operation process, and to complete such a process needs the most basic operation time and computing space. Time and space are the most basic physical limiting factors for computing, and they are both limited. In the 21st century, with the rapid development of computer science, especially storage technology, to exchange space for time has become more and more realistic, therefore, a new mode of computing which surpasses traditional computing capability by decentralization and parallel computation has been proposed. In complexity science this new mode of computing is called emergence computing.

9.3.1 The Connotation of Emergence

In system science, emergence means "the whole is not equal to the sum of parts." A system has many characteristics, and can be represented by the variable *xi*. Therefore, the state composed of *n* types of characteristics can be represented by *n*-dimensional state space, can be marked as X_L. $X_L = \{x_1, x_2, \ldots, x_n\}$. Supposing that the component parts of system $\Sigma(K_1, K_2, \ldots, K_m)$ are $K_1, K_2, \ldots, K_m$, then "the whole is not equal to the sum of parts" can be represented as

$$X_L\left[\sum(K_1, K_2, \ldots, K_\mathrm{m})\right] \neq X_L(K_1) \bigcup X_L(K_2) \bigcup \ldots X_L(K_\mathrm{m})$$

This formula expresses the relationship between the whole and the parts. It is like although a building is composed of bricks and other construction material, it is not simply the sum of these materials.

Intuitively, any system is a whole composed of a large number of micro elements (or elements). When these micro elements interact locally, some completely new characteristics or modes will automatically emerge in the system. This phenomenon is called emergence. For example, the taste of a cake is not the taste of any ingredient the cake is made of. The taste of the cake is also not the mean value of the tastes of the ingredients, such as between the taste of the flour and the taste of the egg. Its taste is far more complex. The taste of the cake exceeds the simple sum of the tastes of all the ingredients. Therefore, the characteristic of emergence is that due to the interaction of the parts, new characteristics emerge. And such characteristics only belong to the whole, not belong to any component, and yet with the characteristics that are not predictable beforehand.

In order to understand the characteristics of emergence, we must study the whole group and its structure instead of only study every single individual element. A simple example is traffic jam (Lee et al. 1999). If you only ask one person who is furious about a traffic jam, you cannot really understand it, even though his car is also part of the reason causing a traffic jam. We can give some more complex examples.

In 1986, the World Cup was held in Mexico. It was during this World Cup that "human wave" first caught the whole world's attention. This phenomenon was called "La Ola," meaning wave. When making the human wave, the audience jumped up group after group in order, raised their arms, and then quickly returned to their seats. The effect was exciting. A group of physicists originally were studying waves on water surface, but later they were quite taken by the magical effect of human wave and decided to study it. They found videos of Mexican human wave from many local stadiums in Mexico and analyzed them. They noticed that the human waves usually rolled clockwise, and always moved at a velocity of "20 seats per second."

In order to find out how the human wave started and was transmitted, researchers used the mathematical model of "incentive medium." This kind of model is usually used for studying non-life phenomena, such as fire's spreading in a forest, or the transmission of electric signal in cardiac muscle tissues, etc. The characteristic of the incentive medium is that it can adjust its states (such as on fire or not) according to the individual elements around it (are the trees nearby on fire?) This model accurately predicted the human wave phenomenon.

This result tells us that by only studying a certain individual's actions, such as standing up or sitting down, we cannot understand the nature of the Mexican human wave. The formation of the Mexican human wave is not rehearsed by someone giving orders with a loud speaker. It has its own life and is a self-organizing behavior.

The mathematical model of the concerted behavior of bird flocks or schools of fish also proves that group action is not centrally controlled. But a group has its collective intelligence, and it is this collective intelligence that helps each individual in the group escape or block predators. Such behavior does not exist in individuals, but is a collective characteristic. How does a bird flock "decide" where to fly to? Study shows that the direction of their flight must be agreed to by all the birds. More importantly, the direction of their flight is usually the best option for the entire bird flock. Each bird plays a small role, and the collective choice of the bird flock will be better than a single bird's choice. Therefore, obvious collective characteristic does not appear in each individual bird, but such characteristic emerges from the interaction and cooperation among birds.

As we know, every tiny ant is a very simple entity. These ants do not have smart brains and can only complete certain simple task of calculation. And yet when thousands of tiny ants gather together, the entire ant colony can display very complex and large-scale emergence phenomenon. For example, emergence behavior can be seen in their foraging activity. Although a single ant is tiny, and has very limited eyesight, and can only see things nearby, when a large number of ants cooperate by exchanging information, they can find the quickest route to carry food back home. This quickest route to carry food is typical emergence behavior of the ant group. In fact, among these ants, there is no king or queen to give orders. All this emergence behavior is entirely the result of the ant group's local interactions.

Similar to the human wave and the ant colony, the regular chirping of crickets also has the characteristic of emergence. There may be many crickets on a tree and they chirp at the same time. Our question is, which one listens to which one? Obviously, they do not have a leader for other crickets listening to its command. But if there is not one, why can they achieve synchronization, and at such same pace? Is it because one cricket listens to all the others' chirping? Or is it because it only listens to a particular cricket? Or is it because it listens to a small number of crickets? Does a certain structure exist in this group? If there is one, how does it play the role?

Actually, whether it is ants, crickets, or people, new collective characteristics can all emerge from the interactions among individuals. Since the beginning of life, life's evolution has experienced many important leaps. In most situations, cooperation and interaction are the most prominent features. And our thoughts are also not the product of one particular neuron. They come from the pattern of neuronal connections, or a kind of network. The research on emergence gives us the following inspirations:

(1) A group means an organic entity (such as a cellular automaton, a multi-agent system, a social network, etc.) consisting of many individuals (such as a cell, an agent, a single person, etc.). It has characteristics that are not in individuals, and these characteristics come from the interaction and cooperation among individuals. Emergence can achieve the effect of "the whole is greater than the sum of parts. Emergence displays an intelligence which can make individuals more intelligent, or complements individual intelligence. For example, an ant colony "has intelligence," even though individual ants do not have such intelligence. A flock of birds decide which direction to fly by considering the will of all the birds. Similarly, a social network formed by the connections among people can do things that not a single person can. A social network can catch and contain information which is transmitted among people and crosses space and time. With the continuous improvement of our hyperlink capabilities, the transmission of information will be more effective, and our interactions more convenient. Social connections that we manage everyday are tremendously different and numerous. All these changes make "network people" like us more like a super human individual in action with the same goal. Anything which is transmitted through social network today will be transmitted farther and faster in the future. With the expansion of the scope of interaction, new characteristics will continue to emerge. The wisdom represented by emergence also tells us:

regarding many complex scientific and technological problems, we not only need to bring into full play individual scientific researcher's freedom of exploration and innovative thinking, but also need their cooperative innovation and depend more on the wisdom and strength of the group. Currently, human society has entered the era of expansive connections and cooperation, as well as big data. On the one hand, the trend of group cooperation is more obvious, on the other, it becomes possible that an individual's role can be amplified through networks, thus influencing more people.

(2) For the past 400 years, in order to study the things for their entirety, scientists have been studying smaller components in things. In the process, they have made some brilliant achievements. For example, dividing life bodies into organs, and then cells, molecules, genes; breaking down matter into molecules, then atoms, basic particles, and quarks. For this purpose, people invented various tools such as the microscope, the supercollider, etc.

However, emergence has provided people a completely new method for understanding the world (the theory of emergence). This theory regards the objects as a whole, which is completely different from each individual element that is a part the object. Also, it is impossible to clearly understand the object as a whole by only studying the parts. This is because that phenomena caused by mutual connections among individual parts do not appear in single individuals and also cannot be restored as individual behavior. Once the mutual connection and interaction are lost, we will have nothing.

Currently, interdisciplinary scientists have turned their attention to the study on how and why parts are combined into a whole, and what are really the rules that determine mutual connections and interactions. Therefore, only by clearly discovering the structure and function of the whole, as well as the characteristics of emergence, can we clearly vision this important scientific trend and understand the essential nature of objects in the world. The idea of cellular automata is exactly that, many complex structures and processes in nature are after all being caused by the simple interactions among numerous basic component units. People believe that various kinds of cellular automata can simulate any evolution processes of complex phenomena.

(3) Emergence has the characteristics of novelty and originality. It makes a system having global properties that are not possessed by the behaviors of its parts (or elements). Therefore, in the evolution process of a system, novel features always keep emerging and new things keep happening. For example, an ant colony emerging out of the very simple behavior of individual ants has ever-changing collective behavioral patterns and group actions, such as various methods of foraging, carrying heavy things, building bridges and nests, etc. Cellular automata rules of life are very simple. Usually 3 to 5 rules can describe the behavior of individual cells. And yet their combination produces various different structures and modes, such as "flashing lamp," "glider," "self-reproducing machine," etc. Even the universal computer can be produced,

and they can simulate all possible things and all lives in the world. These are examples of the emergence of endless new things.

Emergence makes us understand that the global behavior of a system is not the simple addition of the behavior of its parts, due to the reason that a system is full of non-linearity (Dabbaghian et al. 2011). Non-linearity means that the theoretical methods such as trend analysis, equilibrium measurement, sample average, etc., that we induced from traditional observation would not work. Therefore, we need to conduct creative interdisciplinary research of the systems. To be creative means to go beyond traditional knowledge and get closer to the "truth" of objective things. Currently, the study of emergence is not limited to natural sciences, but has expanded to fields such as biology, sociology, economics, management, etc.

Emergence demonstrates the advantage of the self-organization of systems. Organizations in nature cannot possibly be maintained by central control. Order can only be maintained by self-organization. Self-organizing systems can adapt to general environment and respond to changes in the environment. Such responses make a system incredibly flexible and tough, so as to withstand outside disturbances. Such advantage of self-organizing systems makes themselves no match for traditional human technologies (or other-organizing systems). This enlighten us that, during the designing process of decision making mechanisms, we not only need to consider the advantage of central control and management, but also need to fully reflect on the dispersibility in a system's control and management, so as to mobilize the enthusiasm and initiative of sub-systems, to timely respond to the quickly changing outside environment, and make the system as a whole full of vitality and competitiveness.

9.3.2 *Emergence Computation*

To introduce the idea of emergence into a computing system produces the idea of emergence computation (Forrest 1991; Zhang 2011). From the perspective of computation, an emergence system is actually a parallel computing system. In the ant colony's foraging process we mentioned before, each ant is a small operational unit, and the ants can complete a computing task locally and in parallel. The ant colony can then complete complex computing tasks such as finding the shortest way of carrying food or forming complex and beautiful patterns by combing these parallel operational units.

Enlightened by the emergence system which has many advantageous characteristics such as strong anti-interference ability, rich novelty, etc., people came up with a new computing idea, to design a specific computational task beforehand for a given system. But this task is not directly implemented on a computer through traditional programming, but rather by designing a set of rules for micro units' (such as cells or Agent) interaction, to make the final task naturally emerge. That is to say, if the emergence behavior or characteristic of a certain system can be regarded as a certain type of computation, we call this system is performing emergence computation.

Emergence computation has many similarities to emergence simulation. They both use computers to realize a system's emergence phenomenon, but they are also quite different. Emergence simulation aims at making a computer to simulate a real system, to make the simulation to have certain emergence characteristics, while emergence computation has higher requirements: the system not only needs to have emergence characteristics, but also such characteristics must be able to complete a given computational task. That is to say, emergence simulation is to use individual computing processes to realize emergence, while emergence computation requires the emergence of an entire system for completing an actual computing task.

For example, we need to complete a "majority classification" task by the emergence computation of an elementary cellular automaton. The task is very simple: the cellular automaton must distinguish in the initial states of cells whether open states or close states are the majority. If open states are the majority, the final states of all cells need to be changed to open. Similarly, if close states are the majority, the final states of all cells need to be changed to close. If the numbers of open states and close states in the initial states are the same, then there is no answer. However, such situation can be avoided by making the number of cells an odd number. Therefore, the "majority classification" task is also called "density classification."

The problem of "majority classification" is very easy for the computation with current Von Neumann structure.

The CPU of the computer only needs to separately compute the initial open and close states, and to put the computed values in the memory, when computation is completed, read the values in the memory and compare, then set all the cell states as open or close according to the result. A computer with an up-to-date framework can easily complete such a task. The random access memory can be used to preserve the initial states and intermediate values, and the CPU can be used for computing and then making a final comparison, and reset the states.

But a cellular automaton does not have CPU and memory for computation. It only has cells, and each cell only knows its own state and those of its neighbors'. This is quite a common situation. It is in fact the idealization of many real systems. For example, neurons only are connected to a few other neurons in a brain, and yet they must decide whether to trigger, and the strength of triggering, so that the entire triggering mode of a large number of neurons can show specific sensory input. Similarly, ants must decide what to do according to their interactions with a few other ants, so that the entire ant colony can benefit.

Also called elementary cellular automaton is a one-dimensional world of squares, as shown in Fig. 9.5. In it, each square (cell) is composed of two colors, black and white, and the color of each cell at the next moment is only determined by the colors of the cells on its left and right. Since we know that each cell has only two colors, black and white, then, the color combinations of any cell plus the cells on its left and right have altogether 8 possibilities: black, black, black; black, black,

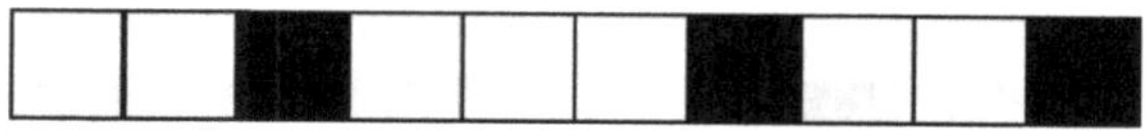

Fig. 9.5 One-dimensional cellular automaton

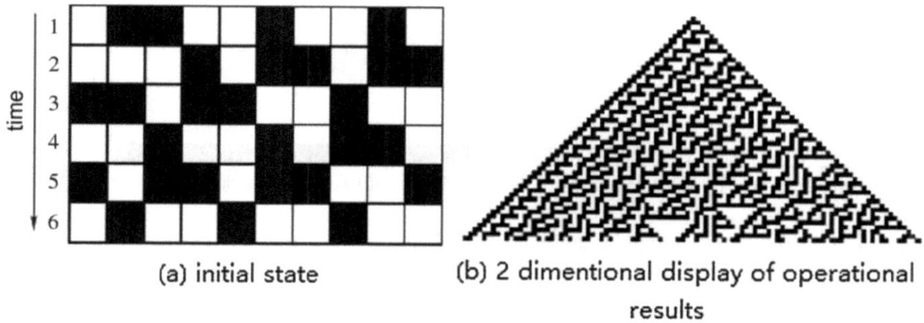

Fig. 9.6 The running of a one-dimensional cellular automaton

white; black, white, black; black, white, white; white, black, black; white, black, white; white, white, white. As long as we designate the color of the current cell at the next moment in all these 8 situations, we can then completely define the rules of this one-dimensional cellular automaton.

We can display the operational situation of the one-dimensional cellular automaton by a two-dimensional figure, as shown in Fig. 9.6. In Fig. 9.6a, each row shows the state of this cellular automaton at a certain moment, and from top to bottom shows the running state of time. Each cell updates its color according to the colors of its neighbors on its left and right. The two-dimensional dynamic figure of the cellular automaton is shown as in Fig. 9.6b.

A one-dimensional cellular automaton is a completely deterministic system. Since the rules are fixed, if the initial state is given (the color arrangement in the first row), the image drawn by the cellular automaton is fixed.

We can totally take this cellular automaton as a computational system. We only need to take the initial state of this cellular automaton as input data, and take the distribution situation of black and white cells after it runs, e.g. 100 steps, as its computational result. Then when a set of input conditions is given, this cellular automaton will complete a series of local operations, and finally give a result at the 100th step. When the cellular automaton's rules are determined, different inputs usually will correspond to different output results. And yet the problem is, in general situations, this cellular automaton will not perform meaningful computation, because its rules are too arbitrary.

Is it then possible to design a kind of appropriate rules for the cellular automaton, to make it being able to perform "majority classification"? Physicist J. P. Crutchfield at The University of California used genetic algorithm to search all possible one-dimensional cellular automata (with different rules), and after continuous evolution, finally found some cellular automata which could complete the

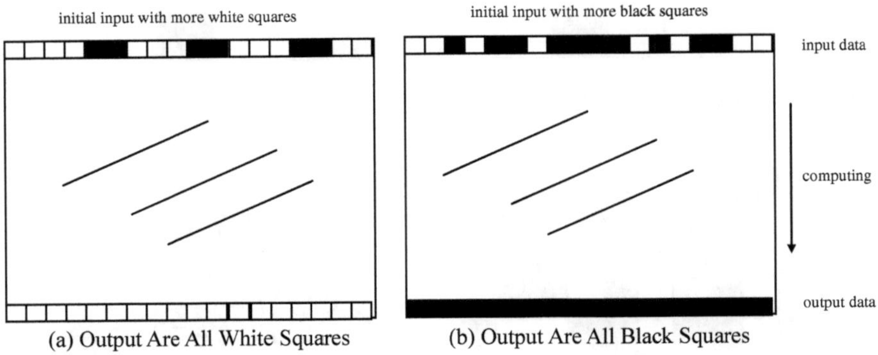

Fig. 9.7 One-dimensional cellular automata completing the density classification task

"majority classification" task. Depending on the initial condition, if black cells are in majority, then the cellular automaton's output result after 100 steps must all be black cells; otherwise, the cellular automaton's output must all be white cells. In this way, if we take the initial black and white cells as input, and the result after 100 steps as output, then this one-dimensional cellular automaton can complete the simple task of "majority (or density) classification", as shown in Fig. 9.7.

The task of majority classification seems quite simple, but is very difficult for cellular automata. This is because each cell can only communicate with its two neighbors on the left and right but cannot see the whole situation at the time of input. In the process of computation, each cell also can only mechanically change colors according to fixed rules and the colors of its two neighbors. There is not a super cell to issue orders to all the cells to determine the operating state of the system. That is to say, this group of cells must learn to coordinate and to cooperate so as to complete a task that is very complex for them.

However, J. P. Crutchfield finally found a kind of one-dimensional cellular automata which can complete the majority classification task by using genetic algorithm. In Fig. 9.8a, initially, black cells are the majority, the cellular automaton correctly gives the answer of all black; in Fig. 9.8b, initially, white cells are the majority, the cellular automaton correctly gives the answer of all white.

In order to clearly see the operating principle of cellular automata, we made marks on Fig. 9.8, filtering out the regular triangular areas, and marked the borders with lines of Greek letters, as "particles." It is shown in Fig. 9.9. We see from the figure that cellular automata can generate 6 different types of particles: γ, η, μ, δ, β, and α. Every type of particle corresponds to a type of borderline. These particles move in time and space, transmitting information from one end of the system to the other, colliding with other particles, producing additional particles or be annihilated as reaction to the collision, so as to complete the computational task which is quite complex for cellular automata.

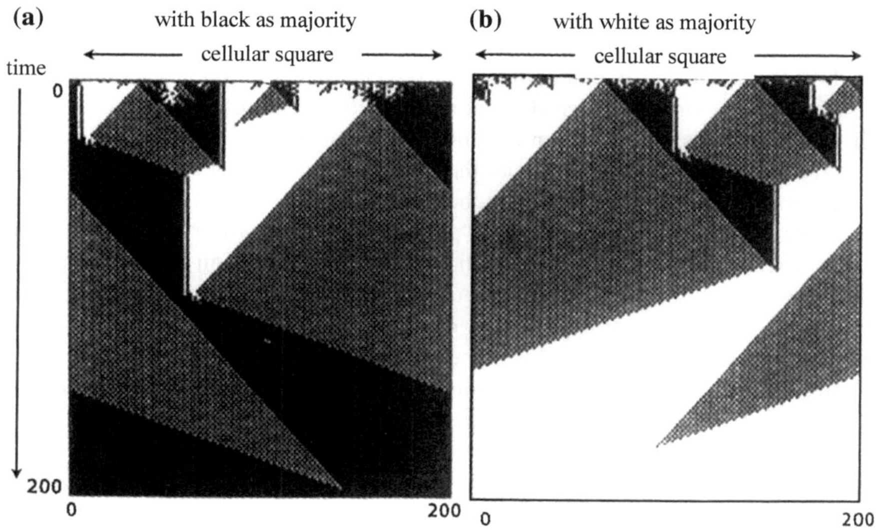

Fig. 9.8 Cellular automata which can complete the task of majority classification

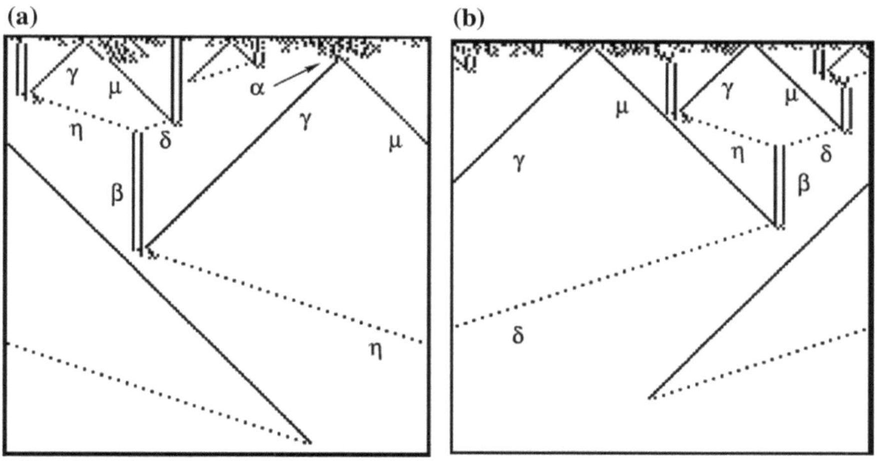

Fig. 9.9 "Particle" collision

To use particles to describe the behavior of cellular automata makes us discover things that cannot be seen by observing only cellular automata rules or only the change of a temporal-spatial figure. This method enables us to explain how cellular automata perform computation from the perspective of information processing. Although particles are a type of description we impose on cellular automata, not something intrinsic with cellular automata. Nevertheless, particles and their interactions can be used as a language to explain distributed computation which uses one-dimensional cellular automata as a background. Even though using this method to understand computation is unconventional, it is quite useful for computation on the system which does not have central control and is distributed in simple individuals, can be taken as a nontraditional computing style.

Crutchfield's research shows that the important reason that simple parallel and interacting cells can complete global computation is that they can make cross-region communication through "particles," so that two or more cells in different regions can interact and realize overall coordination and cooperation. Therefore, a necessary condition for emergence computation is the flow of information. Only the flow of information can complete communication between different regions, so that originally dispersed individuals can be connected into a whole. To use "particles" to describe the work of emergence computation has been recently proposed and still needs further study.

9.4 Future Outlook

1. 20 Unsettled Problems

Nowadays, cellular automata as a type of dynamic model have become a universally adopted modeling method. Their applications have involved majority fields of natural and social sciences. However, as early as 1985, Wolfram raised 20 unsettled problems in cellular automata theory (Wolfram 1985).

(1) What kind of classification capacity can cellular automata produce?
(2) What is the exact relationship between cellular automata's entropy and the Lyapunov index?
(3) What is the geometric analog of cellular space structure?
(4) What statistical characteristics do cellular automata's behaviors have?
(5) In cellular automata's evolution, what remain unchanged?
(6) How to apply thermodynamics to cellular automata?
(7) How is different evolutionary behavior distributed in cellular automata's rule space?
(8) What are the contracting and expanding attributes of cellular automata?
(9) What is the relationship between cellular automata and continuous systems?
(10) What is the relationship between cellular automata and random systems?
(11) How are cellular automata influenced by the noise and other defects?
(12) Will the complexity of one-dimensional cellular automata's regular language be reduced with evolution?
(13) What kind of limit set can cellular automata produce?
(14) What kind of connection is there between cellular automata's computational characteristics and statistical characteristics?

(15) How is the randomness for a cellular automaton to generate sequences?
(16) How wide spread are cellular automata's computational generality and undecidability?
(17) What is the essential nature of cellular automata's unlimited scale?
(18) How wide spread are irreducible cellular automata?
(19) How wide spread are problems which cannot be computed by cellular automata?
(20) Can there be high level description of cellular automata's information processing?

2. **Six Questions for Future Research**

The above open questions are not the same as proving some difficult mathematical problem, nor are they like the mining of the laws behind certain phenomena. Today, 29 years after they were put forward, these open questions have been getting the answer along with the development of information and computer technology. At the same time of solving old problems, new problems keep popping up. The application of cellular automata has long since exceeded the range of computer and mathematics, and has yielded positive results successively in fields such as management, transportation, military, physics, etc. We now provide six questions for future research in accordance with this book's emphasis—the practical applications of cellular automata.

(1) Cellular Automata's Inverse Problem

Cellular automata's inverse problem is to look for the mapping from cellular automata's global behavior to local rules. Since the number of rules is enormous, the search space will be huge, causing such work to be quite difficult. The difficulty of studying the inverse problem directly limits the full development of cellular automata's strong parallel computational ability. Currently, with the aid of evolutionary computational technology (such as genetic algorithm), we have only successfully solved problems such as density classification and synchronization, and yet the research of the inverse problem is only at the initial stage.

(2) Cellular Automata's Information Processing

In essence, cellular automata are a kind of computational tool with strong parallel computing capacity, the applications of cellular automata are based on the characteristics of such "tool". An important reason that the computation of traditional computers is easy to describe is that the existence of tools such as automatic compilation and anti compilation makes the programming language level and the machine code level being able to interchange without any ambiguity. Yet cellular automata have neither compilation tools nor programming language. Therefore, for a computational task, cellular automata do not know how to tell a computer to complete it.

Recently, scientists proposed a "particle" computational method, trying to describe cellular automata's information processing by the interactions among particles. Information is transmitted through the movement of particles, and the collision of particles is the processing of information. Whether particle computation can constitute a set of computational theory needs further study.

(3) The Integration of Cellular Automata with Artificial Intelligence Algorithms

Traditional artificial intelligence algorithms have a common characteristic of completing the convergence process of global optimization through the interactions (the selection crossover operator in genetic algorithm, the pheromone in ant colony algorithm, etc.) of local individuals (such as the genetic individuals in genetic algorithm, the ant individuals in the ant colony algorithm, etc.). In cellular genetic algorithm, we used the "neighbor" relationship of cellular automata to simulate and replace this interaction. Under such unique neighborhood structure of cellular automata, the information of excellent individual receives better continuation and preservation, and the phenomenon of local maximum is effectively overcome.

As aforementioned, an important question in evolutionary computation is how to balance convergence speed with population diversity. Often operators with high efficiency do not lead to good results, while operators with good results do not have high efficiency. The neighborhood structure of cellular automata is good at preserving excellent individuals, but to a certain extent affects the convergence speed. Then, is it possible to design some evolution rules that can well preserve excellent individuals to prevent pre-maturity while improve convergence speed?

(4) Space-Time Prediction Technology Based on Cellular Automata

In recent years, domestic and foreign publications have published many examples about the application of cellular automata in the simulation of space-time phenomena. The examples ranging from fire spreading to the formation of urban morphology, from the evolution of animal population to the change of human land use, even stock prices and the prediction of crime rate. It is not difficult to find that among these problems, almost all the relationships among individuals can be described by very simple rules, and the changes of the states of these relationships depend on the surrounding environment. Using cellular automata to study these problems can control the interactions among individuals on the micro level, so as to study the influence of such interactions on the whole. This is exactly what traditional macro research method unable to do. In the future, more space-time changes with such characteristic can all be simulated by cellular automata.

(5) The Fractal Representation of Cellular Automata

When we observe coast lines and mountains from a distance, we may discover that their shapes are quite irregular. And yet when observing closely, we will discover that their local shapes are similar to the overall shapes. That is to say, on different scales, certain rules are the same in forming the shapes. It is self-similar from global to local. In addition, the evolution of many systems is also a self-organizing evolutionary process, from the initial "chaotic" and "disorderly" state gradually developing into an "orderly" state (Su et al. 2006). Cellular automata happen to possess such similar attribute.

Currently, cellular automata and fractal theory both have found application in the field of urban planning (Couclelis 1997; Wang et al. 2012). In such application, cellular automata still only play the role of describing the change of land use. However, is it possible to go further to establish a connection between fractal dimensions and cellular automata's evolution rules, to use fractal theory to describe cellular automata's computational and evolutionary processes? Currently we have not seen any systematic study on this.

(6) Multi-Dimensional Cellular Automata

In the chapter of "cellular genetic algorithm," from the simulation experiments we could see that, when there are fewer "neighbors," compared to two-dimensional cellular space, the information of excellent individuals has faster transmission speed and better evolutionary efficiency in three-dimensional cellular space. Currently, three-dimensional cellular automata have been widely used in the simulation of experimental phenomena in physics and chemistry. Then, when the dimensions of cellular automata go higher, will their evolutionary behavior simulate more complex phenomena? What is the connection between multi-dimensional cellular automata and the real world? (Christakis and Fowler 2013) This is a question needing further study.

By now, we have come to the end of this book on cellular automata study. In this book, from the perspective of practical applications, we discussed cellular automata's connotation and denotation. The essence of the theme of cellular automata's practical applications can be summarized as follows: the cellular automaton is an important branch of artificial intelligence theory, a powerful tool to explore complexity, a strong proof of the systematic theory of "the whole is greater than the sum of parts," the prototype of parallel computers, an effective supplement to bottom-up and top-down, and is an analytic and simulation modeling method. As a brand new scientific idea, cellular automata are bound to have broad space for development and application prospect.

References

Chopard, B., & Droz, M. (2003). *Cellular automata modeling of physical systems* (Y. Zhu & X. Zhao, Trans.). Beijing: Tsinghua University Press.

Christakis, N. A., & Fowler, J. H. (2013). *Connected* (J. Xue, Trans.). Beijing: Remin University Press.

Couclelis, H. (1997). From cellular automata to urban models: New principles for model development and implementation. *Environment and Planning B, 24*(2), 165–174.

Crutchfield, J. P., & Hanson, J. E. (1993). Turbulent pattern bases for cellular automata. *Physica D: Nonlinear Phenomena, 69*(3–4), 279–301.

Dabbaghian, V., Spicer, V., & Singh, S. K. (2011). The social impact in a high-risk community: A cellular automata model. *Journal of Computational Science, 2,* 238–246.

Forrest, S. (1991). *Emergent computation*. Cambridge: MIT Press.

He, C., Shi, P., Chen, J., et al. (2005). Study of the model of land use situation based on system dynamics and cellular automata models. *Chinese Science, 35*(5), 464–473.

Lee, H. Y., Lee, H. W., & Kim, D. (1999). Dynamic states of a continuum traffic equation with on-ramp. *Physical Review E, 59*(5), 5101–5111.

Li, X., & Ye, J. (2004). Knowledge discovery and geographical cellular automata. *Chinese Science, volume D: Earth Science, 34*(9), 865–872.

Liu, X., & Li, X. (2006). Obtaining cellular automata's nonlinear transformation rules from space with high-dimensional characteristics. *Journal of Geography, 61*(6), 663–672.

Liu, X., & Li, X. (2007). Fisher discriminant and automatically obtaining cellular automata's transformation rules. *Journal of Surveying, 36*(1), 112–117.

Liu, X., Li X., Ye, J., et. al. (2007). Using ant colony intelligence to mine the transformation rules of geographical cellular automata. *Chinese Science, 37*(6), 824–834.

Mitchell, M. (2011). *Complexity: A guided tour* (T. Lu, Trans.). Changsha: Hunan Science & Technology Press.

Su, F., Yao, Lingkan, & Gao, Zhaoning. (2006). The application of fractal cellular automata in borderline self-organization. *Journal of Xinan Jiaotong University, 41*(6), 675–679.

Tero, A., Takagi, S., Saigust, T., et al. (2010). Rules for biologically inspired adaptive network design. *Science, 327*(5964), 439–442.

Tian, X., Duan, X., Liu, X., et al. (2007). Study of cellular automata's quasi-period three behavior based on BPSO. *Complex Systems and Complexity Science, 4*(4), 25–31.

Wang, H., Qiu, Q., Wang, C., et al. (2012). Application of the coupling between fractal and cellular automata to the urban eco planning of Xiamen city. *Environmental Science and Technology, 35*(3), 168–172.

Wolfram, S. (1985). Twenty problems in the theory of cellular automata. *Physica Scripta, T9,* 170–183.

Wu, F. (1998). SimLand: A prototype to simulate land conversion through the integrated GIS and ca with AHP-derived transition rules. *International Journal of Geographical Information Science, 12*(1), 63–82.

Zhang, J. (2011). Overview of emergence computation. *Journal of Wuyi University, 4,* 29–37.

MIX
Papier aus verantwortungsvollen Quellen
Paper from responsible sources
FSC® C105338

If you have any concerns about our products,
you can contact us on
ProductSafety@springernature.com

In case Publisher is established outside the EU,
the EU authorized representative is:
Springer Nature Customer Service Center GmbH
Europaplatz 3, 69115 Heidelberg, Germany

Printed by Libri Plureos GmbH
in Hamburg, Germany